# SOCIAL THEORY

*Social Theory* provides a sophisticated yet highly accessible introduction to classical and contemporary social theories. The author's concise presentation allows students and instructors to focus on central themes. The text lets theorists speak for themselves, presenting key passages from each theorist's corpus, bringing theory to life. The approach allows instructors the opportunity to help students learn to unpack sometimes complex prose, just as it offers inroads to class discussion. Chapters on Addams and early feminism, on Habermas and the Frankfurt School, on Foucault, and on globalization and social movements round out contemporary coverage. The book presents and explains key theories, just as it provides an introduction to central debates about them.

**Berch Berberoglu** is Professor of Sociology and Director of Graduate Studies in the Department of Sociology at the University of Nevada, Reno.

# SOCIAL THEORY

## Classical and Contemporary—A Critical Perspective

*Berch Berberoglu*

Routledge
Taylor & Francis Group

NEW YORK AND LONDON

First published 2017
by Routledge
711 Third Avenue, New York, NY 10017

and by Routledge
2 Park Square, Milton Park, Abingdon, Oxon, OX14 4RN

*Routledge is an imprint of the Taylor & Francis Group, an informa business*

*Library of Congress Cataloging in Publication Data*
Names: Berberoglu, Berch, author.
Title: Social theory: classical and contemporary: a critical perspective / Berch Berberoglu.
Description: 1 Edition. | New York: Routledge, 2016. | Includes bibliographical
references and index.
Identifiers: LCCN 2016030682| ISBN 9781138125483 (hardback) |
ISBN 9781138125490 (paperback) | ISBN 9781315647487 (ebook)
Subjects: LCSH: Sociology–Philosophy. | Sociology–Methodology. |
Sociology–Classification.
Classification: LCC HM585 .B47 2016 | DDC 301.01–dc23
LC record available at https://lccn.loc.gov/2016030682

ISBN: 978-1-138-12548-3 (hbk)
ISBN: 978-1-138-12549-0 (pbk)
ISBN: 978-1-315-64748-7 (ebk)

Typeset in Caslon
by Sunrise Setting Ltd, Brixham, UK

# CONTENTS

# PREFACE

Scholars through the ages have developed social theories to guide them through the process of attaining knowledge to understand society and social phenomena that surround them. The adoption of a theoretical approach in social analysis, especially one that is critical and challenges long-held assumptions about the social world, is therefore an important first step in developing an informed understanding of society and social relations.

My interest in social theory goes back more than four decades, to the early 1970s, when I was first introduced to the great social theorists of the late nineteenth and early twentieth centuries in my undergraduate theory course taught by Larry Reynolds at Central Michigan University. Through his inspiring and engaging lectures on Emile Durkheim, Max Weber, Karl Marx, and other giants of classical social theory, I came to confront some of the central social issues of our time. Later, in a graduate seminar on contemporary social theory, I learned from Larry about the raging controversies in American sociology—from its early beginnings to the Chicago School to Talcott Parsons, Robert Merton, and other proponents of modern functionalism, which dominated the postwar academic scene, to C. Wright Mills and the critical and radical theorizing and activism of a new generation of sociologists in the 1960s, who made an important and lasting contribution to the discipline.

The knowledge I gained through my formal theoretical training in these formative years, however, goes much beyond what I learned about individual theorists, for my broad exposure to social theory during this critical period helped establish a solid foundation for my theoretical studies in the years that followed. For his pivotal role in introducing me to some of the central theoretical positions that I have come to adopt over the years, and in this way for setting me on a most valuable intellectual journey, I thank my mentor, colleague, and friend, Larry Reynolds, in appreciation of his contribution to my theoretical development.

During my graduate studies in the early to mid-1970s, first at the State University of New York at Binghamton and then at Central Michigan University, where I attended seminars and courses taught by James Petras and Blain Stevenson, respectively, and later at the University of Oregon, where I studied toward my doctoral degree under Albert Szymanski, my exposure to and interest in social theory, centered in political economy and class analysis, came to define the parameters of my theoretical orientation in sociology. In this more mature period in my thinking, I came to adopt a more developed, dialectical conception of social analysis informed by the principles of historical materialism. It was also during this most critical period in my intellectual development that I began to see the central, indeed most fundamental, role played by social class in society. Analysis of class structure, class conflict, and class struggle, defined in terms of relations of production, became the basis of my approach to social theory and social research, which continues to inform my theoretical perspective and intellectual work. Throughout this book, the analysis of the positions of each of the classical and contemporary theorists discussed is carried out from the vantage point of this most fundamental social phenomenon—class.

This book was written with the aim of introducing to the beginning college student some of the major classical and contemporary social theorists of the late nineteenth to early twenty-first centuries. Given both the number of prominent social theorists and the scope of the issues addressed over the past century and a half, this book is necessarily selective in both its focus and the depth of its analysis of questions raised by a select number of theorists I have decided to include. Moreover, the analysis presented is both interpretative and critical in its approach toward the subject matter. It is hoped that such an approach will stimulate the beginning student to ponder the critical issues raised by these theorists in a fresh way. In this sense, the book is not intended as a definitive text in social theory but as a supplemental guide for use in introductory sociology and social theory courses to help familiarize students with the works of some of the most prominent social theorists of our time.

The 30 chapters that make up this book were designed to be brief, concise, and to the point, which is expressed whenever possible in the words of the theorists concerned so that the central ideas of each can be presented in their original form. Thus, this introductory book on social theory was designed to serve as an initial stepping-stone to more in-depth analyses of these and other theorists usually covered in more advanced texts specifically prepared for advanced undergraduate and graduate theory courses in sociology. If this book succeeds in stimulating in the beginning student a modicum of interest in social theory—one that will lead to further theoretical studies—then the purpose of this project will have been achieved.

Over the years, many colleagues have contributed to the formation and development of the ideas presented in these pages and, thus, have contributed, directly or indirectly, to the success of this undertaking. I would like to thank Walda Katz-Fishman, Judy Aulette, Jerry Lembcke, Martha Gimenez, John Leggett, Bill Domhoff, Alan Spector, Karl Kreplin, David L. Harvey, Johnson Makoba, David Lott, and Clayton Peoples for their contributions to discussions on various currents in classical and contemporary social theory.

This new book is a revised and expanded edition of the original volume first published in 1993 and which subsequently appeared in its second and third editions in 1998 and 2005. Although there are clear limitations to the scope of any project of this sort, fifteen new chapters have been added to the book since its original publication. Moreover, I have revised and updated several of the original chapters as appropriate. Thus, in many ways this has become a truly new book of its own.

I would like to dedicate this book to my introductory sociology and social theory students, who have, over the years, urged me to undertake this project, which I gladly did to meet this need.

# INTRODUCTION

Social theory is a central component of the analysis of society and social relations that social scientists have adopted as a guide for understanding social reality. The origins of modern social theory go back to the classical Greek philosophers Aristotle, Socrates, and Plato, who had an important influence on subsequent generations of social theorists through the Enlightenment to the late nineteenth and early twentieth centuries. While great social thinkers like Jean Jacques Rousseau, who became one of the leading theorists of the Enlightenment, developed their ideas on the foundations of rationalist and empiricist modes of thought dominant in the seventeenth century, they also generated their own uniquely eighteenth-century concept of society and social relations by integrating into their social analysis the scientific discoveries of thinkers like Isaac Newton, who revolutionized the study of nature and set forth a new standard for scientific research.[1]

The intellectual climate of this period was further enhanced by the French Revolution, which brought an added optimism to the improvement of the human condition. These developments in the eighteenth century, however, led to the conservative reaction of the early nineteenth century and at the same time marked a shift in the direction of social theory, ushering in the social thought of a new stream of theorists: David Hume, Immanuel Kant, Edmund Burke, and Georg Wilhelm Friedrich Hegel.[2]

The postrevolutionary period gave rise, above all, to the emergence not only of a conservative reaction—which, as in the theories of Louis de Bonald and Joseph de Maistre, advocated a return to the prerevolutionary medieval social order—but to two other strands of thought, one that adhered to the preservation of the existing order, as evidenced by the thinking of Auguste Comte, and another that went beyond the status quo in the direction of an egalitarian social order embracing what Karl Marx later called a form of "utopian socialism," as evidenced by the thinking of Henri Comte de Saint-Simon.[3] These two strands established, by the mid-nineteenth century, the conservative and liberal/radical paths that came to define the parameters of competing traditions in the formation of modern sociological theory.

The collective contributions to social theory of the great thinkers of past centuries evolved by the late nineteenth and early twentieth centuries into the alternative theoretical perspectives of Emil Durkheim, Max Weber, and Karl Marx, which most sociologists view as marking a major turning point in classical social theory. These three intellectual giants developed their thinking in direct response to the great social transformations of the eighteenth and nineteenth centuries, a period when the full implications and consequences of life in capitalist society were becoming apparent in all their social, economic, and political dimensions.[4] It was Marx who first developed a comprehensive analysis of the fundamental contradictions of capitalism and established the parameters of discussion and debate on the nature of society and the social order that others, among them Durkheim, Weber, Gaetano Mosca, George Herbert Mead, and Sigmund Freud, later addressed.[5] In fact, as Irving Zeitlin has pointed out in his *Ideology and the Development of Sociological Theory*, Marx's work provoked a response that accounts for many of the theoretical arguments developed by these and other social theorists of this period and prompted, as Zeitlin puts it, "the intense debate with his [Marx's] ghost," one that has shaped, "in a large measure, the character of Western sociology."[6]

Analysis of the various explanations given by classical social theorists concerning the nature of society and social relations provides us with an occasion to examine briefly three fundamentally different theoretical approaches, or what Thomas Kuhn has called paradigms,[7] in classical and contemporary social theory: (1) the organic approach, (2) the individualistic approach, and (3) the organizational approach.

The organic approach, adopted by Durkheim, emphasizes the study of social order. Society in this context is conceived as an organism functioning much as the human body, where the various parts making up the organism contribute to the maintenance of the organism as a whole. Thus, for the smooth functioning of society, each part making up the system must function in organic harmony with the whole. Social order, consensus, equilibrium, and maintenance of the status quo are the central questions taken up for study; disorganization of the family structure, breakdown of the moral order (especially of religion), and the decline in traditional cultural values are social problems typically studied by this approach. Culture, tradition, and long-held social values, seen as the primary motive force of social life, define the source and logic of social relations within this conservative conception of society and the social order, where society is viewed as an entity greater than the individuals it comprises.

The individualistic approach, which Weber adopted as a theoretical expression of the newly emergent capitalist social order, gives primacy to the individual as the motive force of social development. Based on the logic of competition, private enterprise, and individualism as the defining characteristics of the new society in the making, this approach concentrates on the individual as the unit of analysis, emphasizing the importance of such concepts as the actor, personality, the self, motivation, and adaptation. Although Weber and a few others in this tradition also address larger, structural phenomena, such as status, authority, and bureaucracy, the heavy reliance of this approach on human nature as the motive force of society and social relations gives it a primarily microlevel orientation, where problems affecting society are defined in terms of individual deviance, maladjustment, and other problems that can be solved only by the successful reintegration of the individual into the existing social order.

Finally, the organizational approach, articulated by Marx, emphasizes the centrality of social organization and focuses on class relations and class struggles as the motive force of social change and social transformation. This approach highlights the exploitation of labor as the most important, indeed the central, problematic of capitalist society that explains the emergence of class conflict and class struggles under capitalism. The nature of society and the social order, as well as the position of individuals within it, are viewed in terms of the dominant mode of production determined by the social relations of production (or class relations), which define the parameters of the course and direction of broader social relations in society. Instead of the integration of the individual into the dominant culture and morality, as in the conservative organic position, or the adaptation of the individual into society through control of personal deviation from social norms, as in the liberal individualistic position, Marx's organizational approach contends that it is not the individual but the society based on class inequalities, hence class conflict, that is the source of social tensions and instability. Thus, class struggles and struggles for political power are the collective expression of individuals adversely affected in society; individuals who eventually organize and struggle collectively to improve their situation and thereby advance their interests.

The political implications of the three approaches can be delineated rather clearly if one places them in their proper historical contexts. While all three schools of thought developed in direct response to the changing social, economic, and political conditions in the eighteenth and nineteenth centuries, these schools represented the interests of diverse classes that came to define the social context of a declining or ascending order in a most crucial period of epochal social transformation—the transition from feudalism to capitalism and the consolidation of capitalist rule in the nineteenth century.

The organic approach was a conservative reaction to the newly emergent capital-ist order and advocated a return to the old feudal system, wherein society functioned around established traditional cultural precepts, the church was supreme, and the individual was bound to the moral values of the medieval order. Viewing the rising capitalist system as a formula for moral decadence and social decline, the proponents of the organic approach thus argued in favor of social cohesion and social solidarity, which they felt were characteristic of the old moral code of the church.

The individualistic approach, in contrast, lent its support to the rising capitalist order, wherein old traditions were giving way to individual self-advancement in a market-oriented economy founded on private ownership of the means of production, competition, and individualism. The individualistic school viewed the decline of the old order as a step forward in human freedom—freedom from bondage to the church or any other moral authority that dictated the terms of social life and freedom to accu-mulate private capital in accordance with the laws of the market. Thus, this approach was conducive to and, in effect, advanced the interests of the capitalist class against the feudal landlords on the one hand and the wage-earning working class on the other.

Finally, the organizational approach, while supportive of the limited human free-doms achieved under the new social order, criticized the amassing of wealth from private profit based on the exploitation of labor. Thus, it threw its lot in with the oppressed and exploited laboring masses, which it believed would eventually become conscious of their class interests and struggle for the abolition of private property and private profit through a revolutionary transformation of capitalist society, establishing in its place a new egalitarian social order.

Durkheim, Weber, and Marx thus provided three alternative responses to the burn-ing questions of their time and thereby established the parameters of these competing perspectives at the broader theoretical level. These approaches have come to play a central role in the development of social theory over the past century or more and are viewed by most sociologists today as representing the best elements of classical social theory.[8] Although these three theorists have come to define the boundaries of the rival schools of thought in contemporary sociology, other, somewhat less influen-tial theorists of the late nineteenth century to the present have also made important contributions to the development of social theory. In addition to Parsons, Merton, and Mills, theorists as diverse as Vilfredo Pareto, Sigmund Freud, Antonio Gramsci, W. E. B. Du Bois, Nicos Poulantzas, Immanuel Wallerstein, and Goran Therborn have made their mark within the broader parameters of contemporary social theory.

This accumulated source of knowledge over the past century and a half, with par-allel developments in a variety of competing paradigms in social theory, has led to a combination of diverse approaches yielding numerous new theoretical syntheses (e.g., neo-Weberian, neo-Marxist, and neo-Freudian), as well as to the establishment of entire schools of thought cultivated by such intellectual cross-fertilization (e.g., the Frankfurt School of Critical Theory, structural functionalism, symbolic interactionism, feminist theory, and varieties of structuralist theorizing).

More recently, there have emerged "postmodernist" modes of thought, which attempt to explain the contours of the "postcapitalist" social order. Theorists opting for this most recent attempt at critical theorizing, which rejects both mainstream and Marxist analyses of contemporary society, have introduced into their cultural analysis the theory and praxis of "postmodernity," an era that allegedly characterizes contemporary, "postindustrial" society. These self-defined analysts of the "postmodern age," however, have come under strong criticism for promoting yet another fad in social theory rooted in the pessimism prevalent in a period of decline and decay in centers of world capitalism in the closing decades of the twentieth and the opening decades of the twenty-first century.

The theoretical defects in postmodernist discourse on the nature and sources of this transformation notwithstanding, the contemporary crisis of global capitalism has generated intense discussion and debate between and within the leading schools of thought and engendered the emergence of a variety of alternative theoretical positions. Clearly, social theory cannot be divorced from the social context and prevailing material conditions of society. These conditions often give rise to a variety of intellectual responses that evolve into various theoretical positions that attempt to address the social transformations we are experiencing today. Hence, the dialectical interaction between theory and practice over time leads to the accumulation of new knowledge and informs our conception of the social world, thus further contributing to our understanding of the underlying conditions in society. And to accomplish this task fully, this book provides a crucial analytical tool with which to conceptualize and analyze classical and contemporary social theory—and that is class relations and class struggle as the decisive, motive force of social relations and social transformation.

The book is divided into two parts. Part I focuses on classical social theory and examines the works of social theorists of the late nineteenth and early twentieth centuries. Part II provides an analysis of the works of contemporary social theorists of the middle to late twentieth and early twenty-first centuries. It concludes with some reflections on the nature of social theory and its central role in critical intellectual discourse as we enter the twenty-first century.

The theories examined in the chapters that make up this book present a sampling of the rich traditions of both classical and contemporary social theory. By providing an overview of the works of some of the most important theorists of the nineteenth and twentieth centuries from a class standpoint, the book addresses a variety of controversial theoretical issues that have brought social theorizing to the forefront of the critical analysis of society.

## Notes

1   Jean Jacques Rousseau, *The Social Contract* (New York: Dutton, 1950).

2   See, for example, David Hume, *A Treatise of Human Nature* (Oxford: Clarendon Press, 1949); Immanuel Kant, *Critique of Pure Reason* (New York: St. Martin's Press, 1929); Edmund Burke, *Reflections on the Revolution in France* (New Rochelle, NY: Arlington House, 1966); G. W. F. Hegel, *The Philosophy of History* (New York: Dover, 1956); and G. W. F. Hegel, *Science of Logic* (London: Allen and Unwin, 1969).

3   Auguste Comte, *The Positive Philosophy*, 2 vols. (London: Kegan Paul, 1893); Henri de Saint-Simon, *Social Organization, the Science of Man and Other Writings* (New York: Harper & Row, 1964).

4   For an excellent discussion of the changes taking place in western Europe during this period, see Maurice Dobb, *Studies in the Development of Capitalism* (New York: International Publishers, 1963). See also Karl Polanyi, *The Great Transformation* (Boston, MA: Beacon, 1957).

5   See Karl Marx, *Capital*, 3 vols. (New York: International Publishers, 1967).

6   Irving M. Zeitlin, *Ideology and the Development of Sociological Theory* (Englewood Cliffs, NJ: Prentice Hall, 1968), viii.

7   Thomas S. Kuhn, *The Structure of Scientific Revolutions*, 2nd ed. (Chicago, IL: University of Chicago Press, 1970).

8   See, for example, David L. Westby, *The Growth of Sociological Theory* (Englewood Cliffs, NJ: Prentice Hall, 1991), and David Ashley and David Michael Orenstein, *Sociological Theory: Classical Statements*, 5th ed. (Boston, MA: Allyn and Bacon, 2001).

# PART I
# CLASSICAL SOCIAL THEORY

# 1

# HEGEL ON DIALECTICS, THE STATE, AND SOCIETY

Georg Wilhelm Friedrich Hegel (1770–1831) was a German idealist philosopher and social theorist who had a profound impact on subsequent philosophers and social theorists who adopted a rationalist mode of thought. His influence extended beyond the realm of philosophy to affect the thinking of those, like Karl Marx, who adopted and later opposed his ideas, while crediting him with the contributions that he made in formulating a way of looking at the world through the lens of "dialectics." This chapter provides an overview of the Hegelian dialectic and lays bare the philosophical foundations of Hegel's view of the state and society that came to inform his approach to social theory.

## The Hegelian Dialectic

The centerpiece of Hegel's philosophical view of the world is his methodological approach that defines his logic of inquiry to understand society. As a rationalist philosopher, Hegel relied on ideas and metaphysical phenomena. The methodology he adopted was "dialectics"—that is, knowledge derived from an understanding of the unity of opposites. As his approach was based on ideas (or the realm of thought), this meant knowledge is to be attained through the opposition of idea "a" to idea "b" that results in new knowledge embodied in idea "c"—or what came to be known as "thesis" versus "antithesis" leading to "synthesis." Hegel believed that this dialectical mode of thought would lead to the discovery of "the absolute truth," for it is in this way, he argued, the inner logic of the spiritual and material world can be understood.[1] The Hegelian dialectic was viewed by many as an innovative method of attaining knowledge by understanding the oppositional tendencies between sets of ideas. Others, like Karl Marx, adopted this approach to explain the material world in looking at social conflict and struggle between classes as a way of explaining social change and social transformation, which we will explore in Chapter 2.

The Hegelian dialectic was adopted by idealist philosophers and social theorists to understand the source of knowledge and how it developed over time. Based on philosophical rationalizations of the "Idea" and its evolution through the clash of contradictory thought, Hegel aimed to discover the essence of things without reference to their social context and material conditions. The Hegelian idealist dialectics provided a view of the world that was based on pure speculation mixed with religious (or spiritual) reasoning that came to inform subsequent functionalist theorists who claimed to explain the social world through the lens of idealist dialectics. This was the case with Hegel himself, of course, who developed an entire school of thought that became known as Hegelian philosophy.[2]

## The State and Society

Hegel's views on politics and the state were heavily shaped by his idealist philosophy of history and society. Thus, in a typical idealist formulation of the problem, Hegel's concept of the state is based not on any existing state, but on the "*idea* of the state."[3]

In his rational construction of the concept, Hegel viewed the state as having the task of achieving universality (i.e., as caretaker of the "general will"). In this sense, he counter-posed the state's public mission to the private sphere within which civil society functioned. With the state representing the universal community, Hegel assigned to the state the responsibility of combating the harmful effects of civil society based on the individual will. In so doing, he set out to find a moment of mediation between the public and the private spheres to achieve the desired unity.

> The essence of the modern state is that the universal be bound up with the complete freedom of its particular members and with private well-being. . . . The universal must be furthered, but subjectivity on the other hand must attain its full and living development. It is only when both of these moments subsist in their strength that the state can be regarded as articulated and genuinely organized.[4]

To obtain this equilibrium and thus to maintain social order and stability in society, the process requires the functional integration of the individual into the prevailing sociopolitical order led by the state.

> The state is absolutely rational inasmuch as it is the actuality of the substantial will which it possesses in the particular self-consciousness once that consciousness has been raised to consciousness of its universality. This substantial unity is an absolute unmoved end in itself, in which freedom comes into its

supreme right. On the other hand, this final end has a supreme right against the individual, whose supreme duty is to be a member of the state.[5]

In this context, Frederick Copleston points out that for Hegel "the State represents the unity of the universal and the particular" such that "in the State self-consciousness has risen to the level of universal self-consciousness."[6] In this sense, Copleston continues, "The individual is conscious of himself as being a member of the totality in such a way that his selfhood is not annulled but fulfilled."[7] And the state, precisely in this way, becomes the instrument for the expression of collective identity. Thus, for Hegel,

> The State is not an abstract universal standing over against its members: it exists in and through them. At the same time, by participation in the life of the State the members are elevated above their sheer particularity. In other words, the State is an organic unity. It is a concrete universal, existing in and through particulars which are distinct and one at the same time.[8]

Moreover, according to Copleston's further rendering of the Hegelian state, one that highlights its spiritual content, for Hegel,

> The State is the actuality of the rational will when this has been raised to the plane of universal self-consciousness. It is thus the highest expression of objective Spirit. And the preceding moments of this sphere are resumed and synthesized in it."[9]

Rationalizing the primacy of the state, Hegel assigned to the state a supreme, all-powerful position that has clearly religious and metaphysical connotations: referring to it as "this actual God,"[10] he viewed the existence of the state as part of a divine plan, one that "embodies the true, the eternal wisdom of the Spirit—of God."[11] His statement along these lines—written in the original German as "Es ist der Gang Gottes in der Welt, dass der Staat ist," and variously translated into English as "The State is the march of God through the world," "The existence of the State is the presence of God on earth," "The march of God in the world, that is what the state is," or "It is the course of God through the world that constitutes the state"[12]—does, despite the controversy surrounding its precise meaning, convey a link between the state and divine authority that reveals not only its religious or ethically driven character, but also its absolute nature, as some critics have accused Hegel to be promoting.[13]

This sacred, religiously defined idealist conceptualization of the state and society is similar to Emile Durkheim's functionalist definition of society as the supreme entity (conceived in similarly religious terms) to which the individual must submit and conform, if the harmony between the individual and the state and society is to be achieved into a unity—the ideal state and society.

But for Hegel, the state's role and mission is more than that mandated by God; it is sacred not so much because the state represents God's will but because it involved first and foremost the maintenance of order and harmony in the prevailing feudal society threatened by the rise of private capital (i.e., civil society). "Hegel explains the breakdown of the German state by contrasting the feudal system with the new order of individualist society that succeeded it,"[14] writes Marcuse. "The rise of the latter social order," he adds, "is explained in terms of the development of private property."[15] According to Hegel, "The feudal system proper," Marcuse continues, "integrated the particular interests of the different estates into a true community. The freedom of the group or of the individual was not essentially opposed to the freedom of the whole."[16] But, "in modern times," he writes, Hegel believed "exclusive property has completely isolated the particular needs from each other"[17] such that the parts have no relation to the whole. Thus, for Hegel, the only institution that serves to hold society together is the state.

## Critique

The rationalization and legitimization of the state in these terms, however, serve to justify the continued exploitation of the masses by the dominant ruling class through the harmonizing role of the state over society, notwithstanding the claim that this was done under a divine plan devised by God. In reality, this took place within the context of a feudal social order in which the state was ruled by the landowning class, and the church was among the largest landowners, under the pretext of lifting the people to a higher, spiritual level that would usher in true freedom—one based on the unity of the public and private spheres, through their mutual communion.

Suffice it to say, the Hegelian theory of the state and society, based, in essence, on an idealist, metaphysical conceptualization, provides us no better than the ideology of the dominant classes to legitimize their rule and, in the process, to rationalize the reign of a supreme authority exerting its power over the oppressed and exploited laboring masses.

Moving beyond mythical philosophical statements and rationalizations of the state, an analysis of the class nature of the Hegelian ideal state and its role in society reveals its true nature—a utopian ideal that cannot be achieved in its purest form as projected, on the one hand, and an unconditional support for the state that, however "bad" or "sick" it may be, does represent the entire society, on the other hand. It is this authoritative role that Hegel assigns the state, explained in the abstract and divorced from any fruitful understanding of the class nature of society,[18] which, in the final analysis, reinforces his conservative theory of the state as one that rationalizes and legitimizes the exploitation of the laboring masses and their overall place in society in favor of conformity and law and order, rather than helping them liberate themselves from their misery.

In this context, Hegel does not shy away from making his views known on the affinity between his thinking and that of Machiavelli, when he writes:

> Profoundly moved by the situation of general distress, hatred, disorder, and blindness, an Italian statesman grasped with cool circumspection the necessary idea of the salvation of Italy through its unification on one state. . . .

> Machiavelli's fundamental aim of erecting Italy into a state was misunderstood from the start by the blind who took his work as nothing but a foundation of tyranny or a golden mirror for an ambitious oppressor.[19]

Praising *The Prince* and its author for his brilliant work and its relevance to the nature and tasks of the state, Hegel had this to say about Machiavelli:

> You must come to the reading of *The Prince* immediately after being impressed by the history of the centuries before Machiavelli and the history of his own times. Then indeed it will appear as not merely justified but as an extremely great and true conception produced by a genuinely political head with an intellect of the highest and noblest kind.[20]

Aside from his conservative political views and inclinations toward the justification of authoritarian rule—a product of his uncritical acceptance of the prevailing social-economic and political order under both declining feudalism and emerging capitalism, which he accepted as legitimate, including the legitimacy of private property and profit—it took the Young Hegelians, who ended up rebelling against him, to liberate Hegel from the shackles of his own metaphysics and to set his theory free from the influence of conditions so well cultivated by the church and the dominant ruling classes that Hegel himself could not (or did not want to) see for what they were. Doing so otherwise might have forced Hegel to pick up the banner of revolution (as did Marx, Engels, and Lenin) and effect change by smashing the state, not glorifying it, as Hegel did, toward its ideal perfection.

This, of course, had to wait until the mature Marx, like the Young Hegelians before him, was able to turn everything Hegelian, including Hegel himself, on its head and provide us with a materialist conception of history and the state—one that will be taken up in the next chapter.

## Notes

1  G. W. F. Hegel, *Philosophy of Right* (Oxford: Knox, 1942).
2  Hegel, *Philosophy of Right*.
3  Hegel, *Philosophy of Right*, 258.
4  Hegel, *Philosophy of Right*, 260.
5  Hegel, *Philosophy of Right*, 258.
6  Frederick Copleston, *A History of Philosophy*, vol. 7 (New York: Doubleday, 1994), 212.
7  Copleston, *A History of Philosophy*, 212.
8  Copleston, *A History of Philosophy*, 212.
9  Copleston, *A History of Philosophy*, 212.
10  Hegel, *Philosophy of Right*, 213.
11  Irving M. Zeitlin, *Ideology and the Development of Sociological Theory* (Englewood Cliffs, NJ: Prentice Hall, 1968), 52.
12  These series of translations correspond to the following sources, respectively: G. W. F. Hegel, *Selections*, ed. J. Loewenberg (New York: n.p., 1929), 443; E. F. Carritt, "Hegel and Prussianism," in *Hegel's Political Philosophy*, ed. Walter Kaufmann (New York: Atherton, 1970), 36; Hegel, *Philosophy of Right*, 279; C. J. Friedrich, ed., *The Philosophy of Hegel* (New York: Modern Library, 1953), 283.
13  Karl R. Popper, *The Open Society and Its Enemies* (Princeton, NJ: Princeton University Press, 1950).
14  Herbert Marcuse, *Reason and Revolution: Hegel and the Rise of Social Theory* (New York: Oxford University Press, 1941), 53.
15  Marcuse, *Reason and Revolution*, 53.
16  Marcuse, *Reason and Revolution*, 53.
17  Hegel, quoted in Marcuse, *Reason and Revolution*, 53.
18  Hegel's rudimentary class model identifies three general classes in society: the agricultural class (which includes landlords and peasants alike), the commercial class (which includes the business class), and the "universal" class (made up of civil servants in the bureaucracy). Workers in this model are completely left out of the picture—they are not part of any class! See, for example, Shlomo Avineri, *Hegel's Theory of the Modern State* (Cambridge: Cambridge University Press, 1972), 98–109.
19  G. W. F. Hegel, *Political Writings* (Cambridge Texts in the History of Political Thought), ed. Laurence Dickey and H. B. Nisbet (Cambridge: Cambridge University Press, 2010), 219–20.
20  Hegel, *Political Writings*, 219–20.

# 2

# MARX AND ENGELS ON SOCIAL CLASS AND CLASS STRUGGLE

Karl Marx (1818–1883) and Frederick Engels (1820–1895), the most prominent and controversial social theorists of the nineteenth century, provided an analysis of social classes and class struggles in society aimed at understanding the root causes of class inequality based on the exploitation of labor. They stressed that the analysis of class structure, exploitation, and class struggle must be placed within the framework of the dynamics of social change in the world historical process. The crucial task for them, therefore, was to identify and examine the primary motive force of social transformation that defined the parameters of societal development: *class struggle*. Hence, to understand the centrality of class and class struggle in the Marxist analysis of society and social structure, we first briefly discuss the methodological foundation of the Marxist approach—dialectical and historical materialism.

## Dialectical and Historical Materialism

The dialectical method, developed by G. W. F. Hegel, explains phenomena in terms of an endless process of transformation of contradictions resulting from the unity of opposites (i.e., thesis versus antithesis, leading to synthesis). Whereas Hegel applied the dialectical approach to the realm of ideas (i.e., the clash of ideas *a* and *b*, giving rise to idea *c*), Marx and Engels adapted it to the realm of the material world to explain the interaction between ideas (theory) and social reality (practice). Going a step further, Marx and Engels transformed Hegel's dialectical idealism into their materialist dialectics by placing ideas in their social, material context. By applying it to the real world, they were able to explain the structure of social relations, which in class society is based on the struggle between opposing *classes*.

Advancing their materialist conception of social reality, Marx and Engels argue that the material condition of human beings—their real-life experience, their social existence—determines their consciousness. Consequently, the social reality in which humans live molds their thought:

> The production of ideas, of conceptions, of consciousness is at first directly inter-woven with the material activity and the material intercourse of men, the lan-guage of real life. Conceiving, thinking, the mental intercourse of men, appear at this stage as the direct efflux of their material behavior. The same applies to mental production as expressed in the language of the politics, laws, morality, religion, metaphysics of a people.[1]

Elsewhere, Marx states clearly that "it is not the consciousness of men that determines their being, but on the contrary, their social being that determines their conscious-ness."[2] Thus, the material world is prior to and a necessary condition for the emergence of consciousness. This is so because ideas, thoughts, and consciousness are a product of existence, that is, existing conditions of life in society.

Criticizing Hegel's idealist conception of dialectics, Marx and Engels point out that in direct contrast to German philosophy which descends from heaven to earth, here we ascend from earth to heaven. That is to say, we do not set out from what men say, imagine, conceive, nor from men as narrated, thought of, imagined, conceived, in order to arrive at men in the flesh. We set out from real, active men, and on the basis of their real life-process we demonstrate the development of the ideological reflexes and echoes of this life-process.[3]

The starting point in Marx and Engels's analysis of society and social relations is the recognition of human beings as the prime agents of material production, a process that forms the basis of the production and reproduction of human existence. As they put it, "Life involves before everything else eating and drinking, a habitation, clothing and many other things. The first historical act is thus the production of the means to satisfy these needs, the production of material life itself."[4] Hence, in the early stages of history, principal human needs were based and centered on subsistence for the sus-tenance of life.

Through time, humans created and developed tools, skills, knowledge, and work habits—in short, the *forces of production*—to an extent that permitted, for the first time, the accumulation of surplus. Although in most of human history, for thousands of years, human beings lived in classless primitive-communal societies, the accumulation of a social surplus in the form of a surplus product gave rise to the emergence of classes in society. With the development of social classes and class inequality, there emerged historically specific social *relations of production*, or class relations, between those who produced the surplus and those who claimed ownership and control of that surplus (e.g., slaves versus masters, serfs versus landlords, wage laborers versus capitalists). Marx and Engels point out that the forces of production (including the labor process at the point of production) and the social relations of production (class relations) together constitute a society's *mode of production*, or its social-economic foundation, defined as the way in which a society's wealth is produced and distributed—in short, the social-economic system (e.g., slavery, feudalism, capitalism).

Applying these concepts to history and examining the material conditions surrounding the production and reproduction process, in effect the very basis of life itself, Marx and Engels observe that

> The way in which men produce their means of subsistence depends first of all on the nature of the actual means they find in existence and have to reproduce. This mode of production must not be considered simply as being the reproduction of the physical existence of the individuals. Rather it is a definite form of activity of these individuals, a definite form of expressing their life, a definite *mode of life* on their part. As individuals express their life, so they are. What they are, therefore, coincides with their production, both with *what* they produce and with *how* they produce. The nature of individuals thus depends on the material conditions determining their production.[5]

Engels, in a letter to Heinz Starkenburg, further explains the historical-materialist outlook on society this way:

> What we understand by the economic conditions which we regard as the determining basis of the history of society are the methods by which human beings in a given society produce their means of subsistence and exchange the products among themselves (in so far as division of labour exists). Thus the *entire technique* of production and transport is here included. According to our conception this technique also determines the method of exchange and, further, the division of products and with it, after the dissolution of tribal society, the division into classes also and hence the relations of lordship and servitude and with them the state, politics, law, etc.[6]

Once a class society emerges, in which the production process is firmly established, a surplus is generated, and social classes have developed, the relations of production (or class relations) become the decisive element defining the nature of the dominant mode of production, which, in turn, gives rise to the political *superstructure*, including first and foremost the state, as well as other political and ideological institutions that serve the interests of the propertied classes in society. Thus, the superstructure arises from, and becomes a reflection of, the dominant mode of production, which reinforces the existing social order, notwithstanding the fact that the superstructure itself may influence or otherwise effect changes in favor of the long-term interests of the dominant classes in society.[7] As Marx points out,

> In the social production of their life, men enter into definite relations that are indispensable and independent of their will, relations of production which correspond to a definite stage of development of their material productive forces. The sum total of these relations of production constitutes the economic structure of society, the real foundation, on which rises a legal and political superstructure and to which correspond definite forms of social consciousness.[8]

For Marx, then, the relations of production, which he defines as the "relationship of the owners of the conditions of production to the direct producers," disclose "the innermost secret, the hidden basis of the entire social structure, and with it . . . the corresponding specific form of the state."[9] The relations of production, as the decisive element in the mode of production, together with the political superstructure that emerges from it, thus constitute the very basis of the analysis of social classes, class structure, class struggles, and social transformation, according to the Marxist classics. This linkage between the mode of production and the superstructure, which reveals the nature of society and social relations, explains the dynamics of social change and social transformation and is considered by many a milestone in classical social theory.

## Social Class and Class Struggle

In explaining social class and class struggle, Marx and Engels stress that an analysis of the property-based, unequal social relations prevalent in the organization of material production in class society is the key to understanding the nature of a particular social order. Marx and Engels view the position of people in the production process, situated according to their relation to the ownership or control of the means of production, as the decisive element defining class relations in society. It is precisely from these historically specific social relations of production that inequalities arise and lead to class conflict and class struggles, that is, struggles for political power. Thus, referring to class society, Marx and Engels point out, "the history of all hitherto existing society is the history of class struggles."[10]

In capitalist society, for example, two main classes relate to one another in the production sphere: capitalists (owners of capital) and workers (wage labor). The capitalist class owns the means of production and accumulates capital through the exploitation of labor. The working class does not own the means of production but instead uses its labor power to generate value for the capitalists as a condition for its survival. As Marx and Engels point out, capitalist society is thus mainly divided into

> the class of modern capitalists, owners of the means of social production and employers of wage-labor . . . [and] the class of modern wage-laborers who, having no means of production of their own, are reduced to selling their labor-power in order to live.[11]

Under capitalist production, while a portion of the value generated by labor is returned to it for subsistence (wages), a much greater portion goes to the capitalist in the form of surplus value (profits), which, accumulated over time, enhances the wealth and fortunes of the capitalist class vis-à-vis all other classes in society, especially the working class, in both relative and absolute terms.[12]

The accumulation of capital through this process of exploitation under capitalism thus results in disparities in wealth and income between labor and capital, and eventually leads to conflict and struggle between the two classes, extending to realms beyond the production sphere itself. Hence, in this class struggle, write Marx and Engels,

> oppressor and oppressed stood in constant opposition to one another, carried on an uninterrupted, now hidden, now open fight, a fight that each time ended, either in a revolutionary reconstitution of society at large, or in the common ruin of the contending classes.[13]

Marx and Engels conceptualize class at three different, yet related, levels: economic, social, and political. The first of these is identified as the foundation of class analysis, *class-in-itself* (*Klasse-an-sich*). This refers to groups of people who relate to production in the same way, that is, those who have the same property relationships in the productive process (e.g., workers, peasants, landlords, capitalists). Structurally, then, class-in-itself is the logical outcome of the mode of production in all class societies.

Next, at the sociological level is what can be referred to as *social class*. A class-in-itself becomes a social class only when there is a close relationship between the members of a particular class. In this sense, industrial workers (the classic proletariat) constitute a social class in that not only do the members of this class interact in the productive process (in factories, under socialized conditions of production), but they also have a distinct culture, lifestyle, habits—in short, a cohesive, intraclass association, including intermarriage between members of the same class.

Finally, the third and highest level of class is referred to by Marx as that of *class-for-itself* (*Klasse-für-sich*). This means that a *class-in-itself* that has become a social class has attained full consciousness of its interests and goals and engages in common political activity in pursuit of its class interests.

Thus, in capitalist society, the dominant capitalist class, through its control of the major superstructural institutions, obtains political control and disseminates ruling-class ideology, hence assuring its ideological hegemony in society.

At the same time, to prevent the development of class consciousness among the masses and to neutralize and divert their frustration and anger against the system, the dominant class facilitates the development of false consciousness among the working class, that is, the adoption of bourgeois values and ideas in place of working-class ones. This, in turn, serves to block the development of class consciousness among workers and thus delays, to the extent it is successful, the potential for social revolution.

Nevertheless, the material conditions of life that workers experience under capitalism, such as exploitation, unemployment, and poverty, eventually incite workers to organize and rise up against the system. As the working class becomes class conscious and discovers that its social condition is the result of its exploitation by the capitalists, it invariably begins to organize and fight back to secure for itself the economic benefits and political rights denied it in capitalist society, a society wherein the exploitation of labor through the extraction of surplus value is legally assured by the capitalist state.

This exploitation, hence domination, of the working class by capital, Marx points out, will sooner or later lead to class struggle, that is, a struggle for political power: "The conflict between proletariat and bourgeoisie is a struggle of one class against another, a struggle that means in its highest expression a total revolution."[14] "Is there any reason to be surprised," Marx asks, "that a society based on class conflict leads to brutal opposition, and in the last resort to a clash between individuals?"[15] "An oppressed class," he maintains, "is the condition of existence of every society based on class conflict. Thus the liberation of the oppressed class necessarily involves the creation of a new society," adding "only in an order of things in which there are no class conflicts will social evolutions cease to be political revolutions."[16] So long as exploitation and oppression of one class by another continues, the struggle for liberation remains the cornerstone of social emancipation, for it is a struggle to attain political (state) power.

## Political Power and the State

Political power, Marx and Engels point out, grows out of economic (class) power driven by money and wealth, but to maintain and secure their wealth, the dominant classes of society establish and control political institutions to hold down the masses and assure their continued domination. The supreme superstructural institution that historically has emerged to carry out this task is the state.

The emergence of the state coincided with the emergence of social classes and class struggles resulting from the transition from primitive-communal to more advanced modes of production when an economic surplus was first generated. Ensuing struggles over control of this surplus led to the development of the state; once captured by the dominant classes in society, the state became an instrument of force to maintain the rule of wealth and privilege against the laboring masses, to maintain exploitation and domination by the few over the many. Without the development of such a powerful instrument of force, there could be no assurance of the protection of the privileges of a ruling class, who clearly lived off the labor of the masses. The newly wealthy needed a mechanism that

> would not only safeguard the newly-acquired property of private individuals against the communistic traditions of the gentile order, would not only sanctify private property, formerly held in such light esteem, and pronounce this sanctification the highest purpose of human society, but would also stamp the gradually developing new forms of acquiring property, and consequently, of constantly accelerating increase in wealth, with the seal of general public recognition; an institution that would perpetuate, not only the newly-rising class division of society, but also the right of the possessing class to exploit the non-possessing classes and the rule of the former over the latter.
>
> And this institution arrived. The *state* was invented.[17]

Thus, the state developed as an institution as a result of the growth of wealth and social classes:

> Former society, moving in class antagonisms, had need of the state, that is, an organization of the exploiting class at each period for the maintenance of its external conditions of production; that is, therefore, for the forcible holding down of the exploited class in the conditions of oppression (slavery, villeinage or serfdom, wage labor) determined by the existing mode of production. The state was the official representative of society as a whole, its embodiment in a visible corporation; but it was this only in so far as it was the state of that class which itself, in its epoch, represented society as a whole; in ancient times, the state of the slave-owning citizens; in the Middle Ages, of the feudal nobility; in our epoch, of the bourgeoisie.[18]

In *The Origin of the Family, Private Property and the State*, Engels writes,

It is, as a rule, the state of the most powerful, economically dominant class, which, through the medium of the state, becomes also the politically dominant class, and thus acquires new means of holding down and exploiting the oppressed class. Thus, the state of antiquity was above all the state of the slave owners for the purpose of holding down the slaves, as the feudal state was the organ of the nobility for holding down the peasant serfs and bondsmen, and the modern representative state is an instrument of exploitation of wage labor by capital.[19]

Thus, in all class-divided societies throughout history, "political power is merely the organized power of one class for oppressing another."[20]

In modern capitalist society, the state, reflecting the interests of the dominant capitalist class, can thus be identified as the *capitalist state*, for as Marx and Engels point out, this state is nothing more than a political organ of the bourgeoisie adopted for the "guarantee of their property and interests."[21] Hence, "the bourgeoisie has . . . conquered for itself, in the modern representative State, exclusive political sway. The executive of the modern State is but a committee for managing the common affairs of the whole bourgeoisie."[22] In this sense, the struggle of the working class against capital takes on both an economic and a political content:

The more it [the state] becomes the organ of a particular class, the more it directly enforces the supremacy of that class. The fight of the oppressed class against the ruling class becomes necessarily a political fight, a fight first of all against the political dominance of this class.[23]

Seen in this context, the centrality of the state as an instrument of *class rule* takes on an added importance in the analysis of social class and class struggles, for political power contested by the warring classes takes on its real meaning in securing the rule of the victorious class when that power is ultimately exercised through the instrumentality of the state. State rule, in this way, becomes the decisive force determining the class rule of the dominant class and its sway over society.

## Conclusion

We have seen that for Marx and Engels, the concepts of social class and class struggle are central to their analysis of society and social relations. Moreover, their interest in class structure is a result of their larger quest to understand the dynamics of social change and social transformation within the world historical process. In this context, their understanding of the motive force of historical progress and the agents of societal change have brought to the fore the question of political power and the state. Thus, Marx and Engels's focus on production relations, informing their concept of social class, exploitation, and class struggle, as the foundation of the historical-materialist conception of society and social life, including the role of the state and power relations in society, makes an important contribution to classical social theory, as well as to our understanding of class structure in capitalist society. In fact, as we shall see in subsequent chapters, many of the prominent social theorists of the late nineteenth and twentieth centuries either were influenced by the theories of Marx and Engels or developed their own theories in direct opposition to those of the Marxist classics.

## Notes

1 Karl Marx and Frederick Engels, *The German Ideology* (New York: International Publishers, 1947), 13–14.
2 Karl Marx, "Preface to *A Contribution to the Critique of Political Economy*," in *Selected Works*, by Karl Marx and Frederick Engels (New York: International Publishers, 1972), 182.
3 Marx and Engels, *German Ideology*, 14.
4 Marx and Engels, *German Ideology*, 16.
5 Marx and Engels, *German Ideology*, 7.
6 Frederick Engels, "Letter to Heinz Starkenburg," in *Selected Correspondence*, by Karl Marx and Frederick Engels (New York: International Publishers, 1935), 516.
7 See Marx and Engels, *German Ideology*; Karl Marx, *The Poverty of Philosophy* (New York: International Publishers, 1963); Marx, "Preface to *A Contribution to the Critique of Political Economy*"; Karl Marx, *Capital*, vol. 3 (New York: International Publishers, 1967); Frederick Engels, *Anti-Duhring* (New York: International Publishers, 1976), pt. 2; and other writings of Marx and Engels.
8 Marx, "Preface to *A Contribution to the Critique of Political Economy*," 182.
9 Marx, *Capital*, 3:772.
10 Karl Marx and Frederick Engels, "Manifesto of the Communist Party," in Marx and Engels, *Selected Works*, 35.
11 Marx and Engels, "Manifesto of the Communist Party," 35.
12 Surplus value (or gross profits) is that part of the total value created by labor that workers surrender to the owners of the means of production after receiving only a small portion of the total value in the form of wages. Although the end result is the same, the extraction of surplus value from the producers takes on different forms in social formations dominated by different, historically specific mode(s) of production.
13 Marx and Engels, "Manifesto of the Communist Party," 36.
14 Marx, quoted in Ralph Dahrendorf, *Class and Class Conflict in Industrial Society* (Palo Alto, CA: Stanford University Press, 1959), 18.
15 Marx, quoted in Dahrendorf, *Class and Class Conflict in Industrial Society*, 18.
16 Marx, quoted in Dahrendorf, *Class and Class Conflict in Industrial Society*, 18.
17 Frederick Engels, "The Origin of the Family, Private Property and the State," in Marx and Engels, *Selected Works*, 263.
18 Engels, *Anti-Duhring*, 306.

19 Engels, *The Origin of the Family, Private Property and the State*, 263.
20 Marx and Engels, "Manifesto of the Communist Party," 53.
21 Marx and Engels, *German Ideology*, 59.
22 Marx and Engels, "Manifesto of the Communist Party," 37.
23 Frederick Engels, "Ludwig Feuerbach and the End of Classical German Philosophy," in Marx and Engels, *Selected Works*, 627.

# 3

# DURKHEIM ON SOCIETY AND SOCIAL ORDER

Emile Durkheim (1858–1917), one of the eminent social theorists of the late nineteenth and early twentieth centuries, has, with a select few other theorists, shared center stage in classical sociological theory during the past century. Together with the two other giants of classical social theory, Karl Marx and Max Weber, Durkheim has left his mark in sociology as one of the great social thinkers of our time. This chapter examines the major ideas set forth by Durkheim concerning human nature, society, and social order. Limited in scope, our analysis focuses on Durkheim's attempt to develop an organic theory of society.[1]

## Human Nature

Durkheim, in advancing his sociological critique of Western industrial society and its impact on the quality of individual and social life, made a number of key assumptions about human nature that were fundamentally different from and opposed to those of Marx and Engels; for Durkheim, the individual had to be controlled and guided to conform to the existing system, whereas for Marx and Engels, the point was to change the existing exploitative system. Thus, to understand Durkheim and his theory of society and social structure, we must first understand his underlying assumptions about human nature and the individual's role within society and the social order.

"Our first duty," writes Durkheim in his major work, *The Division of Labor in Society*, "is to make a moral code for ourselves."[2] This moral code is crucial, he argues, because it constitutes the very foundation of social solidarity:

> [Moral] discipline . . . is a code of rules that lays down for the individual what he should do so as not to damage collective interests and so as not to disorganize the society of which he forms a part. . . . It is this discipline that curbs him, that marks the boundaries, that tells him what his relations with his associates should be,

where illicit encroachments begin, and what he must pay in current dues towards the maintenance of the community.[3]

But why does Durkheim suggest that we need such a system of social control? Further, why is it "necessary" that the creative expression of individuals be curbed? "The interests of the individual," writes Durkheim, "are not those of the group he belongs to and indeed there is often a real antagonism between the one and the other."[4] Moreover,

> these social interests that the individual has to take into account are only dimly perceived by him: sometimes he fails to perceive them at all, because . . . he is not constantly aware of them, as he is of all that concerns and interests himself. It seems, then, that there should be some system which brings them to mind, which obliges him to respect them, and this system can be no other than a moral discipline.[5]

Durkheim's argument here is both basic and simple: to promote and advance the larger (social) interests of the group and to limit excessive self-interest, the individual must be guided by a "moral code" that implants such values throughout society. To be effective, the adoption of a "moral discipline," he stresses, must take place during early childhood socialization. Durkheim makes this point quite clear when he says,

> Education must help the child understand at an early point that, beyond certain contrived boundaries that constitute the historical framework of justice, there are limits based on the nature of things, that is to say, in the nature of each of us. This has nothing to do with insidiously inculcating a spirit of resignation in the child; or curbing his legitimate ambitions; or preventing him from seeing the conditions existing around him. Such proposals would contradict the very principles of our social system. But he must be made to understand that the way to be happy is to set proximate and realizable goals, corresponding to the nature of each person and not to attempt to reach objectives by straining neurotically and unhappily toward infinitely distant and consequently inaccessible goals.[6]

Thus, through moral discipline "and by means of it alone," Durkheim assures us, "are we able to teach the child to rein in his desires, to set limits to his appetites of all kinds, to limit and, through limitation, to define the goals of his activity."[7] Hence, moral discipline, defined in this way, becomes a mechanism of social control that fulfills the need for integration, conformity, and, in the final analysis, harmony between the individual and society, which in turn helps preserve order in society as a whole.

Durkheim argues that the individual's egoism, if left unchecked, becomes a dangerous force against societal integration and stability. Without a moral commitment to society, the individual, writes Durkheim, fails to strengthen his or her ties to the community. The long-term consequence of such "anomie," or alienation, he argues, is "excessive individualism," the prime cause of "egoistic suicide."

> Excessive individualism not only results in favoring the action of suicidogenic causes, but it is itself such a cause. It not only frees man's inclination to do away with himself from a protective obstacle, but creates this inclination out of whole cloth and thus gives birth to a special suicide which bears its mark.[8]

Such an eventuality "results from the fact that society is not sufficiently integrated at all points to keep all its members under its control."[9] Thus, discipline is necessary, Durkheim insists, not only for the maintenance of social order but for the individual's happiness and moral health as well.

Durkheim's concept of the individual and his or her role in society is, therefore, essentially based on the notion of *conformity*. Only through conformity, according to Durkheim, will both society and the individual be able to survive. Thus, if the lack of conformity leads to serious social and psychological problems, "the only remedy for the ill," such as egoistic suicide, "is to restore enough consistency to social groups for them to obtain a firmer grip on the individual, and for him to feel himself bound to them."[10] Hence, it is the duty of the individual, Durkheim stresses, to be a "good" citizen and a "good" and "productive" worker and to contribute to the social collectivity. To what type of social collectivity, or society, however, Durkheim never tells us.[11]

In attempting to integrate his moralistic theory of society with the real conditions of social existence, Durkheim argues that his "good" and contributing citizen must tolerate oppression. He makes this argument through implication:

> The less one has the less he is tempted to extend the range of his needs indefinitely. Lack of power, compelling moderation, accustoms men to it. . . . [Poverty] is actually the best school for teaching self-restraint. Forcing us to constant self-discipline, it prepares us to accept collective discipline with equanimity.[12]

But why is such an authoritative position granted to society? Why is such an emphasis placed on discipline, self-restraint, and adaptation of the individual to an established moral code or standard in society? And what if such a code is against the interests of the majority of the people in that society?[13]

## Society and Social Order

Durkheim's concept of society is essentially a deterministic one; he views society as an all-embracing entity independent of the individuals that constitute the social collectivity. Society, in Durkheim's theoretical scheme, becomes a real force, having a life of its own. Thus, the structural separation of the "collective conscience" from interaction among individuals at the everyday level means that individuals lack control of their own destinies, and their daily life experiences constitute the manifestation of forces shaping the definition of the greater social reality: "The individual is dominated by a moral reality greater than himself: namely, collective reality."[14]

Likening the nature and functions of society to that of the human organism, Durkheim introduced the notion of "the organic analogy," an idea contending that

> there are a large number of parallels between the functioning of a human organism, with its brain, central nervous system, cells, muscles, and heart and that of a society, with its ideas, classes, division of labor, and culture. The relations among the parts of society are thought to be similar to those among the organs of a human body. As the human body is an organism in which the whole is greater than the sum of its parts, societies can be viewed as social organisms in which their wholes are greater than the sums of their parts. If societies, like human bodies, are viewed as functioning organically, then each subpart must have a function—that is, a role—in contributing to the survival of the entire organism.[15]

Stressing the superiority of society over the individual, Durkheim argues that the individual should conform to the dictates of society in order to preserve the social organism:

> Since the superiority of society to him is not simply physical but intellectual and moral, it has nothing to fear from a critical examination. By making man understand by how much the social being is richer, more complex, and more permanent than the individual being, reflection can only reveal to him the intelligible reasons for the subordination demanded of him and for the sentiments of attachment and respect which habit has fixed in his heart.[16]

Referring to social institutions as the collective expression of forces that make up society, Durkheim points out that these institutions

> will no longer be regarded simply as characterless, ineffective ideological arrangements. Rather they will be felt to be real, living, active forces which, because of

the way they determine the individual, prove their independence of him; which, if the individual enters as an element in the combination whence these forces ensue, at least control him once they are formed.[17]

Thus, for Durkheim, society is superior to and determines the behavior of the individuals that make up the social whole. Accordingly, the individual, Durkheim asserts, must subordinate himself to the larger community if society is to function properly.

Going a step further, Durkheim argues that it is society "that draws us out of ourselves, that obliges us to reckon with other interests than our own":

It is society that has taught us to control our passions, our instincts, to prescribe law for them, to restrain ourselves, to deprive ourselves, to sacrifice ourselves, to subordinate our personal ends to higher ends.[18]

Society, defined in this way, is for Durkheim a sacred, religious entity. Thus, "Religion," writes Durkheim,

ceases to be an inexplicable hallucination and takes a foothold in reality. In fact, we can say that the believer is not deceived when he believes in the existence of a moral power upon which he depends and from which he receives all that is best in himself; this power exists, it is society.[19]

The primary function of religion, according to Durkheim, is to contribute toward the integration of society to encourage a deep sense of moral conformity:

[Religion] is a system of ideas within which the individuals represent to themselves the society of which they are members, and the obscure but intimate relations which they have with it. This is its primary function; and though metaphorical and symbolic, this representation is not unfaithful. Quite on the contrary, it translates everything essential in the relations which are to be explained: for it is an eternal truth that outside of us there exists something greater than us, with which we enter into communion.

That is why we can rest assured in advance that the practices of the cult, whatever they may be, are something more than movements without importance and gestures without efficacy. By the mere fact that their apparent function is to strengthen the bonds attaching the believer to his god, they at the same time really strengthen the bonds attaching the individual to the society of which he is a member, since the god is only a figurative expression of the society.[20]

Thus, in Durkheim's language, the functions of "religion," "god," and "society" become one and the same: they all represent forces of integration, cohesion, conformity, and, in the final analysis, order in society. Here, once again, we see another of Durkheim's repeated attempts to reify society: society, he writes,

> has the chief interest in order and peace; if anomie is an evil, it is above all because society suffers from it, being unable to live without cohesion and regularity. A moral or juridical regulation essentially expresses, then, social needs that society alone can feel.[21]

Thus, Durkheim tells us that to maintain harmony between individuals and between them and their society, a strong sense of social solidarity is needed.

In *The Division of Labor in Society*, Durkheim discusses two kinds of solidarity: (1) mechanical and (2) organic. Mechanical solidarity is based on "states of conscience which are common to all the members of the same society."[22] Thus, it is rooted in likenesses and collective sentiments. "Solidarity which comes from likenesses," writes Durkheim, "is at its maximum when the collective conscience completely envelops our whole conscience and coincides in all its points with it."[23] To clarify the nature of this type of solidarity further, Durkheim points out that "at the moment this solidarity exercises its force, our personality vanishes, as our definition permits us to say, for we are no longer ourselves, but the collective life."[24]

Durkheim is pointing in this passage to the conflict between the collective conscience and the individual. How can this conflict be resolved within the framework of mechanical solidarity? It can be resolved, according to Durkheim, only by moving to a higher level of solidarity, that which he calls "organic." And the division of labor is the mechanism that raises society to that higher level. Thus, the division of labor plays a positive role and becomes the principal social bond among the members of advanced societies, one that reconciles the interests of both the individual and society. Durkheim writes,

> Since mechanical solidarity progressively becomes enfeebled, life properly social must decrease or another solidarity must slowly come in to take the place of that which has gone. The choice must be made. In vain shall we contend that the collective conscience extends and grows stronger at the same time as that of individuals. . . . Social progress, however, does not consist in a continual dissolution. On the contrary, the more we advance, the more profoundly do societies reveal the sentiment of self and of unity. There must, then, be some other social link which produces this result; this cannot be any other than that which comes from

the division of labor. . . . It is the division of labor which, more and more, fills the role that was formerly filled by the common conscience. It is the principal bond of social aggregates of higher types.[25]

In Durkheim's view, then, the division of labor, the specialization of societal functions, brings about two important developments: (1) it enhances one's individuality through detachment from the "common conscience," while (2) it assures a higher level of social solidarity as a result of the assignment of specific functions to individual members of society.

## Conclusion

This chapter presents a brief statement of Durkheim's views concerning human nature and society. And in the process of our analysis we have examined his major theoretical positions regarding society and the social order, developed as a response to the harsh realities of social life under capitalism in the late nineteenth and early twentieth centuries, a response that represents a clear statement of an ideological position transformed into a conservative social theory that Durkheim attempted to develop to contribute to the remedy of problems engendered by emergent industrial capitalism. Although his critique of early capitalist society is laden with attempts to develop a new morality to maintain order in society—hence, in this sense it has conservative political implications—his analysis of the dynamics of society and the social order during this period has broader significance with regard to its overall contribution to classical social theory.

## Notes

1  See, for example, Robert N. Bellah, "Durkheim and History," *American Sociological Review* 24, no. 4 (August 1959): 447–60; Anthony Giddens, *Capitalism and Modern Social Theory* (New York: Cambridge University Press, 1971); Kurt H. Wolff, ed., *Emile Durkheim, 1858–1917* (Columbus, OH: Ohio State University Press, 1960).
2  Emile Durkheim, *The Division of Labor in Society* (New York: Free Press, 1964), 409.
3  Emile Durkheim, *Professional Ethics and Civic Morals* (Glencoe, IL: Free Press, 1958), 14–15.
4  Durkheim, *Professional Ethics and Civic Morals*, 14.
5  Durkheim, *Professional Ethics and Civic Morals*, 14.
6  Emile Durkheim, *Moral Education* (New York: Free Press, 1961), 49.
7  Durkheim, *Moral Education*, 43.
8  Emile Durkheim, *Suicide: A Study in Sociology* (New York: Free Press, 1951), 210.
9  Durkheim, *Suicide*, 373.
10  Durkheim, *Suicide*, 373.
11  We assume here that Durkheim means any society, including the exploitative capitalist society in which he himself lived.
12  Durkheim, *Suicide*, 254.

13 For example, slaves in slave-owning societies and workers in capitalist society are only two cases that raise serious questions about an approach that plays a legitimizing role vis-à-vis the maintenance of order in society.

14 Durkheim, *Suicide*, 38.

15 James W. Russell, *Introduction to Macrosociology* (Englewood Cliffs, NJ: Prentice Hall, 1992), 90–1.

16 Emile Durkheim, *The Rules of the Sociological Method* (New York: Free Press, 1964), 123.

17 Durkheim, *Suicide*, 38–9.

18 Emile Durkheim, *Education and Sociology* (Glencoe, IL: Free Press, 1956), 76.

19 Emile Durkheim, *The Elementary Forms of Religious Life* (London: Allen & Unwin, 1957), 225.

20 Durkheim, *The Elementary Forms of Religious Life*, 225–6.

21 Durkheim, *The Division of Labor in Society*, 5.

22 Durkheim, *The Division of Labor in Society*, 109.

23 Durkheim, *The Division of Labor in Society*, 130.

24 Durkheim, *The Division of Labor in Society*, 130.

25 Durkheim, *The Division of Labor in Society*, 173.

# 4

# WEBER ON BUREAUCRACY, POWER, AND SOCIAL STATUS

Max Weber (1864–1920) is considered by many to be one of the greatest social theorists of the late nineteenth and early twentieth centuries. While he was influenced by the great social thinkers of his period, Weber developed a distinct approach to the analysis of the state, bureaucracy, and power, an approach that constitutes an alternative to both Durkheimian and Marxist conceptions of power, politics, and society.[1] This chapter focuses on Weber's theory of bureaucracy, power, class, and status and provides us with an analysis of their relationship in developing an understanding of the Weberian approach to the study of society.

## Bureaucracy

What distinguishes Weber's analysis of bureaucracy from that of Karl Marx and lends itself to an affinity with classical elite theory is his attempt to assign a quasiautonomous role to the state wherein the bureaucrats appear to be serving their own interests, and the bureaucracy appears to be a power unto itself, with more and more permanent features. Operating at this secondary, institutional level, Weber writes, "bureaucracy is a power instrument of the first order," and adds that "where the bureaucratization of administration has been completely carried through, a form of power relation is established that is practically unshatterable."[2]

In Weber's view, bureaucracies are large-scale, impersonal organizations in which power relations are organized in a top-down hierarchical manner for purposes of efficiently attaining centrally defined goals. Thus, bureaucratic discipline "is nothing but the consistently rationalized, methodically prepared and exact execution of the received order, in which all personal criticism is unconditionally suspended and the actor is unswervingly and exclusively set for carrying out the command."[3]

"The decisive reason for the advance of bureaucratic organization," Weber writes, "has always been its purely technical superiority over any other form of organization."[4]

The fully developed bureaucratic apparatus compares with other organizations exactly as does the machine with the non-mechanical modes of production. Precision, speed, unambiguity, knowledge of the files, continuity, discretion, unity, strict subordination, reduction of friction and of material and personal costs— these are raised to the optimum point in the strictly bureaucratic administration, and especially in its monocratic form.[5]

Outlining Weber's description of the general characteristics of a bureaucratic administrative staff, David L. Westby provides a summary list of the structural features of bureaucratic organization and the characteristics of bureaucratic officialdom:

A   Organizational features

1   Official jurisdictional areas ordered by rules, so that organizational activities are assigned as official duties delimited in a stable way by rules and continuously fulfilled.
2   An established hierarchy of authority under a central authority.
3   Separation of office from private domicile and performance of organizational duties on the basis of written documents maintained in files.
4   Office management presupposes specialized training as the basis for employment.
5   Organizational activities become full-time.
6   Management proceeds according to general rules, the knowledge of which "represents a special technical expertise."

B   Characteristics of officialdom

1   The holding of office is a vocation, meaning that incumbency is based on training and evidence of competence, and that the official is oriented to discharge of office as a "duty."
2   There is a strong relationship between certain organizational characteristics and the extent to which office incumbency determines the status position of the official.
3   The official is appointed.
4   Tenure tends to be for life. This has the effect of contributing to the performance of the organization, but may affect the social status of the official and the technical efficiency of the organization negatively.
5   The official is remunerated by a money salary (and so a money economy is a presupposition of a bureaucracy).

6   The official moves through a career within the organizational hierarchy. This, along with (4) and (5), contributes to the creation of office sinecures in the form of prebends.[6]

In this context of the nature of bureaucratic administration, Weber notes the rise to prominence of the "expert" as a logical outcome of the growth of society and of bureaucracy: "The more complicated and specialized modern culture becomes, the more its external supporting apparatus demands the personally detached and strictly objective expert."[7] Through the possession of technical knowledge, the expert is able to obtain "a position of extraordinary power." Moreover, "bureaucratic organizations, or the holders of power who make use of them," Weber continues, "have the tendency to increase their power still further by the knowledge growing out of experience in the service."[8] But "expertise alone does not explain the power of bureaucracy"; equally important is the bureaucrats' possession of "official information" to which they, and they alone, have direct access—Weber sees this as the "supreme power instrument" of the bureaucracy.[9]

The bureaucratic form of social organization, Weber argues, thus lends itself to the control and domination of society and the individuals within it and generates, as a by-product, a social alienation that puts managers and workers, bureaucrats, and citizens, in opposite camps, thus leading to conflict between those who control and govern and those who are controlled and governed at all levels of society.

Given their logic and organizational structure, bureaucracies, Weber contends, often take on lives of their own, which are often beyond the control of the individual bureaucrats who take part in their daily operation. Thus, according to Weber, once a bureaucracy is firmly in place, it becomes a political force that can very seldom be successfully dismantled or eliminated.

> The individual bureaucrat cannot squirm out of the apparatus into which he has been harnessed. . . . In the great majority of cases he is only a small cog in a ceaselessly moving mechanism which prescribes to him an essentially fixed route of march. . . .
>
> The ruled, for their part, cannot dispense with or replace the bureaucratic apparatus once it exists. . . . Increasingly the material fate of the masses depends upon the continuous and correct functioning of the ever more bureaucratic organizations of private capitalism, and the idea of eliminating them becomes more and more utopian.[10]

The key question then becomes one of determining who controls and directs the complex bureaucratic machine. Unlike the classical elite theorist Robert Michels, Weber does not believe bureaucracy is, in essence, an autonomous power unto itself; rather, it is a tool or instrument of power:

> The bureaucratic structure goes hand in hand with the concentration of the material means of management in the hands of the master. This concentration occurs, for instance, in a well-known and typical fashion in the development of big capitalist enterprises, which find their essential characteristics in this process. A corresponding process occurs in public organizations.[11]

Thus, "the consequences of bureaucracy," Weber concludes, "depend therefore upon the direction which *the powers using the apparatus* give to it."[12] Weber's statement here can be interpreted in two ways: the first assigns primacy to the political process and grants a special role to the bureaucrats—as individuals and as a group—who manage the day-to-day affairs of the political apparatus; the second locates the source of power outside the narrow confines of the political institutions in which individual bureaucrats and the bureaucracy as a whole operate, that is, the economy and class structure of society.

It is not surprising that most contemporary Weberians have separated Weber's analysis of bureaucracy from his generalized theory of class and power in society and, thus, have managed to give a conservative twist to his otherwise controversial analysis, implying that the bureaucracy or the political elite is a power unto itself. Viewed within a broader societal context, however, it becomes clear that bureaucracy and political power to Weber are the manifestations of the real social forces that dominate the social-economic structure of modern society. Thus, to give primacy to the analytic strength of these secondary political concepts would mean that one was dealing with surface phenomena. This is clearly evident, for example, in the works of most contemporary theorists of complex organizations, where power is consistently located within the structure of specific bureaucratic organizations, while bureaucracies are given a logic of their own and conceived in terms of their special power and dynamics. But, to Weber, to understand more fully the logic of bureaucracy and political control, one must examine the nature of property, income, status, and other dimensions of class relations in society. It is here, in his differential conceptualization of class, status, and power based on market relations, that one finds a uniquely Weberian approach in classical social theory.

## Class, Status, and Power

Proponents of the Weberian approach often point out that Weber's theory of stratification and inequality is "multidimensional," while Marx's is "unidimensional," meaning that Weber utilized several equally important concepts to explain social structure and social inequality rather than placing a "narrower" emphasis on social class and class struggle, like Marx.

The key variables in Weber's conceptual scheme are class, status, and power. To Weber, "a 'class' is any group of persons occupying the same class status" or situation.[13] "We may speak of a 'class,'" he writes,

> when (1) a number of people have in common a specific causal component of their life chances, in so far as (2) this component is represented exclusively by economic interests in the possession of goods and opportunities for income, and (3) is represented under the conditions of the commodity or labor markets.[14]

Central to Weber's conceptualization of class is the notion of "life chances," by which he means "the kind of control or lack of it which the individual has over goods or services and existing possibilities of their exploitation for the attainment of receipts within a given economic order."[15]

In the Weberian formulation of class, "class situation" is ultimately "market situation": "According to our terminology," writes Weber, "the factor that creates 'class' is unambiguously economic interest, and indeed, only those interests involved in the existence of the 'market.'"[16]

One's "class situation," then, is expressed by one's access to "a supply of goods, external living conditions, and personal life experiences," all of which are derivative of and determined by the amount of control one has and exercises in the acquisition of income within a particular economic order. And at the center of this control lies, according to Weber, the key (economic) variable of "property."

"'Property' and 'lack of property,'" argues Weber, are "the basic categories of all class situations."[17] In this formulation, one's life chances are "primarily determined by the differentiation of property holdings," and power is derived from the ownership and control of property "which gives [the owners] a monopoly to acquire [highly valued] goods."[18] And since the specific life chances of individuals are created by "the way in which the disposition over material property is distributed . . . this mode of distribution monopolizes the opportunities for profitable deals for all those who [possess property]."[19]

Although Weber defines property somewhat more broadly than Marx to signify wealth and economic power, while Marx defines it as capital or a means of production to effect the exploitation of labor, and although this conception necessarily alters the analytical boundaries of the Weberian versus Marxist definition of the nature, position, and politics of specific classes, it does nonetheless point to the centrality of property relations in the control and execution of power in society.[20]

In addition to the *property class*, which constitutes the determinant core of Weber's class analysis, Weber distinguishes two other types of classes that make up the totality of his class concepts: *acquisition* and *social classes*.[21]

> A class is an "acquisition class" when the class situation of its members is primarily determined by their opportunity for the exploitation of services on the market; the "social class" structure is composed of the plurality of class statuses between which an interchange of individuals on a personal basis or in the course of generations is readily possible and typically observable.[22]

While acquisition classes are based on occupational criteria, as opposed to property ownership, social classes are largely a product of the combination of occupational and property classes: the "working" class, the "lower-middle" classes, the "intelligentsia," and "the classes occupying a privileged position through property and education."[23]

We cannot here go into a detailed description of each one of these classes; suffice it to say that Weber further subdivides the property and acquisition classes into "positively privileged" and "negatively privileged" classes and adds an intermediate category, making up the "middle class." As Weber puts it,

> Positively privileged property classes typically live from property income. This may be derived from property rights in human beings as with slaveowners, in land, in mining property, in fixed equipment such as plant and apparatus, in ships, and as creditors in loan relationships. . . . Finally, they may live on income from securities.
>
> Class interests which are negatively privileged with respect to property . . . are themselves objects of ownership, that is they are unfree [such as slaves].[24]

Although the positively privileged property class's monopoly control over goods, services, wealth, education, high official position, income, accumulated surplus, and other privileges, and the negatively privileged property class's lack of such control and appropriation place Weber's analytic scheme in a position that is analogous to the Marxist conception of exploiting and exploited classes, the logic of such classification is based on an entirely different set of conceptual definitions that separate the two traditions.[25]

"Social status" and "power" are two other major variables in the Weberian theoretical scheme, and we examine them briefly. "Social status," according to Weber, rests on "a typically effective claim to positive or negative privilege with respect to social prestige" derived from "one or more of the following bases: (a) mode of living, (b) a formal process of education . . . and the acquisition of the corresponding modes of life, or (c) on the prestige of birth, or of an occupation."[26]

Thus, within this framework, a social "stratum" "is a plurality of individuals who, within a larger group, enjoy a particular kind and level of prestige by virtue of their position."[27] As Weber puts it elsewhere,

> One might thus say that "classes" are stratified according to their relations to the production and acquisition of goods; whereas "status groups" are stratified according to the principles of their *consumption* of goods as represented by special "styles of life."[28]

And, as Weber's repeated emphasis throughout his writings makes clear, social status is a manifestation of class situation, rooted in property relations, and thus is a derivative of class status.

Finally, the third major concept that is central to the Weberian theoretical scheme is "power." "In general, we understand by 'power,'" writes Weber, "the chance of a man or of a number of men to realize their own will in a communal action even against the resistance of others who are participating in the action."[29] Hence, although economic power is the single most important determinant of power as such, it may itself "be the consequence of power existing on other grounds." What is more, "power, including economic power, may be valued 'for its own sake.'" And, "very frequently the striving for power is also conditioned by the social 'honor' it entails."[30] "Indeed," adds Weber, "social honor, or prestige, may even be the basis of political or economic power, and very frequently has been."[31] Nonetheless, viewed in its ultimate totality, economic power based on property ownership is the crucial determinant of all power in society, according to Weber.

## Conclusion

So, what do we make of Weber's position on bureaucracy, stratification, and class inequality? And what is the relationship between his key concepts, bureaucracy, class, status, and power, vis-à-vis the social collectivity? As we have previously noted and as the implications of the foregoing analysis make sufficiently clear, although Weber viewed these concepts as being relatively independent of one another, he did, nonetheless, stress that in the final analysis, bureaucratic control, social status, and political power are dependent on and determined by class, that is, economic power.

On another level, Weber attempted to deal with a specific manifestation of economic power, namely, power accumulated and exercised at the administrative level of large organizations. He observed that the (vertical) means of administrating large organizations were becoming the dominant fact in all branches of modern society, and the predominant type of organization was becoming the bureaucracy. To sort out clearly the source and linkages of power as it pertains to bureaucratic control, however, Weber's position on bureaucracy must be understood within the context of his analysis of class structure. Framed in this way, we can more clearly comprehend the relationship between bureaucracy, class, power, and property in Weber's theory of modern society, one that has made a great contribution to classical social theory.

## Notes

1  The relationship between the economy, the state, religion, and other spheres of social life are discussed by Weber in his early (1905) work *The Protestant Ethic and the Spirit of Capitalism* (New York: Scribner's, 1948). Here, Weber examines the relationship between Protestantism and the rise of capitalism and concludes that Protestantism played a key role in facilitating the development of capitalism in directly challenging the feudal system prevalent under medieval Catholicism in Europe during this period.
2  Max Weber, *From Max Weber. Essays in Sociology*, ed. and trans. H. H. Gerth and C. Wright Mills (New York: Oxford University Press, 1967), 228.
3  Max Weber, *Economy and Society*, 3 vols. (New York: Bedminster Press, 1968), 3:1149.
4  Weber, *Economy and Society*, 3:973.
5  Weber, *Economy and Society*, 3:973.
6  David L. Westby, *The Growth of Sociological Theory* (Englewood Cliffs, NJ: Prentice Hall, 1991), 430. For an extended discussion of the characteristics of bureaucratic administration and staff, see Weber, *Economy and Society*, 3:956–63.
7  Weber, *Economy and Society*, 3:975.
8  Weber, *Economy and Society*, 1:225.
9  Weber, *Economy and Society*, 3:1418.
10  Weber, *Economy and Society*, 3:987–8.
11  Weber, *Economy and Society*, 3:980.
12  Weber, *From Max Weber*, 1:230; emphasis added.
13  Max Weber, *The Theory of Social and Economic Organization*, ed. Talcott Parsons (New York: Free Press, 1964), 424.
14  Weber, *From Max Weber*, 1:181.
15  Weber, *The Theory of Social and Economic Organization*, 424.
16  Weber, *From Max Weber*, 1:183.
17  Weber, *From Max Weber*, 1:182.

18  Weber, *From Max Weber*, 1:182.

19  Weber, *From Max Weber*, 1:181–2.

20  See Weber, *The Protestant Ethic and the Spirit of Capitalism*. As pointed out earlier, in the Weberian approach, classes, including "property classes," are defined in terms of one's "market situation," whereas in Marxist theory, class relations are based on social relations of production. Also see Chapter 2 of the current book.

21  Weber, *The Theory of Social and Economic Organization*, 424.

22  Weber, *The Theory of Social and Economic Organization*, 424

23  Weber, *The Theory of Social and Economic Organization*, 427.

24  Weber, *The Theory of Social and Economic Organization*, 425.

25  For further discussion on this point, see Chapter 2.

26  Weber, *The Theory of Social and Economic Organization*, 428.

27  Weber, *The Theory of Social and Economic Organization*, 428–9.

28  Weber, *From Max Weber*, 193; emphasis in the original.

29  Weber, *From Max Weber*, 180.

30  Weber, *From Max Weber*, 180.

31  Weber, *From Max Weber*, 180.

# 5

# PARETO, MOSCA, AND MICHELS ON ELITES AND MASSES

This chapter focuses on the political theories of three influential classical elite theorists of the early twentieth century: Vilfredo Pareto (1848–1923), Gaetano Mosca (1858–1941), and Robert Michels (1876–1936). Together, their work on elite formation and oligarchic rule constitutes the core of the classical bureaucratic elite theory of politics.

Classical elite theory maintains that all societies are ruled by elites and that the state is the political instrument by which the vast majority is ruled. This is so, according to this view, because the masses are inherently incapable of governing themselves; therefore, society must be led by a small number of individuals (the elite) who rule on behalf of the masses. This approach to elite rule is quite different from Max Weber's analysis of bureaucracy and political power, and is sharply at odds with Karl Marx's concept of the dominant class, the role of the masses, and the prospects for social change and social transformation.

## Elites and Their Circulation

In his major work, *The Mind and Society*, Pareto sets out to identify a minority of highly talented individuals at the top levels of society who possessed superior personal qualities and wielded great social and political power; distinguishing this group from the great masses of the people, Pareto calls it the *élite*.[1] "So let us make a class of the people who have the highest indices in their branch of activity," writes Pareto, "and to that class give the name of *élite*."[2] Further elaborating on the internal composition of this group, he divides the elite into two (political and social) segments:

A *governing élite*, comprising individuals who directly or indirectly play some considerable part in government, and a *non-governing élite*, comprising the rest. . . .

So we get two strata in a population: (1) a lower stratum, the *non-élite*, with whose possible influence on government we are not just here concerned; then (2) a higher stratum, *the élite*, which is divided into two: *(a)* a governing *élite*, *(b)* a non-governing *élite*.[3]

Within this framework, Pareto sets forth and develops his fundamental idea of the "circulation of elites." By this, Pareto means two diverse processes operative in the perpetual continuity of elite rule: (1) the process in which individuals circulate between the elite and the non-elite, and (2) the process in which a whole elite is replaced by a new one.

The main point of Pareto's concept of the circulation of elites is that the ongoing replenishment of the governing elite by superior individuals from the lower classes is a critical element securing the continuation of elite rule.

> The governing class is restored not only in numbers, but—and that is the more important thing—in quality, by families rising from the lower classes and bringing with them the vigor and the proportions of residues necessary for keeping themselves in power.[4]

A breakdown in this process of the circulation of elites, however, leads to such serious instability in the social equilibrium that "the governing class crashes to ruin and often sweeps the whole of a nation along with it."[5]

In Pareto's reasoning, a "potent cause of disturbance in the equilibrium is the accumulation of superior elements in the lower classes and, conversely, of inferior elements in the higher classes."[6] Hence, "every *élite* that is not ready to fight to defend its position is in full decadence; there remains nothing for it to do but to vacate its place for another *élite* having the virile qualities which it lacks."[7]

Thus, Pareto reaches an inescapable conclusion in his four-volume study: "Aristocracies do not last. Whatever the causes, it is an incontestable fact that after a certain length of time they pass away. History is a graveyard of aristocracies."[8]

The consequences of developments in society are such that they eventually lead to total social transformation, according to Pareto. "Revolutions," he writes,

> come about through accumulations in the higher strata of society . . . of decadent elements no longer possessing the residues suitable for keeping them in power, and shrinking from the use of force; while meantime in the lower strata of society elements of superior quality are coming to the fore, possessing residues suitable for exercising the functions of government and willing enough to use force.[9]

Pareto's explanation of the nature and dynamics of elite rule and their circulation, therefore, rests in large part on the personal qualities of individuals in both elite and non-elite segments of society and their willingness or failure to use force to acquire and retain political power.

Pareto's concern with the decline in legitimacy of the existing order in Italy in the early decades of the twentieth century, together with the rising popularity of Marxism, which he opposed, drove him to fascism. "Fascism, for Pareto," writes Irving Zeitlin,

> seemed not only to confirm his theories but also to hold out hope for a "new era." That he identified with the new order is borne out by the fact that on March 23, 1923, he accepted an appointment as senator—a position he had declined to accept in the pre-fascist government. In a letter to an acquaintance at the time of acceptance, he wrote: "I am happy to see that you are favorably disposed to the new regime, which, in my opinion, is the only one capable of saving Italy from innumerable evils." And, in the same vein, "France will save herself only if she finds her own Mussolini."[10]

"In general," Zeitlin continues, "Pareto's attitude seems to have been that since the pre-fascist regime did not, or could not, save the country from 'anarchy' by legal means, fascism had to do it by force."[11]

## The Political Elite

The fundamental idea that Mosca wanted to develop in his major work, *The Ruling Class*, was a new political theory of power. Like Pareto, Mosca divides people in all societies essentially into two distinct classes: the ruling class (the political elite) and the class that is ruled (the masses). The ruling class always enjoys a monopoly of political power over the masses and directs society according to its own interests:

> In all societies . . . two classes of people appear—a class that rules and a class that is ruled. The first class, always the less numerous, performs all political functions, monopolizes power and enjoys the advantages that power brings, whereas the second, the more numerous class is directed and controlled by the first, in a manner that is now more or less legal, now more or less arbitrary and violent.[12]

This is not merely so with every known society of the past and the present; all societies must be so divided. Herein lies Mosca's argument for the "universal necessity" and "inevitability" of elite rule:

Absolute equality has never existed in human societies: Political power never has been, and never will be, founded upon the explicit consent of majorities. It always has been, and it always will be, exercised by organized minorities, which have had, and will have, the means, varying as the times vary, to impose their supremacy on the multitudes.[13]

Mosca attempts here to establish "the real superiority of the concept of the ruling, or political, class," to show that "the varying structure of ruling classes has a preponderant importance in determining the political type, and also the level of civilization, of the different peoples."[14] Hence, for Mosca, it is not the class structure based on relations of production but the political apparatus of a given society and an organized minority (i.e., the political elite) that controls this apparatus, that determines the nature and movement of society and societal change.[15]

At one point, Mosca writes that "the discontent of the masses might succeed in deposing a ruling class," but, he immediately adds, "inevitably . . . there would have to be another organized minority within the masses themselves to discharge the functions of a ruling class."[16] As Mosca views the specific "functions" of ruling classes in universal terms, he could not envision a state and a society at the service of the laboring masses, as against a ruling class or an "organized minority within the masses."

Mosca's tautological arguments on the "inevitability" of elite rule as expressed above cast a heavy shadow on his work and call into question the accuracy of his observations. The "realistic science" that Mosca wanted to develop, writes Tom Bottomore, was in fact primarily intended to refute Marx's theory of class on two essential points:

First, to show that the Marxist conception of a "ruling *class*" is erroneous, by demonstrating the continual circulation of elites, which prevents in most societies, and especially in modern industrial societies, the formation of a stable and closed ruling class; and secondly, to show that a classless society is impossible, since in every society there is, and must be, a minority which actually rules.[17]

"In the world in which we are living," Mosca wrote quite bluntly, "socialism will be arrested only if a realistic political science succeeds in demolishing the metaphysical and optimistic methods that prevail at present in social studies."[18] Targeting, in particular, Marx and his theory of historical materialism, Mosca argued that his book *The Ruling Class* "is a refutation of it."[19]

Although Mosca believed that the ruling classes throughout history "owe their special qualities not so much to the blood in their veins as to their very particular upbringing"[20] and recognized that "social position, family tradition, the habits of the class in which we live, contribute more than is commonly supposed to the greater or lesser development of the qualities mentioned,"[21] he nonetheless failed to address the social implications of his own position by rejecting the class-struggle analysis of Marx and opting instead for a psychological theory of power based on an individualistic conception of human nature.

## Bureaucratic Organization

Robert Michels, the third influential classical elite theorist, stressed that the source of the problem of elite rule lies in the nature and structure of bureaucratic organization.[22] Unlike Weber, who viewed bureaucracy as a tool of power residing in the market, or Marx, who characterized it as an instrument of the ruling class, Michels argued that the bureaucratic organization itself, irrespective of the intentions of bureaucrats, results in the formation of a bureaucratic/elite-dominated society. Thus, regardless of ideological ends, organizational means will inevitably lead to oligarchic rule: "It is organization which gives birth to the domination of the elected over the electors, of the mandataries over the mandators, of the delegates over the delegators. Who says organization, says oligarchy."[23]

At the heart of Michels's theoretical model lie the three basic principles of elite formation that take place within the bureaucratic structure of political organization: (1) the need for specialized staff, facilities, and, above all, leaders, (2) the utilization of such specialized facilities by leaders within these organizations, and (3) the psychological attributes of the leaders (i.e., charisma).

Michels argued that the bureaucratic structure of modern political parties or organizations gives rise to specific conditions that corrupt the leaders and bureaucrats in such parties. These leaders, in turn, consolidate the power of the party leadership and set themselves apart from the masses. This is so, goes the argument, not only with the so-called democratic organizations of bourgeois society but with Socialist parties as well. Michels, a one-time "Socialist," thought that if Socialist parties, dedicated as they were to the highest egalitarian values, were undemocratic and elitist, then all organizations had to be elitist.

"Even the purest of idealists who attains to power for a few years," he wrote, "is unable to escape the corruption which the exercise of power carries in its train."[24] For Michels, this pointed to the conservative basis of (any) organization, since the *organizational form*, as such, was the basis of the conservatism, and this conservatism was the inevitable outcome of power attained through political organization. Hence, "political organization leads to power, but power is always conservative."[25]

Based on this reasoning, one might think that Michels was an anarchist; he was not. He insisted that any organization, including those of the anarchists, was subject to the "iron law":

> Anarchism, a movement on behalf of liberty, founded on the inalienable right of the human being over his own person, succumbs, no less than the Socialist Party, to the law of authoritarianism as soon as it abandons the region of pure thought and as soon as its adherents unite to form associations aiming at any sort of political activity.[26]

This same phenomenon of elitism/authoritarianism, argued Michels, also occurs at the individual level. Hence, to close the various gaps in his theory, Michels resorted to human-nature-based tautological arguments: once a person ascends to the leadership level, he becomes a part of his new social milieu to the extent that he would resist ever leaving that position. The argument here is that the leader consolidates his power around his newly acquired condition and uses that power to serve his interests by perpetuating the maintenance of that power. In order to avoid this and eliminate authoritarianism, which comes about in "associations aiming at any sort of political activity," one must not "abandon the region of pure thought"! Herein lay the self-serving conservatism of Michels, who in the latter part of his life turned, like Pareto before him, to the cause of Italian fascism.

In his introduction to a recent edition of Michels's book *Political Parties*, Seymour Martin Lipset writes,

> Michels, who had been barred from academic appointment in Germany for many years . . . left his position at the University of Basle to accept a chair at the University of Perugia offered to him personally by Benito Mussolini in 1928.[27]

Lipset goes on to point out, "Michels found his charismatic leader in Benito Mussolini. For him, Il Duce translated 'in a naked and brilliant form the aims of the multitude.'"[28] Finally, Michels "died as a supporter of fascist rule in Italy."[29]

## Conclusion

The three major proponents of elite theory—Pareto, Mosca, and Michels—provided a political theory of elites that they believed explains the nature and dynamics of power in modern society. Best exemplified in Mosca's characterization of the ruling class as the governing elite of full-time politicians in charge of the state apparatus and society in general, classical elite theory has argued in favor of a theory centered on bureaucratic organization, particularly in the sphere of politics. Hence, in a manner different from Weber's characterization of bureaucracy, which he viewed as a tool of power lodged in the economic (market) sphere, classical elite theorists, especially Mosca and Michels, argue that power in society resides in government and the governing elite.

Given its contempt for the masses and its acceptance of elite rule over them as an inevitable outcome of the bureaucratic organization prevalent in modern politics, classical elite theory lends itself to antipopular, reactionary conclusions with important political implications that are quite different from Weber's formulation of the question and diametrically opposite to Marx and Engels's ideas regarding the prospects for change and social transformation in society today.

## Notes

1  Vilfredo Pareto, *The Mind and Society*, 4 vols. (New York: Harcourt, Brace, 1935).
2  Pareto, *Mind and Society*, 3:1423.
3  Pareto, *Mind and Society*, 3:1423–4; italics in the original.
4  Pareto, *Mind and Society*, 3:1430–1.
5  Pareto, *Mind and Society*, 3:1431.
6  Pareto, *Mind and Society*, 3:1431.
7  Pareto, *Mind and Society*, 1:40.
8  Pareto, *Mind and Society*, 3:1430.
9  Pareto, *Mind and Society*, 3:1430.
10  Irving M. Zeitlin, *Ideology and the Development of Sociological Theory* (Englewood Cliffs, NJ: Prentice Hall, 1968), 194.
11  Zeitlin, *Ideology and the Development of Sociological Theory*, 194.
12  Gaetano Mosca, *The Ruling Class* (New York: McGraw-Hill, 1939), 50.
13  Mosca, *Ruling Class*, 326.
14  Mosca, *Ruling Class*, 51.
15  Mosca, *Ruling Class*, 329.
16  Mosca, *Ruling Class*, 329.
17  Tom Bottomore, *Elites and Society* (Baltimore, MD: Penguin, 1966), 17–18.
18  Mosca, *Ruling Class*, 327.
19  Mosca, *Ruling Class*, 447.
20  Mosca, *Ruling Class*, 62.
21  Mosca, *Ruling Class*, 63.
22  Robert Michels, *Political Parties* (New York: Free Press, 1968).
23  Michels, *Political Parties*, 365.
24  Michels, *Political Parties*, 355.
25  Michels, *Political Parties*, 333.
26  Michels, *Political Parties*, 327–8.
27  Seymour Martin Lipset, "Introduction," in Michels, *Political Parties*, 33.
28  Lipset, "Introduction," 32.
29  Lipset, "Introduction," 38.

# 6

# SIMMEL ON SOCIAL RELATIONS AND GROUP AFFILIATIONS

*Clayton D. Peoples*

Georg Simmel (1858–1918), a German sociologist and contemporary of Max Weber, leaves a mixed legacy as a social theorist. While some consider his work extremely important in the advancement of social thought,[1] others downplay the importance of his work and note a lack of substantive integration in his writings because he wrote about a wide variety of topics.[2] Questions of substantive integration aside, his works do provide a perspective unique to sociology at the time he was writing—a focus on the "micro," or on social relations and group affiliations. This focus on the micro in Simmel's work paved the way for subsequent theorizing in the social-psychological tradition in sociology from Cooley and Mead onward, ultimately leading to the development of *symbolic interactionism*. This chapter illuminates and critiques Simmel's micro perspective.

## Social Relations

For Simmel, social relations are what make the individual, and, thus, what ultimately creates society.[3] He therefore argues that we must look at the micro social relations between individuals or entities to understand the larger social structures of society:

> If one wants to understand the real web of human society with its indescribable dynamics and fullness, the most important thing is to sharpen one's eyes for . . . beginnings . . . for forms of relationship which are merely hinted at and are again submerged, for their embryonic and fragmentary articulations.[4]

Simmel then compels us to first look at the simplest forms of social relations in *The Dyad and the Triad*. A dyad refers to the relationship that "operates between two elements" and is "the simplest sociological formation."[5] The dyad carries considerable significance despite its simplicity. For instance, Simmel notes that if one wishes to share a secret, the best way to keep track of the secret is to share it with just one other person via a dyadic relationship; assuming the person is not a gossip, the secret will live and die within that dyad.[6] This illustrates, however, the fragility of a dyad. A dyad is a precarious yet sacred relationship because the exit of one element causes the relationship itself to cease existing. A triad, however, extends the relationship by one element, which has a number of implications for dyad preservation and beyond.

A triad is a relationship among three elements, essentially adding a "third element" to a dyad. Simmel asserts the significance of the third element in remarking, "It is sociologically very significant that isolated elements are unified by their common relation to a phenomenon which lies outside of them."[7] This third element can serve a number of different roles. Simmel highlights two roles, in particular: (1) serving as a tying bind, and (2) serving as a mediating force.[8] Examples of a third element serving as a tying bind could include a person who creates a stronger tie between two people, such as a child strengthening the bond between parents due to their mutual love for that child. A less direct example, however, might involve a church (so, in this case, the "third element" is not a person, per se, but, instead, is an entity or group) linking two people who adhere to that church's beliefs. Examples of a third element serving as a mediating force can include both an objective outsider brought in to help resolve a conflict between two entities, and also a less objective insider who has a vested interest in the outcome of a dispute.

Simmel's *The Dyad and the Triad*, while useful at directing us toward the complexities of even the simplest social relations, does very little to help us connect these relations to larger social structures. Importantly, central questions concerning the structure of power in relationships, inequality, and, ultimately, class conflict are inadequately addressed in *The Dyad and the Triad*. To get a better sense of Simmel's views on these issues, we need to consult his other writings.

## Power Relationships

Simmel writes about power relationships in the context of "domination," focusing on situations in which one person or entity has consistent power over subordinates. He suggests that there are two types of domination: (1) authority and (2) prestige.[9] Simmel contends that authority in general requires at least some level of legitimacy or acceptance among the people; prestige, on the other hand, does not require legitimacy—prestige arises out of emotional appeal (as with the fervor surrounding celebrities) or brainwashing. Simmel further distinguishes, then, between different forms of authority, much as Weber did in his writings. One form of authority rests on true ability, such as the authority granted to a leader whose actions genuinely fulfill the needs of the group. The other form of authority, however, borders on mere prestige, as it rests on illusion—for instance, in cases where an unable leader is merely propped up by a religion, military, or state.

After categorizing different types of domination, Simmel discusses the social dynamics surrounding domination. He portrays domination as a reciprocal process involving both the dominators and the subordinates: "Nobody, in general, wishes that his influence completely undermine the other individual. He rather wants his influence . . . to act back upon him."[10] In this reciprocal process, both the dominators and the subordinates are in a mutually interdependent relationship whereby they each need the other. Simmel makes this clear by invoking the adage, "the master is the slave of his slaves."[11] But why is it that subordinates fail to seize power in light of this interdependence? Why do subordinates infrequently revolt against their dominators? Simmel argues that the subordinates in fact consent to being dominated, which is why the domination continues. This is clear when he writes, "The [subordinate] participates in a sociological event that requires his . . . [consent]."[12] In so doing, Simmel demarcates domination from power relationships that rely on outright coercion as a means of influence/control. But his contention that domination rests on the consent of subordinates requires explanation.

Simmel provides us with a partial explanation for his ideas concerning consent, noting that "power relationships demand a price for freedom . . . a price many are unwilling to pay."[13] This "price for freedom" is not physical harm, as with coercion, but, instead, is embarrassment, ostracism, etc. Put differently, subordinates may consent to continuing in a relationship that disadvantages them because doing what is necessary to change the power dynamic and break away from the situation (i.e., question the status quo, mobilize, revolt) may carry the costs of stigmatization (i.e., being labeled a "radical") or worse. His explanation concerning consent may help us begin to understand why acquiescence so often exists in situations of inequality, such as when workers do not mobilize against their capitalist exploiters. Nonetheless, his explanation still leaves a considerable gray area concerning both (a) fear of coercion as a disincentive to mobilization, which is arguably distinct from both outright coercion and consent, and (b) the role of false consciousness—a phenomenon described by Marx and Engels that is produced by the fetishism of commodities and capitalist ideological hegemony, leading subordinates to unwittingly buy into the existing system.

In summary, Simmel's work on power relationships provides us with some useful insights into types of domination and the dynamics of power relationships, as well as partial insights into the role of consent in maintaining power differentials and inequality. This work does not, however, provide us with any insights into the structural sources of power differentials and inequality. For instance, it fails to answer how it is that one ends up in a position of "dominator" in the first place. Nor does this work provide us with insights into how power relationships play out in a grander sense—that is, how class-based groups congeal and act in solidarity against one another. Perhaps his work on money will help fill this gap.

## Philosophy of Money

In *The Philosophy of Money*, Simmel provides an analysis of the role of money in society as a standardized currency through which value is affixed to objects, ideas, services, etc. As the title suggests, it is a rather philosophical piece rather than being purely sociological. That said, it offers insights that are certainly of interest from a sociological perspective.

The book is essentially divided into two sections: an "analytical part" and a "synthetic part." In the analytical part, Simmel argues first that there is a tension to be overcome between the subjective value of things and a more objective approach. The emergence of money is the standardizing force that bridges the gap between subjective value and objective value. Although he does not delve too much into the history of the development of monetary systems, he does nonetheless note that money has shifted over time from a substance with value in and of itself to a functional part of exchange relations.

Arguably, money initially had its own intrinsic value. This is especially true in situations in which coins or other monetary instruments were literally composed of precious metals such as silver or gold. Over time, though, Simmel notes that money has also taken on a symbolic value—it is worth something *and* can be used in exchange for various desired goods and services. Simmel is sure to point out that money is not solely symbolic in its value today, but, instead, has simply gained functional utility in representing value in exchanges.

In the synthetic part of Simmel's *The Philosophy of Money*, he moves the discussion into the realm of sociology. For instance, he comments on the role of money in shifting the relationships between people. Prior to the advent of monetary systems, Simmel argues, relationships were personal. With the shift toward a money economy, relationships become more impersonal. This, however, is not all bad for Simmel: he contends that these impersonal relationships actually allow for more personal freedom. In this sense, he argues that money itself has helped lead to more freedom, albeit indirectly.

Simmel also comments, importantly, on the role of money in labor processes and class relations. He acknowledges the importance of the labor theory of value and its assertion that workers are paid less than the value of their labor (and that the surplus goes to capitalists in the form of profit). He examines the issue further, though, and contends that there are many facets of the value of labor that ought to be dissected. For instance, Simmel makes a distinction between the value of an item produced in the labor process and the value of what he terms the "labor power" that went into producing the item. He also explores the value of mental effort and argues that this mental labor, if you will, is not simply reducible to the same metric as, say, manual labor.

In summary, although still very micro in orientation, Simmel's work on money begins to provide some insights into structural sources of power differentials and inequality. In particular, the section in which he examines the value of labor from a number of different angles at least acknowledges the larger structural forces that bring rise to class differences—especially in reference to the labor theory of value. This work still does not, however, provide insights into how, for instance, class-based groups coalesce and act against one another. For this we must turn to his work on groups.

## Group Affiliations

In *The Web of Group Affiliations*, Simmel discusses different types of group formations as well as the micro social processes governing how these groups form, such as through recognized similarities in economic position and overlapping interests. In terms of class, Simmel writes about position in relation to capital and how this can be a basis for the formation of class-based groups. For instance, in introducing the working class, he writes:

> The [working class] exemplifies a group-formation based on a pervasive social awareness . . . . No matter what the job of the individual worker may be . . . the very fact that he is working for wages makes him join the group of those who are paid the same way. The workers' identical relation to capital constitutes the decisive factor, i.e. wage labor is in a similar condition in the most diversified activities and all those are organized who find themselves in this condition.[14]

Simmel then goes on to describe how those in the working class can form associations (i.e., labor unions) to defend their interests, noting that "workers have joined associations according to logical or formal criteria of like interests"[15] and that such associations can help workers "obtain more favorable working conditions not for the individual worker but for labor as a whole."[16] This is critical for mobilizing against management and the capitalist class in general:

The purpose of forming such a syndicate was . . . that in this way the individual occupation could put pressure on the management, for which the isolated strength of each group would not have sufficed . . . . Only this made a "general strike" possible, since such a strike would not serve the purpose of a single trade, but would be called in order to force through a recognition of political rights for labor as a whole . . . .[17]

Simmel argues that similar processes are at work in the coalescence of the capitalist class and its related associations, creating a formidable force against labor in struggles at the base:

Similar relations occur when employers in different types of business form a coalition. The employer in one type of business is essentially indifferent towards the employer-employee relations in another. The aim of the coalition is only to strengthen the position of employers as a whole as opposed to labor as a whole . . . . Already in 1892 an association of employers was formed in the United States in view of the strikes of workers which were getting out of hand. This association of employers was designed to oppose labor with party-like solidarity and resistance.[18]

Simmel recognizes that it is not only in the base, though, that the capitalist class mobilizes against the working class. He notes capitalist class solidarity and how it impacts events occurring in the superstructure (particularly political decisions) using the example of merchants: "The merchant joins other merchants in a group which has a great number of common interests [including] legislation on issues of economic policy . . . ."[19]

In sum, Simmel provides keen insights into the micro-social bases of class formation and class solidarity—both for the working class and for the capitalist class—in *The Web of Group Affiliations*. Additionally, he provides an analysis that properly places the interests of these groups in opposition, examining the potential for class mobilization and conflict in both the base and the superstructure. All of his class analysis, though, is from the micro perspective that is characteristic of his work; he does not address the larger structural conditions leading to class formation, solidarity, mobilization, or conflict, nor does he provide us with any predictions concerning how class conflict may transform the larger system from which it was created.

## Conclusion

Simmel will likely continue to have a mixed legacy as a social theorist. Some argue his work is highly influential on sociology, particularly American sociology coming out of the Chicago School;[20] yet others question the sociological relevance of his writings and even Simmel's seriousness about the field.[21] No matter one's opinion of his work, it is clear Simmel provided a unique perspective on the subject matter of sociology by focusing on the micro in his writings, orienting us toward the examination of social relations and group affiliations.

While Simmel's focus on the micro processes of society obscures larger structural considerations and leaves a number of important macro-level questions unanswered, there is still a lot to be taken from his micro perspective. For instance, Simmel provides us with valuable insights into the nature of power in relationships. He also helps us better understand some of the micro social processes underlying class formation, solidarity, mobility, and conflict. So while Simmel's work virtually ignores the larger structural context of society and its institutions, his work should not be discarded, as it can prove useful in orienting us toward the micro processes underlying the larger structural forces in society. Moreover, Simmel's micro perspective arguably helped give rise to the *symbolic interactionist* paradigm in sociology.

As already noted, Simmel argued that social relations influence the individual. Indeed, he goes so far as to say that "society arises from the individual, and the individual arises out of [social relations]."[22] In this statement, Simmel places social relations at the foundation of the social world; importantly, too, he argues that the individual—which could include self, personality, etc.—is a product of social relations/interactions. This is very similar to the arguments that theorists such as Charles Horton Cooley and George Herbert Mead would make concerning the development of self and personality in their development of *symbolic interactionism*. As such, Simmel's ideas on the individual and social relations were a precursor to, and likely an influence on, the formative ideas of *symbolic interactionism*.

## Notes

1. See, for example, Lewis A. Coser and Bernard Rosenberg, eds., *Sociological Theory: A Book of Readings*, 2nd ed. (New York: Macmillan, 1962).
2. David Ashley and David Michael Orenstein, eds., *Sociological Theory: Classical Statements*, 5th ed. (Boston, MA: Allyn and Bacon, 2001), 162.
3. Georg Simmel, "The Web of Group Affiliations," in *Conflict and the Web of Group Affiliations* (New York: The Free Press, 1955), 163.
4. Georg Simmel, "The Dyad and the Triad," in *The Sociology of Georg Simmel* (Glencoe, IL: The Free Press, 1950), 151.

5  Simmel, *The Sociology of Georg Simmel*, 122.

6  Simmel, *The Sociology of Georg Simmel*, 123.

7  Simmel, *The Sociology of Georg Simmel*, 146.

8  Simmel, *The Sociology of Georg Simmel*, 147–50.

9  Georg Simmel, "Domination, a Form of Interaction," in *The Sociology of Georg Simmel*, ed. and trans. Kurt H. Wolff (Glencoe, IL: The Free Press, 1950), 181–6.

10  Simmel, *The Sociology of Georg Simmel*, 181.

11  Georg Simmel, "Superiority and Subordination as Subject Matter of Sociology," *American Journal of Sociology* 2, no. 2 (1896): 167–89.

12  Simmel, *The Sociology of Georg Simmel*, 184.

13  Simmel, *The Sociology of Georg Simmel*, 182.

14  Simmel, *Conflict and the Web of Group Affiliations*, 172.

15  Simmel, *Conflict and the Web of Group Affiliations*, 174.

16  Simmel, *Conflict and the Web of Group Affiliations*, 175.

17  Simmel, *Conflict and the Web of Group Affiliations*, 174–5.

18  Simmel, *Conflict and the Web of Group Affiliations*, 175–6.

19  Simmel, *Conflict and the Web of Group Affiliations*, 155.

20  Donald N. Levine, Ellwood B. Carter, and Eleanor Miller Gorman, "Simmel's Influence on American Sociology, I," *American Journal of Sociology* 81, no. 4 (1976): 813–45.

21  Randall Collins, *Four Sociological Traditions* (New York: Oxford University Press, 1994), 112–14.

22  Simmel, *Conflict and the Web of Group Affiliations*, 163.

# 7

# COOLEY AND MEAD ON HUMAN NATURE AND SOCIETY

*Larry T. Reynolds*

In the closing decades of the nineteenth century and the opening decades of the twentieth, Charles Horton Cooley (1864–1929) and George Herbert Mead (1863–1931), along with the pragmatist John Dewey, represented the very best that the philosophical camp of social idealism had to offer. They helped found a major new variety of social-psychological reasoning that was later to be called *symbolic interactionism*. Their concern with the fate of the person caught up in the massive process of industrialization, differently addressed by Emile Durkheim, Max Weber, and Karl Marx, led them to focus on the relationship between the individual and the collectivity. Herein lies their contribution. This chapter, therefore, focuses on Cooley's and Mead's views on self and society.

## Society and the Individual

From Cooley's perspective, "The imaginations which people have of one another are the solid facts of society."[1] Society lives in the minds of the members constituting the social unit, and this is precisely what makes the unit something very real as far as its members are concerned. Cooley equates mental and social life, but he also notes that society has a structure and that structure evinces the characteristics of a complex organism:

[Society] is a complex of forms of processes each of which is living or growing by interaction with the others, the whole thing being so unified that what takes place in one part affects all the rest. It is a vast tissue of reciprocal activity, differentiated into innumerable systems, some of them quite distinct, others not readily traceable, and all interwoven to such a degree that you see different systems according to the point of view you take.[2]

Cooley obviously prefers to focus not on individuals but on society, but only as society is maintained in the imaginations or minds of individuals. He simultaneously avoids the overpowering social determinism of classic organicism and the instinct- or propensity-driven model of extreme individualism. Given his conception of the nature of human collectivities, it is not difficult to see how Cooley reaches the conclusion that the individual and society are but two sides of the same coin, which is to say, inseparable.

Cooley also develops a methodology compatible with his theories of self and society. If "the imaginations which people have of one another are the solid facts of society," it follows that in order to best understand social life, one must somehow gain access to these "imaginations," which are not directly accessible when one simply observes external behavior. As these "imaginations," these "ideas," are, in a sense, accessible only to those that experience them, Cooley advocates a methodological strategy termed "sympathetic introspection." One is to place oneself in touch with society's members and sympathetically try to imagine life as these members live it. One seeks, then, to detail, describe, and understand the imagination of others because these imaginations are the solid facts of society. One needs to imagine as others imagine.

Given Cooley's views on the nature of human society and how best to study it, he develops two concepts to facilitate the task: (1) the *primary group*, and (2) the *looking-glass self*. These two concepts dovetail nicely with his conception of society and also allow him to work out his view of human nature.

## The Primary Group and the Looking-Glass Self

In looking at the primary group and the looking-glass self, it must be kept in mind that, for Cooley, the concepts of group and self are dynamically intertwined. The self develops in a group context, and the primary group is the true seat of self-development. Primary groups are important for three reasons: (1) they are the building blocks for more complex social relationships, (2) they are the mechanisms through which the self evolves, and (3) they are the linkage points between the larger social order and its human elements, individuals. Cooley defines primary groups as follows: "By primary groups I mean those characterized by intimate face-to-face association and co-operation. They are primary in several senses, but chiefly in that they are fundamental in forming the social nature of the ideas of individuals."[3]

From Cooley's vantage point, the self is developed and defined in the course of interaction with others; it is a social product produced, for the most part, in the primary group. This social product is best referred to as a looking-glass self in that the child obtains an identity only with the realization that a picture, idea, or image of oneself "reflects" other people's perceptions. What is reflected is the imaginations of others concerning the individual. The self resides in the mind of society's members; it constitutes an imaginative act. The specific social reference for the self, argues Cooley,

> takes the form of a somewhat definite imagination of how one's self—that is, any idea he appropriates—appears in a particular mind, and the kind of self-feeling one has is determined by the attitude toward this attributed to the other mind. A social self of this sort might be called the reflected or looking-glass self.[4]

In simple terms, "We always imagine, and in imagining, share, the judgments of the other mind."[5] Cooley's notion of the looking-glass self has three components: (1) our imagination of how we appear to others, (2) our imagination of how others judge our appearance, and (3) our resultant self-feelings, which are produced by such imaginings.

This conceptualization of self and the way it is formed has important consequences. Sheldon Stryker summarizes them as follows:

> [T]here is and can be no individuality outside of the social order; individual personality is a "natural" development from existing social life and the state of communications among the persons sharing that life; and, the expectations of others are central to this development.[6]

Cooley's writings, especially those on human nature, self, and society, contained food for future social-psychological theory.

## Mind, Self, and Society

Following Cooley's line of reasoning, Mead argues that the full range of truly human conduct unfolds only in the course of the association of actors with one another. Human life is, in essence, social life, group life. And social life is essentially a matter of cooperative behavior. According to Mead, humans cooperate because they have the ability to take the other's point of view, to mentally place themselves in the position of the other, and in so doing, to take that other's point of view into account. In short, we are able to form a conception of the perspectives held by other persons. We can and do act in concert because we share common expectations both for our own behavior and that of others. Our more complex forms of social organization, such as social institutions and even society itself, mirror this same process. This is clearly seen in Mead's definition of social institutions: "[T]he institutions of society are organized forms of groups or social activity—forms so organized that the individual members of society can act adequately and socially by taking the attitudes of others toward these activities."[7] With the understanding of others' behaviors that results from putting oneself in their place, the person structures her or his conduct in a manner that allows it to fit in with the behavior of others. In carrying on common action, group members influence themselves and others in a similar fashion. Mead puts this in the following terms:

> The very stimulus which one gives to another to carry out his part of the common act affects the individual who so affects the other in the same sense. He tends to arouse the same activity in himself which he arouses in the other.[8]

Among these stimuli that people present to others are *gestures*. A gesture is a portion of an act that nevertheless stands for the whole act. When an individual makes a gesture (e.g., displays a clenched fist), the person who is the recipient of the gesture completes in her or his imagination the act that the gesture stands for. The recipient projects the gesture into the future: "I am going to get punched." The recipient understands the act the gesture stands for; the gesture's meaning is taken. Happily, people have the ability to respond to their own gestures. Therefore, they can attach to their own gestures the same meaning that others attach to them; the individual can complete the act just as others complete it. When shared meanings attach to gestures, they become significant symbols.

A system of significant symbols, of linguistic elements, constitutes a language. Through the use of language, human society and the human individual communicate. Individuals, because they can respond to their own gestures, can share each other's experiences, forge a common basis for organized social life, and in cooperation establish a society. Human behavior is social in character, not only because we respond to the behavior of others but because the behavior of others is incorporated into our own behavior, and ours is incorporated in theirs. According to Mead, we can respond to ourselves as others respond to us, and because we do, we imaginatively share the behavior of our fellow citizens. Our relationship with others is a product of our ability to respond to our own gestures and imaginatively to place ourselves in the position of others:

> We are more or less seeing ourselves as others see us. We are unconsciously addressing ourselves as others address us. . . . We are calling out in the other

person something we are calling out in ourselves, so that unconsciously we take over these attitudes. We are unconsciously putting ourselves in the place of others and acting as others act.[9]

Thus is human society possible, and this society is the source of the social genesis of both selves and minds.

## The Self

From Mead's perspective, the most important thing about human society is that it is made up of persons with selves. If you are capable of acting toward yourself as you act toward others, then you have a self. To possess a self means that you can respond to yourself as an object. It means that you have the capacity to gain perspective on yourself by looking back as others would look on you.

The existence of human society necessarily implies the existence of role taking; role taking, in turn, is the underlying mechanism producing the self. Through the process of role taking, the individual becomes capable of treating himself as an object, becomes capable of gaining and maintaining "social distance" from himself. The self develops during childhood, and childhood activity plays an instrumental role in that development because, through initial attempts at role taking, the child begins to gain a modicum of social distance from himself. This takes place through the three stages described below.

The first stage can be labeled the *imitation* or *preparatory* stage. During this stage, the child begins, through the process of meaningless imitation, to gain a small amount of social distance from himself. Lacking any real comprehension of what he is doing, the child imitates, or does, things that others around him are doing. A two-year old girl pretending to read a magazine with her father is starting to extricate herself from herself. She is engaging in the initial process of role taking: she is incipiently placing herself in the position of her father and acting like him.

In the second, or *play*, stage, the child gains additional distance from self by exaggerating the imitation process. The child in sequential fashion pretends to be several different people. Actual role playing is starting to take place. As the child is here directing activity toward herself by taking the roles of others, a self is now being formed. Evidence of this self formation presents itself when the child refers to herself in such terms as "Scarlet is sleepy" or "Scarlet is a good girl." The child is now not only seeing herself from the perspective of others but is actually beginning to take on these perspectives as her own. During the *play* stage, the child has yet to develop a consistent, or uniform, vantage point from which to view self.

During the final, or *game*, stage, the child develops the ability to simultaneously take on a number of roles. He must simultaneously respond to several other people's expectations. The child can now respond to what Mead calls "the generalized other." He now sees the community of interests as over and against the interests of any one other. Children can now view themselves from the perspective of the group, community, or even society as a whole. Once a child has taken on this generalized standpoint, he can conduct himself in a consistent, organized fashion. The self can be viewed from a consistent standpoint. The game stage is the stage of completing the self, but while the self is a process that develops in stages, it is a process that has its own definite elements, or structures.

While the self is best conceptualized as a social process within the individual, it involves two "distinguishable phases" called the "I" and the "me," respectively.[10] The impulsive and spontaneous tendencies of the actor are represented by the "I"; it is the unpredictable, unorganized, uncertain, and undirected component in human experience. It is the spontaneous spark of energy within the individual. The "I" is a manifestation of both natural needs and impulses; it is a process of thinking, as well as acting, and because it represents the unpredictable and spontaneous, its presence means that human beings will never be the completely passive agents, the mere reflections of the larger social order, that conservative theorists are pleased to see them as being.

The "me" phase of the self represents the group's common meanings, definitions, expectations, values, and understandings. Depending on the situation, the "me" may comprise a specific other or the generalized other. It represents the incorporated other(s) within the individual.[11]

Human acts start in the form of the "I" and tend to terminate in the form of the "me." However, while the "me" establishes limits within which the "I" must act, if "the stress becomes too great, these limits are not observed, and an individual asserts himself in perhaps a violent fashion." When this happens "the 'I' is the dominant element over and against the 'me.'"[12] Typically, the "me" provides direction to an ongoing act, while its initial propulsion comes from the "I." The act is a product of the dynamic interplay between the two phases of the self. Conformity appends to the "me" and novelty to the "I"; the "me" represents society's influence on the individual, and the "I" represents the person's impact on society. It is in the give and take between the "I" and "me" phases of self that novel experience becomes possible, while social control becomes, at least partly, "self control."

## The Mind

As Mead points out, "the origin of minds and the interaction among minds become mysteries" if one assumes the existence of individual minds and then attempts to derive social life and processes from them. He rejects such an approach and, as he did with respect to the self, argues instead that mind is a social product: "Mind arises through communication by a conversation of gestures in a social process or context of experience."[13] It is through communication by means of significant symbols that mind arises, and the mind is present when the person employs such symbols in interacting with the self. The gestures and significant symbols pointed to by Mead are extremely important; only by means of them can thinking take place.

Mead's analysis of mind starts with a consideration of the relationship of the person to her or his environment. The relationship of the individual to the environment is one of adaptation. People, in a sense, determine which aspects of the environment they are going to pay attention to, but their selective reaction to the environment is not automatic. There is typically a hesitancy before overt action, and when overt behavior is inhibited, when one is mentally contemplating alternative courses of subsequent action, when one is assessing the future consequences of present behavior in terms of past experience, then mind is present.

Minded behavior, or thinking, arises in the face of problems, in the light of the blockage of the act; as Mead puts it, "All analytic thought commences with the presence of problems."[14] Minded behavior is simply contemplating in the light of previous experience the possible consequences of different lines of future conduct before selecting the one alternative to be acted on. Past, present, and future all come together in this process called mind. This process of minded behavior dictates that humans construct their acts in the course of their responses to their environments.

Mead points out that people respond to what he called *objects*. Objects are plans of action; people perceive things in terms of experiences they would have if a plan of action were carried out toward that object. One sees objects in terms of the use to be made of them or the action to be directed toward them. Objects exist only when we indicate them to ourselves. To indicate something to oneself is to take others into account. As "others' definitions" are implicated in our indicating objects to ourselves, objects are largely shared, or social, objects. Hence, while we indeed select those objects that make up our social habitats, we do so on a social, as well as an individual, basis.

Cooperative social activity forms the matrix out of which communication arises, and such communication is, in turn, the very process out of which mind arises. During the course of interacting with others, some initial gestures of the human infant are favorably received. Soon, certain gestures come to have common meanings for both the child and his associates. Such consensually agreed upon gestures Mead calls "conventional gestures." Through these conventional gestures and additional linguistic symbols, the child learns the "meanings," or definitions, of the collectivity to which he belongs, learns to take the role of others, and develops the ability to think. A socially generated mind not only enables the individual to adjust to society but, in turn, makes possible society's continued existence.

Mead's working conceptualization of mind, self, and society furthered the development of social-psychological theorizing in the United States.

## Conclusion

Cooley and Mead played a key role in shaping the most sophisticated variety of social behaviorism currently found in American sociology, the social-psychological framework known as symbolic interactionism. Their strong emphasis on the group, especially the primary group, as the basic molder of individual behavior and as the "real place" one has to look first to explain such conduct became a cornerstone in social-psychological theory. Their concepts of the looking-glass self and the social self impact heavily on contemporary treatments of personality. Their views on the importance of gestures, symbols, and language in shaping behavior and integrating society are still in force among sociologists and social psychologists alike. Both Cooley and Mead favored those methodological techniques, strategies, and devices that are today called *qualitative approaches* and find favor among a large number of sociologists.

While the approach represented by Cooley and Mead has its shortcomings (e.g., it is fairly ahistorical and needs to provide a better analysis of large-scale societal structures, including social classes), one real measure of their success stands out in that many of their insights are taken for granted by today's social psychologists.

## Notes

1 Charles Horton Cooley, *Human Nature and Social Order* (New York: Scribner's, 1902), 87.
2 Charles Horton Cooley, *Social Process* (New York: Scribner's, 1918), 28.
3 Charles Horton Cooley, *Social Organization* (New York: Scribner's, 1909), 23.
4 Cooley, *Human Nature and Social Order*, 151–2.
5 Cooley, *Human Nature and Social Order*, 152–3.
6 Sheldon Stryker, *Symbolic Interactionism* (Menlo Park, CA: Benjamin Cummings, 1980), 29.
7 George Herbert Mead, *Mind, Self and Society: From the Standpoint of a Social Behaviorist* (Chicago, IL: University of Chicago Press, 1934), 261.
8 Mead, *Mind, Self and Society*, 137.
9 Mead, *Mind, Self and Society*, 68–9.
10 Mead, *Mind, Self and Society*, 178.

11  Bernard N. Meltzer, *The Social Psychology of George Herbert Mead* (Kalamazoo, MI: Western Michigan University Center for Sociological Research, 1964), 17.
12  Mead, *Mind, Self and Society*, 210.
13  Mead, *Mind, Self and Society*, 55.
14  George Herbert Mead, "Suggestions Toward a Theory of Philosophical Disciplines," *Philosophical Review* 9 (1900): 2.

8

# FREUD ON THE DEVELOPMENT OF SOCIETY AND CIVILIZATION

This chapter examines the contributions of Sigmund Freud (1856–1939) to social theory with his concept of human nature, the origins and development of society and civilization, and the nature of religion and religious phenomena. While Freud is generally known for his psychological approach to the study of human relations, his analysis of individual behavior within the context of society and social relations, especially the impact of social institutions on the individual, constitutes a major contribution to classical social theory.

The controversies surrounding the development of a psychoanalytic theory of society in the early part of the twentieth century have given rise to a number of critical approaches to Freudian psychology.[1] Some controversial figures, such as Wilhelm Reich, have attempted to develop a Marx–Freud synthesis to explore the political sources of mass psychology and explain the rise of fascism in Germany.[2] Focusing on the cultural, ideological, and philosophical dimensions of Freudian theory, others, such as Erich Fromm and Herbert Marcuse, have developed their own distinct versions of this synthesis that informs a critical analysis of modern society.[3]

## Human Nature and Character Structure

Freud viewed the individual as an organism driven by an instinctual energy called *libido*. Contrary to the arguments of some who have set forth a narrow, vulgar interpretation of libido purely as a sexual drive, others have maintained that the Freudian libidinal instinct

> is manifested not only in childhood sexuality, attachment to parents and brotherly love, but in art, work, aggression and just about all forms of human behavior involving emotional commitment including the feelings associated with the concepts "self-respect," "human dignity," "fraternity" and "equality."[4]

Moreover, Freud's broader characterization of libido as a more generalized drive for human satisfaction can be deduced from his observation suggesting that creative work may provide a primary release for libidinal energies:

> The possibility [work] offers of displacing a large amount of libidinal components, whether narcissistic, aggressive or even erotic, on to professional work and on to the human relations connected with it lends it a value by no means second to what it enjoys as something indispensable to the preservation and justification of existence in society. Professional activity is a source of special satisfaction if it is a freely chosen one—if, that is to say, by means of sublimation, it makes possible the use of existing inclinations, of persisting or constitutionally reinforced instinctual impulses.[5]

Focusing on the inner workings of human behavior, Freud concludes that there exist two contradictory processes: "After long doubts and vacillations," he writes, "we have decided to assume the existence of only two basic instincts, *Eros* and the destructive instinct."[6]

> The aim of the first of these basic instincts is to establish ever greater unities and to preserve them thus—in short, to bind together; the aim of the second, on the contrary, is to undo connections and so to destroy things. We may suppose that the final aim of the destructive instinct is to reduce living things to an inorganic state. For this reason we also call it the *death instinct*. . . .
>
> In biological functions the two basic instincts work against each other or combine with each other.[7]

These basic instincts, Freud tells us, represent "forces which we assume to exist behind the tensions caused by the needs of the id."[8] Furthermore, "they represent the somatic demands upon mental life. . . . [T]hey are the ultimate cause of all activity."[9]

These instincts, then, lie at the very core of human personality or character structure, and through the dynamic parts or mechanisms of this structure, one relates to others and to the external world. The three component parts of the individual's character structure, in the Freudian model, are the *id*, the *ego*, and the *superego*; together, they form the topography of the mind.

"The power of the id," Freud asserts, "expresses the true purpose of the individual organism's life. This consists in the satisfaction of its innate needs."[10] "In the id there are no conflicts; contradictions and antitheses exist side by side, and often equalize matters between themselves by compromise formations. . . . [E]verything which goes on in the id is unconscious and remains so."[11] Consequently,

> the core of our being, then, is formed by the obscure id, which has no direct relations with the external world and is accessible even to our own knowledge only through the medium of another agency of the mind. . . .
> The id, which is cut off from the external world, has its own world perception.[12]

In short, according to Freud, the id is our instinctual nature; it represents the drive for the satisfaction of our innate needs.

The ego, in contrast, is the organized part of the id. It mediates the demands of the id, on the one hand, and the realities of the external world, as well as the superego, on the other. In Freud's words,

> the ego is in control of voluntary movement. It has the task of self-preservation. As regards *external* events, it performs that task by becoming aware of the stimuli from without. . . . As regards *internal* events, in relation to the id, it performs that task by gaining control over the demands of the instincts, by deciding whether they shall be allowed to obtain satisfaction, by postponing that satisfaction to times and circumstances favorable in the external world or by suppressing their excitations completely.[13]

Finally, the superego, according to Freud, is the conscience of internalized cultural prohibitions. To the extent that these prohibitions imposed on individuals by society or civilization come to repress and frustrate libidinal energies, aggression is the result. If such aggression is not channeled and released through some social mechanism, then the individual can become neurotic. Otherwise, the collective yearning to release repressed libidinal energies may trigger a social response with revolutionary political implications!

### The Origins and Development of Society and Civilization

Society and civilization, in Freudian theory, have their roots in the material conditions of human social existence. Hence, for Freud, the rise and development of human societies must be explained through a concrete analysis of the social world. "Human civilization," Freud explains,

> includes on the one hand all the knowledge and capacity that men have acquired in order to control the forces of nature and extract its wealth for the satisfaction

of human needs, and, on the other hand, all the regulations necessary in order to adjust the relations of men to one another and especially the distribution of the available wealth. The two trends of civilization are not independent of each other.[14]

The development of civilization, Freud argues, is thus the result of the physiological imperatives of survival (i.e., food, shelter, and physical security) and the society's need to organize social relations to maintain social order. "If we go back far enough," Freud writes, "we find that the first acts of civilization were the use of tools, the gaining of control over fire and the construction of dwellings."[15] At a certain point in history, humans realized that it would be to their advantage to work in cooperation with others to overcome the immense difficulties posed by nature, which threatened human survival. This cooperative work among individuals led to the formation of groups that were mutually beneficial for all. In Freud's words,

> After primal man had discovered that it lay in his own hands, literally, to improve his lot on earth by working, it cannot have been a matter of indifference to him whether another man worked with or against him. The other man acquired the value for him of a fellow-worker, with whom it was useful to live together. Even earlier, in his ape-like prehistory, man had adopted the habit of forming families, and the members of his family were probably his first helpers.[16]

For Freud, then, civilization is rooted in an individual's relationship with nature and with other individuals—in developing the necessary technology to sustain life and in satisfying his or her social needs. Thus, Freud gives us a materialist analysis of the rise and development of society and civilization. He argues that the human group has its roots in the material conditions of its social existence in nature and that the mechanism that facilitates this process is the family.

The family, through the social relationships it engages in, channels instinctual energies and forms the child's character structure. Through this process, the family thus becomes the mechanism that produces and socializes children who are fitted to the social roles that society requires them to fulfill. In this way, the family comes to play a key role in rationalizing and reinforcing the existing social order.[17]

The role of the family in facilitating the preservation of the modern social order is a central one in the Freudian view, as the social and class structure of society is transmitted to future generations through the socialization process that develops and matures within the family. Thus, "the social relationships of the family . . . channels instinctual energies and forms the child's character structure."[18] And with the development of this character structure, the family passes on to future generations the socially accepted roles that one's offspring acquire.

The recognition by some Marxist theorists of the process surrounding the role of the family in facilitating the maintenance of the status quo led to the development of the Marx–Freud synthesis in the earlier part of the twentieth century. The proponents of this approach developed their analysis to examine the reasons for the prevalence of false consciousness among the working class and how it can be transformed into class consciousness, which the working-class family can promote to advance its class interests.

A recent proponent of this approach, Albert Szymanski, points out that, in his analysis of the family, Freud

> mistakenly assumes the logic of the family triad to be universal among "civilized" homo sapiens. The early synthesizers of Marx and Freud, on the other hand, put the family in historical context, recognizing Freud's universal family for the bourgeois family it is. They understood that families in different societies and different classes would have different logics and consequently would produce different typical character structures.[19]

To maintain their control over society, the dominant classes, through the institutions they control, which in turn have great influence on the family, channel behavior to conform to the values promoted by the existing social order. Thus, the development of a character structure that conforms to the prevailing status quo

> results in passive and dependent people who have internalized the necessities of class society and the capital accumulation process. Political conservatism among the masses of the oppressed thus becomes firmly rooted. False-consciousness among people who should be among the most active supporters of revolution is securely anchored by these mechanisms in the very psychology of the oppressed.[20]

Moreover,

> Conservatism and reaction in all its forms—religion, nationalism, fascism, etc.—on the one hand ward off rational impulses [to freedom, dignity and self-determination] and on the other offer substitute gratifications in aggressive behavior towards other "races" and nations or against the very groups and individuals which advocate liberation. Racism, fascism and extreme nationalism are thus firmly rooted in the character structures of large segments of the oppressed.

These phenomena are consequently far more than mere attitudes, values, norms, or prejudices; they are based in the organization of our psychic energies.[21]

Thus, in order to eliminate these phenomena, which block the development of class consciousness, one "must remove the source of the energy behind such behavior, not just 're-educate,' i.e., the libidinal repression necessitated by the logic of capitalism must be eliminated by destroying that logic itself."[22]

## Religion

Religion and religious ideas, for Freud, are likewise the manifestations of material conditions in social life; they reflect the basic social organization of society. Hence, religious phenomena, Freud argues, must be explained from the standpoint of a materialist understanding of social reality, one that locates religion within the confines of the prevailing social order and social relations. Perhaps one of the clearest statements of Freud's social conception of religion can be found in the following passage:

> Religion . . . is an attempt to get control over the sensory world, in which we are placed, by means of the wish world which we have developed inside us as a result of biological and psychological necessities. But it cannot achieve its end. Its doctrines carry with them the stamp of the times in which they originate, the ignorant childhood days of the human race.[23]

Arguing that religion plays an illusory role and mystifies the nature of human relations in society, Freud proclaims the abolition of religion as the first step toward the demystification of social reality, hence clearing the way for the realization of true human potential. In his dialogue with his imaginary opponent in *The Future of an Illusion*, Freud argues that "religious doctrines . . . should cease to be put forward as the reasons for the precepts of civilization."[24] Moreover, "those historical residues," he adds,

> have helped us to view religious teachings, as it were, as neurotic relics, and we may now argue that the time has probably come, as it does in an analytic treatment, for replacing the effects of repression by the results of the rational operation of the intellect. We may foresee, but hardly regret, that such a process of remolding will not stop at renouncing the solemn transfiguration of cultural precepts, but that a general revision of them will result in many of them being done away with.[25]

"[R]eligious doctrines will have to be discarded," Freud insists,

> no matter whether the first attempts fail, or whether the first substitutes prove to be untenable.... [I]n the long run nothing can withstand reason and experience, and the contradiction which religion offers to both is all too palpable.[26]

Through the abolition of religion, then, humanity will be able to free itself from illusions and actively intervene in history to liberate itself from repression and move toward the satisfaction of truly human needs, needs that precisely form the very core of the human experience.

## Conclusion

The above analysis of the Freudian approach in classical social theory reveals a number of strands in the application of psychoanalytic theory to explain social reality. We have argued that once they are stripped of their biological connotations, Freud's arguments in essence are socially based and concern the inner workings of social life, which he was able to express through his materialist analysis of society and the social order within which the individual is situated. Thus, for Freud, the discontented individual becomes stressed because society limits individual behavior by repressing his or her innate psychological drives for freedom and independence. Further, the major institutions of society, such as the family, the state, and religion, play a pivotal role in perpetuating this condition to maintain social order. However, failing to provide a dialectically informed class analysis of the prevailing social realities, Freud was unable to see that these very same institutions can also become key instruments of change that help transform society and achieve genuine freedom for the individual and the social collectivity.

The significance of the Freudian model is such that, if interpreted within its social and material context (i.e., the context of class relations within capitalist society), it can add an important dimension to sociological analysis and, thus, make a valuable contribution to classical social theory.

## Notes

1  For a critical analysis of the origins and development of psychoanalysis in the United States, see Harry K. Wells, *The Failure of Psychoanalysis* (New York: International Publishers, 1963); and C. P. Oberndorf, *A History of Psychoanalysis in America* (New York: Grune, 1953). See also Martin Jay, *The Dialectical Imagination* (Boston, MA: Little, Brown, 1973), chap. 3.

2  See, for example, Wilhelm Reich, *Character Analysis* (New York: Orgone Institute Press, 1949); Wilhelm Reich, *The Mass Psychology of Fascism* (New York: Farrar, Strauss, and Giroux, 1970); and Wilhelm Reich, *Sex Pol: Essays, 1929–1934* (New York: Random House, 1972).

3 For a sampling of Fromm's writings, see Erich Fromm, *Beyond the Chains of Illusion* (New York: Simon and Schuster, 1962); and Erich Fromm, *The Crisis of Psychoanalysis* (New York: Holt, Rinehart, Winston, 1970). For some of Marcuse's most influential works, see Herbert Marcuse, *One Dimensional Man* (Boston, MA: Beacon Press, 1964); and Herbert Marcuse, *Eros and Civilization* (New York: Vintage Books, 1968).

4 Albert Szymanski, "The Revolutionary Uses of Freudian Theory," *Social Praxis* 5, nos. 1–2 (1976): 46.

5 Sigmund Freud, *Civilization and Its Discontents* (New York: Norton, 1962), 27.

6 Sigmund Freud, *An Outline of Psychoanalysis* (New York: Norton, 1949), 20.

7 Freud, *An Outline of Psychoanalysis*, 20–1.

8 Freud, *An Outline of Psychoanalysis*, 19.

9 Freud, *An Outline of Psychoanalysis*, 19.

10 Freud, *An Outline of Psychoanalysis*, 19.

11 Sigmund Freud, *The Question of Lay Analysis* (Garden City, NY: Doubleday Anchor, 1950), 36, 38.

12 Freud, *An Outline of Psychoanalysis*, 108–9.

13 Freud, *An Outline of Psychoanalysis*, 15–16.

14 Sigmund Freud, *The Future of an Illusion* (Garden City, NY: Doubleday Anchor, 1961), 2–3.

15 Freud, *Civilization and Its Discontents*, 37.

16 Freud, *Civilization and Its Discontents*, 46.

17 Szymanski, "The Revolutionary Uses of Freudian Theory," 32.

18 Szymanski, "The Revolutionary Uses of Freudian Theory," 30.

19 Szymanski, "The Revolutionary Uses of Freudian Theory," 30.

20 Szymanski, "The Revolutionary Uses of Freudian Theory," 36.

21 Szymanski, "The Revolutionary Uses of Freudian Theory," 36.

22 Szymanski, "The Revolutionary Uses of Freudian Theory," 36.

23 Sigmund Freud, *New Introductory Lectures on Psychoanalysis*, ed. and trans. James Strachey (New York: Norton, 1990), 168.

24 Freud, *The Future of an Illusion*, 72.

25 Freud, *The Future of an Illusion*, 72–3.

26 Freud, *The Future of an Illusion*, 88–9.

# 9

# ADDAMS AND EARLY WOMEN SOCIAL THEORISTS

*Mary Jo Deegan*

Women were central to the establishment of sociology as a discipline between 1890 and 1920. Their vision differed significantly from that of white male sociologists based in leading academies and/or widely recognized today as founding figures. The women's ideas and practices challenged patriarchy and, therefore, all the established, classical approaches to theory now recognized as definitive. The women's challenges included an emphasis on theory and practice as united and processual, and they argued that the ideal society was cooperative, pacifist, inclusive of women and children, and emergent from the liberal values of democracy and civil rights. Several dozen women who shared these theoretical stances are introduced in my volume on *Women in Sociology*.[1] The most central figure in this group was Jane Addams (1860–1935) who co-founded an institution, Hull-House. This social settlement focused the work and commitments of many other female sociologists who worked in the academy, the community, and social movement organizations, often in the United States but also globally.

In this chapter I introduce Addams as a person, a theorist, an activist, and a leader in sociological theory and practice within the context of the Hull-House School of Sociology and other early women social theorists associated with it in the late nineteenth and early twentieth centuries.

## Jane Addams and Her Biographical Location

Jane Addams is a recognized world leader with a sweeping mind, personal charisma, and an innovative intellectual legacy. She is one of the most important female sociologists who has ever lived. From 1890 to 1935, she was the leader of dozens of women in sociology, although after 1920 most of these women were forced out of sociology and into other fields such as social work, home economics, applied psychology, pedagogy, and administration in higher education.[2]

Addams was born on September 6, 1860 in the Midwestern small town of Cedarville, Illinois. She was profoundly influenced by her father, John Addams, a Hicksite Quaker, state senator, and mill owner, but she did not know her mother, Sarah Weber, who died when Addams was two years old. In 1877 Addams entered Rockford Female Seminary, in Rockford, Illinois, one of the pioneering colleges for women. After she graduated in 1881, she entered an extended period of unhappiness and depression. In August, her father died and his absence left her confused and despairing. She entered the Women's Medical College in Philadelphia in the fall, but she soon returned to Illinois. Ill and surrounded by family problems, Addams drifted for a year. Finally taking some action, in 1883 she traveled to Europe but she remained frustrated for the next two years until she returned to Europe. Addams received the equivalent of a graduate education during these extended journeys where she practiced and learned a number of languages including Italian, German, French, and Greek. She visited art galleries, museums, as well as becoming familiar with numerous cultures and customs.

In her second European trip and accompanied by her college friend Ellen Gates Starr, Addams found a direction for her life after visiting the social settlement Toynbee Hall in London's East End. This group served the exploited working classes and supported artisans who harmonized their interests in art, labor, and the community. Toynbee Hall provided a model in 1889 for Addams and Starr to co-found their social settlement, Hull-House, in Chicago. Hull-House became the institutional anchor for women's gender-segregated work in sociology and a liaison with the most important male sociological center during this era, the University of Chicago.

### Life and Labor at Hull-House (1889–1935)

The 1890s were lively, controversial years at Hull-House where anarchists, Marxists, Socialists, unionists, and leading social theorists congregated.[3] John Dewey, George Herbert Mead, and W. I. Thomas, among others, were frequent visitors, lecturers, and close friends of Addams. Chicago pragmatism was born through their collegial contacts and intellectual exchanges.[4] A groundbreaking sociological text, *Hull-House Maps and Papers,* was published by Hull-House residents in 1895, predating and establishing the interests of the early Chicago male sociologists.[5]

Author of thirteen books and hundreds of articles, Addams continued her educational efforts through lectures across the country. She led social reform organizations, campaigned for the Progressive Party, and helped to found numerous government agencies and programs, such as Workers' Compensation and civil service. She practiced and advocated "radical democracy," arguing that equality must extend beyond citizenship rights and pervade all aspects of economic and social life. "Economic democracy" was similar to Fabian socialism enacted in England in their welfare state. "Social democracy" included a commitment to African Americans and cultural pluralism. "Political democracy" referred to civil rights and political participation, including winning women's suffrage.[6] She sought not only answers to problems, but answers in the best interests of all, including the poor and disenfranchised. Nonviolence permeates all of Addams's thought. I call her work for a nonviolent democracy "*Satyagraha democracy*," due to its alliance with Mahatma Gandhi and her adoption of the nonviolent concepts of passive resistance and Satyagraha, the latter a term referring to nonviolence as a political and spiritual force.[7]

Her thought and practice is called "feminist pragmatism": an American theory uniting liberal values and a belief in a rational public with a cooperative, nurturing, and liberating model of the self, the other, and the community. Education and democracy are significant mechanisms to organize and improve society.

Feminist pragmatists study "social behavior" and believe each "individual" is born with rudimentary, flexible instincts or "impulses." Infants primarily learn by observing, imitating, and responding to the gestures of others, particularly their parents. They can abstract the meaning of "gestures," particularly "vocal gestures," and generalize about "the other, the group, the community, and institutions." This "process" allows the individual to develop a "mind, intelligence, a self, and the ability to take the role of the other." The self learns organized "attitudes" of "the community" toward "social situations." People sharing the same neighborhood and community develop "shared experience (which is the greatest of human goods." The self emerges from others and is not in conflict with others unless it is taught to be in conflict. "Education" is a major way to learn about one's community, participate in group decisions, and become a "citizen."

Women who obey the rules governing the home and family follow "the family claim." When they work for others outside the home, they follow "the social claim." Conflicts between these claims can result in "social disorganization," where competing values and attitudes on the same situation are legitimated simultaneously. This creates an instability in society, whereby "women become a resource for social change." Women in public life can utilize their cooperative worldview to implement the goals of democracy. The female world is based on the unity of the female self, the home, the family, and face-to-face interactions with neighbors in a community. Women can take this pattern and extend it to nurturing others, as "bread givers engaged in bread labor." Their model for the home and family, when extended to the larger social situation, is called "civic housekeeping." Women can be leaders in a new "social consciousness," indicated in "newer ideals of peace." A sign of this awakening consciousness is "the integration of the objective with the subjective." This is organized through "social movements in labor, social science, and women." The modern city is a new location for these social changes.

Women learn "folk wisdom" and share a culture based on female myths such as the Corn Mother. This unity crosses racial/ethnic lines while it supports and respects differences including variation by class, age, race, religion, education, sexual preference, and disability. Democracy emerges from different groups, and represents these distinct perspectives, histories, communities, and characteristic structures of the self. Social change must articulate and respond to these various groups' commonalities and differences. "Old women" also learn and pass on legends, cherish the good in others, develop "woman's Memory," and engage in "perfecting the past." Because women are not full members of the male world, they are in an ideal situation to "challenge war, disturb conventions, integrate industry, react to life, and transform the past." "Women's obligation" is to help create and distribute the world's food supply. The modern woman's family claim is built on a "consumer role" that should critique and change industry.

Reuniting the woman and society through economic productivity empowers the woman to make better choices in the home and the marketplace. "New perspectives on women" can develop through the use of rational facts; alternative attitudes; new social situations; the new social sciences, especially sociology; and changed economics. This can occur through the development of "working hypotheses" that enter a social situation and change it, thereby generating new working hypotheses. This process is called "social reconstruction." Women's clubwork is another source for social change and education.

## The Hull-House School of Sociology

Literally thousands of people attended Hull-House each week, and a smaller group of this large body of supporters included community leaders, academics, and female sociologists. A prominent segment of the last group were five women who held marginal positions in the department of sociology at the University of Chicago.[8] They, in turn, formally trained a large number of students in the ideas and practices of Hull-House. Within the academy they were aligned with Chicago pragmatists who trained another significant group of professionals.[9] After 1920, the five women were largely segregated from sociology and moved into the School of Social Service Administration, and their students primarily entered social work and not sociology. A lengthy analysis of this process is available in my book, *Annie Marion MacLean and the Chicago Schools of Sociology, 1894–1934*.[10]

Areas of concentration within feminist pragmatism and the Hull-House School of Sociology form separate literatures, including the study of: (1) the city, (2) crime,[11] (3) the use of qualitative and quantitative methodology,[12] (4) the lifecourse, (5) social class, work, occupations, and labor relations, (6) the process of making and enjoying art and aesthetics,[13] (7) play,[14] (8) education, (9) social movements, (10) ethics, (11) the development of an international consciousness and political apparatus, (12) immigration, (13) law, (14) African American life and racial discrimination,[15] (15) socioautobiographies, (16) gender,[16] (17) feminine values and the natural environment or "ecofeminist pragmatism,"[17] (18) pacifism and nonviolence,[18] and (19) prophetic pragmatism.[19] Each area often involved dozens[20] of scholars and activists with Addams as a central figure uniting these disparate interests and activities.

Addams participated in all of these specialties. They each involved formal publications, popular writings and speeches, voluntary organizations, and civic leadership in the latter. As a national and international social network they played major roles in articulating and implementing feminist pragmatism.

As a pacifist prior to World War I, Addams was lauded as a "good woman." With the building of patriotic feeling from 1914 until America's entry into the war in 1917, she increasingly became the target of animosity and personal attack. In 1914 Addams and her sister sociologists had organized the first, and still largest, group of international female pacifists into the Women's International League of Peace and Freedom.[21] By 1917 she was socially and publicly ostracized. She went from being a saint to a villain. Booed off speaking platforms, abandoned by her friends, colleagues, and, most notably, other sociologists, Addams was a social pariah. This was an agonizing time for her. Committed to her values, based on "female" ideals, she maintained her pacifist position. The culmination of her politically untouchable status occurred in 1919, when she was targeted by the U.S. Government as the most dangerous person in America. At this point her major role as a sociologist diminished and she was ostracized by succeeding generations of sociologists, until recently. The overwhelming majority of female sociologists followed her commitment to peace, and they, too, were ostracized from the profession.

In 1920, women were granted the franchise, and to Addams this was a major victory. Contrary to her expectation of a powerful women's vote, this decade led to an eclipse of the former power of women activists, including Addams. Progressive leadership was squelched and the liberal vision of a changing, optimistic, and scientifically rational society was accepted less and less. Sociologists increasingly applied an androcentric perspective to their definition of the field.

Addams gradually resumed her pubic leadership during the 1920s, but the devastating impact of the Great Depression once more called for radical social analysis and social change. Addams, again, became a distinguished world leader. Winner of the Nobel Peace Prize in 1931, she spoke for many of the values and policies adopted during the New Deal, especially in social security and other government programs which altered American capitalism. (Her colleague and friend Emily Green Balch employed the principles of the Hull-House School of Sociology in her work and was awarded the Nobel Peace Prize in 1946.) Dying in 1935, Addams was mourned worldwide as a great leader and interpreter of American thought.

In addition to Addams's relation to Chicago pragmatism, she analyzed sociological traditions in Britain, including empiricism, social surveys, social settlements, Fabian socialism, and the Arts and Crafts movement. She was interested in the work of Charles Ashbee, Beatrice Webb, Charles Booth, Patrick Geddes, John Ruskin, and Canon Barnett. Addams was also influenced by Russian sociologists, especially the pacifism and art of Leo Tolstoy and the analysis of the human relationship to the land articulated by Petr Kropotkin. Addams seriously considered the Germanic tradition of sociology enacted by Karl Marx and Frederick Engels,[22] but her dedication to a cooperative, and not a conflict, model based on the triple foundation for human behavior, including play and art, as well as the Marxist emphasis on labor, made this tradition unworkable for her.

There is a vast literature on Addams, most of it emphasizing her biography, social work, and public role in American society.[23] There is a serious lack of study of her intellectual apparatus: her theory of the arts, including the theater, pageants, drama, literature, sculpture, pottery, and the aesthetics of nature; her life-long commitment to political theory; and her vast influence in American race relations, especially between whites, Mexican-Americans, and African Americans. This dearth of scholarship in these major areas of her work significantly limits our understanding of her ideas and accomplishments.

A large literature exists in several other fields, especially in Women's Studies, which criticizes white, middle-class women, early social workers, reformers, and philanthropists as conservative, exploitative, and oppressive. Addams is often the symbolic leader of these various groups and sometimes emerges as a contemporary symbol of the villainy of benevolent ignorance or intentional evil. Thus, she is sometimes mentioned superficially in texts where she is stereotyped as a racist, assimilationist, essentialist, and atheoretical meddler.

Addams is recognized increasingly in textbooks, but often only a paragraph or, at most, a page is included. Her implicit criticism of the dominant approaches in sociology is usually omitted, as is her alliance with Chicago pragmatism. This latter problem arises from the misinterpretation of Chicago pragmatism as limited to microsociology and rational face-to-face interaction divorced from progressive politics and emotions.[24] The dozens of feminist pragmatists who were allies of Addams are excluded from the annals of sociology in the process.[25]

The general scholarship noted above contrasts with the early studies of Addams as a sociologist before 1920, when she was highly integrated into the sociological literature, frequently spoke before the American Sociological Society, and published in the *American Journal of Sociology*. Addams's stellar leadership in sociology was erased until the publication of my work often noted here in the endnotes.[26] Rediscovering her role and influence in sociology is increasingly visible and understood within the profession.

## Conclusion

Addams's intellectual legacy as a feminist pragmatist has been obscured, misunderstood, and sometimes distorted. She articulated radical changes in American life and politics, altering the possibilities for human growth and action for the poor, the working class, immigrants, people of color, youth, the aged, and women. This work was organized into multiple areas of specialization, with dozens of women in sociology assuming leadership in this broad and inclusive approach. This social network was extremely powerful and united, but they were vulnerable to an almost complete removal from the profession after World War I. Their work was defined by patriarchs as outside the boundaries of the discipline.

Addams was a central figure in applied sociology between 1892 and 1920 and led a large and powerful cohort of women whom she profoundly influenced. Contemporary scholars often document and either praise or deplore Addams's significant contributions to public life, but her intellectual stature is barely appreciated. Her legacy in sociology, and the large network of scholars who followed her, is particularly hidden within the mainstream literature in the discipline. Her profound influence on the course and development of sociology is only suggested in most sociological textbooks, books, and articles. A growing number of scholars are analyzing this great, alternative heritage and tradition in American sociology. They envision a new horizon for a more just and liberated society.

## Notes

1  Mary Jo Deegan, ed., *Women in Sociology* (Westport, CT: Greenwood Press, 1991).
2  Mary Jo Deegan, *Jane Addams and the Men of the Chicago School, 1892–1918* (New Brunswick, NJ: Transaction Press, 1988).

3 Jane Addams, *Twenty Years at Hull-House* (New York: Macmillan, 1910).

4 Darnell Rucker, *The Chicago Pragmatists* (Minneapolis, MI: University of Minnesota Press, 1969).

5 Residents of Hull-House, *Hull-House Maps and Papers* (New York: Crowell, 1895).

6 See Mary Jo Deegan, "Jane Addams on Citizenship in a Democracy," *Journal of Classical Sociology* 10, no. 3 (2010), 217–38.

7 See Jane Addams, "Tolstoy and Gandhi," *Christian Century* 48, no. 47 (1931), 1485–8; and Tom Gilsenan, "Peacemakers and Friends: Jane Addams and Gandhi," www.mkgandhi-sarvodaya.org/articles/addamsgandhi.htm (accessed 8 February 2007).

8 These women were Edith Abbott, Sophonisba P. Breckinridge, Mary E. McDowell, Annie Marion MacLean, and Marion Talbot. Other Hull-House women who taught sociology in the Extension Division included Jane Addams, Julia Lathrop, and Florence Kelley. I refer to this group as the female Chicago School of Sociology, and Patricia Lengermann and Jill Niebrugge refer to them as the Women of the Chicago School of Sociology. See Mary Jo Deegan, "Women in Sociology, 1890–1930," *Journal of the History of Sociology* 1 (1978): 11–34; Mary Jo Deegan, *Annie Marion MacLean and the Chicago Schools of Sociology, 1894–1934* (New Brunswick, NJ: Transaction Press, 2014). See entries on Abbott, Breckinridge, Kelley, and MacLean in *Women in Sociology*; and Patricia Madoo Lengermann and Jill Niebrugge, eds., *The Women Founders: Sociology and Social Theory, 1830–1930* (New York: McGraw-Hill, 1998). There were numerous other female sociologists in this network including Charlotte Perkins Gilman, Ida B. Wells-Barnett, and Fannie Barrier Williams. See Fannie Barrier Williams, *A New Woman of Color: The Collected Writings of Fannie Barrier Williams*, ed. and intro. Mary Jo Deegan (DeKalb, IL: Northeastern Illinois University, 2002).

9 See a detailed description of this alliance in Mary Jo Deegan, "Play from the Perspective of George Herbert Mead," in *Play, School, and Society*, ed. and intro. Mary Jo Deegan (New York: Peter Lange, 1999), xix–cxii; and Mary Jo Deegan, *Self, War, and Society: The Macrosociology of George Herbert Mead* (New Brunswick, NJ: Transaction Publishers, 2008).

10 Deegan, *Annie Marion MacLean*.

11 Mary Jo Deegan, "Katharine Bement Davis: Her Theory and Praxis of Feminist Pragmatism," *Women & Criminal Justice* 14, nos. 2–3 (2003): 15–40; Elizabeth Neeley and Mary Jo Deegan, "George Herbert Mead on Punitive Justice: A Critical Analysis of Contemporary Practices," *Humanity & Society* 29, no. 1 (2005): 71–83.

12 Deegan, *Jane Addams*.

13 Mary Jo Deegan and Ana-Maria Wahl, "Introduction: Ellen Gates Starr and Her Journey toward Social Justice and Beauty," in *On Art, Labor, and Religion*, ed. and intro. Mary Jo Deegan and Ana-Maria Wahl (New Brunswick, NJ: Transaction Publishers, 2003), 1–35.

14 Deegan, "Play."

15 Mary Jo Deegan, *Race, Hull-House, and the University of Chicago: A New Conscience against an Ancient Evil* (Westport, CT: Greenwood Press, 2002).

16 Mary Jo Deegan, *Gender at Hull-House and the University of Chicago: Exploring the Origins and Influence of Feminist Pragmatism, 1889–2011* (Amherst, NY: Cambria Press, 2014).

17 Mary Jo Deegan and Christopher Podeschi, "The Ecofeminist Pragmatism of Charlotte Perkins Gilman: The Herland Sagas," *Environmental Ethics* 23, no. 1 (2001): 19–36.

18 See Jane Addams, Emily G. Balch, and Alice Hamilton, *Women at The Hague: The International Peace Congress of 1915* (Amherst, NY: Humanity Books, 2003).

19 Cornel West, *The American Evasion of Philosophy* (Madison, WI: University of Wisconsin Press, 1989).

20  Lists of names of such women are found in Deegan, *Women in Sociology* and in *Race, Hull-House, and the University of Chicago*. In the latter book, over 70 names are included and such an analysis of each specialization could be constructed.

21  See Addams, Balch, and Hamilton, *Women at The Hague*. The Women's International League for Peace and Freedom (WILPF) now involves approximately 700,000 active members and is the founding model for over 400 female pacifist organizations globally.

22  See analyses of these usually neglected traditions in sociology in Deegan, *Jane Addams*.

23  See, for example, Allen F. Davis, *American Heroine* (New York: Oxford University Press, 1973).

24  All of these errors are addressed in the following books: George Herbert Mead, *Play, School and Society*, ed. and intro. Mary Jo Deegan (New York: Peter Lang, 1999); George Herbert Mead, *Essays in Social Psychology*, ed. and intro. Mary Jo Deegan (New Brunswick, NJ: Transaction Publishers, 2001); and Deegan, *Self, War, and Society*.

25  An excellent critique of this distortion of the history of the profession is found in Joe R. Feagin, Hernan Vera, and Kimberly Ducey, *Liberation Sociology*, 3rd ed. (Boulder, CO: Paradigm, 2014).

26  An important recognition of her work is found in her inclusion as one of the top fifty sociologists. See Mary Jo Deegan, "Jane Addams," in *Fifty Key Sociologists: The Formative Theorists*, ed. John Scott (London: Routledge, 2007), 3–8.

# 10

# VEBLEN ON THE LEISURE CLASS AND CONSPICUOUS CONSUMPTION

Among the conventional social theorists of the late nineteenth and early twentieth centuries, Thorstein Bunde Veblen (1857–1929) earned himself a prominent place as a harsh critic of advanced industrial society through his writings on the "leisure class" and "conspicuous consumption," which he argues are the twin culprits of the long-term decline and decay of modern capitalist society.[1] This is so because the dominant wealthy leisure class has increasingly become a parasitic idle class set against the industrious laboring masses who toil to maintain modern society. Like Karl Marx before him, Veblen also ventures into an analysis of the evolution of society through various stages of development—from primitive to modern—but his historical typology varies widely from Marx's, especially in terms of the agents of social change and transformation. Unlike Marx, Veblen seeks the transformation of contemporary capitalist society not through the organized will of the exploited working class, but through the technocratic ingenuity of the engineers and intellectuals in whom he places his trust to transform society and societal institutions.

## The Evolution of Society and Social Order

Although influenced by Marx's analysis of modes of production and types of societies that Marx had identified as having gone through a series of historic transformations, Veblen develops his peculiar set of societal types that he claims was the basis of social development from earlier times to the present. He argues that human history evolved through three stages, from savagery to barbarism to capitalism, with a future society that he characterizes as a new industrial republic with social-democratic features. According to Veblen, the savage stage was communal, egalitarian, and devoid of social classes (a stage similar to what Marx called primitive communism). Speaking of "communities of primitive savages in which there is no hierarchy of economic classes," Veblen writes: "The scheme of life of these groups at the time of their earliest contact with Europeans seems to have been nearly typical, so far as regards the absence of a leisure class."[2] This was followed by "barbarism," according to Veblen. In this stage of social development, private property arose, classes began to form, and divisions along class lines led to conflict and exploitation of the masses—a stage characteristic of various types of precapitalist societies (from despotism to slavery to feudalism):

> The evidence afforded by the usages and cultural traits of communities at a low stage of development indicates that the institution of a leisure class has emerged gradually during the transition from primitive savagery to barbarism; or more precisely, during the transition from a peaceable to a consistently warlike habit of life.[3]

Veblen explains that the emergence of a leisure class under barbarism is an outcome of the accumulation of wealth based on private property that was acquired by outright looting. "The loot," writes Veblen, "may become [private] property and be accumulated in sufficient mass to make a difference between rich and poor."[4] Slavery and feudalism were the dominant social systems of the barbarian stage, and Veblen is quick to point out that they served the interests of the dominant leisure class:

> The effect of slavery in its best day, and of landed wealth in medieval and early modern times, was to make the community's industrial efficiency serve the needs of slave-owners in the one case and of the land-owners in the other.[5]

This development took a new turn with the rise of capitalism, from its mercantile (commercial) beginnings to its full-scale industrial and financial forms, as the capitalism that flourished through the industrial revolution brought with it the expansion of science and technology during the eighteenth century. The evolution and development of capitalism from this point on ushered in the process of capital accumulation, wealth and income polarization, and the emergence of a new parasitic leisure class, especially as industrial capitalism gradually became transformed into a financial one. Finance capital thus epitomized for Veblen all the negative consequences of a new idle class that accumulated its wealth through speculation, manipulation, and all kinds of non-productive schemes that enriched them at the cost of forcing many on the lower rungs into poverty and destitution that affected the great majority of laboring people in society.

## The Theory of the Leisure Class

Adopting a Darwinian evolutionary perspective and an institutionalist approach to social and economic analysis, Veblen attempts to address the underlying conflict and contradictions in contemporary capitalist society in terms of the fundamental divisions between those who possess wealth and are idle and those who engage in productive work through their labor. In his *The Theory of the Leisure Class* ([1899] 1915), Veblen identifies the "leisure class" as an idle class characterized by a lack of productive economic activity (as with masters in slave society, landlords in feudal society, and capitalists in modern capitalist society).[6] This applies especially to the financiers under modern capitalism who make their fortunes from non-productive financial pursuits as distinct from the industrious entrepreneurs and their highly technical staff (the engineers), who, together with manual labor, constitute those who Veblen views to be "industrious" and productive.

Although the leisure class is considered by Veblen as the top crust of the wealthy elite that engages in frivolous activities that do not contribute much to society, hence they have much time and money at their disposal to live an opulent life, he looks upon labor and productive members of society as the ones carrying society forward through their hard work that contributes to overall societal development. This dichotomy between productive and unproductive segments of society defines for Veblen the contradiction of modern society and social life that creates tensions in social relations and holds back social-economic progress and development.

The modern leisure class that Veblen speaks of often in his writings is obviously a product of the emergence and evolution of capitalism, but he does not identify this class based on its position in the ownership of capital and its relations with labor, let alone see this relationship as an exploitative one. This is so because he has no problem in accepting the entrepreneur of the previous century as industrious, engaging in activities that built the basis of a capitalist economy and society. On the contrary, he admires those capitalists engaged in productive activity, such as in manufacturing, construction, and the production of useful goods and services, as distinct from banking, finance, and speculative investments that he sees as having no real basis in the economy. The inclusion of industrial capitalists in his "industrious class," along with the engineers and wage laborers, however, creates a serious problem in differentiating class distinctions in modern capitalist society, notwithstanding the fact that one could consider his classificatory scheme as another form of stratification and class divisions in society, as with Max Weber's schema of classes based on status, power, and privilege, or the elite theorists' take on classes based on political considerations, as well as other competing definitions of social relations by theorists discussed in previous chapters.

## Conspicuous Consumption

The central characteristic of the leisure class, according to Veblen, is its "conspicuous consumption." It is this form of behavior by the leisure class that gives its members their character in order to exhibit their wealth: "in order to gain and hold on to the esteem of men," writes Veblen, "it is not sufficient merely to possess wealth or power. The wealth and power must be put in evidence, for esteem is awarded only on evidence."[7] This "evidence" of exhibiting wealth by the leisure class develops in tandem with their indulgence of "conspicuous consumption":

> Leisure held the first place at the start, and came to hold a rank very much above wasteful consumption of goods. . . . Its ascendency is furthered by the fact that leisure is still fully as effective an evidence of wealth as consumption. . . . [However,] consumption has gained ground, until, at present, it unquestionably holds the primacy.[8]

Referring to "the growth of conspicuous leisure and consumption," Veblen argues that

> the utility of both alike for the purpose of reputability lies in the element of waste that is common to both. In the one case it is a waste of time and effort, in the other it is a waste of goods. Both are methods of demonstrating the possession of wealth, and the two are conventionally accepted as equivalents.[9]

It is through such conspicuous consumer behavior, Veblen contends, that wealthy members of the leisure class reassure themselves of having and holding on to power, and have those in other classes to emulate them to keep the latter attracted to the system through a false sense of achievement that possessions and consumption may provide. This may also serve to block the development of awareness and consciousness of the true meaning of work and industriousness that Veblen so fondly admires. It is here, in the possession of goods and levels of consumption as a path to upward mobility that may distort the development of class consciousness among the working class, that Veblen could have alluded to in explaining why workers have failed to challenge the leisure class, rather than longing to imitate the latter's distorted consumption habits. But Veblen was not interested in addressing relations of exploitation between labor and capital that would have forced him to develop, as Marx had done, a revolutionary view that would call into question the entire corrupt and wasteful system. Instead, Veblen's obsession with the misbehavior of the leisure class, as against his own standards of industriousness, led him to criticize the leisure class for its misplaced ethics and morality that also inflicted those on the lower rungs of society. It is for this reason that Veblen develops a pessimistic view of the prospects for society and social change, and, hence, remains ambivalent about the future.

Coming from a humble background and fond of hard work in creating value through productive activity that makes an important contribution to society, and social-economic development in general, Veblen despises the parasitic behavior of the rich—those living in opulence and mindlessly spending money that they accumulated from speculative and shady dealings that he views as immoral and indefensible, as well as harmful to society. And in this context, he is compelled to develop sympathy toward those who live a disciplined life based on high principles and morals in making a genuine contribution to society and social life through which they also help elevate their own status as useful and productive members of society. But in the absence of a social agency in his analytical scheme to make things right, he is hard put to envision a future that would liberate society from the madness inflicted upon it by the powers that be.

## Conclusion

An ardent critic of the excesses of the wealthy elite and their conspicuous consumption, Veblen provides a sharp criticism of the leisure class, blaming it for the ills of advanced capitalist society. Borrowing much from Marx and adding his own distinct understanding of the inner workings of capitalism and its inherent contradictions, Veblen provides an uncompromising attack on finance capital—in particular, its unproductive, speculative, and parasitic segments—and exposes its corrosive nature. Thus, to the extent that he has been able to expose the fault lines of capitalism and its impending ill fate, Veblen could be viewed as a critic of the system and its excesses. But his criticisms of the capitalist system and the capitalist class fall far short of a clear and concise understanding of the nature, dynamics, and contradictions of the system that has kept workers exploited and oppressed for so long. Failing to develop an understanding of the system's fault lines based on class and class conflict between labor and capital that would highlight the exploitation of labor, Veblen, in the end, is unable to provide us a clear and concise understanding of the problems generated by the system that he so passionately criticizes. For that we must return to Marx and his analysis of the nature and dynamics of class relations under capitalism.

## Notes

1 Thorstein Veblen, *The Theory of the Leisure Class: An Economic Study of Institutions* (New York: The Macmillan Company, [1899] 1915).
2 Veblen, *The Theory of the Leisure Class*, 6.
3 Veblen, *The Theory of the Leisure Class*, 7.
4 Thorstein Veblen, *The Instinct of Workmanship* (New York: Macmillan, 1914), 157.
5 Thorstein Veblen, "On the Nature of Capital: Investment, Intangible Assets, and the Pecuniary Magnet," *Quarterly Journal of Economics* 23, no. 1 (1908): 528.

6  Veblen, *The Theory of the Leisure Class*.
7  Veblen, *The Theory of the Leisure Class*, 36.
8  Veblen, *The Theory of the Leisure Class*, 91–2.
9  Veblen, *The Theory of the Leisure Class*, 85.

# 11

# KARL MANNHEIM AND THE SOCIOLOGY OF KNOWLEDGE

*Martin Orr*

Karl Mannheim (1893–1947) was among the first to advance a sociology of knowledge. A seminal influence upon subsequent contributions to sociological theory, diverse figures, from Robert K. Merton to C. Wright Mills, acknowledged the importance of his ideas upon their intellectual development. In one of the first attempts to synthesize the theories of Marx and of Weber, Mannheim's contributions to the development of the sociology of knowledge are foundational. *Ideology and Utopia*, far and away his most important work, was conceived and written in the context of political struggle. Aristocratic landowners, liberal-bourgeois capitalists, revolutionary Communists, and the fascist reaction were vying for power in the years between the first and second World Wars. A refugee from fascism in Hungary and then in Germany, his thought was shaped by these trials. Motivated by the clash of political ideas that he observed, Mannheim explored some of the most interesting philosophical and political questions in the discipline of sociology.

*Ideology and Utopia* advances the central thesis of the sociology of knowledge—that ideas are, at least in part, socially determined and tied to the various locations in a social structure. First, Mannheim offers a sociological explanation for the development of the sociology of knowledge, tracing it from the concept of "ideology" to Marx's materialist account of the relationships between theory and practice. Second, seeking to apply this understanding, Mannheim surveys the political ideologies of his era, focusing on how each portrays the relationship between theory and practice, and explaining each as the reflection of the interests of various classes and strata. Third, stepping back, Mannheim argues that, at the most fundamental level, contemporary societies are divided between the powerful and wealthy versus the powerless and impoverished. Their interests in either conserving or abolishing a given social order are the basis of two opposing streams of thought—ideologies and utopias. While the former blinds one to the fragility of the status quo, the latter may lead to an overly optimistic assessment of the potential for social change. Given this, he argued that a synthetic perspective is required in order to understand society and history adequately.

### The Theory of Ideology and the Sociology of Knowledge

For Karl Mannheim, the guiding principle of the sociology of knowledge is that "there are modes of thought which cannot be adequately understood as long as their social origins are obscured."[1] To better comprehend our own understanding of the world, we have to acknowledge that "every perception is and must be ordered and organized into categories," but that the "extent . . . to which we can organize and express our experience in such conceptual forms is, in turn, dependent upon the frames of reference which happen to be available at a given historical moment . . . ."[2] Mannheim's insight is that, in order to evaluate what we know, sociology is indispensable—in fact, in order to understand sociology itself, we must view it as a thought-system that undergoes socially determined historical development. In *Ideology and Utopia*, Mannheim's first task is to employ the sociology of knowledge to explain the sociohistorical origins of the sociology of knowledge itself.

Mannheim argues that the sociology of knowledge is the culmination of earlier explorations of the concept "ideology." The original use of the term, which Mannheim calls the "particular conception of 'ideology,'" is simply skepticism of the ideas and statements of a political opponent. The opponent's propositions "are regarded as more or less conscious disguises of the real nature of the situation . . . [ranging] all the way from . . . calculated attempts to dupe others to self-deception."[3] However, this "particular conception of 'ideology'" challenges only some of an opponent's assertions, and only in terms of the content of their claims. That is, it is assumed that we and our opponents can agree upon the standards by which we can decide upon what is or isn't true. Mannheim suggests that this use of the particular conception "ideology" proceeds through a purely psychological analysis of interest: what are the motivations that underlie particular statements?

A next step, what he calls the "total conception of 'ideology,'" is a development of German philosophy—the contributions of Kant, Hegel, and, ultimately, Marx. Kant pointed out that consciousness is not fragmented, but is a unified whole. Hegel advanced this understanding by situating consciousness socially, but ahistorically, in *Volksgeist*—a "folk spirit" abstracted from reality as a timeless attribute of a people and their culture. Marx's elaboration of the concepts "class ideology" and "class consciousness" superseded speculative philosophy and completed the development of the "total conception of 'ideology.'" Consciousness is indeed a structured whole, but it is grounded in historically and socially specific relationships of power. In contrast to the particular conception of "ideology," a challenge to a particular individual's claims, the total conception of ideology calls into question not only specific assertions of an individual, but the entire *Weltanschauung* (worldview) of one's political opponent. Their conceptual framework and criteria of validity are called into question, and traced to their sociohistorical setting and their structured interests in the future of their society. With the emergence of the total conception comes the awareness that not only are individual representatives of particular sociopolitical positions guilty of conscious or unconscious falsification, *they are incapable of thinking correctly*. With Marx, Mannheim argued that "correct" thinking comes to be seen as that which is relevant to political practice: "A theory . . . is wrong if in a given practical situation it uses concepts and categories which, if taken seriously, would prevent man from adjusting himself at that historical stage."[4]

Mannheim argued, however, that Marx's theory of ideology did not constitute a fully developed sociology of knowledge—it was merely a "specific formulation of the total conception of 'ideology.'" Mannheim proposed a "general formulation":

> With the emergence of the general formulation of the total conception of ideology, the simple theory of ideology develops into the sociology of knowledge. What was once the intellectual armament of a party is transformed into a method of research in social and intellectual history generally. To begin with, a given social group discovers the "situational determination" of its opponents' ideas. Subsequently the recognition of this fact is elaborated in an all-inclusive principle according to which the thought of every group is seen as arising out of its life conditions.[5]

Charging that Marx and Engels sought only to explain the ideology of the capitalist class, Mannheim believed that he had identified a theoretical framework for understanding the social origins of *all* systems of thought, including Marxism. Because of the pejorative connotations of the concept "ideology," Mannheim substituted the term "perspective": a "subject's whole mode of conceiving things as determined by his historical and social setting."[6] Mannheim sought to analyze all perspectives, to demonstrate that political thought in all cases is socially determined.

This presented a problem. As Mannheim acknowledged, the sociology of knowledge must confront a conundrum—the problem of relativism. The apparent paradox is that the central thesis of the sociology of knowledge (that knowledge is a function of social forces) undermines the credibility of all knowledge-claims—including the claim that knowledge is a function of social forces. But Mannheim argues that the sociology of knowledge is not relativistic, but relational:

> Relativism is a product of the modern historical-sociological procedure which is based on the recognition that all historical thinking is bound up with the concrete position in life of the thinker . . . . But relativism combines this historical-sociological insight with an older theory of knowledge which was yet unaware of the interplay between conditions of existence and modes of thought, and which modelled its knowledge after static prototypes such as might be exemplified by the static proposition $2 \times 2 = 4$. This older type of thought, which regarded such examples as the model of all thought, . . . led to the rejection of all those forms of knowledge which were dependent upon the subjective standpoint and the social situation of the knower, and which were, hence, merely "relative."[7]

Relational knowledge derives from the thinker's social context, which exists within a set of social relationships. Ideas are not formed haphazardly in isolation from other groups, but are shaped as groups relate to one another. In the process truth is approached: "Knowledge arising out of experience in actual life situation, though not absolute, is knowledge none the less."[8] Moreover: "[T]he fact that our thinking is determined by our social position is not necessarily a source of error. On the contrary, it is often the path to political insight . . . ."[9] The implication of the sociology of knowledge is not that knowledge is merely relative, but that there are some kinds of knowledge for which it is impossible to conceive of absolute truth unrelated to social context—knowledge for which truisms like $2 \times 2 = 4$ are not adequate models. For Mannheim, political thought is the exemplar of this. Having tied political perspectives to social relationships, the "question then arises: which social standpoint *vis-à-vis* history offers the best chance for reaching an optimum of truth?"[10]

## The Prospects of Scientific Politics

Not unlike Marx, Mannheim developed a theory of knowledge that explains thought by reference to social stratification. While Mannheim employs a Weberian approach to stratification, emphasizing status and social groups, he often returns to class, class struggle, and class interests as fundamental to the sociology of knowledge. Like Weber, Mannheim is often concerned with social strata and all subcultural groupings, but with Marx he acknowledges that class is the keystone:

[Of] all the above-mentioned social groupings and units class stratification is the most significant, since in the final analysis all the other social groups arise from and are transformed as parts of the more basic conditions of production and domination . . . .[11] It is just this correlation between base and superstructure which has become the inescapable foundation of every modern sociology of culture.[12]

For Mannheim, since the sociology of knowledge seeks to identify the social bases of thought, a prior understanding of the organization of society is required. Mannheim believes that all social groupings are associated with specific worldviews, but *Ideology and Utopia* emphasizes relationships between classes as key to the understanding of ideological and political struggle.

Mannheim applies the sociology of knowledge most masterfully in his discussion of the major political perspectives emergent since the collapse of feudalism in Europe. He identifies five distinct political philosophies: Bureaucratic Conservatism, Conservative Historicism, Liberal-Democratic Bourgeois Thought, the Socialist-Communist Conception, and Fascism. Each of these is the reflection of a specific position in the structure of society, and each understands the relationship between political theory and political practice differently. In these passages, Mannheim offers a sociology of knowledge explanation for modern political ideologies.

Bureaucratic Conservatism, the perspective of bureaucratic functionaries, treats problems of politics as problems of administration. Because the origins of the law fall outside of the scope of administrative activity, this group tends to ignore the structural interests that underpin the law. As a result, revolutionary practice is taken as merely the irrational disturbance of order. Conservative Historicism, the expression of a reactionary aristocracy challenged by the revolutions in the United States and France, focuses on the irrationality of history. History is seen as entirely beyond comprehension—the development of non-rational forces. From this perspective there can be no scientific politics. Politics cannot be taught and the hereditary instincts of the nobility are required. Liberal-Democratic Bourgeois thought is associated with the capitalist class, triumphant over the aristocracy. Here, the attempt is made to rationalize political struggle, and the "irrational" aspects of power—interests, perspectives, class conflict, and the anarchy of the market—are ignored. Intellectualistic and rationalistic, there is radical separation of theory from practice—the truth may be achieved only through the process of debate and discussion in parliaments, and in the "marketplace of ideas."

The Socialist-Communist Conception, exemplified by Marxism, is the theory of an ascendant class, the proletariat, concerned only with long-term success. Given that, the deception of oneself or of others is pointless. With the emergence of this perspective, the relationship between theory and practice undergoes a fundamental transformation. Theory, a function of practice, informs practice. The success or failure of our practice requires the modification of our theory. Marxism, while recognizing the irrationality of class conflict and the anarchy of capitalism, does not try to conceal it. Without despairing of the attempt to understand history, Marxism explains class struggle without denying historical specificity and contingency.

Early in Mannheim's life, a fifth contender for political power emerged: Fascism. Mannheim portrayed Fascism as "activistic and irrational".[13] For the fascist there is no logic to history, and so the interpretation of history is pointless. All historical knowledge is fictitious and self-deceptive (although the manipulation of history can be of value in controlling the masses). History is shaped by the decisive deeds of the aspiring elite. Procedure, heredity, reason, and science are irrelevant—the putsch is what molds the future. Having lived in the era of pogroms, street thugs, and Brown Shirts, Mannheim saw fascism as the expression of socially uprooted and loosely integrated groups. Under other circumstances, he might have noticed how capitalists cultivated "loosely integrated groups" and rallied around the fascist banner. Since democracy entails the rule of majorities, and since under capitalism workers are the majority, democracy must be curtailed in order to perpetuate class domination.

## Ideological and Utopian Mentalities

Having offered sociology of knowledge explanations for the emergence of the sub-discipline and for the perspectives underpinning contemporary political thought, Mannheim makes a more general distinction. "Ideologies" and "Utopias," he argues, are two "mentalities" behind all perspectives, related to group interest in the conservation or abolition of a given social order. Whereas "ideologies arise in groups which control the social and political means of power," Mannheim says that utopian thought arises among the governed and oppressed groups which strive for emancipation."[14] As Mannheim puts it:

> There is implicit in the word "ideology" the insight that in certain situations the collective unconscious of certain groups obscures the real condition of society both to itself and to others and thereby stabilizes it .... [R]uling groups can in their thinking become so interest-bound to a situation that they are simply not able to see certain facts which would undermine their sense of domination.[15]

As for utopias, "the groups driven into opposition to the present order will be oriented towards the first stirrings of the social order for which they are striving and which is being realized through them."[16] Both ideologies and utopias, he argued, inhibit an accurate understanding of society and history. While ideologies blind those wedded to the status quo to the potential for change, oppressed groups "unwittingly see only those elements in the situation which tend to negate it . . . . [W]ishful representation hides certain aspects of reality . . ., and [t]heir thinking is incapable of correctly diagnosing an existing condition of society."[17]

Given his belief that both ideologies and utopias distort our perception of social reality, Mannheim ultimately placed his hopes in "the classless stratum" of "socially unattached intellectuals." Through the "scrutiny of their own social moorings and the quest for the fulfillment of their mission as the predestined advocate of the intellectual interests of the whole,"[18] the intelligentsia is capable of arriving at a synthetic "total orientation."[19] In the end, after finding final refuge in England, Mannheim even more directly addressed himself to elites rather than to workers: rather than an advocate of revolution, Mannheim's was an appeal for wise planning on the part of the powerful so as to ensure stability and security for both the elites and the masses.[20]

## Conclusion

Much of twentieth-century sociological theory can be interpreted as a series of attempts to reconcile and synthesize Karl Marx and Max Weber. *Ideology and Utopia* can be read as one of the first such attempts. Often described as a "bourgeois Marxist," Mannheim, while raised in a Hegelian and Weberian tradition, remained a student of Marx. While Mannheim adopted Weber's model of stratification, he was more willing to acknowledge that class is the fundamental scaffolding of all other systems of inequality. While attempting to find a place "above" political struggle, Mannheim still regards proletarian opposition to bourgeois domination as a source of insight, and acknowledges that it played a central role in the development of the sociology of knowledge. He generally seeks a Weberian "interpretive understanding" of the relationship between social structure and ideas rather than trying to develop Marx's theory of history, but he is also appreciative of what he recognizes as Marx's sophisticated understanding of the relationship between theory and practice.[21] Still, despite his willingness to acknowledge a debt to Marx, in the end, it is doubtless true that "[for] Mannheim, Marxism is to be superseded rather than generalized or extended."[22]

As a result of attempts to distance himself from a thoroughgoing class analysis of knowledge, Mannheim offers a problematic synthesis. Robert K. Merton argues that, given the diversity of the sources from which he drew, Mannheim's work was unnecessarily eclectic, suffering from "a fundamental instability in his conceptual framework."[23] As Lewis Coser puts it, "He who goes to Mannheim to learn from him an integrated and consistent way of reasoning on the relation of knowledge to society is bound to be disappointed."[24] Mannheim, one would think, would encourage us to put his own thought into a historical context. He was the privileged son of a manufacturer, yet a student of Lukacs. He was a comfortable and relatively mainstream academic in the tradition of Simmel and Weber, yet he was twice a political refugee from fascism and anti-Semitism. Given this, it is no wonder that Mannheim's thought is less than consistent. While it is true that he fails to provide a definitive theory of the relationship between society and knowledge, Karl Mannheim made important contributions to our understanding of the social origins of our own values and beliefs. As such, he will long remain a provocative thinker worthy of study.

## Notes

1  Karl Mannheim, *Ideology and Utopia: An Introduction to the Sociology of Knowledge*, Preface by Louis Wirth, trans. Louis Wirth and Edward A. Shils (New York: Harcourt, Brace and Company, 1949), 14.
2  Mannheim, *Ideology and Utopia*, 77.
3  Mannheim, *Ideology and Utopia*, 49.
4  Mannheim, *Ideology and Utopia*, 85.
5  Mannheim, *Ideology and Utopia*, 69.
6  Mannheim, *Ideology and Utopia*, 239.
7  Mannheim, *Ideology and Utopia*, 70.
8  Mannheim, *Ideology and Utopia*, 76.
9  Mannheim, *Ideology and Utopia*, 111.
10  Mannheim, *Ideology and Utopia*, 71.
11  Mannheim, *Ideology and Utopia*, 247–8.
12  Karl Mannheim, *Structures of Thinking*, ed. David Kettler, Volker Meja, and Nico Stehr, trans. Jeremy J. Shapiro and Shierry Weber Nicolsen (Boston, MA: Routledge & Kegan Paul, 1982), 177.
13  Mannheim, *Ideology and Utopia*, 119.
14  Henk E. S. Woldring, *Karl Mannheim: The Development of his Thought: Philosophy, Sociology and Social Ethics, with a Detailed Bibliography* (New York: St. Martin's Press, 1986), 195.
15  Mannheim, *Ideology and Utopia*, 36.
16  Mannheim, *Ideology and Utopia*, 176.
17  Mannheim, *Ideology and Utopia*, 36.
18  Mannheim, *Ideology and Utopia*, 140.
19  "Critics will . . . conveniently simplify my thesis of the easily refutable proposition that the intelligentsia is an exalted stratum above all classes or that it is privy to revelations. [M]y claim was merely that certain types of intellectual have a maximum opportunity to test and employ the socially available vistas and to experience their inconsistencies." Karl Mannheim, *Essays in the Sociology of Culture*, ed. and trans. Ernest Mannheim and Paul Kecskemeti (London: Routledge & Kegan Paul, 1956), cited in A. P. Simonds, *Karl Mannheim's Sociology of Knowledge* (Oxford: Clarendon Press, 1978), 131.

20  Irving M. Zeitlin, *Ideology and the Development of Sociological Theory* (Englewood Cliffs, NJ: Prentice Hall, 1968), 312.

21  Mannheim, *Ideology and Utopia*, 259–60 (emphasis mine), and cf. 239n; W. Suchting, "Knowledge and Practice: Towards a Marxist Critique of Traditional Epistemology," *Science and Society* 47, no. 1 (1983): 29–30; and Gunter W. Remmling, "Marxism and Marxist Sociology of Knowledge," in *Towards the Sociology of Knowledge: Origin and Development of a Sociological Thought Style*, ed. Gunter W. Remmling (New York: Humanities Press, 1973), 245–7.

22  Brian Longhurst, *Karl Mannheim and the Contemporary Sociology of Knowledge* (New York: St. Martin's Press, 1989), 71.

23  Robert K. Merton, *Social Theory and Social Structure*, 3rd ed. (New York: Free Press, 1968), 545.

24  Lewis A. Coser, *Masters of Sociological Thought: Ideas in Historical and Social Context* (New York: Harcourt Brace Jovanovich, 1971), 429.

# 12

# GRAMSCI AND LENIN ON IDEOLOGY, THE STATE, AND REVOLUTION

While the classical elite theorists Vilfredo Pareto, Gaetano Mosca, and Robert Michels held the masses in contempt and sided with the ruling classes as the engines of social development, V. I. Lenin (1870–1924) and Antonio Gramsci (1891–1937), like Karl Marx and Frederick Engels before them, threw in their lot with the laboring masses and saw the working class as the leading revolutionary force to transform capitalist society. This chapter takes a brief look at the central arguments of Gramsci and Lenin on the nature and role of the state and ideological hegemony and explores the underlying class contradictions of capitalist society, which, they argued, would lead to its revolutionary transformation.

## Class Struggle and the State

Outlined in its clearest and most concise form in his classic work *The State and Revolution*, Lenin explains that in all class societies, the *class essence* of the state's rule over society is rooted in domination and exploitation by a propertied ruling class of the propertyless oppressed class.

> In our epoch, every state in which private ownership of the land and means of production exists, in which capital dominates, however democratic it may be, is a capitalist state, a machine used by the capitalists to keep the working class and the poor peasants in subjection.[1]

Democracy in capitalist society, Lenin points out, is always bound by "the narrow limits set by capitalist exploitation, and consequently always remains, in effect, a democracy for the minority, only for the propertied classes, only for the rich."[2]

> Freedom in capitalist society always remains about the same as it was in the ancient Greek republics: freedom for the slave-owners. Owing to the conditions

of capitalist exploitation, the modern wage slaves are so crushed by want and poverty that "they cannot be bothered with democracy," "cannot be bothered with politics"; in the ordinary, peaceful course of events, the majority of the population is debarred from participation in public and political life. . . .

Democracy for an insignificant minority, democracy for the rich—that is the democracy of capitalist society. . . .

Marx grasped this *essence* of capitalist democracy splendidly when, in analyzing the experience of the Commune, he said that the oppressed are allowed once every few years to decide which particular representatives of the oppressing class shall represent and repress them in parliament![3]

"People always have been the foolish victims of deception and self-deception in politics," Lenin continues elsewhere, "and they always will be until they have learnt to seek out the *interests* of some class or other behind all moral, religious, political and social phrases, declarations and promises."[4]

In class society, Lenin points out, the state has always been "an organ or instrument of violence exercised by one class against another."[5] And in capitalist society, this violence is exercised by the capitalist class against the working class. In an important passage in *The State and Revolution*, Lenin stresses that the state in capitalist society is not only the political organ of the capitalist class; it is structured in such a way that it guarantees the class rule of the capitalists and, short of a revolutionary rupture, its entrenched power is practically unshakable:

A democratic republic is the best possible political shell for capitalism, and, therefore, once capital has gained possession of this very best shell . . . it establishes its power so securely, so firmly, that *no* change of persons, institutions or parties in the bourgeois-democratic republic can shake it.[6]

The question remains: with the obvious contradictions and conflicts between labor and capital, and with the ever-more visible unity of capital and the state, how is capital able to convince broad segments of the laboring masses of the legitimacy of its class rule and the rule of the capitalist state over society?

## Ideological Hegemony

In explaining the process by which the capitalist class disseminates its ideology through control of the state and its dominance over society, Gramsci draws attention to the ideological apparatuses of the capitalist state and introduced the concept of bourgeois cultural and ideological *hegemony*.[7] He stresses that it is not enough for the capitalist class simply to take control of the state machine and rule society directly through force and coercion; it must also convince the oppressed classes of the legitimacy of its rule: "The state is the entire complex of practical and theoretical activities with which the ruling class not only justifies and maintains its dominance, but manages to win the active consent of those over whom it rules."[8] Through its dominance of the superstructural organs of the state, the ruling class controls and shapes the ideas, hence consciousness, of the masses. Thus,

> Hegemony involves the successful attempts of the dominant class to use its political, moral, and intellectual leadership to establish its view of the world as all-inclusive and universal, and to shape the interests and needs of subordinate groups.[9]

With the acceptance of its ideas and the legitimization of its rule, the capitalist class is able to exercise control and domination of society through its ideological hegemony at the level of the superstructure, with the aid and instrumentality of the state. Gramsci, writes Martin Carnoy, "assigned to the State part of this function of promoting a single (bourgeois) concept of reality, and, therefore, gave the State a more extensive (enlarged) role in perpetuating class,"[10] hence preventing the development of working-class consciousness. As such,

> it was not merely lack of understanding of their position in the economic process that kept workers from comprehending their class role, nor was it only the "private" institutions of society, such as religion, that were responsible for keeping the working class from self-realization, but it was the *State itself* that was involved in reproducing the relations of production. In other words, the State was much more than the coercive apparatus of the bourgeoisie; the State included the hegemony of the bourgeoisie in the superstructure.[11]

Although the dialectics of the accumulation process, which involves first and foremost the exploitation of labor, ultimately results in class struggle, civil war, and revolution to seize state power, the ideological hegemony of the ruling class, operating through the state itself, prolongs bourgeois class rule and institutionalizes and legitimizes exploitation. Gramsci argues that "the system's real strength does not lie in the violence of the ruling class or the coercive power of its state apparatus, but in the acceptance by the ruled of a 'conception of the world' which belongs to the rulers."[12] "False consciousness," or the lack of working-class consciousness and the adoption of bourgeois ideas by the laboring masses, Gramsci argues, is the result of a complex process of bourgeois ideological hegemony that, operating through the superstructural (i.e., cultural, ideological, religious, and political) institutions of capitalist society, above all the bourgeois state, has come to obtain the consent of the masses in convincing them of the correctness and superiority of the bourgeois worldview.

> In his doctrine of "hegemony," Gramsci saw that the dominant class did not have to rely solely on the coercive power of the State or even its direct economic power to rule; rather, through its hegemony, expressed in the civil society *and* the State, the ruled could be persuaded to accept the system of beliefs of the ruling class and to share its social, cultural, and moral values.[13]

"The philosophy of the ruling class," writes Giuseppe Fiori, "passes through a whole tissue of complex vulgarizations to emerge as 'common sense': that is, the philosophy of the masses, who accept the morality, the customs, the institutionalized behavior of the society they live in."[14] "The problem for Gramsci then," Fiori continues,

> is to understand *how* the ruling class has managed to win the consent of the subordinate classes in this way; and then, to see how the latter will manage to overthrow the old order and bring about a new one of universal freedom.[15]

The increasing awareness of the working class of this process, hence the development of working-class consciousness, stresses Gramsci, helps expand the emerging class struggle from the economic and social spheres into the sphere of politics and ideology, so the struggle against the capitalist ideology promoted by the bourgeois state and other ruling-class institutions becomes just as important, perhaps more so, as the struggle against capital develops and matures in other spheres of society. Countering the ideological hegemony of the capitalist class through the active participation of workers in their own collective organizations, the class-conscious organs of workers' power—militant trade unions, workers' political parties, and so forth—come to play a decisive role in gaining the political support of the laboring masses. In turn, through their newly gained awareness of their own class interests, the workers transcend the bounds of bourgeois ideological hegemony and develop their own counter (proletarian) political outlook, a process that accelerates with the further development of a proletarian class consciousness. Thus, as the struggle against the state becomes an important part of the class struggle in general, the struggle against capitalism takes on a truly political and ideological content.

Gramsci's contribution to the Marxist theory of the state and of bourgeois ideological hegemony, then, both affirms and extends the analyses of the Marxist classics and advances our understanding of the processes of ruling-class domination and hegemony and the responses needed for the revolutionary transformation of capitalist society.

## The State and Revolution

Writing in August 1917, on the eve of the Great October Socialist Revolution in Russia, Lenin points out both the class nature of the state and, more important, the necessity of its revolutionary overthrow:

> If the state is the product of the irreconcilability of class antagonisms, if it is a power standing *above* society and "*alienating* itself *more and more* from it," it is clear that the liberation of the oppressed class is impossible not only without a violent revolution, *but also without the destruction* of the apparatus of state power which was created by the ruling class and which is the embodiment of this "alienation."[16]

Thus, for Lenin, the transformation of capitalist society involves a revolutionary process in which a class-conscious working class, led by a disciplined workers' party, comes to adopt a radical solution to its continued exploitation and oppression under the yoke of capital and exerts its organized political force in a revolutionary rupture to take state power.

The victory of the working class in this struggle for power and control over society leads to the establishment of a Socialist workers' state. The Socialist state constitutes a new kind of state ruled by the working class and the laboring masses. The cornerstone of a workers' state, emerging out of capitalism, is the abolition of private property in the major means of production and an end to the exploitation of labor for private profit.

The establishment of a revolutionary dictatorship of the proletariat (as against the dictatorship of capital) distinguishes the Socialist state from its capitalist counterpart. As the class essence of the state lies at the heart of an analysis of the nature and role of the state in different epochs throughout history, the class nature of the Socialist state gives us clues to the nature and role of the state in a Socialist society developing toward communism. For, as Marx points out in *Critique of the Gotha Program*, the dictatorship of the proletariat (i.e., the class rule of the working class) is a transitional phase between capitalism and communism:

Between capitalist and communist society lies the period of the revolutionary transformation of the one into the other. Corresponding to this is also a political transition period in which the state can be nothing but *the revolutionary dictatorship of the proletariat*.[17]

During this period, the state represents and defends the interests of the working class against capital and all other vestiges of reactionary exploitative classes, which, overthrown and dislodged from power, attempt in a multitude of ways to recapture the state through a counterrevolution.

"The theory of the class struggle, applied by Marx to the question of the state and the socialist revolution," writes Lenin,

leads as a matter of course to the recognition of the *political rule* of the proletariat, of its dictatorship, i.e., of undivided power directly backed by the armed force of the people. The overthrow of the bourgeoisie can be achieved only by the proletariat becoming the *ruling class*, capable of crushing the inevitable and desperate resistance of the bourgeoisie, and of organizing *all* the working and exploited people for the new economic system.[18]

In this context, then, the proletarian state has a dual role to play: (1) to break the resistance of its class enemies (the exploiting classes), and (2) to protect the revolution and begin the process of Socialist construction.

## The Withering Away of the State

The class character of the new state under the dictatorship of the proletariat takes on a new form and content, according to Lenin: "During this period the state must inevitably be a state that is democratic *in a new way* (for the proletariat and the propertyless in general) and dictatorial *in a new way* (against the bourgeoisie)."[19] Thus,

*simultaneously* with an immense expansion of democracy, which *for the first time* becomes democracy for the poor, democracy for the people, and not democracy for the money-bags, the dictatorship of the proletariat imposes a series of restrictions on the freedom of the oppressors, the exploiters, the capitalists.[20]

Used primarily to suppress these forces and build the material base of a classless, egalitarian society, the Socialist state begins to wither away once there is no longer any need for it. As Engels points out,

The first act in which the state really comes forward as the representative of society as a whole—the taking possession of the means of production in the name of society—is at the same time its last independent act as a state. The interference of the state power in social relations becomes superfluous in one sphere after another, and then ceases of itself. The government of persons is replaced by the administration of things and the direction of the processes of production. The state is not "abolished," *it withers away*.[21]

In this sense, the state no longer exists in the fully matured Communist stage, for there is no longer the need in a classless society for an institution that is, by definition, an instrument of class rule through force and violence. Lenin writes,

Only in communist society, when the resistance of the capitalists has been completely crushed, when the capitalists have disappeared, when there are no classes (i.e., when there are no distinctions between the members of society as regards their relation to the social means of production), *only* then "the state . . . ceases to exist," and "*it becomes possible to speak of freedom*." Only then will a truly complete democracy become possible and be realized, a democracy without any exceptions whatever.[22]

It is in this broader, transitional context that the class nature and tasks of the state in Socialist society must be understood and evaluated, according to Lenin.

Thus, Lenin characterizes the period of transition to Communist society as exhibiting an infinitely higher form of democracy than that found in capitalist society, for democracy under socialism, he argues, is democracy for the masses, democracy for the great majority of the laboring population working together to build an egalitarian, classless society.

## Notes

1 V. I. Lenin, "The State," in *On Historical Materialism*, by Karl Marx, Frederick Engels, and V. I. Lenin (New York: International Publishers, 1974), 641.

2 V. I. Lenin, "The State and Revolution," in *Selected Works in Three Volumes*, by V. I. Lenin (Moscow: Progress Publishers, 1975), 2:301.

3 Lenin, "The State and Revolution," 2:301–2.

4 V. I. Lenin, "The Three Sources and Three Component Parts of Marxism," in *Selected Works in One Volume*, by V. I. Lenin (New York: International Publishers, 1971), 24.

5 Lenin, "The State and Revolution," 2:374.

6 Lenin, "The State and Revolution," *Selected Works*, 2:247.

7  By *hegemony*, Gramsci meant the ideological predominance of the dominant ruling class(es) over the subordinate. At the same time, and in response to this, he introduced the concept of counterhegemony, which occurs when the proletariat, with the aid of "organic" intellectuals, exerts hegemony and exercises its superiority over society through the establishment of a proletarian Socialist state.

8  Antonio Gramsci, *Prison Notebooks* (New York: International Publishers, 1971), 244.

9  Martin Carnoy, *The State and Political Theory* (Princeton, NJ: Princeton University Press, 1984), 70.

10  Carnoy, *The State and Political Theory*, 66.

11  Carnoy, *The State and Political Theory*, 66; emphasis in the original.

12  Giuseppe Fiori, *Antonio Gramsci, Life of a Revolutionary* (London: New Left Books, 1970), 238.

13  Carnoy, *The State and Political Theory*, 87.

14  Fiori, *Antonio Gramsci*, 238.

15  Fiori, *Antonio Gramsci*, 238.

16  Lenin, "The State and Revolution," 242; emphasis in the original.

17  Karl Marx, "Critique of the Gotha Programme," in *Selected Works*, by Karl Marx and Frederick Engels (New York: International Publishers, 1972), 331; emphasis in the original. For an extended discussion of the concept of the "dictatorship of the proletariat," see Etienne Balibar, *On the Dictatorship of the Proletariat* (London: NLB, 1977).

18  Lenin, "The State and Revolution," 255; emphasis in the original.

19  Lenin, "The State and Revolution," 262; emphasis in the original.

20  Lenin, "The State and Revolution," 302; emphasis in the original.

21  Frederick Engels, *Anti-Duhring* (New York: International Publishers, 1976), 307.

22  Lenin, "The State and Revolution," 302–3; emphasis in the original.

# 13

# KOLLONTAI ON CLASS, GENDER, AND PATRIARCHY

This chapter examines the contributions of Alexandra Kollontai (1872–1952) to the study of gender, patriarchy, and the position of women in capitalist society and provides an analysis of her views on women's oppression and the processes engendering the social emancipation of women.[1]

Kollontai was one of the most outspoken proponents of women's rights at the beginning of the twentieth century. Keenly aware of the oppression of women in capitalist society and adamantly opposed to the patriarchal structures imposed on women that assured their subordination over the centuries, Kollontai, like other Marxist critics of her time, took up the study of the women's question to advance the cause of women's rights and thereby contribute to women's total social emancipation. To this end, she undertook a serious study of the nature and dynamics of women's oppression in contemporary capitalist society and, thus, helped develop a theory and practice for the liberation of women.

## Capitalism, Patriarchy, and the Women's Question

The principal idea in the Marxist approach adopted by Kollontai to the women's question, which sharply differed from the approach adopted by her feminist contemporaries, was the recognition of existing social relations, above all, relations of production or class relations, as the determinant of various aspects of life in class society, including the subordination and oppression of women. "The conditions and forms of production," Kollontai writes in *The Social Basis of the Women's Question*, "have subjugated women throughout human history, and have gradually relegated them to the position of oppression and dependence in which most of them existed until now."[2] Pointing out that "specific economic factors were behind the subordination of women"[3] throughout history, she argues,

A colossal upheaval of the entire social and economic structure was required before women could begin to retrieve the significance and independence they had lost. . . . The same forces which for thousands of years enslaved women, now, at a further stage of development, are leading them along the path of freedom and independence.[4]

This is so because class society in general and capitalism in particular are producing and reproducing class contradictions. By drawing more and more women into the labor force and exploiting them at a level much higher than working men, Kollontai argues, capitalism is inevitably contributing to the future liberation of women as women begin to organize and struggle alongside men for the liberation of their class, the working class, an observation similar to the one made earlier by Frederick Engels.

Kollontai's analysis of the nature and sources of women's oppression leads her to look for a class solution to the emancipation of women. The rights of women, she argues, cannot be achieved while society is organized on the basis of private profit. Going beyond the critique of capitalism and the exploitation of labor in general, Kollontai places the interests of women workers at the forefront of her analysis and examines the struggles of working women and their families in the late nineteenth-century capital-ist society that preceded the bourgeois (middle- and upper-class) women's suffragist movement that emerged later during this period, bringing into sharp focus the class content of women's rights under capitalism.

Examining the origins of the bourgeois women's movement, Kollontai traces the development of a broader struggle for women's rights as it unfolded during the sec-ond half of the nineteenth century. Viewing the condition of women from a class perspective, Kollontai differentiates the interests of working-class women from those of bourgeois and petty-bourgeois women and argues that well before the birth of the bourgeois women's movement, working-class women had entered the world of labor and struggled for their rights as part of the struggles of the working class in general. This class-based approach to the women's question allows her to reach different polit-ical conclusions than the bourgeois feminists of her time and lays bare the ideological split that defined the two leading positions in the early women's movement.

## Class, Gender, and Feminism

Providing a class-analysis approach to the study of women's position in capitalist soci-ety, Kollontai, like Rosa Luxemburg and Clara Zetkin, defines the rights and interests of women on the basis of their class position, not their gender alone. She develops a sharp critique of the feminist movement for representing the interests of only a segment of the female population—bourgeois women. Siding with the working class politically and advocating the transformation of capitalist society and the building of socialism, Kollontai focuses her attention on working women and sees their emancipation as part of the process of emancipation of the working class from capitalist exploitation.

Stating her position in sharp contrast to that of the feminists, Kollontai frames the women's question in strictly class terms. "The women's world," she writes, "is divided, just as is the world of men, into two camps":

> The interests and aspirations of one group of women bring it close to the bourgeois class, while the other group has close connections with the proletariat, and its claims for liberation encompass a full solution to the woman question.[5]

She goes on to point out that although both of these groups advocate the liberation of women from their historic oppression, their goals and interests are different because "each of the groups unconsciously takes its starting point from the interests of its own class."[6]

Bourgeois women and women of the working class have distinct and contradictory class interests that override their identity as women, according to Kollontai. The women's suffragist movement, for example, was led by bourgeois feminists, such as Susan B. Anthony, who advocated women's empowerment and gender equality through the right to vote, without the transformation of existing capitalist society. But for Kollontai, whereas the feminists may have envisioned that the extension of the franchise would empower women in general, hence provide opportunities for them to rise to leadership positions within the upper class to which the suffragists belonged or with which they identified, it would do little to ameliorate the oppressive conditions suffered by women of the working class, let alone advance their interests as working women to improve their lot under the capitalist system. Thus, while the struggles of the suffragists would lead to their empowerment and gaining rights traditionally reserved to bourgeois men, such struggles, Kollontai argues, would bring greater power to bourgeois women to advance their own specific class interests as distinct from the interests of working-class women.

The class essence of women's rights, as manifested in the position of women in society with respect to labor, is clearly driven home in Kollontai's works when she focuses on the problems of working women as they experience them in their daily lives. The abstract, generalized pronouncements of feminist organizations, advocating women's rights in a broader context of female oppression in capitalist society, are thus given concrete meaning in Kollontai's works as she addresses the manifestations of exploitative class relations based on private profit. The exploitation of labor, especially female labor, takes on a special class meaning, differentiating the experiences and thereby the interests of women of different classes, a distinction that has important political implications as well. Much of Kollontai's writing that directly addresses the feminists makes this point very clearly.

"The feminists," she points out, "seek equality in the framework of the existing [capitalist] class society; in no way do they attack the basis of this society. They fight for prerogatives for themselves [for women of their own privileged class], without challenging the existing prerogatives and privileges."[7] Thus, "however apparently radical the demands of the feminists," Kollontai argues,

> one must not lose sight of the fact that the feminists cannot, on account of their class position, fight for that fundamental transformation of the contemporary economic and social structure of [capitalist] society without which the liberation of women cannot be complete.[8]

The liberation of working women, and of women in general, cannot therefore be achieved without a major transformation of the existing capitalist social order, which requires, for Kollontai, a revolutionary restructuring of the social, economic, and political life that defined the cultural parameters of society in the early twentieth century.

## Social Revolution and the Liberation of Women

The fundamental question for Kollontai regarding the liberation of women is the nature and source of change, which divided the women's movement along class lines. Should women's struggles primarily focus on the manifestations of existing exploitative relations in capitalist society, or should they confront head-on the very structures of capitalism that have generated these manifestations in the first place? Kollontai puts the question this way: "Can political equality in the context of the retention of the entire capitalist-exploiter system free the working woman from that abyss of evil and suffering which pursues and oppresses her both as a woman and as a human being?"[9] And she answers it as follows:

> The more aware among proletarian women realize that neither political nor juridical equality can solve the women's question in all its aspects. While women are compelled to sell their labor power and bear the yoke of capitalism, while the present exploitative system of producing new values continues to exist, they cannot become free and independent persons.[10]

Thus, the aim of the women workers, Kollontai points out, "is to abolish all privileges deriving from birth or wealth"; in this sense, they are "fighting for the common class cause, while at the same time outlining and putting forward those needs and demands that most nearly affect themselves as women, housewives and mothers."[11] The struggles of working women, therefore, "are part and parcel of the common workers' cause!"[12]

> There was a time when working men thought that they alone must bear on their shoulders the brunt of the struggle against capital, that they alone must deal with the "old world" without the help of their womenfolk. However, as working-class women entered the labor market by need, by the fact that husband or father is unemployed, working men became aware that to leave women behind in the ranks of the "non-class-conscious" was to damage their cause and hold it back. The greater the number of conscious fighters, the greater the chances of success. . . .
>
> Every special, distinct form of work among the women of the working class is simply a means of arousing the consciousness of the woman worker and drawing her into the ranks of those fighting for a better future. . . . [The] meticulous work undertaken to arouse the self-consciousness of the woman worker is serving the cause . . . of the unification of the working class.[13]

It is in this context of the broader interests of the working class as a whole that Kollontai develops her understanding of the interplay between class, gender, and patriarchy and identifies the centrality of the exploitation of labor for private profit as the basis of the oppression and exploitation of working women in capitalist society.

## Notes

1  For a brief biographical sketch of Kollontai, see the excellent compilation on numerous female social theorists by Mary Jo Deegan, ed., *Women in Sociology* (Westport, CT: Greenwood Press, 1991), 231–8. See also Sheila Rowbotham, *Women, Resistance, and Revolution* (New York: Penguin, 1972), 134–60.

2  Alexandra Kollontai, "The Social Basis of the Women's Question," in *Selected Writings of Alexandra Kollontai*, ed. Alix Holt (Westport, CT: Lawrence Hill, 1978), 61.

3  Kollontai, "The Social Basis of the Women's Question," 58.

4  Kollontai, "The Social Basis of the Women's Question," 61.

5  Kollontai, "The Social Basis of the Women's Question," 59.

6  Kollontai, "The Social Basis of the Women's Question," 59.

7  Kollontai, "The Social Basis of the Women's Question," 59.

8  Kollontai, "The Social Basis of the Women's Question," 59–60.

9  Kollontai, in I. M. Dazhina, *Alexandra Kollontai: Selected Articles and Speeches* (New York: International Publishers, 1984), 33–4.
10  Kollontai, in Dazhina, *Alexandra Kollontai*, 34.
11  Kollontai, in Dazhina, *Alexandra Kollontai*, 64.
12  Kollontai, in Dazhina, *Alexandra Kollontai*, 64.
13  Kollontai, in Dazhina, *Alexandra Kollontai*, 62–5.

# 14

# DU BOIS AND FRAZIER ON RACE, CLASS, AND SOCIAL EMANCIPATION

This chapter examines the ideas of two of the most prominent African American social theorists of the early twentieth century, William Edward Burghardt Du Bois (1868–1963) and Edward Franklin Frazier (1894–1962).[1] Together, Du Bois and Frazier set the standard for the study of race relations in the United States in the early decades of the twentieth century and made a major contribution to social theory on the relationship between race and class.

## Race Relations and the Color Line

At the beginning of the twentieth century, in 1901, Du Bois proclaimed, "The problem of the twentieth century is the problem of the color line."[2] Subsequently, Frazier, following his mentor, undertook the study of race relations in America to expose the predicament of African Americans, documenting the class nature of their oppression. Despite differences in their approach (the former focusing on race and the latter on class), together Du Bois and Frazier have made a significant contribution to the sociology of race and race relations in America in the twentieth century.

Du Bois, writes Meyer Weinberg, "was one of the greatest intellectuals America ever produced. If the intellectual is a tensor between scholarship and social action, Du Bois fulfilled the role with the highest distinction."[3] In his foreword to Manning Marable's biography of Du Bois, John Milton Cooper, Jr. writes,

> W. E. B. Du Bois ranks, along with Frederick Douglass, Booker T. Washington, and Martin Luther King, Jr., as one of the four greatest black Americans in the nation's history. Like them, he was a leader of his people and a man who sought to share fully in their lot. . . . [M]ore than any other person, he uncovered and interpreted black Americans' African roots and theorized about their ties to the larger nonwhite world. Du Bois deserves the title of first and greatest Afro-American.[4]

"There is no outstanding Afro-American creative figure of the twentieth century," writes another distinguished historian and editor of Du Bois's numerous works, Herbert Aptheker, "who did not, at some point, draw inspiration and gather aid directly from their Dean."[5] Indeed, Du Bois was the most celebrated intellectual and social activist in the African American community until his death in 1963.

Frazier, while a graduate student at Howard University, was among those exposed to Du Bois's ideas, ideas that shaped the content and direction of studies taken up by a new generation of African American intellectuals in subsequent decades. "Frazier's work and self-identity," writes Anthony Platt, "were consistently driven by a sense of moral outrage at any kind of social inequality and a relentless, burning hatred of racism."[6]

> Although his contributions were much more modest, Frazier was no less political than Du Bois. They made different kinds of contributions and operated in different arenas, but, like Du Bois, it was a rare day when Frazier did not think about the struggle against inequality.[7]

Concerned at the same time with the social makeup of the African American community and its internal class dynamics, which were in the process of maturation, Frazier addressed the developing class distinctions that increasingly determined the nature and dynamics of social relations among African Americans in the mid-twentieth century—trends that developed further in the latter part of the century.[8]

Placed in historical context, the ideas and works of Du Bois and Frazier provide us with much insight into the social condition of African Americans over the past 200 years and give us the tools of analysis to develop an interpretation of their predicament in American society.

## From Slavery to Freedom: The Predicament of African Americans

Under slavery and formal freedom, the African American experience is captured brilliantly in the works of Du Bois, whose great-grandfather was a slave. Born barely two years after the end of the Civil War, Du Bois became keenly aware of the experience of slavery in the social, economic, political, and psychological makeup of African Americans in the closing decades of the nineteenth century.

The slave system in the South set the parameters of life for millions of African American slaves who were denied citizenship and basic human rights for more than a century.

With the new world came fatally the African slave trade and Negro slavery in the Americas. There were new cruelties, new hatreds of human beings, and new degradations of human labor. The temptation to degrade human labor was made vaster and deeper by the incredible accumulation of wealth based on slave labor, by the boundless growth of greed, and by world-wide organization for new agricultural crops, new techniques in industry, and world-wide trade.[9]

The slaves, Du Bois explains, "could be bought and sold, could move from place to place only with permission, were forbidden to learn to read or write, legally could never hold property or marry."[10] This oppressive condition that the slaves experienced continued until the late nineteenth century.

Then came the war, which was not started with the idea of liberating the slaves, but which soon showed the North that freedom for the Negro was not only a logical conclusion of the war, but the only possible physical conclusion. Two hundred thousand black men were drafted in the army and the whole slave support to the Confederacy was threatened with withdrawal. Insurrection was in the air and the emancipation of the slaves was needed to save the Union. . . .

The Negro was freed as a penniless, landless, naked, ignorant laborer. Very few Negroes owned property in the South; a larger number of the race in the South were field hands, servants of the lowest class.[11]

Over the years, the ex-slaves became transformed into farm laborers and then into industrial workers in the mines and mills of modern capital as wage labor. Thus, during the century following emancipation, more and more African Americans became part of an expanding working class, and the African American community in general began to undergo internal social differentiation such that a more complex class structure began to emerge among African Americans. The intersection of race and class thus took on new meaning in the discussions and debates that began to surface among African American intellectuals in addressing the problems of race and class in contemporary American society.

## The Question of Race and Class

The changing dynamics of the developing class structure among African Americans led Du Bois and Frazier to take up a closer examination of the relationship between race and class.

Du Bois had earlier (at the turn of the twentieth century) observed that "the problem of the twentieth century is the problem of the color line," and by the early 1920s, he had rejected the class analysis approach to the study of African Americans by asking, "How far, for instance, does the dogma of the 'class struggle' apply to black folk in the United States today?"[12] He answered it this way: "The colored group is not yet divided into capitalists and laborers. There are only the beginnings of such a division. In one hundred years, if we develop along conventional lines, we would have such fully separated classes."[13] Although he continued to hold on to these views during the 1930s and 1940s, Du Bois was always aware of the potential development of classes and class conflict among African Americans if the current trends of capitalist expansion in America were to encroach on their communities in the future:

> The main danger and the central question of the capitalistic development through which the Negro-American group is forced to go is the question of the ultimate control of the capital which they must raise and use. If this capital is going to be controlled by a few men for their own benefit, then we are destined to suffer from our own capitalists exactly what we are suffering from white capitalists today.[14]

By the mid-twentieth century, the dynamics of the changing class structure among African Americans that was manifesting itself in their communities convinced Du Bois to supplement his earlier observations by stating,

> [During the 1930s] I repudiated the idea that Negroes were in danger of inner class division based on income and exploitation. Here again I was wrong. Twenty years later, by 1950, it was clear that the great machine of big business was sweeping not only the mass of white Americans ... [but] it had also and quite naturally swept Negroes into the same maelstrom.[15]

He went on to point out that with the fall of official segregation in public accommodations and schools, African Americans "will be divided into classes even more sharply than now."[16] By 1960, Marable points out, "Du Bois argued that 'class divisions' within Negro communities had so divided blacks 'that they are no longer [one] single body. They are different sets of people with different sets of interests.'"[17]

Adopting more and more a class-analysis approach to the race question, Du Bois during his later years (in the 1950s and early 1960s) began to develop, as Gerald Horne points out, "firm and decided views about the basis for race discrimination" in class terms: "He continually pointed to the wage differential between black and white workers as the material basis for racism."[18] In this way, Horne observes, "Du Bois was edging away" from his earlier view that "the problem of the twentieth century is the problem of the color line" and "edging toward the view that the twentieth century's problem was labor."[19]

Frazier, like Du Bois, also went through a transformation in his ideas on the causes and consequences of racism. Going beyond his earlier, social-psychological studies of race relations and the African American family, Frazier's views about racism later became more and more informed by social class.[20] "Influenced by the class-based theories of left intellectuals and organizations," writes Platt, "by the 1930s . . . his writings tended to reinterpret the history of race relations through a prism of exploitation."[21]

"The introduction of the Negro into America," Frazier points out, "was due to the economic expansion of Europe," and "the fate of Negro slavery was determined by economic forces"; in this sense, "the Negro's status in the United States," he stresses, "has been bound up, in the final analysis, with the role which the Negro has played in the economic system."[22] Framing the problem in these broader historical and structural terms, Frazier, as Platt points out, "located the fundamental roots of racism in the dynamics of class relations on a global scale."[23]

### Racism, Class Conflict, and Social Emancipation

Both Du Bois and Frazier understood the dynamics of racism as a manifestation of class conflict. They understood, therefore, that social emancipation would be the outcome of a resolution of the struggle between the chief opposing classes in society. Although Du Bois's views on the forms the struggle would take differed from Frazier's, both agreed on the necessity for social change to end exploitation and bring about peaceful relations between the races.

Whereas Du Bois argues in favor of gradual transformation of social relations through reforms, Frazier opts for a more concrete assessment of the historical record and sees no other viable alternative to resolve the race question except radically transforming the existing social-economic order. Thus, earlier in the century, Du Bois expected "changes to come mainly through reason, human sympathy, and the education of children" and "gravely doubt[ed] if, in the future, there [would] be any real recurrent necessity for upheaval."[24] However, the absence of any progress in race relations in subsequent decades led to his skepticism about the viability of this approach in the later years of his life as he became more and more critical of the persistent inequalities of the existing social order.

Frazier's stance was much more forceful and direct, allowing no pessimism of will or resolve. In contrast to Du Bois and his reformist approach, Frazier argued that there could be "no fundamental changes in race relations . . . unless these changes are brought about in connection with some revolutionary movement."[25] However well intentioned, "the accumulation of goodwill will not do it," he added, because "the present racial situation is bound up with the present economic and social system."[26]

Frazier's understanding of the relationship of race to the contradictions of capitalism in the late twentieth century led him to draw optimistic conclusions about the possibility of black–white unity within the working class, targeting the capitalists as the source of racial oppression and class exploitation—exploitation of an increasingly multiracial, multinational working class. Drawing his optimism on this score from the effects of the Great Depression on the working class in the 1930s and observing the "spread of radical ideas among working class Negroes through cooperation with white workers,"[27] Frazier projects that "as the Negro may become an integral part of the proletariat . . . the feeling against his color may break down in the face of a common foe."[28] Clarifying his position on the interplay of race, class, and social emancipation "in the urban environment," he writes, the African American worker "is showing signs of understanding the struggle for power between the proletariat and the owning classes, and is beginning to cooperate with white workers in this struggle which offers the only hope of his complete emancipation."[29]

Despite their differences in the strategy and tactics of the struggle against racism and racial oppression, Du Bois and Frazier were two of the most prominent African American intellectuals and social activists of the twentieth century. In their own distinct ways, they gave their utmost to this struggle and worked toward the building of a society based on equality among all citizens, regardless of race, gender, or class. In this sense, these two champions of human rights were among the pioneers of the modern civil rights movement that emerged toward the end of their lives. Yet, some three decades after their deaths, and a century after the pronouncements of Du Bois on "the problem of the color line," racism and racial oppression continue to afflict American society. And in response, the fight against racism and for social justice continues to grow and intensify today, in the early years of the twenty-first century.

## Notes

1  See James E. Blackwell and Morris Janowitz, eds., *Black Sociologists: Historical and Contemporary Perspectives* (Chicago, IL: University of Chicago Press, 1974).

2  W. E. B. Du Bois, "The Freedman's Bureau," *The Atlantic Monthly* 87, no. 519 (1901): 354.

3  Meyer Weinberg, ed., *W. E. B. Du Bois: A Reader* (New York: Harper & Row, 1970), xv.

4  John Milton Cooper, Jr., "Foreword," in *W. E. B. Du Bois: Black Radical Democrat*, by Manning Marable (Boston, MA: Twayne, 1986), vii.

5  Herbert Aptheker, "W. E. B. Du Bois: Struggle Not Despair," *Clinical Sociology Review* 8, no. 1 (1990): 62–3. For an extensive list of Du Bois's works, see Herbert Aptheker, *Annotated Bibliography of the Published Writings of W. E. B. Du Bois* (Millwood, NY: Kraus-Thomson, 1973).

 6  Anthony M. Platt, *E. Franklin Frazier Reconsidered* (New Brunswick, NJ: Rutgers University Press, 1991), 3.

 7  Platt, *E. Franklin Frazier Reconsidered*, 3.

 8  For an analysis of these developments, see E. Franklin Frazier, *Black Bourgeoisie* (Glencoe, IL: Free Press, 1957).

 9  W. E. B. Du Bois, "The White Masters of the World," in *The Writings of W. E. B. Du Bois*, ed. Virginia Hamilton (New York: Crowell, 1975), 201–2.

10  W. E. B. Du Bois, "The Social Effects of Emancipation," in Weinberg, *W. E. B. Du Bois: A Reader*, 71.

11  Du Bois, "The Social Effects of Emancipation," 72.

12  W. E. B. Du Bois, "The Class Struggle," in Weinberg, *W. E. B. Du Bois: A Reader*, 341.

13  Du Bois, "The Class Struggle," 341.

14  Du Bois, "The Class Struggle," 342–3.

15  Du Bois, quoted in Gerald Horne, *Black & Red: W. E. B. Du Bois and the Afro-American Response to the Cold War, 1944–1963* (Albany, NY: SUNY Press, 1986), 224.

16  W. E. B. Du Bois, "Negroes and the Crisis of Capitalism in the United States," *Monthly Review* 4, no. 12 (1953): 482–3.

17  Manning Marable, *W. E. B. Du Bois: Black Radical Democrat* (Boston, MA: Twayne, 1986), 207.

18  Horne, *Black & Red*, 225.

19  Horne, *Black & Red*, 224.

20  For his earlier studies, see, for example, E. Franklin Frazier, *The Negro Family in the United States* (Chicago, IL: University of Chicago Press, 1939). His later views on the relationship of race and class are developed in E. Franklin Frazier, *The Negro in the United States* (New York: Macmillan, 1949); and E. Franklin Frazier, *Race and Culture Contacts in the Modern World* (New York: Knopf, 1957).

21  Platt, *E. Franklin Frazier Reconsidered*, 164.

22  Frazier, quoted in Platt, *E. Franklin Frazier Reconsidered*, 164.

23  Platt, *E. Franklin Frazier Reconsidered*, 219.

24  Du Bois, "The Class Struggle," 341.

25  Frazier, quoted in Platt, *E. Franklin Frazier Reconsidered*, 186.

26  Frazier, quoted in Platt, *E. Franklin Frazier Reconsidered*, 186.

27  Frazier, quoted in Platt, *E. Franklin Frazier Reconsidered*, 164.

28  Frazier, quoted in Platt, *E. Franklin Frazier Reconsidered*, 163.

29  Frazier, quoted in Platt, *E. Franklin Frazier Reconsidered*, 164.

# PART II
# CONTEMPORARY SOCIAL THEORY

# 15

# PARSONS, MERTON, AND FUNCTIONALIST THEORY

This chapter examines the central ideas presented in the works of Talcott Parsons (1902–1979), Robert K. Merton (1910–2003), and other functionalist theorists who came to dominate American sociology during the 1950s.[1] Incorporating and synthesizing various Durkheimian and Weberian notions into their conception of the American society of the early to mid-twentieth century, Parsons and Merton developed a mainstream theory of society and social relations that went well with the conservative era of 1950s McCarthyism. Critically analyzing the functionalists' conservative views on human nature, social organization, and the social system, this chapter exposes Parsonian functionalism as a theory that has served as an ideology to rationalize and legitimize the prevailing system of mid-twentieth-century U.S. capitalism.

## Human Nature

In the process of developing a theory of social systems, Parsons and other functionalists have made a number of assumptions about human nature. These assumptions constitute an integral part of contemporary functionalist theory. In this sense, the functionalist view of social organization, society, and the social system cannot be understood clearly unless we first comprehend the nature and theoretical underpinnings of these assumptions concerning the place of the individual in the social system.

In the Parsonian scheme, the basic alternatives that, in certain combinations, orient the individual actor to his or her culture and social system are referred to as the *pattern variables*.[2] These are the dichotomies of (1) affectivity versus affective neutrality, (2) self-orientation versus collectivity orientation, (3) universalism versus particularism, (4) achievement versus ascription, and (5) specificity versus diffuseness.[3] Parsons believes that the value orientation of the culture in which the individual finds himself or herself can be described in terms of these dichotomies. The individual learns this value orientation through the process of socialization and social control, which together facilitate the internalization of society's values. This internalization of value-orientation patterns by individuals keeps society going, according to Parsons.

Merton's approach to norms and values is likewise based on a process wherein an individual's values correspond to roles by way of "role performance."[4] Through this process, the person responds to other individuals only in terms of the defined expectations of acceptable behavior between them. Hence, this near-mechanical view of individuals allows for the subsequent development of conformity and equilibrium.

Going beyond the traditional Parsonian frame of functional analysis and introducing into the model "middle-range" theories that can be empirically examined, Merton has contributed an additional dimension to contemporary functionalist theory by identifying *manifest* and *latent functions*.[5] Manifest functions are those that are recognized and intended by the participants, whereas latent functions are those that are not recognized and have unintended consequences: "The distinction between manifest and latent functions was devised to preclude the inadvertent confusion, often found in the sociological literature, between conscious *motivations* for social behavior and its *objective consequences*."[6]

Thus, while poverty in capitalist society is a deplorable condition of life for some (unemployed and poorly paid) segments of the population who find themselves in such a condition, it also serves as a latent function to justify the necessity for hard work so that employed workers continue to generate profits for their employers, with the threat that failing to do so will force them into unemployment and poverty. Hence, as in this case, latent functions are often the result of actions designed to benefit powerful social forces in society—forces that have an interest in securing conformity to the dominant values, ideas, and norms in society.

The individual, according to Parsons, Merton, and other functionalists, is built on the notion of conformity. Conformity of individuals is seen as crucial for the maintenance of the system. To illustrate this point clearly, Parsons explicitly states that

> the concept of "integration" . . . is a mode of relation of the units of a system by virtue of which, on the one hand, they act so as collectively to avoid disrupting the system and making it impossible to maintain its stability, and, on the other hand, to "co-operate" to promote its functioning as a unity.[7]

Thus, "the well-integrated personality," writes Parsons,

> feels an obligation to live up to expectations in his variously defined roles, to be a "good boy", to be a "good student," an "efficient worker," and so on. . . . The

element of obligation in this sense is properly treated as "disinterested." It is a matter of "identification" with a generalized pattern, conformity with which is "right."[8]

According to the functionalist view, then, individuals acquire a sense of satisfaction when their behavior fulfills the expectations of the social group or society to which they belong and which sets the standards for individual behavior in varied social settings. As a result, the fulfillment of these goals becomes a motivational objective of individuals so that their resultant behavior is oriented toward the attainment of these goals. In this way, society achieves the integration of individuals into the social system and, thereby, secures social order and stability in the system. The crucial part in Parsons's system, then, is the internalization of value patterns by individuals in order to assure the maintenance of the social system. This internalization, Parsons argues, "constitutes the strategic element of [the] basic personality structure" because it is only in this way that social order can be obtained.[9]

Merton's equally central concern with conformity and integration leads him to observe that deviation from the norms established in society is a result of role or status strain or a response to the divergence between socially established common goals and differently distributed means. Acknowledging the prevalence and impact of such strains on society, Merton introduces into his model elements that are "dysfunctional" to the system.[10] Deviance is one such element that represents a dysfunctional relationship of the individual to society. If the deviance exceeds the acceptable range of tolerance and if the deviant cannot be persuaded to adopt an alternative role, the resultant variance and diversity within the social system creates the need for social control.[11] Thus, with the imposition of social control to maintain both the value patterns of a society, as well as the motivation of its members, Parsons and Merton bring us full swing into their stable, functional social system.

## Society and the Social System

The modern functionalists see society as a system of interdependent parts that are integrated through institutionalized norms and patterns of behavior.[12] Such integration, argues Parsons, assures the maintenance of the social system:

> Solidarity is the generalized capacity of agencies in the society to "bring into line" the behavior of system units in accordance with the integrative needs of the system, to check or reverse disruptive tendencies to deviant behavior, and to promote the conditions of harmonious cooperation.[13]

Thus, the functionalist view of society is concerned with the relationship of equilibrating forces between the various parts of the system. As each part or unit of the system is given equal importance, any change in one part will affect all the others. To maintain conditions of stability within the system, society must be in a state of "equilibrium," one that promotes the survival and maintenance of the prevailing social system. Such rationalization, however, has led critics to charge that modern functionalist theory legitimizes mid-twentieth-century dominant capitalist ideology. Indeed, this is clearly evident in their discussion of social classes, politics, and the state.

Generally, the functionalists see social classes and class inequality as naturally occurring phenomena in all societies at all times. In their classic essay, "Some Principles of Stratification," Kingsley Davis and Wilbert Moore speak of "the *universal necessity* which calls forth stratification in *any* social system."[14] Moreover, "the main functional necessity explaining the universal presence of stratification," write Davis and Moore, "is precisely the *requirement* faced by *any* society of placing and motivating individuals in the social structure."[15]

> Inevitably, then, a society must have, first, some kind of rewards that it can use as inducements, and second, some way of distributing these rewards differentially according to positions. The rewards and their distribution become a part of the social order, and thus give rise to stratification.[16]

This is so, Davis and Moore categorically state, in "every society, no matter how simple or complex."[17]

Such an assertion, however, is based on the functionalist (ideological) assumption that stratification is "functionally necessary" to ensure the maintenance of the existing social system and not a scientific analysis of historical reality. "Functional theories," comments Arthur Stinchcombe, "are like other scientific theories: they have empirical consequences which are either true or false. Deciding whether they are true or false is not a theoretical or ideological matter but an empirical one."[18] As the wealth of data available on a large number of previous societies shows, almost all (98 percent) of hunting and gathering (primitive-communal) societies do not have a class system or structured social inequality, while the remaining 2 percent have become "stratified" as a result of contact with more advanced societies.[19] Hence, as humans have lived in hunting and gathering societies as the predominant form of social organization for most of human history, it is clear that the historical evolution of *Homo sapiens* for thousands of years has been unquestionably highly democratic and egalitarian. Only in more recent times do we begin to see the development of class systems, hence of class inequality.[20]

To his credit, Melvin M. Tumin, a functionalist himself, has expressed strong criticism of the Davis–Moore thesis, refuting the latter's contentions on inequality and stratification. In fact, Tumin's critical analysis of the problem leads him to reach almost exactly the opposite conclusions from those of Davis and Moore, as he specifies various "negative functions, or dysfunctions, of institutionalized social inequality," such as "human ignorance, war, poverty."[21] Responding to the Davis–Moore thesis on the functional necessity of inequality, Tumin raises some important issues that challenge this view. He writes,

> Since a theoretical model *can* be devised in which all other clearly indispensable major social functions are performed, but in which inequality as motive and reward is absent, how then can we account for stratification in terms of structural and functional necessities and inevitabilities?[22]

Extending his analysis to account for the key mechanism that perpetuates structured social inequality, "an essential characteristic of all known kinship systems," writes Tumin,

> is that they function as transmitters of inequalities from generation to generation. Similarly, an essential characteristic of all known stratification systems is that they employ the kinship system as their agent of transmission of inequalities.
>
> To the extent that this is true, then it is true by definition that the elimination from kinship systems of their function as transmitters of inequalities (and hence the alteration of the definition of kinship systems) would eliminate those inequalities which were generation-linked.
>
> Obviously, the denial to parents of their ability and right to transmit both advantages and disadvantages to their offspring would require a fundamental alteration in all existing concepts of kinship structure. At the least, there would have to be a vigilant separation maintained between the unit which reproduces and the unit which socializes, maintains and places. In theory, this separation is eminently possible. In practice, it would be revolutionary.[23]

Indeed it would! By curbing the transfer of wealth and property through the alteration of the nature and function of the kinship structure, it is indeed possible to bring up a new generation of individuals without a significant level of social inequality.

## Power, Politics, and the State

Turning to politics, Parsons and other contemporary functionalists have characterized the modern U.S. state as a democratic institution whose primary function is to secure order within the system.[24] Representing the interests of society as a whole, the state coordinates the other major institutions of society—economic, educational, religious, and so on—and advances both the general social welfare and that of the individuals within it. Thus, for the functionalists, while the state provides strong, effective leadership and represents institutionalized power and authority vis-à-vis individual citizens, its actions reflect widespread and diverse interests that exist in society, interests that the functionalists claim are well represented within the state. As the supreme guardian of "representative democracy," the state thus fulfills its role in carrying out its social tasks, while ensuring its democratic control by society—a view that is at odds with Marx's characterization of the state as an instrument of the dominant capitalist class, as well as with Weber's view of it as a tool of powerful propertied interests in society.

"Power," writes Parsons, "is a generalized facility or resource in the society":

> It has to be divided or allocated, but it also has to be produced and it has collective as well as distributive functions. It has the capacity to mobilize the resources of the society for the attainment of goals for which a general "public" commitment has been made, or may be made. It is mobilization, above all, of the action of persons and groups, which is *binding* on them by virtue of their position in the society.[25]

Thus, for Parsons, the state maintains an autonomous role for itself as the sole public authority and at the same time assures the equal distribution of power across competing political groups in society. "This tension in functionalist thinking on the state between a view of the necessity for a strong, modernizing, central co-ordinator on the one hand, and a relatively equal distribution of social powers on the other," observes one critic, "reflects the cross-pulls from two allegedly functional pre-requisites: the need for autonomy and the need for integration."[26] By distributing its control among a broad range of social groups and preventing its monopolization by any one group, the state, according to the functionalists, thus paves the way for political competition and "pluralist democracy."[27]

Empirical reality, however, is much different from what contemporary functionalists would have us believe. While functionalists such as Robin Williams argue that "no 'rule by monopoly' is in sight in the American economy" and "corporate shares are held by large numbers of individuals," and further, that the American pattern of power distribution is "the balancing of interests and compromising of conflicts through multiple power-centers, numerous separate channels of influence, and the subdivision of politi-cal authorities,"[28] the true extent of wealth and ownership and of political power can be illustrated as follows: the top 10 percent of American families own 78 percent of real estate, 90 percent of all publicly held corporate stocks, 90 percent of all bonds, and 94 percent of net business assets.[29] Moreover, the top 0.5 percent of all families own nearly half of all corporate stocks and bonds and nearly two-thirds of all business assets.[30] Further, the two hundred largest U.S. corporations, many of which are mutu-ally controlled through interlocking directorates, control more than 75 percent of all corporately held assets and account for nearly two-thirds of total net profits.[31]

## Conclusion

The functionalist conception of human nature, society, and politics examined in this chapter reveals that contemporary functionalists have uncritically accepted the exist-ing class structure of capitalist society as given and have thus contributed, implicitly or explicitly, toward the maintenance of the prevailing social order and the perpetuation of dominant capitalist ideology. This has opened the way to a barrage of criticism of modern functionalism for being nothing more than an ideological expression of the capitalist system in the United States.

The functionalist contention that in America political power resides with many diverse and equally powerful groups reflecting the interests of the vast majority of the population has similarly come under strong criticism in recent decades. In the late 1950s, critics, led by C. Wright Mills, began to provide a powerful critique of Parsonian functionalism that set the stage for subsequent debates within sociology. Expanding this effort during the 1960s and 1970s, G. William Domhoff and numer-ous other critical sociologists were instrumental in widening the critique of modern functionalism and, thus, breaking its decades-long monopoly over social theory.

Through such critique of the ideological implications of modern functionalist theory vis-à-vis its earlier intellectual hegemony within sociology, more and more sociologists have come to understand clearly the dynamics of recent developments in contemporary sociological theory. The contributions to this critique through alterna-tive theoretical formulations provided by Mills and Domhoff are discussed in the next two chapters of this book.

## Notes

1  Although this chapter addresses two different versions of contemporary functionalist theory—
   Parsonian and Mertonian, or what C. Wright Mills called "grand theory" and "abstracted
   empiricism," respectively—we use the term *functionalism* when referring to both versions.
2  Talcott Parsons, *The Social System* (New York: Free Press, 1951), 67.

3  Parsons, *The Social System*, 67.
4  Robert K. Merton, *Social Theory and Social Structure* (New York: Free Press, 1968), 390–4.
5  Merton, *Social Theory and Social Structure*, 114–18.
6  Merton, *Social Theory and Social Structure*, 114.
7  Talcott Parsons, *Essays in Sociological Theory*, rev. ed. (Glencoe, IL: Free Press, 1954), 71.
8  Parsons, *Essays in Sociological Theory*, 56–7.
9  Parsons, *The Social System*, 228.
10  Merton, *Social Theory and Social Structure*, 105.
11  Merton, *Social Theory and Social Structure*, 230–48.
12  Harry M. Johnson, *Sociology: A Systematic Introduction* (New York: Harcourt, Brace, 1960).
13  Talcott Parsons, cited in Chandler Morse, "The Functional Imperatives," in *The Social Theories of Talcott Parsons*, ed. Max Black (Englewood Cliffs, NJ: Prentice Hall, 1961), 126.
14  Kingsley Davis and Wilbert E. Moore, "Some Principles of Stratification," *American Sociological Review* 10, no. 2 (1945): 242.
15  Davis and Moore, "Some Principles of Stratification," 242.
16  Davis and Moore, "Some Principles of Stratification," 243.
17  Davis and Moore, "Some Principles of Stratification," 243.
18  Arthur L. Stinchcombe, "Some Empirical Consequences of the Davis–Moore Theory of Stratification," *American Sociological Review* 28, no. 5 (1963): 808.
19  Gerhard Lenski, *Power and Privilege* (New York: McGraw-Hill, 1966); Eleanor B. Leacock, "Introduction," in *The Origin of the Family, Private Property and the State*, by F. Engels (New York: International Publishers, 1972).
20  See Albert Szymanski, *Class Structure: A Critical Perspective* (New York: Praeger, 1983), chap. 2.
21  Melvin Tumin, "Some Principles of Stratification: A Critical Analysis," *American Sociological Review* 18, no. 4 (1953): 394; and Melvin Tumin, "Reply to Kingsley Davis," *American Sociological Review* 18, no. 6 (1953): 672.
22  Tumin, "Reply to Kingsley Davis," 672.
23  Tumin, "Reply to Kingsley Davis," 672.
24  Talcott Parsons, *Societies: An Evolutionary Approach* (Englewood Cliffs, NJ: Prentice Hall, 1966); and Talcott Parsons, "On the Concept of Political Power," in *Sociological Theory and Modern Society*, by T. Parsons (New York: Free Press, 1967).
25  Talcott Parsons, *Structure and Process in Modern Societies* (New York: Free Press, 1960), 221.
26  Roger King, *The State in Modern Society* (Chatham, NJ: Chatham House, 1986), 15.
27  S. N. Eisenstadt, ed., *Modernization: Protest and Change* (Englewood Cliffs, NJ: Prentice Hall, 1966), cited in King, *The State in Modern Society*, 15.
28  Eisenstadt, *Modernization*, 15.
29  Jerry Kloby, "Increasing Class Polarization in the United States: The Growth of Wealth and Income Inequality," in *Critical Perspectives in Sociology*, ed. Berch Berberoglu (Dubuque, IA: Kendall/Hunt, 1991), 44.
30  Kloby, "Increasing Class Polarization in the United States," 44.
31  United States Bureau of the Census, *Statistical Abstract of the United States, 1990* (Washington, DC: Government Printing Office, 1990), 541.

# 16

# MILLS ON THE POWER ELITE

One of the earliest and most powerful critics of Talcott Parsons and structural functionalism in American sociology was C. Wright Mills (1916–1962). Challenging the domain assumptions of the discipline sustained by the functionalist mainstream in the conservative 1950s, Mills soon became one of the most outspoken and controversial social theorists of the postwar period in the United States. Taking on the discipline's domain assumptions single-handedly, Mills called for what he termed "the sociological imagination" to untangle some of the most critical issues of our time—power, politics, and society.[1] Writing at the height of the Cold War and the McCarthy witch hunts of the 1950s, Mills provided a devastating critique of establishment sociology by launching an all-out attack on Parsonian functionalism, which had played an important role in rationalizing the status quo, thereby promoting the existing social order and reinforcing unequal power relations in society.

This chapter examines Mills's ideas on the American power structure that he developed as a critique of pluralism. Focusing on his analysis of power relations at the highest levels of American society, the chapter provides a critical overview of his concept of political power, which he presented as an important corrective to the conservative theories of Parsons and what came to be known as Parsonian sociology.

## The Power Elite

Influenced by Max Weber, Gaetano Mosca, Vilfredo Pareto, and Karl Marx, Mills develops an institutional theory of political power, one based on an articulation of the combined expression of a "power elite." Rejecting the Marxist contention that the capitalist class, through its control of the government, is also a ruling class,[2] Mills adopts an institutional approach, believing that power has shifted from owners of the means of production (or capitalists) to managers and functionaries of the key institutions of American society—the economy, the polity, and, especially, the military.

Such a view forces Mills to focus on high-ranking individual policymakers, especially generals and admirals, whom he considered as part of the higher circles that make up the power elite:

> Within American society, major national power now resides in the economic, the political, and the military domains. . . . As each of these domains has coincided with the others, as decisions tend to become total in their consequence, *the leading men* in each of the three domains of power—*the warlords, the corporation chieftains, the political directorate*—tend to come together, to form the power elite of America.[3]

The power elite, Mills continues, is composed of those who are "in command of the major hierarchies and organizations of modern society": "They rule the big corporations. They run the machinery of the state and claim its prerogatives. They direct the military establishment. They occupy the strategic command posts of the social structure".[4] "The power to make decisions of national and international consequence," Mills points out,

> is now so clearly seated in political, military, and economic institutions that other areas of society seem off to the side. . . . The scattered institutions of religion, education and family are increasingly shaped by the big three, in which history-making decisions now regularly occur. . . . This triangle of power is now a structural fact, and it is the key to any understanding of the higher circles in America today.[5]

The critical point in Mills's analysis of the power elite is not the mere identification of the elite in the three key institutions that constitute the American power structure, but the interrelationship between these institutions and between members of the elite that control and direct them:

> The shape and meaning of the power elite today can be understood only when these three sets of structural trends are seen at their point of coincidence. . . . Accordingly, at the top of this structure, the power elite has been shaped by the coincidence of interest between . . . the professional politicians . . . the corporate chieftains and the professional warlords.[6]

The interrelationship between these institutions and between their top leadership is such that retired generals become corporate executives and serve on the boards of directors of large corporations that sell inflated military hardware through lucrative defense contracts signed by old associates in the military, while corporate executives who enter politics serve the interests of big business once they hold key government posts that facilitate the passage of legislation favorable to corporate interests. Thus, as the linkage between big business and the government becomes consolidated, so, too, does the control of the state by business interests become solidified, thereby diminishing the prospects for open discussion and debate on public policy:

> The shift of corporation men into the political directorate has accelerated the decline of the politicians in the Congress to the middle levels of power; the formation of the power elite rests in part upon this relegation. It rests also upon the increased official secrecy behind which great decisions are made without benefit of public or even of Congressional debate.[7]

## The Rise of the Military

Corresponding to the increased influence over and control of the government by big business, Mills also sees the rise of the military and its more direct role and influence in political affairs, as exemplified by Gen. Dwight D. Eisenhower's ascendance to the presidency in the 1950s. "In so far as the structural clue to the power elite today lies in the enlarged and military state," writes Mills, "that clue becomes evident in the military ascendancy."[8] In a chapter of *The Power Elite* titled "The Military Ascendancy," Mills points out, "As the United States has become a great world power, the military establishment has expanded, and members of its higher echelons have moved directly into diplomatic and political circles."[9] Moreover, "the military order, once a slim establishment in a context of civilian distrust, has become the largest and most expensive feature of government."[10]

> The high military have gained decisive political and economic relevance. The seemingly permanent military threat places a premium upon them and virtually all political and economic actions are now judged in terms of military definitions of reality: the higher military have ascended to a firm position within the power elite of our time.[11]

The ascendancy of the military goes far beyond the institutional boundaries of the political and economic order, according to Mills. The military establishment, he argues, is attempting to extend its power into the civilian sphere by molding public opinion in favor of a military definition of reality:

It is not only within the higher political and economic, scientific and educational circles that the military ascendancy is apparent. . . .

The military manipulation of civilian opinion and the military invasion of the civilian mind are now important ways in which the power of the warlords is steadily exerted.[12]

The increasing power of the military (and its top leadership) in civilian affairs, Mills contends, "points to the tendency of military men . . . to pursue ends of their own, and to turn other institutional areas into means for accomplishing them."[13] As a result, since World War II, he argues, "those who command the enlarged means of American violence have come to possess considerable autonomy, as well as great influence, among their political and economic colleagues."[14] The generals, he adds, "are now more powerful than they have ever been in the history of the American elite; they have now more means of exercising power in many areas of American life which were previously civilian domains."[15]

### Conclusion

The close association of big business, the government, and the military and between the heads of each of these institutions led Mills to conclude that, together, this collection of powerful men constituted the center of power in American society, with the military, through its direct presence in the executive branch, wielding a disproportionate power stemming from the entry of the Pentagon into power politics.

Developments since 1960, however, have shown that the prominence of the military in politics was in effect an outcome of postwar popular sentiment toward a general (Eisenhower) who led the United States to victory in World War II rather than evidence of the rise of the military, as such, to the center stage of power politics, as Mills's empiricist observations had led him to believe. Critics have pointed out that, all appearances to the contrary, his exaggerated emphasis on the rise of the military, hence, his (unwarranted) attribution of extraordinary powers to the "warlords," which Mills's critics contend the latter lacked, has had a lopsided effect on Mills's tripartite model of the power elite.[16] Countering Mills's argument on this point, G. William Domhoff, for example, has pointed out that

if the United States in the postwar era has adopted what Mills called a military definition of reality, it is because this was chosen by leading big business members of the power elite on the basis of their understanding of national goals and international events, not because it was somehow foisted on them by the military.[17]

Along these lines, one can argue that despite the rise to prominence of several generals over the past few decades (such as Gen. William Westmoreland during the Vietnam War in the late 1960s and early 1970s, Gen. Norman Schwarzkopf during the first Gulf War in the early 1990s, and Gen. Colin Powell as secretary of state during the post-September 11 invasion of Afghanistan in 2001 and Iraq in 2003), the recent military posture of the United States around the world during the Cold War and in the post-Soviet/post-Cold War era of U.S. global hegemony continues to be a manifestation of U.S. economic power in the world and is driven by economic considerations (such as access to oil in the Middle East and Central Asia). It is thus orchestrated by powerful U.S. capitalist interests who control the state and who, through the state, unleash military force to maximize capitalist profits to secure U.S. global domination.

A more serious criticism of Mills, brought out in subsequent work on the U.S. power structure launched by Domhoff and others in the 1960s and 1970s, is the absence in Mills's analysis of a connection between the power elite and what Domhoff calls "the social upper class."[18] Herbert Aptheker, for example, has pointed out that Mills's

> projection of the concept of a triangular power elite, which he explicitly offers in preference to that of a ruling class, is based on a misconception of "ruling class." Moreover, in his tripartite division of the wielders of control he avoids comparing the relative weight of each of the three and tends to ignore the central depository of power—the financial overlords.[19]

This misconception of the source of power in American society prevented the development of a structural analysis of power linked to class until Domhoff's introduction into the discussion of the central role of the "upper class" in government through the former's transformation from a cohesive social-economic class into a "governing class"—a topic we address in the next chapter.

## Notes

1  See C. Wright Mills, *The Sociological Imagination* (New York: Oxford University Press, 1959); and C. Wright Mills, *The Power Elite* (New York: Oxford University Press, 1956). See also C. Wright Mills, *White Collar: The American Middle Classes* (New York: Oxford University Press, 1951).

2  Mills, *The Power Elite*, 277.

3  Mills, *The Power Elite*, 6, 9; emphasis added.

4  Mills, *The Power Elite*, 4.

5  C. Wright Mills, "The Structure of Power in American Society," in *Power, Politics, and People: The Collected Essays of C. Wright Mills*, ed. Irving Louis Horowitz (New York: Oxford University Press, 1963), 27.

6  Mills, *The Power Elite*, 276.

7   Mills, "The Structure of Power in American Society," 35.

8   Mills, *The Power Elite*, 275.

9   Mills, *The Power Elite*, 202.

10  Mills, "The Structure of Power in American Society," 28.

11  Mills, "The Structure of Power in American Society," 28.

12  Mills, *The Power Elite*, 219, 221–2.

13  Mills, *The Power Elite*, 222.

14  Mills, *The Power Elite*, 202.

15  Mills, *The Power Elite*, 202.

16  See G. William Domhoff and Hoyt B. Ballard, eds., *C. Wright Mills and the Power Elite* (Boston, MA: Beacon Press, 1968).

17  G. William Domhoff, *The Higher Circles: The Governing Class in America* (New York: Vintage, 1971), 139.

18  For an extended discussion on this point, see Chapter 17.

19  Herbert Aptheker, *The World of C. Wright Mills* (New York: Marzani and Munsell, 1960), 19–20.

# 17

# DOMHOFF ON THE POWER STRUCTURE AND THE GOVERNING CLASS

Taking Mills's analysis of the American power structure one step further, G. William Domhoff (1936– ) has made an important contribution to our understanding of the social basis of political power by linking the upper class to the major political institutions of American society, especially the state—a relationship embodied in the concept of the "governing class."[1] This chapter explores Domhoff's ideas on the American power structure, which he, like Mills, developed as a critique of pluralist theory. Examining his analysis of the governing class in America, the chapter provides a critical overview of his concept of political power in the United States that goes beyond Mills's characterization of the power elite.

## The Power Structure

In his now classic *Who Rules America?* Domhoff took a giant step forward beyond Mills's pioneering study of the power elite by looking behind the movers and shapers of American domestic and foreign policy. Attempting to understand the common interests of the leading forces of the power structure and their connection to the social upper class of wealthy owners of the giant corporations, Domhoff discovered that through a multitude of political processes the upper class has, through direct and indirect mechanisms of control and domination of government, become a ruling, or governing, class. This became especially the case as U.S. corporations got more and more involved in shaping state policy during the Vietnam War in the 1960s and 1970s.

Clarifying the meaning of the concepts of "power elite," "upper class," and "governing class," Domhoff makes explicit his own analysis of the American power structure and thus sets himself apart from that developed by Mills. The "power elite," Domhoff points out, "encompasses all those who are in command positions in institutions controlled by members of the upper (governing) class."[2] In this sense, Domhoff's definition of the power elite is similar to Mills's concept, that is, an elite made up of the top functionaries of the leading institutions of American society, but goes beyond Mills's tripartite model of power, in that Domhoff differentiates the position of the power elite from that of the upper class. Referring to the former, "This power elite," Domhoff argues,

> is the *leadership group* of the upper class as a whole but it is *not the same thing as the upper class*, for not all members of the upper class are members of the power elite and not all members of the power elite are part of the upper class. It is members of the power elite who take part in the processes that maintain the class structure.[3]

What distinguishes Domhoff's approach from that of Mills is Domhoff's focus on the central problematic of "whether or not the institution [that the power elite serves] is *controlled by members of the upper class*,"[4] for it is this *class control* that is decisive, *not* the particular characteristics or motives of the power elite per se, as Mills had emphasized. "Thus," Domhoff continues,

> if we can show that members of the upper class control the corporations through stock ownership and corporate directorships, the military through the Department of Defense, and the corporate law profession through large corporate law firms and major law schools, we will have gone a long way toward demonstrating that *the aims of the American power elite*, as defined by either Mills or this book, *are necessarily those of members of the upper class*.[5]

Domhoff defines the upper class as a social class "made up of rich businessmen and their families" and points out that it is "closely knit by such institutions as stock ownership, trust funds, intermarriages, private schools, exclusive city clubs, exclusive summer resorts, debutante parties, foxhunts, charity drives, and, last but not least, corporation boards."[6] In short, the upper class, Domhoff points out, is based on "great wealth and unique life styles of intermarrying and interacting families of high social standing."[7] After a detailed examination of the position and connections of the wealthy in America, Domhoff concludes: "There is in the United States an intermarrying social upper class, based upon business wealth, that has a rather definite set of boundaries which are guarded by . . . exclusive institutions."[8] Going a step further, Domhoff raises the central question of his inquiry: "Is this social upper class, with its several institutional focal points and its several means of assimilating new members, also a 'governing class'?"[9] And, if so, what is the process by which the American upper class becomes a national governing class?

## The Upper Class as Governing Class

In both *Who Rules America?* and *The Higher Circles: The Governing Class in America*, Domhoff documents how the upper class is in fact a cohesive social class based on the ownership of the large corporations and banks, and that this class, through its control of numerous private and public institutions, has become a "governing class."[10] He defines the governing class as

> a social upper class which owns a disproportionate amount of the country's wealth, receives a disproportionate share of the country's yearly income, contributes a disproportionate number of its members to governmental bodies and decision-making groups, and dominates the policy-forming process through a variety of means.[11]

Domhoff goes on to show how, through numerous institutional mechanisms, the social upper class becomes a bona fide governing class.

After extensive study and analysis of the relationship between the upper class, the power elite, and the key governmental institutions of American society, Domhoff concludes: "Members of the American upper class and their employees control the Executive branch of the federal government, . . . the Judicial branch and the regulatory agencies," including "the military, the CIA, and the FBI."[12] Moreover, the upper class is well represented in and has substantial influence over the legislative branch and has an impact on other key institutions, including universities, foundations, clubs, advisory councils, and numerous other organizations.[13] Through this control and domination of the key governmental and social institutions of American society, the upper class has become a governing class, according to Domhoff.

Whereas Domhoff had in his earlier work avoided the use of the term "ruling class" because, as he put it, it is "a term that implies a Marxist view of history"[14] (with which he apparently did not want to be identified), opting instead for "the more neutral term 'governing class,'"[15] in his later works—beginning with *The Powers That Be: Processes of Ruling Class Domination in America*—Domhoff drops the term "governing class" and substitutes in its place the concept of the "ruling class"—a concept he had rejected a decade earlier.[16]

In the opening chapter of *The Powers That Be*, titled "The Ruling Class and the Problem of Power," Domhoff defines the term "ruling class" as follows:

> By a ruling class I mean a clearly demarcated social class which has "power" over the government (state apparatus) and underlying population within a given

nation (state). Evidence for the "power" of a ruling class can be found in such indicators as:

1   A disproportionate amount of wealth and income as compared to other social classes and groups within the state;
2   A higher standing than other social classes within the state on a variety of well-being statistics;
3   Control over the major social and economic institutions of the state;
4   Domination over the governmental processes of the country.[17]

In a broader sense, then, the "ruling class is a social class that subordinates other social classes to its own profit or advantage"[18] and dominates the major institutions of society, especially the state, to advance its class interests.

Differentiating his concept of the "ruling class" from Mills's "power elite," Domhoff writes: "C. Wright Mills first introduced the concept of a power elite into the sociological literature as a substitute for 'ruling class.'"[19] In contrast, Domhoff states,

I define the power elite as the leadership group or *operating arm* of the ruling class. It is made up of active, working members of the ruling class and high-level employees in institutions controlled by members of the ruling class.[20]

"The difference between Mills' definition and mine," Domhoff continues,

lies in the fact that (1) I do not assume *a priori* that any institutionally based group is by definition part of the power elite, as Mills did in so designating leaders within corporate, military and governmental bureaucracies; and (2) I have grounded the power elite in a social class. Using this approach, it is possible to determine empirically which parts of the economy and government can be considered direct outposts of the ruling class by virtue of disproportionate participation by members of the power elite.[21]

"Both of these concepts—ruling class and power elite," Domhoff concludes, "are important in an examination of how America is ruled, for they bring together the class-rule and institutional-elite perspectives" of power in American society.[22]

## Conclusion

Domhoff's analysis of power in American society, through the introduction of the concept of the "governing class," has provided an added dimension to Mills's approach to politics and the state. However, despite his significant contribution to power-structure research and substantial improvement over Mills's concept of the power elite, Domhoff has been criticized for paying insufficient attention to class relations and class struggle beyond the instrumental identification of control of the state and other institutions of American society by the governing (or ruling) upper class. Marxist critics have faulted him for having focused too much on the institutional aspects of the policy-formation process and for ignoring a class analysis of the capitalist political economy that incorporates a dialectical approach to class. Moreover, Domhoff's loose usage of the term "upper class" has led to further criticism of his overall model, which he has built outside the Marxist problematic of the ruling *capitalist* class.

While Domhoff in his book *The Power Elite and the State* attempts to correct this shortcoming by injecting an element of class analysis into his new theory of power and the state, he, like Mills, continues to reject Marxist theories of the state and opts instead for an eclectic approach in line with his previous studies of power in the United States.[23] Thus, although he clearly states that "the relationship between states and social classes [is] the crucial issue of this book," Domhoff criticizes the efforts of the structural Marxists by asserting that "they abandoned the study of social power in general for more narrow concerns such as 'class structure' or 'state power.'"[24] Rejecting the Marxist approach and anticipating criticisms of the eclectic theoretical position he has come to adopt in his studies of the U.S. power structure during the past twenty-five years, Domhoff admits,

> After all those years spent wandering in the empirical wilderness, surrounded on every side by pluralists, structural Marxists, and utility maximizers . . . I hope the eclecticism of my view . . . does not continue to create confusion for the pigeon-holers, taxonomists, and single-cause theorists who now dominate discussions of power in America.[25]

Domhoff's objections to structural Marxism notwithstanding, to develop a more comprehensive understanding of the relationship between class, power, and the state, we turn in the next chapter to the debate on the theory of the capitalist state—a debate that has taken center stage in Marxist circles for over four decades.

## Notes

1 See G. William Domhoff, *Who Rules America?* (Englewood Cliffs, NJ: Prentice Hall, 1967); and G. William Domhoff, *The Higher Circles: The Governing Class in America* (New York: Vintage, 1971). For the relationship of Domhoff's work to that of Mills, see G. William Domhoff and Hoyt B. Ballard, eds., *C. Wright Mills and the Power Elite* (Boston, MA: Beacon Press, 1968).

2 Domhoff, *Who Rules America?* 10.

3  G. William Domhoff, *Who Rules America Now? A View for the '80s* (New York: Simon & Schuster, 1983), 2.

4  Domhoff, *Who Rules America?* 10; emphasis added.

5  Domhoff, *Who Rules America?* 10.

6  Domhoff, *Who Rules America?* 4.

7  Domhoff, *The Higher Circles*, 32.

8  Domhoff, *Who Rules America?* 33.

9  Domhoff, *Who Rules America?* 5.

10  See Domhoff, *The Higher Circles*, 103–9, and Domhoff, *Who Rules America?* 156. See also G. William Domhoff, *The Powers That Be: Processes of Ruling Class Domination in America* (New York: Vintage, 1978), chap. 1.

11  Domhoff, *The Higher Circles*, 109.

12  Domhoff, *Who Rules America?* 84, 131.

13  Domhoff, *Who Rules America Now?* chaps. 4 and 5.

14  Domhoff, *Who Rules America?* 3.

15  Domhoff, *Who Rules America?* 3.

16  See Domhoff, *The Powers That Be*.

17  Domhoff, *The Powers That Be*, 12.

18  Domhoff, *The Powers That Be*, 13.

19  Domhoff, *The Powers That Be*, 13–14.

20  Domhoff, *The Powers That Be*, 13; emphasis added.

21  Domhoff, *The Powers That Be*, 14.

22  Domhoff, *The Powers That Be*, 14–15.

23  See G. William Domhoff, *The Power Elite and the State* (New York: Aldine de Gruyter, 1990).

24  Domhoff, *The Power Elite and the State*, xviii, 7. Domhoff writes, "I believe that the Marxian analysis of the state in democratic capitalist societies is wrong because it incorporates a false homology between the economy and the state that distorts its view of the state and creates a tendency to downplay the importance of representative democracy." Domhoff, *The Power Elite and the State*, 8.

25  Domhoff, *The Power Elite and the State*, xix, 14–15.

# 18

# ALTHUSSER, POULANTZAS, AND MILIBAND ON POLITICS AND THE STATE

This chapter focuses on the views of three contemporary Marxist theorists, Louis Althusser (1918–1990), Nicos Poulantzas (1936–1979), and Ralph Miliband (1924–1994), on politics and the state in capitalist society. Concerned with the base–superstructure problematic (i.e., the relationship of the social-economic base to the political superstructure) and the nature and role of the capitalist state, these theorists provide us with the framework for an informed analysis of the debates on the state and politics in late capitalist society.

## Ideology and the Political Superstructure

In the late 1960s, Althusser reintroduced into Marxist discourse V. I. Lenin's and Antonio Gramsci's contributions on ideology and the state and provided an extended discussion on the basic concepts of historical materialism. Althusser played a key role in the effort to revitalize critical thought on the subject by incorporating Gramsci's notion of ideological hegemony into his own analysis of "ideological state apparatuses."[1]

In linking the political superstructure to the social-economic base, or mode of production, Althusser argues in favor of the classical Marxist position, which identifies the superstructure as determined "in the last instance" by the base: "The upper floors," he writes in reference to the political superstructure, "could not 'stay up' (in the air) alone, if they did not rest precisely on their base."[2] Thus, the state, the supreme political institution and repressive apparatus of society, "enables the ruling classes to ensure their domination over the working class, thus enabling the former to subject the latter to the process of surplus-value extortion."[3] This is so precisely because the state is controlled by the ruling class. And such control makes the state, and the superstructure in general, dependent on, and determined by, the dominant class in the base.

In his essay "Ideology and Ideological State Apparatuses," Althusser expands his analysis of the base–superstructure relationship to include other superstructural institutions—cultural, religious, educational, legal, and so on. As the hegemony of the ruling class in these spheres becomes critical for its control over the dominated classes and society in general, the class struggle takes on a three-tiered attribute, consisting of the economic, political, and ideological levels. Central to the process of ruling-class ideological domination is the installation by the ruling class of the dominant ideology in the ideological state apparatuses (i.e., the political institutions, schools, media), according to Althusser.

> The ideology of the ruling class does not become the ruling ideology by virtue of the seizure of state power alone. It is by the installation of the ideological state apparatuses in which this ideology is realized itself that it becomes the ruling ideology.[4]

The relationship between ruling-class domination and the dominant ideology is also emphasized by Poulantzas, who further develops Althusser's conceptualization of ideology, situating it in the context of class domination and class struggle. "The dominant ideology, by assuring the practical insertion of agents in the social structure," Poulantzas points out, "aims at the maintenance (the cohesion) of the structure, and this means *above all* class domination and exploitation."[5]

> It is precisely in this way that within a social formation ideology is dominated by the ensemble of representations, values, notions, beliefs, etc. by means of which class domination is perpetuated: in other words it is dominated by what can be called the ideology of the dominant class.[6]

This Althusserian conception of the relationship between the base and the superstructure, especially the state and the ideological state apparatuses, informs Poulantzas's analysis of classes, class struggle, and the state, and forms the basis of recent discussion and debate on the Marxist theory of the state.

## The Poulantzas–Miliband Debate on the Capitalist State

The Poulantzas–Miliband debate on the nature and role of the capitalist state in the early 1970s prompted renewed interest in Marxist theorizing on the capitalist state during the past two decades.[7] In this debate, one position emphasized the direct and indirect control of the state by the dominant capitalist class, and another emphasized the structural requirements of the capitalist system affecting the state and its "relative autonomy." These two views correspond to the so-called instrumentalist and structuralist positions associated with Miliband and Poulantzas, respectively. Central to the debate are questions related to the class nature of the state, the relationship between different classes and the state, and the notion of relative autonomy in the exercise of state power.[8]

In his original formulation of the problem in *The State in Capitalist Society*, Miliband approaches the question of the state via a critique of the pluralist models still dominant in political sociology and mainstream political theory. In so doing, he provides an approach and analysis that earns his work the unwarranted label "instrumentalism." Critiques of his work, reacting to this instrumentalism, have resulted in the formulation of a counterposition labeled "structuralism."

The central question addressed in the initial formulation of the instrumentalist problematic has been a determination of the role of the state in a society dominated by capitalist social relations. In this context, Miliband's study of the capitalist state focuses on the special relationship between the state and the capitalist class and on the mechanisms of control of the state by this class that, de facto, transform the state into a *capitalist state*.

In contrast, Poulantzas, representing the so-called structuralist position, focuses on the structural constraints of the capitalist system that limit the state's autonomy and force the state to work within the framework of an order that yields results invariably favorable to the dominant capitalist class. According to this view, the state becomes a *capitalist* state by virtue of the system of production itself in capitalist society, even in the absence of direct control of the state apparatus by capitalists.

It should be pointed out, however, that the degree of lack of direct control of the state apparatus by the capitalist class determines the degree of the state's relative autonomy from this class. And this relative autonomy in turn gives the state the necessary freedom to manage the overall interests of the capitalist class and rule society on behalf of the established capitalist order.

The central problem for these competing views of the state is not so much whether the state in capitalist society is a capitalist state—they agree that it is—but how that state becomes a capitalist state. Far more than their limited academic value, the answers to this question have immense political implications because the debates surrounding this issue originally emerged in Europe among Marxists and local Communist parties in response to the pivotal political question regarding the strategy and tactics of taking state power under advanced capitalism.

## Instrumentalism Versus Structuralism

Let us briefly look at the fundamentals of the instrumentalist-versus-structuralist problematic and show, in the process, that the dichotomy has been ill conceived as, ultimately, both Miliband and Poulantzas in later reformulations of their positions basically accept the validity of their critics' conclusions.

To start with, in his initial formulation of the problem, Miliband writes,

> In the Marxist scheme, the "ruling class" of capitalist society is that class which owns and controls the means of production and which is able, by virtue of the economic power thus conferred upon it, to use the state as its instrument for the domination of society.[9]

Miliband expounded this seemingly instrumentalist statement through his focus on "patterns and consequences of personal and social ties between individuals occupying positions of power in different institutional spheres."[10] Concentrating on a study of the nature of the capitalist class, the mechanisms that tie this class to the state, and the specific relationships between state policies and class interests,[11] Miliband leaves himself open to charges of voluntarism and instrumentalism.

In contrast, Poulantzas argues that "the *direct* participation of members of the capitalist class in the state apparatus and in the government, even where it exists, is not the important side of the matter."[12] What is crucial to understand, according to Poulantzas, is this:

> The relation between the bourgeois class and the state is an *objective relation*. This means that if the *function* of the state in a determinate social formation and the *interests* of the dominant class in this formation *coincide*, it is by reason of the system itself: the direct participation of members of the ruling class in the state apparatus is not the *cause* but the *effect*, and moreover a chance and contingent one, of this objective coincidence.[13]

In this formulation, the functions of the state are broadly determined by the structural requirements of the capitalist mode of production and the constraints placed on it by the structural environment in which the state must operate. Given these parameters of operation, the state obtains relative autonomy from the various fractions of the capitalist class in order to carry out its functions as a capitalist state on behalf of the capitalist system. Thus, Poulantzas accepts the control of the state by the capitalist class through direct and indirect means but assigns to it relative autonomy vis-à-vis any one fraction of that class.[14] Hence, in this formulation, the capitalist state is the state of the capitalist class and serves the interests of that class as a whole; at the same time, it maintains relative autonomy from that class's various fractions.

## Convergence of the Two Views

Miliband, defending himself against vulgar instrumentalist interpretations of his argument, later concedes that the state can and must have a certain degree of autonomy from the capitalist class. Referring to Karl Marx and Frederick Engels's assertion that "the modern state is but a committee for managing the common affairs of the whole bourgeoisie," Miliband writes,

> This has regularly been taken to mean not only that the state acts *on behalf* of the dominant class . . . but that it acts *at the behest* of that class which is an altogether different assertion and, as I would argue, a vulgar deformation of the thought of Marx and Engels. . . . [T]he notion of common affairs assumes the existence of particular ones; and the notion of the whole bourgeoisie implies the existence of separate elements which make up that whole. This being the case, there is an obvious need for an institution of the kind they refer to, namely the state; and the state *cannot* meet this need without enjoying a certain degree of autonomy. In other words, the notion of autonomy is embedded in the definition itself, is an intrinsic part of it.[15]

Elsewhere, Miliband addresses this question more directly: "Different forms of state have different degrees of autonomy. But all states enjoy some autonomy or independence from all classes, including the dominant classes."[16] Nevertheless,

> the relative independence of the state does not reduce its class character: on the contrary, its relative independence makes it *possible* for the state to play its class role in an appropriately flexible manner. If it really was the simple "instrument" of the "ruling class," it would be fatally inhibited in the performance of its role.[17]

He goes on to argue that

> the intervention of the state is always and necessarily partisan: as a class state, it always intervenes for the purpose of maintaining the existing system of domination, even where it intervenes to mitigate the harshness of that system of domination.[18]

Thus, Miliband takes a big step toward reconciliation with the relative autonomy thesis, while retaining the core of his argument in seeing the capitalist state as an institution controlled by the capitalist class as a whole.

Poulantzas, in his later writings, also moves in a direction away from his earlier position on relative autonomy. He admits that in the current monopoly stage of capitalism, the *monopoly fraction* of the capitalist class dominates the state and thereby secures policies in its own favor over other fractions of the bourgeois power bloc.[19] This situation, he adds, poses problems to the state's traditional role as "political organizer of the general interest of the bourgeoisie" and "restrict[s] the limits of the relative autonomy of the state in relation to monopoly capital and to the field of the compromises it makes with other fractions of the bourgeoisie."[20] The political crisis resulting from this fractional domination and fragmentation, argues Poulantzas, leads to a crisis of the bourgeois state.[21]

## Conclusion

With these later reformulations of state theory by both Poulantzas and Miliband, we see a convergence of the two positions and arrive at the general conclusion that the state in capitalist society is both controlled by and, simultaneously, relatively autonomous of the various fractions of the capitalist class, in order to perform its functions in advancing the interests of the capitalist class as a whole and, at the same time, maintain its legitimacy over society. This "relative autonomy," however, is rapidly being undermined by the hegemonic (monopoly) fraction of the capitalist class, which, as a result, is blocking the state's effectiveness in fulfilling its political role as the "executive committee" of the entire bourgeoisie.

More recently, some neo-Weberian theorists have introduced an alternative, "state-centered" approach that grants greater (not less) autonomy to the state and views state managers as autonomous agents who are independent of the prevailing class structure in society. We provide a critical analysis of this approach in the next chapter.

### Notes

1  See Louis Althusser, *For Marx* (London: Penguin, 1969); and Louis Althusser, *Lenin and Philosophy and Other Essays* (New York: Monthly Review Press, 1971). See also Louis Althusser and Etienne Balibar, *Reading Capital* (London: New Left Books, 1970).
2  Althusser, *Lenin and Philosophy and Other Essays*, 135.
3  Althusser, *Lenin and Philosophy and Other Essays*, 137.
4  Althusser, *Lenin and Philosophy and Other Essays*, 185.
5  Nicos Poulantzas, *Political Power and Social Classes* (London: Verso, 1973), 209.
6  Poulantzas, *Political Power and Social Classes*, 209.

7   The debate began with a review of Ralph Miliband's *The State in Capitalist Society* (New York: Basic Books, 1969) by Nicos Poulantzas in "The Problem of the Capitalist State," *New Left Review*, no. 58 (1969), to which Miliband responded in the next issue of the same journal. See Ralph Miliband, "The Capitalist State—Reply to Nicos Poulantzas," *New Left Review*, no. 59 (1970). See also Nicos Poulantzas, *Political Power and Social Classes*; Ralph Miliband, "Poulantzas and the Capitalist State," *New Left Review*, no. 82 (1973); and Nicos Poulantzas, "The Capitalist State: A Reply to Miliband and Laclau," *New Left Review*, no. 95 (1976). Among Poulantzas's later works, see *Classes in Contemporary Capitalism* (London: New Left Books, 1975) and *State, Power, Socialism* (London: Verso, 1978). Miliband's subsequent arguments can be found in his "Political Forms and Historical Materialism," in *Socialist Register, 1975*, ed. R. Miliband and J. Saville (London: Merlin Press, 1975) and *Marxism and Politics* (London: Oxford University Press, 1977).

8   See David Gold, Clarence Y. H. Lo, and Erik Olin Wright, "Some Recent Developments in Marxist Theories of the Capitalist State," pts. 1 and 2, *Monthly Review* 27, nos. 5–6 (1975); Gosta Esping-Andersen, Roger Friedland, and Erik Olin Wright, "Modes of Class Struggle and the Capitalist State," *Kapitalistate*, nos. 4–5 (1976); Albert Szymanski, *The Capitalist State and the Politics of Class* (Cambridge, MA: Winthrop, 1978); Bob Jessop, *The Capitalist State* (New York: New York University Press, 1982); Martin Carnoy, *The State and Political Theory* (Princeton, NJ: Princeton University Press, 1984).

9   Miliband, *The State in Capitalist Society*, 23.

10  Gold, Lo, and Wright, "Some Recent Developments in Marxist Theories of the Capitalist State," 33.

11  Gold, Lo, and Wright, "Some Recent Developments in Marxist Theories of the Capitalist State," 32–3.

12  Poulantzas, "The Problem of the Capitalist State," 73.

13  Poulantzas, "The Problem of the Capitalist State," 73.

14  Poulantzas, *Political Power and Social Classes*; and Poulantzas, *State, Power, Socialism*.

15  Miliband, "Poulantzas and the Capitalist State," 85.

16  Miliband, *Marxism and Politics*, 83.

17  Miliband, *Marxism and Politics*, 87.

18  Miliband, *Marxism and Politics*, 91.

19  Nicos Poulantzas, "The Political Crisis and the Crisis of the State," in *Critical Sociology: European Perspectives*, ed. J. W. Freiberg (New York: Irvington, 1979), 374–81.

20  Poulantzas, "The Political Crisis and the Crisis of the State," 375.

21  Poulantzas, "The Political Crisis and the Crisis of the State," 357–93.

# 19

# TRIMBERGER, BLOCK, AND SKOCPOL AND NEO-WEBERIAN THEORIZING

This chapter examines a number of contemporary attempts at neo-Weberian theorizing on the state and society by theorists influenced by the Weberian school—Ellen Kay Trimberger, Fred Block, and Theda Skocpol. Providing a revised Weberian political theory of state–society relations, which also includes elements of elite theory that we discussed in Chapter 5, these theorists stress the autonomy of the state vis-à-vis the dominant and dominated classes and characterize the state as a source of power independent of the contending class forces.[1] In what follows, we present a critical analysis of the main arguments advanced by these theorists and contrast their views with the Marxist theory of the state discussed in Chapters 12 and 18.

## Autonomous Bureaucrats and Political Power

Trimberger, in her book *Revolution from Above*, attempts to develop a neo-Weberian theory of the state and society, arguing that the state should be seen as playing an independent role and state bureaucrats as independent agents free of class control. "A bureaucratic state apparatus, or a segment of it can be said to be relatively autonomous," Trimberger writes, "when those who hold high civil and/or military posts satisfy two conditions":

> (1) They are not recruited from the dominant landed, commercial or industrial classes; and (2) they do not form close personal and economic ties with these classes after their elevation to high office. Relatively autonomous bureaucrats are thus independent of those classes which control the means of production.[2]

Trimberger goes on to argue that "dynamically autonomous bureaucrats enter the class struggle as an *independent* force, rather than as an instrument of other class forces."[3] Going a step further, she contends that these bureaucrats "have a distinctive class position" and that they can "use their control over state resources—coercive, monetary, and ideological—to destroy the existing economic and class order."[4] Moreover,

> even in polities where the state bureaucracy is subordinate to a party and parliamentary system controlled by [dominant] class interests ... relatively autonomous military officers have the potential for breaking this institutional subordination by force.[5]

If, as Trimberger contends, these "autonomous" bureaucrats hold on to no particular class interests of their own (or those of other classes), it is not clear why they would be "acting to destroy an existing economic and class order" in crisis situations.[6] Trimberger fails to explain (1) the class ideology of these bureaucrats (which is substantially, but not exclusively, determined by their class origin); (2) the class interests they intend to serve (which is related to the above considerations of origin, ideology, or both); and, most important, (3) the structural consequences of policies pursued by these bureaucrats and their positive or negative impact on different classes.

Trimberger's general contention that "control of the governing apparatus is a source of power independent of that held by class"[7] constitutes a departure from the Marxist theory of the state discussed in the previous chapter. She confirms this departure by stating that

> neither the Marxist nor the non-Marxist political sociology of Third World societies has looked at the relationship between the state apparatus and dominant classes as an *independent* variable determining the type and rate of change in the transition from agrarian to industrial societies.[8]

In this sense, the approach taken by Trimberger on this issue is, in effect, a restatement of a revised version of the Weberian position.

## State Managers and Power Politics

An extension of this line of reasoning has led other theorists in a pluralist direction where, as evidenced in Block's argument, the state and state officials become "autonomous agents" so that they acquire independence from the capitalist class and, further, determine policy over the heads of this class, including the formulation of policies that sometimes go against the interests of the capitalists as a whole.[9]

In his controversial article "The Ruling Class Does Not Rule," Block attacks Nicos Poulantzas's structuralist position as "a slightly more sophisticated version" of instrumentalism and proposes to replace it with his own reformulation of the problem. The underlying argument advanced by Block against the structuralist–instrumentalist problematic discussed in Chapter 18 rests on his conception of the role of "state managers," who, according to Block, are autonomous agents functioning in their own self- (or positional) interests and are not consciously engaged in the protection of the interests of the capitalist class as such. Thus, Block introduces into the debate "autonomous state managers" controlled by no one and subservient to no particular class interests other than their own, although they are forced to formulate policies within the framework of an environment that includes both capitalist domination of the economy and class struggle between the two contending class forces, the capitalists and the workers. This becomes clear when Block states, "State managers do have an interest in expanding their own power, including their own power to manage the economy."[10] To back this claim up, Block writes, "German capitalists were reduced to being functionaries, albeit highly paid functionaries, of the Nazi state that was acting in its own profoundly irrational interests."[11]

Elsewhere, Block asserts that "the rationality of the capitalist state emerges out of the three-sided relationship between state managers, capital and subordinate classes."[12] Referring to his own theoretical formulation, and distancing himself from Marxism, he writes,

> The virtue of this model is that it allows one to get away from the standard Marxist methodological tool of assuming that state policies always reflect the intentionality of a social class or sector of a class. It renders obsolete the procedure of looking for a specific social base for any particular state policy.[13]

He goes on to assert,

> One can say that a policy objectively benefited a particular social class, but that is very different from saying that this social class, or sector of a class, subjectively wanted the policy or that its intentions were a critical element in policy development.[14]

This leads him to conclude, "The road to analytic confusion in Marxism is paved with an exaggerated concern with class intentionality."[15]

Block's critique of Marxism, for its "narrow focus on 'class struggles,'" has, during the past decade, taken him down what he calls a "post-Marxist" path to a rejection of historical materialism altogether. In his recent book *Revising State Theory*, Block continues to see the state as an autonomous agent, arguing that politics is "irreducible" and that social struggles, such as those around race and gender, cannot be explained as manifestations of class struggle.[16] Advocating a position that would "go beyond Marxism," Block asserts, "The answers that Marx offered no longer suffice, and just as Marx sought to transcend Hegel, so too, those who pursue the Post-Marxist project seek to transcend Marx."[17] This, he feels, would free him to introduce into his analysis

> many other collective actors organized around race, gender, age, sexual orientation, religious orientation, or shared views about the environment or the arms race. In place of a narrow focus on "class struggles," the emphasis would be on a broad range of social struggles.[18]

Block's seemingly "broader" reformulation of state theory, which allows state managers considerable autonomy, while bringing in a multitude of social actors beyond classes, unfortunately turns out to be a "slightly more sophisticated version" of recent neo-Weberian approaches rather than a new attempt at a reconstruction of prevailing Marxist theories of the state and society.

## Class, State, and Society: A State-Centered Approach

Other neo-Weberian theorists, like Skocpol, have adopted an approach similar to that of Trimberger and Block in conceptualizing the state as an independent force and, in the process, have come to embrace a more elaborate, "state-centered" approach, rejecting the Marxist position on the class nature of the state.[19] Influenced by Weberian theory, Skocpol in her book *States and Social Revolutions* attempts to counter the classical Marxist position on the relationship of the state to the mode of production and the class basis of politics and the state.[20] She writes,

> In contrast to most (especially recent) Marxist theories, this view refuses to treat states as if they were mere analytic aspects of abstractly conceived modes of production, or even political aspects of concrete class relations and struggles. Rather it insists that states are actual organizations controlling (or attempting to control) territories and people.[21]

Arguing in favor of the view that the state is an entity with "an autonomous structure—a structure with a logic and interests of its own,"[22] Skocpol examines the French, Russian, and Chinese revolutions in terms of the centrality of the state's role in "acting for itself." Adopting an "organizational" and "realist" perspective on the state,[23] "state and party organizations," she argues, must be viewed "as *independent* determinants of political conflicts and outcomes."[24] Thus, for Skocpol "the state organizations . . . have a more central and autonomous place" because, like Trimberger and Block, she sees in the state "potential autonomy of action over . . . the dominant class and existing relations of production."[25]

In this reformulation of the class–state problematic, the state is divorced from and opposed to existing social classes and acts in accordance with its distinct interests, based primarily on the maintenance of internal order and competition against external forces (i.e., other states) threatening its survival.

> The state normally performs two basic sets of tasks: It maintains order, and it competes with other actual or potential states. . . . [T]he state's own fundamental interest in maintaining sheer physical order and political peace may lead it— especially in periods of crisis—to enforce concessions to subordinate-class demands. These concessions may be at the expense of the interests of the dominant class, but not contrary to the state's own interests in controlling the population and collecting taxes and military recruits.[26]

Thus,

> If state organizations cope with whatever tasks they already claim smoothly and efficiently, legitimacy . . . will probably be accorded to the state's form and rulers by most groups in society. . . . Loss of legitimacy, especially among the crucial [politically powerful] groups, tends to ensue with a vengeance if and when . . . the state fails consistently to cope with existing tasks, or proves unable to cope with new tasks suddenly thrust upon it by crisis circumstances.[27]

"The political crises that have launched social revolutions," writes Skocpol, "have not at all been epiphenomenal reflections of societal strains or class contradictions. Rather, they have been direct expressions of contradictions centered in the structures of old-regime states."[28] Thus, to understand better those processes by which the state has taken center stage in history, Skocpol suggests "the need for a more state-centered approach" in studying states and social revolutions.[29]

## Conclusion

Contrary to the Trimberger, Block, and Skocpol formulations, one could argue that although the state can, and sometimes does, gain limited autonomy from the direct control of the main class forces in society (especially during periods of crises), this autonomy by no means implies the class neutrality of the state and its agents, or that the state and state officials are "above class."

Clearly, the state cannot be seen in terms distinct from class forces and class struggles in society. However independent it may at times appear to be, the state, as the supreme superstructural institution in society, is in the final analysis a reflection of the underlying mode of production defined by the definite relations of production that characterize the class nature of that state.

This understanding of the materialist dynamics of history lies at the heart of Marx's class analysis, which we discussed at the beginning of this book. In the closing chapters of this book, we return to this theme, exploring a more complete understanding of the relationship between the state and society and revealing the real nature of politics and the state.

Before returning to historical materialism and class analysis, however, we take up in the next few chapters other important theories that address aspects of society and social relations characteristic of life under contemporary capitalism.

## Notes

1 See Ellen K. Trimberger, *Revolution from Above: Military Bureaucrats and Development in Japan, Turkey, and Peru* (New Brunswick, NJ: Transaction Books, 1978); Theda Skocpol, *States and Social Revolutions: A Comparative Analysis of France, Russia and China* (Cambridge: Cambridge University Press, 1979); Fred Block, "The Ruling Class Does Not Rule: Notes on the Marxist Theory of the State," *Socialist Review*, no. 33 (1977).
2 Trimberger, *Revolution from Above*, 4.
3 Trimberger, *Revolution from Above*, 5; emphasis added.
4 Trimberger, *Revolution from Above*, 4.
5 Trimberger, *Revolution from Above*, 4.
6 Trimberger, *Revolution from Above*, 4–5.
7 Trimberger, *Revolution from Above*, 7.
8 Trimberger, *Revolution from Above*, 8.
9 See Block, "The Ruling Class Does Not Rule"; and Fred Block, "Class Consciousness and Capitalist Rationalization: A Reply to Critics," *Socialist Review*, nos. 40–1 (1978).
10 "Class Consciousness and Capitalist Rationalization: A Reply to Critics," 218.
11 "Class Consciousness and Capitalist Rationalization: A Reply to Critics," 219.
12 Fred Block, "Marxist Theories of the State in World System Analysis" (paper, First Annual Political Economy of the World System Conference, American University, Washington, DC, 1977), 8.
13 Block, "Marxist Theories of the State in World System Analysis," 8.
14 Block, "Marxist Theories of the State in World System Analysis," 8.
15 Block, "Marxist Theories of the State in World System Analysis," 8.
16 Fred Block, *Revising State Theory* (Philadelphia, PA: Temple University Press, 1987), 17–18, 34–5.
17 Block, *Revising State Theory*, 35.

18  Block, *Revising State Theory*, 18.
19  Acknowledging the affinity of his approach to state theory to Skocpol's "state-centered" approach, which we discuss later in the chapter, Block writes, "The systematization of a state-centered approach in the work of Theda Skocpol has been the other important new development in state theory. Skocpol has energetically argued that both the liberal and the Marxist traditions have been society-centered, explaining what goes on in the state as a function of what goes on in society. Her alternative is a state-centered approach that would provide a corrective to the standard view by stressing the diverse ways in which the state structures social life." Block, *Revising State Theory*, 20.
20  Skocpol, *States and Social Revolutions*. For an acknowledgment of this and other influences on Skocpol's views, see Skocpol, *States and Social Revolutions*, 301n73 and 301n77.
21  Skocpol, *States and Social Revolutions*, 31.
22  Skocpol, *States and Social Revolutions*, 27. In developing this view of the state, Skocpol cites the works of Trimberger and Block, among others, and states, "I have been very greatly influenced by these writings, and by personal conversations with Trimberger and Block." Skocpol, *States and Social Revolutions*, 301n73.
23  Skocpol, *States and Social Revolutions*, 31.
24  Theda Skocpol, "Political Response to Capitalist Crisis: Neo-Marxist Theories of the State and the Case of the New Deal," *Politics and Society* 10, no. 2 (1981): 199.
25  Skocpol, *States and Social Revolutions*, 31.
26  Skocpol, *States and Social Revolutions*, 30.
27  Skocpol, *States and Social Revolutions*, 31–2.
28  Skocpol, *States and Social Revolutions*, 29.
29  Skocpol, *States and Social Revolutions*, 29.

# 20

# HOMANS ON SOCIAL EXCHANGE

*Larry T. Reynolds and Alice L. Littlefield*

Social exchange theory is a perspective with a long history in social science circles, extending from Adam Smith and Jeremy Bentham through Peter Blau, Richard Emerson, Mancur Olson, James Coleman, John Thibaut, and Harold Kelley, to such contemporary practitioners as Karen Cook, Michael Hechter, David Willer, Linda Mohn, John Roemer, and John Elster. In this chapter, we focus on George Caspar Homans (1910–1989) as exchange theory's trailblazer among American sociologists. Homans not only presented the theory in its clearest and most forceful form, he became the intellectual lightning rod for the adverse reaction it engendered. Homans was the exchange theorist's theorist, and his writings on exchange constitute one of the best-known reactions against collectivist explanations of human behavior.

## A Move toward Exchange

*Marriage, Authority and Final Causes*, a sixty-five-page pamphlet published in 1955, marks Homans's move away from his previous sociological orientation in the direction of exchange theory.[1] This approach takes more definite form in a 1958 article in which he views all human interaction in terms of *exchange*, a type of bargaining:

> Interaction between persons is an exchange of goods, material and non-material. This is one of the oldest theories of social behavior, and one that we still use everyday to interpret our own behavior, as when we say, "I found so-and-so rewarding"; or "I got a good deal out of him"; or, even, "Talking with him took a good deal out of me."[2]

In this article, Homans speaks of costs, profits, rewards, influence, and distributive justice, all concepts developed in his later writings on exchange. In fact, most of his subsequent work mirrors the topics found here in embryonic form.

Homans's "all the world's a market" analogizing is, in part, a reaction against Talcott Parsons and his followers' attempts to impose functionalism on sociology. As Homans sees it, the functionalists have it backwards; we should not be studying society first and individuals last. Rather, we must first examine simple social behavior because "what happens when two or three persons are in a position to influence one another [is] the sort of thing of which those massive structures called 'classes,' 'firms,' 'communities,' and 'societies' must ultimately be composed."[3]

## Market Meets Maze: Economics and Behavior

Homans expands considerably the ideas contained in the 1958 article in his 1961 book *Social Behavior: Its Elementary Forms*,[4] in which he lays out a sociological theory quite compatible with the folk wisdom of American society. Here Homans assumes, as do most citizens of the United States, that people are materialistic, profit-motivated, and self-interested; that competition is a lever of progress; that market exchange is good exchange; and that capitalism is not only the best, but the most natural, form of economic organization.

Many sociologists admired this book, and many others took it to task. In response to his critics, Homans argues once again in a 1974 revised edition that the best way to conceptualize human interaction is to treat it as exchange. He introduces eleven concepts from which he generates the theory's six key postulates. Four of the concepts are taken from classical economics; the remaining seven derive from the behaviorist theory of the psychologist B. F. Skinner.

## The Concepts

The eleven concepts that constitute the core of Homans's theory of social exchange are as follows:

1 *Activity*: Behavior attempting to elicit a reward.
2 *Cost*: An activity that is punishing or an alternative reward that is foregone in order to get still another reward.
3 *Distributive Justice*: Activities involving the calculation of whether costs and investments have led to a "fair" profit by individuals in an exchange.
4 *Interaction*: Behaviors in which people direct their activities in order to derive rewards and avoid punishments from each other.

5 *Investments*: A person's relevant past activities (e.g., skills, education, and expertise) and social characteristics (e.g., sex, age, and race), which are brought to the situation and evaluated by both the person and those with whom one is interacting.

6 *Norms*: Verbal statements or activities in which people communicate the kinds of activities that should or should not occur in a situation.

7 *Profit*: Rewards, minus the costs and investment, for engaging in a given activity.

8 *Quantity*: The number of units of an activity (whether rewarding or punishing) emitted and/or received over a particular period of time.

9 *Rewards*: Anything a person receives or any activity directed toward one that the person defines as valuable.

10 *Sentiments*: Activities in which individuals communicate their "internal dispositions," such as liking/disliking or approving/disapproving of each other.

11 *Value*: An activity's degree of reinforcement or capacity to meet needs of an individual, whether one's own activity or activity directed toward the individual.

Employing these concepts, Homans proceeds to enumerate the key postulates, or basic assumptions, from which nearly everything else in his exchange theory flows.

## The Basic Propositions

Homans's perspective on elementary social behavior is anchored in Skinner's operant conditioning principles, which Homans argue "are the general explanatory propositions of all the social sciences."[5] He sees all large social features as comprising nothing more than varying combinations of elementary forms of social behavior, the building blocks of complex organizations, social institutions, and social classes. Homans's basic propositions, as modified for the second edition of *Social Behavior: Its Elementary Forms*, are as follows:

1 *The Stimulus Proposition*: "If in the past the occurrence of a particular stimulus, or set of stimuli, has been the occasion on which a person's action has been rewarded, then the more similar the present stimuli are to the past ones, the more likely the person is to perform the action, or some similar action, now."[6]

2 *The Success Proposition*: "For all actions taken by persons, the more often a particular action of a person is rewarded, the more likely the person is to perform that action."[7]

3 *The Value Proposition*: "The more valuable to a person the result of his action, the more likely he is to perform the action."[8]

4 *The Deprivation-Satiation Proposition*: "The more often in the recent past a person has received a particular reward, the less valuable any further unit of that reward becomes for him."[9]

5 *The Aggression-Approval Proposition*: "When a person's action does not receive the reward he expected, or receives punishment he did not expect, he will be angry; he becomes more likely to perform aggressive behavior, and the results of such behavior become more valuable to him. . . . When a person's action receives reward as expected, especially a greater reward than he expected, or does not receive punishment he expected, he will be pleased; he will become more likely to perform approving behavior, and the results of such behavior become more valuable to him."[10]

6 *The Rationality Proposition*: "In choosing between alternative actions, a person will choose that one for which, as perceived by him at the time, the value, *V*, of the result, multiplied by the probability, *P*, of getting the result, is the greater."[11]

By offering us these propositions, Homans feels that he has spelled out the true elementary forms of social behavior and related them to the most fundamental of the social processes and that larger social features, such as social classes and institutions, flow from them. As Homans sees it, out of basic exchange processes, human social organization, at the group and institutional levels, emerges. The emergence follows a pattern, and according to Jonathan Turner, it is characterized by the following accelerating process:

> 1) Men with capital (reward capacity) "invest" in creating more complex social relations that increase their rewards and allow those whose activities are organized to realize a "profit." 2) With increased rewards, these men can invest in more patterns of organization. 3) Increasingly complex patterns of organization require, first of all, the use of generalized reinforcers, and then, the codification of norms to regulate activity. 4) With this organizational base, it then becomes possible to elaborate further the pattern of organization, creating the necessity for differentiation of subunits that assure the stability of the generalized reinforcers and the integrity of norms. 5) With this differentiation, it is possible to expand even further the networks of interaction, since these are standardized means for rewarding activities and codifying new norms as well as enforcing old rules.[12]

From the vantage point of Homans's exchange theory, large-scale social forms are constructed with the outward expansion of reward capacity, are maintained when they meet individual needs, and begin to crumble when these needs are no longer met.

The six propositions and the eleven concepts detailed above are the corpus of Homans's theory of social exchange. He intends for them to explain those features of individual and social life he feels merit attention. But the word "explain" holds a different meaning for him than it does for most of his fellow sociologists. To him, "explain" simply means that if you can show how a given conclusion is a direct deduction from two or more propositions, then you have not only explained the conclusion, but you have said about all you can or need to say about it.[13]

For Homans, a sociological theory is not a series of well-worded, interrelated statements about the sum and substance of social life. It is instead a deductively connected set of laws, and these laws are all psychological in nature; none of them are sociological. Homans successfully relaunches exchange theory along the individualistic route Adam Smith first set for it. His works have met with considerable acclaim, but his variety of exchange theory has some serious shortcomings.

## Criticisms

Morton Deutsch has pointed out that Homans's exchange theory is incapable of accounting for novel experience,[14] and Peter Ekeh has argued that Homans's approach offers an intellectual justification for exploitation, suffers from internal inconsistency, and uses inappropriate data for supporting its basic propositions.[15] Bengt Abrahamsson has attacked Homans on methodological grounds, arguing that he often employs tautological concepts rather than analytical ones.[16] Rodney Needham has also argued that Homans uses "superficial statistical correlations in place of intensive analysis" and that his exchange theory presents an overly rational image of people. Needham has also pointed out that Homans's theory is culturally and temporally limited in its applicability.[17]

Others have emphasized Homans's weak treatment of social organization and social structure,[18] a flaw his theory shares with other forms of social behaviorism, and pointed to the overwhelmingly conservative bias of his approach.

## Conclusion

Homans's exchange theory has the virtue of being clearly written. It just as clearly requires considerable modification if it is to provide us with an adequate account of larger societal features such as complex organizations, social institutions, social classes, and society itself. Homans's work has served to focus sociologists' thinking on economic matters, but the dominant role of the contemporary nation-state and of corporate capitalism has led him to believe that social behavior is economic behavior and that human behavior and market behavior are identical—a flaw that stems from a narrow understanding of social structure and social relations and casts doubt on the perspective's ability to explain the diversity of human behavior.

## Notes

1 George C. Homans and David Schneider, *Marriage, Authority, and Final Causes* (Glencoe, IL: Free Press, 1955).
2 George C. Homans, "Social Behavior as Exchange," *American Journal of Sociology* 63, no. 6 (1958): 598.
3 Homans, "Social Behavior as Exchange," 597.
4 George C. Homans, *Social Behavior: Its Elementary Forms*, rev. ed. (New York: Harcourt, Brace and Jovanovich, 1974).
5 Homans, *Social Behavior*.
6 Homans, *Social Behavior*, 22–3.
7 Homans, *Social Behavior*, 16.
8 Homans, *Social Behavior*, 25.
9 Homans, *Social Behavior*, 29.
10 Homans, *Social Behavior*, 37 and 39.
11 Homans, *Social Behavior*, 43.
12 Jonathan Turner, *The Structure of Sociological Theory* (Homewood, IL: Dorsey Press, 1974), 260–1.
13 George C. Homans, "Contemporary Sociological Theory," in *Handbook of Modern Sociology*, ed. Robert E. L. Faris (Chicago, IL: Rand McNallly, 1964), 951.
14 Morton Deutsch, "Homans in the Skinner Box," *Sociological Inquiry* 34, no. 2 (1964): 156–65.
15 Peter Ekeh, *Social Exchange Theory: The Two Traditions* (Cambridge, MA: Harvard University Press, 1974), 127.
16 Bengt Abrahamsson, "Homans on Exchange," *American Journal of Sociology* 76, no. 2 (1970): 273–85.
17 Rodney Needham, *Structure and Sentiment: A Test Case in Social Anthropology* (Chicago, IL: University of Chicago Press, 1962), 4.
18 Larry T. Reynolds, *Interactionism: Exposition and Critique*, 3rd ed. (Dix Hills, NY: General Hall, 1993), 154–7.

# 21

# THE FRANKFURT SCHOOL OF CRITICAL THEORY

*Lauren Langman*

Among critical studies of early twentieth-century modern capitalist society in Europe, we find the emergence of a school of thought that provided a philosophical critique of contemporary capitalist society that resulted in the formation of what became known as the Frankfurt School of Critical Theory. Max Horkheimer (1895–1973) and Theodor Adorno (1903–1969) were the pioneers of this new school of thought that sought to explore the dynamics and contradictions of contemporary capitalist society focused on the deconstruction of capitalist ideological hegemony—one that Antonio Gramsci and other Marxist theorists had been grappling with at about the same time in the early to mid-1920s. Later, after the onslaught of the Great Depression, others, such as Erich Fromm (1900–1980) and Herbert Marcuse (1898–1979), became identified with and further developed the theoretical framework of the early pioneers and brought into their analysis elements of Freudian psychology that later facilitated the growth and development of critical theory in a new and different intellectual direction.

## The Rise of Critical Theory: Social and Historical Context

In 1923 a number of German Marxist scholars formed the Institute for Social Research at the University of Frankfurt and thus established the Frankfurt School of Critical Theory. While rooted in the Marxist critique of capitalism, its earliest studies were devoted to labor movements and growing anti-Semitism in Germany. In 1930, Max Horkheimer, a then young Hegelian-Marxist philosopher, was appointed Professor of Philosophy at the University of Frankfurt. He soon became the Director of the Institute, which then led to major shifts in its orientation.

Horkheimer encouraged the Institute to move toward developing a broad, multilevel, interdisciplinary, emancipatory critique of modern capitalist society, incorporating the then recent discovery of Marx's writings on alienated labor which estranged and objectified the worker, and thwarted his or her freedom and self-realization. Moreover, the Institute gave serious attention to Marx's critiques of ideology and "commodity fetishism" (which characterized the products produced by workers as things, not as social relations). Further, given influential critiques of Karl Korsch that defended the role of philosophy and George Lukacs's analysis of the "reification" of consciousness, due to the "rational" nature of bourgeois thought that turned people and relationships into "things," the Institute attempted to revise and update Marx's nineteenth-century critique of capitalist society to the conditions of twentieth-century industrial capitalism with its modern assembly lines, new technologies of mass production, and the expansion of monopoly capital. Further, twentieth-century critique needed to consider the new electronically based mass media, namely radio and film, that shaped worldviews, political attitudes, and values. Finally, the Institute attempted to incorporate more recent theoretical perspectives of both Max Weber and Sigmund Freud into the critique of domination.

In the late 1920s, there was a worldwide Depression. In Germany, there was growing unrest due to increasing unemployment, runaway inflation, and a weak Weimar government little able to change the course of events and stabilize the economy. This led to a number of crises of political, economic, and cultural legitimacy. Between its economic meltdown, rampant hyperinflation, and an impotent government, there were frequent protests in the streets and quite often conflicts between the progressive left and a growing reactionary right. It is this context of economic and political crises and a rise in anti-Semitism that brought to power the ultra-right-wing Nazi regime.

The Frankfurt School began interrogating how and why the atavistic barbarism of Nazism, extolling anger, hatred, death, destruction, and evil, could erupt and gain significant support in what had been one of the most culturally advanced societies in the world. In order to understand the rise of fascism, they launched a number of studies and critiques of fascist ideology starting with alienation, the psychodynamics of Nazi supporters, the appeal of its political spectacles, and the seminal role of the then new forms of mass-mediated propaganda. Their pioneering efforts would have considerable impact on later sociological theory and research. But given the rise of Nazism, the largely Jewish, Marxist intellectuals of the Institute left Germany, eventually moving to the United States primarily living in New York and California. By 1933, aided by the votes of many angry, alienated workers, dissatisfied with Socialist or Communist parties, lured by Hitler's charisma, Nazi ideology and its propaganda, the Nazis gained political power. The world would soon face the most massive, horrific war in history in which unprecedented barbarism was implemented through technically advanced forms of industrial warfare, and unprecedented genocide in the Nazi concentration camps in which the roundups, transportation of victims, and the mass production of death were rationally administered. Eleven million died in the Holocaust. Meanwhile, American atomic bombs annihilated the cities of Hiroshima and Nagasaki in Japan.

## Toward a Critical Theory of Society

The Critical Theorists undertook a number of major philosophical and empirical investigations producing hundreds of books, articles, and notes. Given the breadth of their concerns, we can just note what may be relevant for sociological perspectives, beginning with the sources and formation of knowledge, sometimes considered the facts–values problem. How we see, construct, and interpret the world, and, thus, act accordingly, is shaped by our historical context and our social position in society—namely class, race, gender, etc. How then do we select or create our knowledge of the world? As philosophers trained in the traditions of German Idealism, the critical theorists argued that people actively constructed their worlds (Kant). But while people's views of the world were socially constructed, they nevertheless contained embedded "invisible" ruling class ideologies that disposed seeing the world in certain ways that sustained class domination (Marx). More specifically, whereas for the eighteenth-century philosophers of the Enlightenment like Kant, Reason promised freedom and liberation from domination, superstition and ignorance; instead, Reason, became "instrumentalized" as part of the ruling class ideology, oriented to attain particular political and economic goals, namely power and profits, while indifferent to the dehumanizing consequences of those goals. The logic of the physical sciences, what Weber called "functional or purposive reason," and what Horkheimer and Adorno termed "Instrumental Reason," became the dominant form of Reason, seeking to most efficiently foster science, commerce, and capitalist profits, as well as administer public or private institutions. This logic reduced people and relationships to objects and entities that produced and/or consumed commodities, and, in either case, they created great wealth for the capitalist classes. Reason, then, served ideological functions, distorting consciousness and eroding critique, as well as celebrating capitalist "modernity" as benevolent, as desirable, and as "progress" by rendering production, administration, and even war and genocide more efficient. But when applied to the human sciences and/or administration, Reason served the goals of capitalist domination through the logic of scientific objectivity and rationality which fostered passivity and uncritical acceptance of existing social relationships. By considering the importance of culture, especially in their ideological critique of Reason, the Frankfurt scholars initiated a "cultural Marxism" focused on the critique of capitalist ideology and mass psychology that sustained the economic system. Their goal was to forge a social philosophical analysis of the current age that would advance an emancipatory critique of capitalist domination. But that critique was now updated and informed by then recent developments in the social and psychological sciences.

### Horkheimer and Adorno: The Pioneers of Critical Theory

One of the foundational works of the Frankfurt School was Adorno and Horkheimer's *The Dialectic of Enlightenment*, which argued how the promise of emancipation became a form of domination, an analysis based on Marx's writings on alienation and ideology.[1] Written during their exile from Nazi Germany and World War II, while living in the United States, the elite German intellectuals never felt comfortable in the land of mass conformity, anti-intellectualism, crass commercialism bordering on hucksterism, and its lowbrow popular culture. There was always a fear that the United States itself might turn fascist; thus, the book often embraced pessimism. Yet as Adorno later stated, philosophy was needed. Domination was still present and philosophy keeps the spirit of critique alive that would encourage resistance and transcendence. The book focused on the cultural logic of twentieth-century modernity, the privileging of rationality, "Instrumental Reason," and the science and technology that had shaped capitalist ideology.

Horkheimer and Adorno attempted to resurrect Marx's critique of ideology in general and the specifics of "commodity fetishism" in which the social relationships that produced the commodity form were reduced to things with abstract value. A central theme of their critique, echoing Nietzsche, argued that the progressive Enlightenment values of liberty, equality, democracy, and brotherhood actually served to hide, yet maintain, new, modern forms of domination, hierarchy, and intolerance that dehumanized people, truncated human potential, and led to new forms of immiseration. The Enlightenment had promised freedom, liberation from fear, and the emancipation of humanity from domination that had been sustained by ignorance, superstition, and/or the "God ordained" doctrines of the feudal church–state elite that normalized the relationships of the aristocrats and peasants. Notwithstanding its emancipatory promise, the Enlightenment (with its celebrations of Reason instrumentalized) had ambivalent, dialectical consequences and itself became problematic based upon new forms of domination, (1) over nature, (2) domination from within, and (3) the domination of some people, the bourgeoisie, over others, the workers.

How then did the conditions that led to unprecedented progress in science, medicine, and industry lead to fascism, genocide, and weapons of mass destruction? Reason had become irrational. While the quest for freedom and emancipation had been an essential moment of the Enlightenment, the "rational" culture, political, economic, and legal institutions of modernity, based on empiricism, positivism, and objectivity, led to the loss of freedom as capitalism and its science and technologies flourished. The privileging of empiricism, and "objectivity," the logic of accounting and science, while seemingly objective, became itself a form of domination, alienation, and dehumanization in so far as humanity was reduced to a series of measurements. Fascism, with its emotion-laden rituals, charismatic leaders, and recreation of an "imagined community," provided a variety of emotional gratifications that had been suppressed by rationality—from idealization of the leader and nation, to anger and hatred for the Other.

Horkheimer and Adorno did not simply reject the Enlightenment as such, but saw the intertwining of two processes: "[M]yth is already Enlightenment, and Enlightenment reverts to mythology."[2] Earlier forms of religion and philosophy contributed to the progressive moments of the Enlightenment, while modernity with its ideological and destructive factors has reactionary elements. The danger of each comes when denying change. Such change emerged from "determinate negation" in which immanent critique serves to differentiate truth from ideological distortion that "discloses each image as a script. It teaches us to read from [the image's] features the admission of falseness which cancels its power and hands it over to truth."[3] Perhaps the most widely known chapter of *The Dialectic of Enlightenment* was the critique of the "culture industries" that was initially inspired by the brilliant use of mass media by the Nazis, who were masters of crafting an ideology that promised to restore German greatness which was articulated in emotion-arousing propaganda as well as carefully choreographed, highly moving, inspiring spectacles. The Nazis promised to provide the people, the *Volk*, with pride and economic benefits—to make Germany great again. When the Frankfurt School theorists moved to the United States, primarily to New York and Hollywood, they began to see that America's mass culture was produced by large corporations, "culture industries" that produced entertainment with films, records, books, and radio programs for profit—yet these products also served a similar propaganda function as in Germany, to distract and divert, to reproduce the system. A number of cultural products were systematically mass-produced; nearly identical, standardized products with little genuine differentiation fell into clearly defined genres that would not only stupefy, distract, and divert, but celebrate the status quo, the "superiority of America and goodness of Americans." Like any other form of production, mass production required only a few basic, standardized themes or plots; most forms of recorded music, Broadway stage musicals, films, and, eventually, television provided endless, yet fungible variations that would both entertain and distract to ultimately foster obedience to the status quo and the reproduction of domination—now largely done through advertising and consumerism fostering a "pseudo-individuality" devoid of critical, indeed any social or political, concern.

The notion of "culture industries" has, however, been criticized as fostering "cultural dupes" when a great many media researchers have shown that people actively interpret cultural products and often develop their own interpretations and meanings. Moreover, certain elements of mass culture do in fact challenge and/or subvert dominant ideologies, as there are many books, movies, and television programs that do offer critiques of capitalism.

### *Max Horkheimer*

As both the director of the Institute, and one of its intellectual luminaries, Horkheimer was extremely influential in changing the direction of the Institute to focus on ideology and contradictions between self and society, facts and values, and theories and practices. One of Horkheimer's most widely read essays, "Traditional and Critical Theory", was an attempt to summarize the work of the Institute, its philosophical and methodological stances, and guide its future agendas—especially its early transition from more orthodox Marxism to a more comprehensive critical theory that displayed more concern with the nature of ideology, Reason, entertainment, and, indeed, psychoanalytic insights into human suffering.[4]

Perhaps it was an accident of history, when Horkheimer assumed leadership of the Institute in 1930, that Freud published *Civilization and its Discontents*. Freud had claimed that civilization inevitably required instinctual repression that was maintained by the superego; guilt-based suffering enabled people to live in harmony and cooperate, to work together, and sublimate their desires into beauty, order, and cleanliness. People might seek pleasure, and perhaps momentarily find it through intoxicants, yet they would remain plagued by a sense of guilt. But civilization was the basis of humanity's collective suffering. (Psychoanalysis might relieve enough personal suffering to enjoy the collective suffering of the human race.) But Horkheimer would disagree: suffering was not inevitable; it was historically variable, and "man's striving for happiness is to be recognized as a natural fact requiring no justification."[5] The origin of modern suffering instead was due to the particular irrational, capitalist social arrangements that were nevertheless insinuated within the superego, as was the case with capitalism that economically and culturally enabled greater general prosperity and seemingly political freedom, but at the cost of suffering alienation, dehumanization, and the endless competition for individual gain that provided the basis for a warped sense of self-esteem. But capitalism, indifferent to social welfare and the common good, might provide some individuals with ersatz status and elusive power—neither of which could ever provide the genuine happiness found in love and productive work. Indeed, with more rational, Socialist arrangements, people would find more genuine forms of community, self-fulfillment, and dignity and, in turn, be happier. Critical theory could be helpful in attaining that end, especially by helping the working classes understand their circumstances and see themselves as a major force in history and envision an alternative—much as Marx and Engels had attempted in the *Manifesto*.

Horkheimer suggested that we need a broader, Marxist critical theory that attends to human suffering and locates that suffering as the consequence of capitalist social relationships. Thus, an emancipatory theory based on immanent critique requires a "presentation of societal contradictions [which] is not merely an expression of the concrete historical situation but also a force within it to stimulate change, then [the critical theorist's] real function emerges."[6] But whether or not the critical theorist can actually become a force for social change is problematic, and, like much of critical theory, Horkheimer is often ambivalent, articulating both hope for genuine emancipation and the alleviation of human suffering, as well as pessimism as to whether or not this might happen. Although modern capitalism, extolling science and technology, has on the one hand led to a great deal of progress, "after an enormous extension of human control over nature, it finally hinders further development and drives humanity into a new barbarism."[7] Note! As Horkheimer reminded us, traditional theory needs to understand its own historical context; as we have noted, one of the primary contexts of early critical theory was the rise of fascism and the exile of the Institute to the United States. But to the critical theorists, the future barbarism of fascism was already evident in 1936 with Hitler's support for Franco—immortalized in Picasso's painting *Guernica*, depicting massive bombings against civilians. Moreover, some of the early research on authoritarianism, especially the use of projective tests, revealed intense sadomasochism and the extolling of death that clearly anticipated the Nazi death camps. (And Hitler's final exhortation to defeated German armies in Russia was to fight until death.)

As was noted earlier, critical theory attempted to incorporate Freudian theory into its critique of domination and hopes for liberation. In his classical essay on "Authority and the Family," Horkheimer made several important points, beginning with the fact that the family largely functioned as an obedience factory instilling compliance to patriarchal authority.[8] Moreover, the authority patterns based on a particular form of political-economic system, mediated through identification with the father's own superego, could then endure for several generations beyond the time of their origin—tendencies toward submission to authority typical of earlier times might well persist for generations. But at the same time, Horkheimer noted that in late capitalism, many of the functions of the family, including the role of the father in socialization, had been taken over by a variety of social institutions, schools, hospitals, museums, etc., and, as a result, the actual authority of the father had waned, disposing a certain degree of ego weakness. There was a resulting need to submit to a powerful authority as a compensation, but that disposed authoritarianism, compliance to leaders, and disposed hatred toward real or imagined others. Such characters, always fearful, always angry, could never be at peace with themselves.

### Theodor Adorno

While Adorno was an extremely prolific writer, he first became known to the broader American academic world when he became the director of the Authoritarian Personality study.[9] Whereas surely Adorno was influenced by Reich and Fromm (see below), and despite his critique of empiricism in social science, he directed a large-scale study of authoritarianism in the United States which developed and utilized the F-scale (F for fascism)—a measure that included a number of items ranging from childrearing practices to attitudes toward obedience and leadership, reflecting the degree of authoritarianism, a tendency to submit to idealized authority, to demand compliance from subordinates, and direct aggression toward subordinates, outgroups, or both. The authoritarian character was likely to submit to legitimate authority, embrace the values and beliefs of the leadership they accepted, and tolerate, if not express, aggression toward various outgroups, especially minorities and/or foreigners. Thus, authoritarians were psychologically disposed to embrace fascism. Adorno feared that, notwithstanding the democratic traditions of America, recalling de Tocqueville's warning of the "tyranny of the majority," given the weakness of social ties and the power of culture industries to shape public opinion, there was an underlying fear that America, like Germany, might embrace fascism. Despite values of democracy and equality, significant numbers of Americans were highly authoritarian and, in turn, intolerant—many were racist, xenophobic, and anti-Semitic. In the original study, authoritarianism was also associated with conformity, anti-intraception (looking within oneself), intolerance of ambiguity, closed mindedness, paranoia, superstition, etc. We might note that the study of authoritarianism has remained an important topic in social psychology, and is even used by some political scientists, especially when looking at current trends in American society.

Based on his study of authoritarianism, one of his more ingenious applications of the study came from Adorno's reading of the astrology column in the daily newspaper.[10] Why might some people believe that far-off planets and stars, the latter years away, might influence their daily lives? Astrology offers less than erudite people simple explanations for life and guidance that gives them a sense of superiority by being "in the know"—but really, the belief in external forces controlling one's destiny is little more than an optimistic conformity, a fascism on the cheap. Adorno states,

> astrological ideology resembles, in all its major characteristics, the mentality of the "high scorers" of the Authoritarian Personality. . . . Moreover, by strengthening the sense of fatality, dependence, and obedience, [astrology] paralyses the will to change objective conditions in any respect and relegates all worries to a private plane promising a cure-all by the very same compliance which prevents a change of conditions. It can easily be seen how well this suits the overall purpose of the prevailing ideology of today's cultural industry; to reproduce the status quo within the mind of the people.[11]

No discussion of Adorno would be complete without noting his dismissal of American jazz. Adorno, as a product of the haute bourgeois culture of Germany, was also a trained musician who studied, and subsequently published a number of books on, musicology. As brilliant and insightful as he surely was, he was also a cultural elitist who looked down on the genuine expressions of popular culture typical of the people at the lower ends of the social spectrum. Moreover, he suggested that jazz disposed people to the embrace of fascism.

It is rare in the history of ideas that men like Adorno and Horkheimer might work together so closely and jointly influence an intellectual legacy that developed when fascism began to spread throughout Europe—and let us not forget that a number of prominent Americans supported Hitler and the Nazi party. Their work remains a significant body of ideas that remain relevant to current society. Nevertheless, their broad philosophical concerns, rooted in the Marxist critique of capitalist domination, primarily its concerns with alienation, domination, and ideology, has not just endured, but, given the contradictions of contemporary global capital, many of the issues and debates that emerged in Nazi Germany are still with us. But not only have Horkheimer and Adorno provided us with enduring social and philosophical insights; their work brought together a number of other renowned scholars who also contributed to the lasting legacy of the Frankfurt School.

## Critical Social Psychology

Understanding fascism required more than a critique of its political economy and ideology; it also required the embrace of Freudian depth psychology in order to recognize the unconscious aspect of character, the typically hidden, repressed emotional factors, desires, repression, and ambivalence that explained how and why certain people could become so motivated to embrace various kinds of irrationality—indeed, the utter evil of mass slaughter. For Freud, civilization required the repression of sexual and aggressive drives. In the course of early socialization in the family, young children internalized the values of their parents as an enduring aspect of their character, namely the superego—the conscience. Influenced by Freud, but attracting little recognition at the time, the Marxist psychoanalyst Wilhelm Reich suggested that Freud failed to differentiate civilization in general from its capitalist forms which required docile, compliant workers in factories, offices, and retail stores, with the "requisite," compliant personality type, obedient authoritarians, fostered by an authoritarian family that would attempt to repress sexuality and aggression to instill compliance with the demands of work. But that repression fostered anger that was, in turn, directed toward scapegoats.

In order to free people of the sexually repressive, capitalist ideology internalized within the superego to enable a peaceful Socialist society, Reich initiated what he called the Sex-Pol movement (Sexual Politics) which encouraged teenagers to freely explore their own sexuality and enjoy that sexuality in a guilt-free atmosphere that he thought would be politically liberating. Such ideas were quite shocking at that time. He was thrown out of both the Communist party and the International Psychoanalytic Association. Nevertheless, his ideas on the family, sexual repression, and compliance with authority disposing the mass psychology of fascism influenced the Frankfurt School and their subsequent concerns with the psychodynamics of the family, the superego, authoritarianism, and group psychology.

As the critical theorists developed their various theories of capitalist modernity, they moved further and further away from orthodox Marxism. They did not see class conflict as the basis of all history and social change. Nor did they see socialism as inevitable; barbarism was just as likely. They did not see the working class as the agent of change since they had been placated by the welfare state and co-opted by bourgeois ideologies that became intrinsic aspects of their character. When the working class subsequently embraced consumer-based identities and lifestyles, and enjoyed the many diversions and escapes of mass culture, they were no longer seen as the agent of progressive social change; rather, they had become a conservative force. These perspectives came from psychoanalytic understandings.

### Erich Fromm

Erich Fromm, a sociologist-turned-psychoanalyst, introduced psychoanalytic concepts to the Frankfurt School. As a sociologist, he developed an important theory of "social character"—a certain pattern or cluster of psychological traits and qualities that was the most frequently found in a particular population at a given time. Moving away from Freud's biological determinism to a more social–relational perspective, he suggested that at particular times people developed a "social character" that was psychologically prepared to do that which the society demanded they do: feudalism demanded a receptive character; early capitalism a hoarding character; and late industrial-consumer capitalism, a market character. Each type was well adapted to its era, but that adaptation was a "pathology of normalcy" in which people suffered. For Fromm, with the rise of capitalism, there was a "fear of freedom," powerlessness, isolation from others, and meaninglessness that fostered a great deal of anxiety. People attempted to "escape that freedom" through various "mechanisms of escape," especially authoritarian submission, aggression, and conformity.[12] Attuned to Weber's argument that the embrace of Protestantism alleviated the "salvation anxiety" of the petit bourgeois classes, Fromm suggested that a similar dynamic was at work in the embrace of Hitler and Nazism.[13] Moreover, fascism provided emotional releases and gratifications that rationality had suppressed.

Fromm initiated a number of studies of authoritarianism and found that a significant number of workers were highly authoritarian and psychologically disposed to support Hitler and National Socialism. This early research revealed that a certain "character type," the highly repressed, sadomasochistic authoritarian character, was likely to display a number of distinct qualities, beginning with structuring the world in terms of relationships of domination and subordination. Such a character was always deferential and obedient to superior authority, while demanding compliance and submission from those below; they valued strength and toughness and tended to be highly aggressive, yet would often project that aggression outward to various "enemies," real or imagined. Authoritarians were highly conformist, cognitively rigid, and thought in terms of either–or, black and white dualisms without nuance. When beset by economic hardships and social uncertainty, the authoritarian character would become angry, anxious, and fearful; to escape freedom, loneliness, and powerlessness, they would submit to a powerful leader who would "love" his followers in exchange for their absolute obedience. Such leaders would forge new kinds of social ties to the *Volk*. Meanwhile, to further comfort the anger and discontents of the masses, and provide targets for their aggression, the Nazis targeted scapegoats like the Jews who were seen as responsible for the humiliation and suffering of Germany. Nazism alleviated much of the anxiety and uncertainty of their followers, especially when the early policies of the Nazis provided economic growth and security. The appeal of fascism and reception to its propaganda thus depended on (1) the psychological gratifications it gave to the individual, (2) a reactionary ideology that provided people with meaning in a world grown more and more rational, impersonal, and "heartless", while (3) its martial music, choreographed rallies, midnight rituals, and its social organizations like the Hitler Youth gave people a sense of community through submission to the leader. In this context, the German ruling classes supported Hitler as the bulwark against communism.

### Herbert Marcuse

Herbert Marcuse was one of the first scholars to offer a systematic critique of Marx's theory of alienation—a concern that would shape all of his subsequent thought, even when moving from alienated labor to alienated consumerism. In his earlier work, Marcuse had implicitly accepted Wilhelm Reich's notion that sexual repression sustained capitalist domination.[14] Sexual freedom would enable political freedom. Although early capitalism had once required the "surplus repression" of desire to maintain (capitalist) civilization and motivate work, in his later book, *One-Dimensional Man*, Marcuse argued that late capitalism, with its relative affluence and consumerism, fostered "repressive de-sublimation" (a colonized form of seeming sexual freedom) that made people feel free while being entrapped.[15] The sexual revolution may have freed sexuality from guilt-based repression, but mass media, especially advertising, colonized desire and inculcated "false needs" which were gratified in the intertwining of sexuality and consumer behavior that integrated the person into the society. Thus, consumerism was an integral part of capitalist ideology that legitimized the capitalist system. Workers might well face domination and alienation in the factory, offices, or stores, but they could enjoy consumerism as a form of privatized hedonism that surely compensated for tedious, onerous work. Between a small house, a new car, and trips to Disneyland they were quite happy. Marcuse's *One-Dimensional Man* showed how mass media and its consumerist ideology fostered the cheerful robots of bureaucratic capitalism. The privatized hedonism of consumer capitalism, whether buying or consuming goods, co-opted freedom and agency in ways that would limit any possibilities that critical thought and resistance might erupt to challenge, if not, indeed, overcome, the prevailing social order. Meanwhile, "one dimensional, uncritical rational thought" sustained bureaucratic capitalism and the impersonally administered capitalist society, while masking his or her domination. Nevertheless, despite the spurious commodified gratifications, there were still various forms of alienation, malaise, and discontent with capitalism's superficial culture that denied people being recognized as unique, worthwhile individuals who might seek their own creative self-realization.

Arguing that "contented" workers, qua consumers, would not be the revolutionary classes, Marcuse suggested that college youth together with minorities might be the vanguards of "great refusals" against the meaninglessness and emptiness of America's postwar consumer capitalism, as well as its aggressive "imperialist" adventures.[16] During the 1960s, there were massive protest movements against America's war in Vietnam. Marcuse became a folk hero to progressive youth involved in what was called the "movement." Meanwhile, a growing counterculture rejected the shallowness, superficiality, and conformity of the times. Instead they extolled the joys of drugs and sex and rock 'n' roll to become the vanguard of the "sexual revolution." Today, finding authentic selfhood, especially through gratifying work and living within meaningful communities, has become even more difficult given the stagnating or declining income of most people, especially youth, who have been hit especially hard—fostering current "great refusals" from Occupy Wall Street to the support for Socialist presidential candidate Bernie Sanders.

In one of his most insightful analyses, Marcuse showed how the very language of news magazines and television broadcasts was highly slanted and biased in subtle ways that would sustain the ruling classes both economically and politically. Mainstream news, whether print journalism or television, systematically slants, biases, and suppresses critical coverage and quite often slants information, if not lies, in ways that support corporate interests as well as the interests of the state. There is a very long and dark history of how the United States ruthlessly suppressed various progressive leftist causes and organizations that might challenge capitalism, such as the Wobblies (IWW, the Industrial Workers of the World), and even jailed Socialists such as Eugene V. Debs. After World War II there was a rabid anti-communism McCarthyism that was little challenged by the mass media. The justifications for the war in Vietnam (the fictitious attack on American ships in Tonkin Bay) could well have been crafted by the Nazis who created a false-flag operation to "justify" the Nazi attack on Poland. More recently, the media were complicit in mobilizing mass support for George Bush in the invasion of Iraq by repeating the fabrications that Iraq had weapons of mass destruction about to be launched at America. Little mention was made in the mass media of the three independent investigations in Iraq that failed to find any evidence of weapons of mass destruction. This became one of the greatest foreign-policy disasters in American history, and more than a million died.

Thus, while, as noted, the "culture industry" thesis has been challenged as itself being "one dimensional" and assuming people were easily duped, the legacy of the Frankfurt School fostered media studies inquiries and initiated questions about the political role of mass media. The dominant categories of "one-dimensional thinking" and support for the ruling classes became an essential part of capitalist ideology. The analysis of the culture industries by the Frankfurt School is quite compatible with

Gramsci's notion of hegemony as the ideological control of culture to foster "willing assent" on the part of the masses to the domination by a particular historic bloc (the coalition of elites that control society). It still remains the case that most forms of mass media today, owned by giant corporations, are shaped by dominant class interests to secure both social stability of the prevailing capitalist system and corporate profits.

## The Next Legacy of Critical Theory

By the late 1960s, a new generation of Critical Theorists had emerged. Among them was Jürgen Habermas, former assistant to Adorno, often considered the most important philosopher of the late twentieth century. Habermas's critical theory should be first understood in terms of his early work on the public sphere, epistemology, and legitimation crises, and his later work on a communications theory of society.

### The Public Sphere

For Habermas, the rise of print media, especially pamphlets, journals, and even the growing postal service, enabled the emergence of a bourgeois "public sphere" where (affluent male) people could meet, debate, and argue various truth claims to arrive at certain social understandings.[17] Thus, we began to see the rise of "public opinion" that eventually became a major political force sustaining the leadership claims of the rising bourgeoisie whose growing economic power, together with Enlightenment ideologies embracing freedom and democracy, would eventually lead to the overthrow of monarchies. But, eventually, in face of rapid growth and commercialization of mass media, the critical aspects of the public sphere would wane. We might note that some critical scholars have suggested otherwise. For example, Nancy Fraser has argued that Habermas's perspective was limited to bourgeois males, but in the late twentieth century we began to see a number of counter public spheres—especially the proliferation of various feminist public spheres which, however marginalized by conservative forces, have nevertheless challenged patriarchal domination and shifted public opinion such that there is now much greater toleration for female participation, as seen in growing numbers of women in sports, business, science, the academy, and politics.[18] Similarly, the Internet has enabled the proliferation of thousands upon thousands of websites where various political values and agendas might be debated, members recruited, and various social/political movements organized. These might range from various left, progressive, or socialist organizations to right-wing conservative organizations, and even reactionary Islamic fundamentalist ones as seen in the very skillful use of social media by ISIS.

## Epistemology

In his work on the nature of knowledge—for example, epistemology—Habermas differentiated rational/technical interests which were concerned with *controlling the world*, the practical/hermeneutic interests of *understanding the world* and other people, and emancipatory/critical interests in *overcoming domination*.[19] Echoing earlier critiques of Instrumental Reason, the "colonization of the life world" meant that the realm of "practical interests" had been taken over by rational technical interests which then became a form of domination, fostering passivity as well as marginalizing alternative forms of emancipatory thought and/or alternative forms of social organization as "unpractical."

## Legitimation Crisis

Habermas's work also examined the nature of crises, student protests in the 1960s, and other political activities that challenged the system.[20] And much like his teachers, there was little interest in workers' movements (perhaps because workers lost a worker-based identity and had embraced an amorphous, "middle-class" consumer-based identity and become part of the social forces defending and protecting the status quo). He argued that there were a number of likely crises of legitimacy at the level of the system: namely, that the economy was not working, the polity was dysfunctional, and/or the culture was no longer relevant or meaningful. Such crises migrated to the life world of identity and motivation, evoking strong emotions from anger and indignation to fear and anxiety. At such times, people were likely to withdraw loyalty to the system and either reject the system, as did the various retreatist hippie movements, or perhaps embrace social movements for change, such as feminism, antiwar, or ecology. Today, many of the social justice movements have arisen as capitalism has failed people and lost its legitimacy. Indeed, this has been seen in the Arab Spring, Occupy Wall Street, and, most recently, Black Lives Matter.

## Communication Theory of Society

Over time, Habermas's interests shifted as he attempted to develop a comprehensive theory of society in which communication and meaning led to the attenuation of concerns with political economy.[21] Habermas, duly noting the English analytic philosophers, examined the nature of communication, an aspect of "species being" about which Marx said little. His version of critical social theory attempted to incorporate Max Weber's notions of rationality with Alfred Schutz's concerns with "life world," Parsons's structural functionalism, and George Herbert Mead's symbolic interactionism. In his attempt to resurrect the "uncompleted project of modernity," he argued that communication, an essential aspect of humanity, needed to be analyzed further. Building upon "ordinary language" philosophy (John Searle, J. L. Austin) and the developmental theories of Jean Piaget and Lawrence Kohlberg, he argued that utterances ("speech acts") have a goal of mutual understanding and recognition. But for various reasons, with modernity, instrumental rationality now dominates all spheres of life, leading to distorted communication. He argued that capitalist markets, the modern state, and its bureaucratic organizations, embracing Instrumental Reason, colonized the life world and hindered communicative competence. But with this move, Habermas made a decided shift away from concerns with capitalism, and his more recent work focused on questions of justice, European integration, and constitutionalism.

## The Relevance of the Frankfurt School of Critical Theory Today

The Frankfurt School of Critical Theory has had a considerable influence in social theory that is often not recognized. Yet its concerns with ideology, power, bureaucratic logic, mass culture, social movements, mass media, and consumerism have been quietly absorbed, often with little acknowledgment, into other perspectives—and in the process, some of its fundamental critiques of capitalism and its hegemonic ideologies sustaining its "administered societies" have generally been slighted. However, while there are very few scholars who clearly identify themselves as working in the traditions of the Frankfurt School, almost all general discussions of social theory dealing with the above concerns allude to that very broad and very rich perspective.

Today, there are a number of critical theory scholars whose work is important for sociological theory. Perhaps these might include Moishe Postone, who has rekindled the concerns with Marx's value theory; Harry Dahms, who has been rethinking alienation and globalization; Robert Antonio, who has also been concerned with globalization and ecology; and David Smith, who has been very concerned with authoritarianism and genocide.[22] I have argued elsewhere that an updated psychoanalysis still provides trenchant insights into such diverse realms as social character, consumerism, alienation, nationalism, aspects of popular culture, and the alternative globalization movements, and have done this within the context of a critical theory of American culture and character.[23] Several political scientists, such as Stephen Bronner, Timothy Luke, Fred Alford, and Michael Thompson should also be noted.[24] So, too, philosophers like Douglas Kellner, Andrew Feenberg, and Arnold Farr, developing the ideas of Marcuse, should be mentioned.[25]

Moreover, there has been a resurgence of interest in some of the other early Frankfurt School scholars such as Walter Benjamin and Ernest Bloch.[26] Critical theory, with its multi-disciplinary, dialectical approach to society as a totality, is clearly a value-laden progressive, if not radical, position that is highly critical of advanced capitalist society that depends upon the alienation, exploitation, and dehumanization of the worker, and indeed the suppression of human freedom for all. But it is not, nor can it really be, one of the dominant schools of social thought—especially at a time in which neoliberalism has insinuated itself in the academy. But at the same time, the power of its logic, its capacities to reveal and clarify what might otherwise be obscured, means that critical theory will remain an enduring part of social theory whose influence extends far and wide, even to those who would reject its premises and conclusions.

## Conclusion

As has been noted, critical theory poses a number of barriers to general acceptance, beginning of course with its Marxist roots, notwithstanding its critique of many of the central tenets of Orthodox Marxism. It quite clearly rejects the notions of "value free" rationality as ethically "neutral" since, as has been shown, rationality becomes one of the legitimating factors of modern consumer capitalism. Moreover, perhaps more so than other sociological theories, critical theory presupposes a certain familiarity with philosophical traditions, especially with Hegel, Voltaire, and Rousseau. Furthermore, its radical interdisciplinary orientation, which includes concerns that range from individual psychodynamics to popular culture to science and technology, runs quite contrary to the ever greater specialization and narrower expertise fostered by most academic disciplines and the departments they call home.

Nevertheless, the legacy of the Frankfurt School endures as a rich tradition examining both the dysfunctions and travesties of the present age, as well as inspiring hope that, however bleak events may be today, the contradictions between the emancipatory promises of the Enlightenment and the actual conditions of our times can only impel more sustained critique, resistance, and progressive mobilizations that yet dare to envision utopian futures. Let us indeed hope so, as the alternative to a democratic, post-capitalist world is the barbarism of a Mad Max world surviving upon the detritus of failed societies in which warlords fight for the leftover scraps of what had been called "advanced civilizations."

## Notes

1 Max Horkheimer and Theodor W. Adorno, *The Dialectic of Enlightenment* (Palo Alto, CA: Stanford University Press, [1944] 2002).

2 Horkheimer and Adorno, *The Dialectic of Enlightenment*, xviii.

3 Horkheimer and Adorno, *The Dialectic of Enlightenment*, 18.

4 Max Horkheimer, "Traditional and Critical Theory," in *Critical Theory: Selected Essays*, ed. Max Horkheimer (New York: Continuum, [1937] 1972), 188–243.

5 Horkheimer, "Traditional and Critical Theory," 44.

6 Horkheimer, "Traditional and Critical Theory," 215.

7 Horkheimer, "Traditional and Critical Theory," 227.

8 Max Horkheimer, "Authority and the Family," in *Critical Theory: Selected Essays*, ed. Max Horkheimer (New York: Continuum, 1972), 47–128.

9 Theodor Adorno, Else Frenkel-Brunswik, Dan Levinson, and Nevitt Sanford, *The Authoritarian Personality* (New York: Harper and Row, 1950).

10 Theodor Adorno, *The Stars Down to Earth* (New York: Routledge, 1994).

11 Adorno, *The Stars Down to Earth* (New York: Routledge, 1994), 121.

12 Erich Fromm, *Escape from Freedom* (New York: Holt, Rinehart, 1941). See also Adorno, Frenkel-Brunswik, Levinson, and Sanford, *The Authoritarian Personality*.

13 Fromm, *Escape from Freedom*; Adorno, Frenkel-Brunswik, Levinson, and Sanford, *The Authoritarian Personality*.

14 Herbert Marcuse, *Eros and Civilization* (New York: Vintage Books, 1968).

15 Herbert Marcuse, *One-Dimensional Man* (Boston, MA: Beacon Press, 1964).

16 Herbert Marcuse, *Essay on Liberation* (Boston, MA: Beacon Press, 1969).

17 Jürgen Habermas, *The Structural Transformation of the Public Sphere* (Cambridge, MA: MIT Press, 1989).

18 Nancy Fraser, "Rethinking the Public Sphere: A Contribution to the Critique of Actually Existing Democracy," *Social Text* 25/26 (1990), 56–80.

19 Jürgen Habermas, *Knowledge and Human Interests* (London: Polity Press, 1986).

20 Jürgen Habermas, *Legitimation Crisis* (Boston, MA: Beacon Press, 1975).

21 Jürgen Habermas, *The Theory of Communicative Action*, vols. 1–2 (Boston, MA: Beacon Press, 1984).

22 Moishe Postone, *Time, Labor and Social Domination* (Cambridge: Cambridge University Press, 1996); Harry Dahms, "Affinities between the Project of Dynamic Theory and the Tradition of Critical Theory: A Sketch," in *Theorizing the Dynamics of Social Processes*, ed. Harry Dahms (Bingley: Emerald, 2010), 81–9; Robert Antonio, *Marx & Modernity* (Hoboken, NJ: Wiley-Blackwell, 2002); David Norman Smith, "Charisma and Critique," in *Current Perspectives in Social Theory*, ed. Harry Dahms (Bingley: Emerald, 2011).

23 Lauren Langman and George Lundskow, *God, Gold, Guns and Glory* (Leiden, Netherlands: Brill Press, 2016).

24 Steve Bronner, *Critical Theory: A Short Introduction* (New York: Oxford University Press, 2011); Timothy Luke, *Ecocritique: Contesting the Politics of Nature, Economy, and Culture* (Minneapolis, MN: University of Minnesota Press, 1997); C. Fred Alford, *Melanie Klein and Critical Social Theory* (New Haven, CT: Yale University Press, 1989); Michael Thompson, *The Domestication of Critical Theory* (Lanham, MD: Rowman and Littlefield, 2016).

25 Douglas Kellner, ed., *Collected Papers of Herbert Marcuse*, vols. 1–6 (New York: Routledge, 2005–14); Andrew Feenberg, *The Philosophy of Praxis: Marx, Lukács and the Frankfurt School* (London: Verso Press, 2014); Arnold Farr, *Critical Theory and Democratic Vision: Herbert Marcuse and Recent Liberation Philosophies* (Lanham, MD: Lexington Books, 2009).

26 One of the most important literary critics of the twentieth century, Walter Benjamin's essays on art, literature, and history remain essential to current cultural criticism. Walter Benjamin, *Illuminations* (New York: Houghton Mifflin, 1969). An important aspect of critical theory has been not just to critique capitalism, but to offer an alternative vision. Bloch, using Freud's theory of dreams and wish fulfillments, offered a vision of human fulfillment as much broader than simply owning tools. Ernst Bloch, *The Principle of Hope*, vols. 1–3 (Cambridge, MA: MIT Press, 1986).

# 22

# GOFFMAN AND GARFINKEL ON DRAMATURGY, ETHNOMETHODOLOGY, AND EVERYDAY LIFE

*Larry T. Reynolds and Nancy J. Herman*

This chapter examines two "sociologies of everyday life," *dramaturgy* and *ethnomethodology*, as represented in the writings of Erving Goffman (1922–1982) and Harold Garfinkel (1917–2011), respectively. These are, in a sense, social behaviorist approaches in that their prime concern is with detailing human behavior at the interpersonal level, as distinct from historical, comparative, or structural analyses of society and social relations. Thus, Goffman's and Garfinkel's work should be placed within the context of the approaches taken by Charles Horton Cooley and George Herbert Mead, the functionalists, and George Caspar Homans's theory of social exchange, all of which were explored in previous chapters.

## Goffman and Self-Presentation

A leading influence among social psychologists and the principal spokesperson for symbolic interactionism's dramaturgical approach was Erving Goffman. Influenced by Kenneth Burke's use of the dramaturgical metaphor, Goffman's early work is built on a single and simple premise: when people interact, they do so through the use of symbolic devices that they employ in an attempt to "manage" the impressions others receive from them. His first major book, *The Presentation of Self in Everyday Life*, makes evident Goffman's preference for treating life as a theater in which we stage, or put on, shows for one another. In it he informs us,

> The perspective employed in this report is that of the theatrical performance; the principles derived are dramaturgical ones. I shall consider the way . . . the

individual . . . presents himself and his activity to others, the ways in which he guides and controls the impressions they form of him, and the kinds of things he may and may not do while sustaining his performance before them.[1]

An examination of Goffman's early work clearly reveals that he conceptualizes human social behavior as a series of "performances" by "actors" who strive to present themselves (who "give" and "give off" "expressions" designed to create an "impression") as being exactly who and what they claim to be. Social behavior is a performance whose ultimate aim is to convince others of the authenticity of one's self. Operating either solo or in concert with their fellow actors and actresses as a team of players, people "stage shows" or "give performances" during which they "read social scripts," "enact routines," and "play parts" that utilize "props" and "settings." These performances are given in "front regions," which is to say, before an "audience." The performances are "prepared" in society's "back regions." During these moments of preparation, when one is not "on stage," opportunities arise for anticipating whether one's performance will be well or ill received by the intended audience. The end product of a performance is the audience's "imputation" of a particular kind of self to the "character" being performed.[2]

The Presentation of Self in Everyday Life is not the only work in which one may catch the general flavor of Goffman's dramaturgical orientation. His book Interaction Ritual: Essays in Face-to-Face Behavior contains a fairly representative set of his ideas.[3] Here he deals with the fact that individuals interact so as to maintain both their own "faces" and those of other parties involved in the interaction. In this work, he also deals with the nature of deference and demeanor, with embarrassment, with alienation, with mental symptoms and tacit rules, and with the deliberate taking of avoidable risks in interaction.

Goffman's contribution to sociological theory in general and symbolic interactionism in particular goes beyond the application of his dramaturgical framework. In Asylums: Essays on the Social Situation of Mental Patients and Other Inmates, he makes an important contribution to the "labeling perspective" favored by many interactionists.[4] Goffman here applies the same social-psychological analysis that appears in The Presentation of Self in Everyday Life. In studying mental patients, tuberculosis patients, military recruits, prisoners, and cloistered monks and nuns, Goffman coins the term "total institution," which refers to places of work, residence, and confinement where large numbers of similarly defined individuals are physically and symbolically separated from the outside world. This separation has profound negative implications for self and identity. In such institutions, large numbers of people are subjected to a regimented schedule. All aspects of their lives are conducted without privacy in the same locations under the supervisory body of the institution. As Goffman sees it, total institutions, through their rules, regulations, procedures, and treatment of the inmates, function to humiliate and degrade individuals. Such structures serve to strip away the patient's/recruit's/novice's sense of dignity and self-worth and reduce him or her to total dependency on the hierarchical powers of the institution.[5]

Speaking of this process as "mortification of self," Goffman states that once in a total institution, it is virtually impossible to maintain positive, non-deviant self-images and identities. Individuals are physically separated from those on the outside who validate such identities and self-conceptions. Self is stripped through a number of procedures: individuals are often physically stripped of their clothing, belongings, jewelry, money, and other personal items, all important components of their "identity kit." Moreover, they may be bathed, given a haircut, and issued institutional clothing. As a result, they come to resemble all others in the institution. More importantly, they are proffered a new identity, as "mental patient," "army recruit," or "prisoner," an identity that is reinforced on a daily basis by staff and other inmates alike. Through the entire structure of the total institution, with its rewards and punishments, an individual gradually comes to accept his or her new definition of self and its corresponding role and status.[6]

In a second study, *Stigma: Notes on the Management of Spoiled Identity*, Goffman considers the presentation of self by a number of persons, including minorities, ex-psychiatric patients, prisoners, the obese, the blind, little people, and so forth, and how they manage their "spoiled identities."[7] For Goffman, all of these people possess a stigma, a characteristic or attribute that is considered by society as a deviation from normalcy. Goffman defines three basic types of stigma: (1) abominations of the body, which include various physical deformities, such as missing limbs; (2) blemishes of individual character, which are qualities or actions influentially based on the individual's having engaged in acts such as drug use, swinging, homosexuality, mental illness, and so forth; and (3) tribal stigmas, which are stigmas of race, religion, and nation. Regardless of the type, all stigmas denote individuals' spoiled identities; they are disvalued and conceived of as undesirable in the eyes of others.[8]

Goffman makes the distinction between "discredited" and "discreditable" identities. In terms of the former, individuals possess stigmas that are either readily apparent or known to others. Paraplegics, a woman with a seeing-eye dog, and an obese man all possess discredited identities in Goffman's view. In terms of the latter, some individuals possess stigmas that are not readily apparent or known to others. Consider the case of the impotent male, the infertile female, a hermaphrodite, or a former psychiatric patient—their deviant attributes are not obvious to others. Such people, then, possess discreditable deviant identities.

Goffman contends that it is a continual effort on the part of both the discredited and the discreditable to attempt to manage such information about themselves. To be sure, deviants expend a great deal of time and energy at this never-ending task. As strategists, negotiators, and expert managers, such people employ a number of stratagems and techniques to mitigate the stigma of their "failing" on their daily rounds. Such stratagems include deviance disavowal (normalization), total concealment, selective concealment, therapeutic disclosure, and preventive disclosure.[9]

But while Goffman has indeed made a major contribution to symbolic interactionism, it should be noted that his later work has tended to move in a different direction. His book *Frame Analysis: An Essay on the Organization of Experience* clearly departs from the central concerns of most interactionists.[10] In fact, feeling that Goffman's later work is better characterized as structuralism than as interactionism, George Gonos notes that "Goffman's work stands opposed to the central tenets and most basic assumptions of symbolic interactionism."[11]

In *Frame Analysis*, Goffman is out to examine not impression management but life's microstructures. He no longer feels bound by W. I. Thomas's dictum that situations defined as real may be real in their consequences. As Goffman sees things, "Defining situations as real certainly has consequences, but these may contribute very marginally to the events in progress."[12] Furthermore, he apparently has come to think that people seldom come up with new definitions of a situation on their own. Instead, they simply avail themselves of the definitions that "society" has provided.

The main thrust of *Frame Analysis* is "to isolate some of the basic frameworks of understanding available in our society for making sense out of events and to analyze the special vulnerabilities to which these frames of reference are subject."[13] Here, Goffman has come to the position that sees human behavior as a product of simple adherence to society's rules and regulations. This view is, of course, anathema to most symbolic interactionists as they favor a creative and less reactive picture of human action. This may, in part, account for the fact that while Goffman's works are indeed read by symbolic interactionists, he has, of late, attracted few interactionists to his banner. Furthermore, his later writings have come under fire by such well-known symbolic interactionists as Herbert Blumer and Norman K. Denzin. In fact, as very few interactionists would today identify themselves as dramaturgists, the dramaturgical approach may not remain a major variant of symbolic interactionism for much longer. As it consistently either ignores or inadequately treats such issues as social class, social power, and social structure, its demise may be difficult to lament.[14]

## Garfinkel and Ethnomethodology

While ethnomethodology can be said to have its precursors, its evolution is somewhat unlike that of most other theories. It really did not take off as a school of thought until it was given a name by University of California, Los Angeles, sociologist Harold Garfinkel.[15] Emerging out of phenomenology, Garfinkel's ethnomethodology seeks to understand the methods people employ to make sense out of their worlds. It seeks to uncover the taken-for-granted assumptions underlying social interaction. Commonplace activities are characterized by an implicit order that occurs during the course of the interaction itself. This order serves to make our social situations "accountable," to use Garfinkel's term. For him, ethnomethodological studies "analyze everyday activities as members' methods for making those same activities visibly-rational-and-reportable-for-all-practical-purposes, that is, 'accountable' as organizations of commonplace activities."[16]

By ethnomethodologists' reasoning, the assumptions of sociology are no different than the taken-for-granted assumptions made by non-sociologists in the course of carrying out their everyday activities. And ethnomethodology is, above all, concerned with "the ways in which shared meanings . . . come to be taken for granted in human society."[17] As Paul Filmer et al. note, "sociology is, in an important sense, itself an everyday activity."[18] Thus, in approaching sociology as a form of everyday activity and in seeking to explain that activity, the ethnomethodologists have been led to look at sociology's own taken-for-granted assumptions. That, in itself, may be enough to occasion mainstream sociology's "contemptuous rejection" of ethnomethodology, but ethnomethodologists' questioning of one sociological assumption in particular is almost enough to guarantee it. That assumption is the assumption of order, and its handling by the ethnomethodologists tells us something about ethnomethodology as a perspective.

As Nicolaus Mullins informs us, ethnomethodologists do not even directly examine the various manifestations of social order, such as social structure and social organization; they focus instead "on the process by which members manage to produce and sustain *a sense of social structure*."[19] For ethnomethodology "social order [is] a convenient fiction people allow each other to entertain so that mutual activity can proceed."[20]

Garfinkel argues that social order, or social reality, is not something that is simply "out there." Social realities "emerge relative to our particular position in social and cultural matrixes"; hence, "exactly *what* system of reality is defined as warranting our trust varies." These assumed realities "come to define . . . the ways in which the relationships themselves are interpreted and carried out during interaction."[21]

The ethnomethodologists, then, are concerned with the methods employed by both sociologists and non-sociologists, by the observer and the observed alike, in constructing their everyday realities. If the sociologists' constructed realities differ too greatly from the constructed realities of their subjects, or if sociologists fail to realize that their realities, too, are simply constructions, or social products, the process of understanding will be impeded.

We need to know "how people go about constructing in their own minds and conversations a view of the social world around them," write Randall Collins and Michael Makowsky. "People act as if reality were solid, given, and unambiguous, but the social world they communicate about is actually fluid, highly subject to interpretation, and not easily discoverable."[22] Thus, as Garfinkel points out, to develop an understanding of the meaning of people's everyday activities, ethnomethodologists set themselves the task of analyzing social situations in which people interact: "Their study is directed to the tasks of learning how members' actual, ordinary activities consist of methods to make practical actions, practical circumstances, common sense knowledge of social structures, and practical sociological reasoning analyzable."[23]

In order to approach such "practical activity in everyday life," Garfinkel and other ethnomethodologists employ a variety of concepts such as "reflexivity," "accounting," "practical reasoning," "typification," and "documentary interpretation" in an attempt to disclose:

> (1) the nature of and extent to which various orders of meanings are *carried* in ordinary and common everyday exchanges of utterances, (2) the *underlying sense of meaning* tacitly accepted yet ordinarily unacknowledged by members involved in communication, (3) the *exchange* of intersubjectively meaningful *understanding* derived from communication, and (4) the nature of everyday exchanges as they constitute for members a sense of *rational, rule-like character* and thus are seen by members as making "sense."[24]

How, in short, can the commonplace be made visible? Garfinkel replies, "Procedurally it is my preference to start with familiar scenes and ask what can be done to make trouble."[25] This approach is aimed at achieving a better understanding of commonsense knowledge and behavior by first rendering them problematic. Only by disrupting the "routine" are the very taken-for-granted assumptions that make the social world a routine place more clearly revealed.

By Garfinkel's reasoning, there is more than one objective world and more than one "correct" way of structuring it: "The question is not one of what is the objective world and what is objective knowledge, but what are the varieties of objective knowledge."[26]

Garfinkel seeks to shake people up, to unsettle their daily routines, and in the process of watching them put their "lives back together" and "their houses back in order," to unearth and better understand the very processes by which social realities are constructed and social worlds rendered intelligible in the first place. In Garfinkel's words,

> under the breach of the expectancies of everyday life, given the conditions for the optimal production of disturbance, persons should shift in exhibited confusion in an amount that is coordinate with the original extent of their grasp of the "natural facts of life."[27]

Garfinkel argues that people's adherence to society's rules

> is not necessarily a product of their value commitments or belief in such rules. It may merely be . . . the anticipatory anxiety that prevents [them] from permitting a situation to develop, let alone confronting a situation, in which [they have] the alternative of acting or not with respect to a rule.[28]

People may then fail to challenge, break, or change rules not because of a belief in the essential correctness of the rules but because fear and anxiety prevent them from doing so. Much of our knowledge of the "rules" confers on these selfsame rules a character that has never been submitted to any test, and as Garfinkel points out, "the more important the rule, the greater is the likelihood that knowledge is based on avoided tests."[29] The implication here is that "insofar as the sociologist ignores this—that fear, anxiety, and ignorance, not positive value commitments, often account for compliance—he makes real persons in society into judgmental dopes."[30] One does not have to agree with Garfinkel's implicit image of people as being little more than "blundering fools" in order to see that he has touched bedrock with his critique of conventional sociology's "over-socialized conception" of human nature. But, as Irving Zeitlin notes in speaking of one of Garfinkel's studies,

> This experiment, and the principle it illustrates, has more implications than Garfinkel explicitly draws out; it has critical and even revolutionary implications in that it points directly to the potential flexibility, contingency, and changeability of institutions. It brings out clearly that institutions often regarded as necessary are merely those whose necessity has not been tested.[31]

Garfinkel's failure to spell out in detail the most radical implications of his findings is a characteristic shared by many ethnomethodologists. In some cases, this reluctance may be a product of the belief that commonsense, everyday knowledge is "adequate and valid, with nothing more to be said about it."[32] It may also, in part, be a result of the fact that much of Garfinkel's ethnomethodology focuses on those microscopic features of social reality whose political implications for the larger social world are especially difficult to ascertain. Ignoring society's larger structural features comes at a price. In our opinion, that price is too high.

## Conclusion

In this chapter, we have glimpsed the strengths and weaknesses of the dramaturgical and ethnomethodological approaches by focusing on the works of Goffman and Garfinkel. On the positive side of the ledger, both perspectives detail the richness of social life in concrete social settings. They allow sociologists to "feel close" to their human subjects, to see things as their subjects would see them. On the ledger's other side, the microscopic, astructural aspects of both orientations not only result in an inadequate treatment of larger societal features, but put rather sharp limits on their historical and cross-cultural applicability. Such limited, small-scale social-psychological approaches both ignore class relations and provide only a partial explanation of social reality, which, placed in a broader context of human social relations, reveals merely a small segment of social life that is conditioned by social forces at the larger, structural level.

## Notes

1 Erving Goffman, *The Presentation of Self in Everyday Life* (Garden City, NY: Doubleday, 1959), xi.

2 Bernard N. Meltzer, John W. Petras, and Larry T. Reynolds, *Symbolic Interactionism: Genesis, Varieties and Criticism* (London: Routledge & Kegan Paul, 1975), 68.

3 Erving Goffman, *Interaction Ritual: Essays in Face-to-Face Behavior* (Garden City, NY: Doubleday, 1967).

4 See Erving Goffman, *Asylums: Essays on the Social Situation of Mental Patients and Other Inmates* (Garden City, NY: Doubleday, 1961).

5 Goffman, *Asylums*.

6 Goffman, *Asylums*.

7 Erving Goffman, *Stigma: Notes on the Management of Spoiled Identity* (Englewood Cliffs, NJ: Prentice Hall, 1963).

8 Goffman, *Stigma*.

9 Goffman, *Stigma*.

10 Erving Goffman, *Frame Analysis: An Essay on the Organization of Experience* (Cambridge, MA: Harvard University Press, 1974).

11 George Gonos, "'Situation' Versus 'Frame': The 'Interactionist' and the 'Structuralist' Analyses of Everyday Life," *American Sociological Review* 42, no. 6 (1977): 855.

12  Goffman, *Frame Analysis*, 1.

13  Goffman, *Frame Analysis*, 10.

14  Larry T. Reynolds, *Interactionism: Exposition and Critique*, 3rd ed. (Dix Hills, NY: General Hall, 1993), 102.

15  See Harold Garfinkel, *Studies in Ethnomethodology* (Englewood Cliffs, NJ: Prentice Hall, 1967).

16  Garfinkel, *Studies in Ethnomethodology*, vii.

17  Meltzer et al., *Symbolic Interactionism*, 79.

18  Paul Filmer, Michael Phillipson, David Silverman, and David Walsh, *New Directions in Sociological Theory* (Cambridge, MA: MIT Press, 1973), 210.

19  Nicolaus Mullins, "Text of a Speech Delivered at the ASA Convention," in *The Sociology of Sociology*, ed. Larry T. Reynolds and Janice Reynolds (New York: McKay, 1973), 195.

20  William Skidmore, *Theoretical Thinking in Sociology* (Cambridge: Cambridge University Press, 1975), 260.

21  Meltzer et al., *Symbolic Interactionism*, 79.

22  Randall Collins and Michael Makowsky, *The Discovery of Society* (New York: Random House, 1972), 209.

23  Garfinkel, *Studies in Ethnomethodology*, viii.

24  Jack N. Mitchell, *Social Exchange, Dramaturgy, and Ethnomethodology: Toward a Paradigmatic Synthesis* (New York: Elsevier, 1978), 133–4.

25  Garfinkel, *Studies in Ethnomethodology*, 37.

26  Harold Garfinkel, "Perception and the Other" (unpublished PhD diss., Harvard University, 1952).

27  Garfinkel, *Studies in Ethnomethodology*, 65.

28  Garfinkel, *Studies in Ethnomethodology*, 70.

29  Garfinkel, *Studies in Ethnomethodology*, 70.

30  Irving M. Zeitlin, *Rethinking Sociology: A Critique of Contemporary Sociology* (Englewood Cliffs, NJ: Prentice Hall, 1973), 187.

31  Zeitlin, *Rethinking Sociology*, 187.

32  Zeitlin, *Rethinking Sociology*, 187.

# 23

# WILSON AND WILLIE ON RACE, CLASS, AND POVERTY

Nearly half a century after the great debate on race and class prompted by W. E. B. Du Bois's and E. Franklin Frazier's contrasting positions on this important question, the publication in 1978 of William Julius Wilson's book *The Declining Significance of Race* set into motion a new round of debate led by Charles Vert Willie on the nature and role of race and class in the United States today. This chapter examines the central issues raised in this debate by providing a forum for Wilson's and Willie's views on this important and controversial topic.

## Wilson on Race and Class

Describing his book *The Declining Significance of Race* as "a study of race and class in the American experience," Wilson points out that its focus is "a rather significant departure" from that of his previous book, *Power, Racism, and Privilege*, in which, he says that he "paid little attention to the role of class in understanding issues of race."[1] "I now feel that many important features of black and white relations in America," he writes, "are not captured when the issue is defined as majority versus minority and that a preoccupation with race and racial conflict obscures fundamental problems that derive from the intersection of class with race."[2] Wilson goes on to state,

> Race relations in America have undergone fundamental changes in recent years, so much so that now the life chances of individual blacks have more to do with their economic class position than with their day-to-day encounters with whites. In earlier years the systematic efforts of whites to suppress blacks were obvious to even the most insensitive observer. Blacks were denied access to valued and scarce resources through various ingenious schemes of racial exploitation, discrimination, and segregation, schemes that were reinforced by elaborate ideologies of racism. But the situation has changed. However determinative such practices were for the previous efforts of the black population to achieve racial equality

. . . they do not provide a meaningful explanation of the life chances of black Americans today.[3]

In building his case for a macrosociological, historical analysis of the process of transformation that the African American community has undergone since the days of slavery, Wilson identifies three distinct stages in the development of race relations in the United States:

> Stage one coincides with antebellum slavery and the early postbellum era and may be designated the period of *plantation economy and racial-caste oppression*. Stage two begins in the last quarter of the nineteenth century and ends at roughly the New Deal era and may be identified as the period of *industrial expansion, class conflict, and racial oppression*. Finally, stage three is associated with the modern, industrial, post-World War II era, which really began to crystallize during the 1960s and 1970s, and may be characterized as the period of *progressive transition from racial inequalities to class inequalities*.[4]

In the antebellum period and in the period from the mid-nineteenth to the mid-twentieth century, "Racial oppression was deliberate, overt, and is easily documented, ranging from slavery to segregation."[5] However, since the middle of the twentieth century, "many of the traditional barriers have crumbled under the weight of the political, social, and economic changes of the civil rights era. A new set of obstacles has emerged from basic structural shifts in the economy."[6] "These obstacles," Wilson explains, "are therefore impersonal but may prove to be even more formidable for certain segments of the black population."[7]

> Specifically, whereas the previous barriers were usually designed to control and restrict the entire black population, the new barriers create hardships essentially for the black underclass; whereas the old barriers were based explicitly on racial motivations derived from intergroup contact, the new barriers have racial significance only in their consequences, not in their origins. In short, whereas the old barriers bore the pervasive features of racial oppression, the new barriers indicate an important and emerging form of class subordination.[8]

Thus, "in the modern industrial period," Wilson writes, "fundamental economic and political changes have made economic class position more important than race,"[9] such that "as the influence of race on minority class-stratification decreases . . . [economic] class takes on greater importance in determining the life chances of minority individuals."[10] Adopting a Weberian approach to class in contemporary American society, Wilson writes:

> The clear and growing class divisions among blacks today constitute a case in point. It is difficult to speak of a uniform black experience when the black population can be meaningfully stratified into groups whose members range from those who are affluent to those who are impoverished. This of course has not always been the case, because the crystallization of a black class structure is fairly recent.[11]

Wilson argues that the social-economic and political changes in American society during the course of the twentieth century have led to the development of a class structure that has fostered a growing class division among African Americans, such that in "the last quarter of the twentieth century a deepening economic schism seems to be developing in the black community, with the black poor falling further and further behind middle- and upper-income blacks."[12]

> On the one hand, poorly trained and educationally limited blacks of the inner city, including that growing number of black teenagers and young adults, see their job prospects increasingly restricted to the low-wage sector, their unemployment rates soaring to record levels (which remain high despite swings in the business cycle), their labor-force participation rates declining, their movement out of poverty slowing, and their welfare roles increasing. On the other hand, talented and educated blacks are experiencing unprecedented job opportunities that are at least comparable to those of whites with equivalent qualifications. The improved job situation for the more privileged blacks in the corporate and government sectors is related both to the expansion of salaried white-collar positions and to the pressures of state affirmative action programs.[13]

"In view of these developments," Wilson writes, "it would be difficult to argue that the plight of the black underclass is solely a consequence of racial oppression, that is, the explicit and overt efforts of whites to keep blacks subjugated," adding, "in the same way that it would be difficult to explain the rapid economic improvement of the more privileged blacks by arguing that the traditional forms of racial segregation and discrimination still characterize the labor market in American industries."[14] Wilson concludes, "The recent mobility patterns of blacks lend strong support to the view that economic class is clearly more important than race in predetermining job placement and occupational mobility."[15]

## Willie on the Persistence of Race and Racism

"Race is one of the most sensitive and sure indicators of the presence or absence of justice in our society," writes Willie.[16] "To repress the guilt of racial discrimination through denial and other means," he adds, "is to permit injustice to fester and erupt from time to time in race riots and other forms of rebellion."[17] Contrary to Wilson's position, with which he disagrees, Willie argues that "race has not declined but continues as a significant variable differentiating blacks from whites at all income levels."[18] He goes on to argue that "racial discrimination is one of the major factors contributing to economic deprivation among blacks."[19]

In contradistinction to Wilson's thesis of the declining significance of race and the increasing importance of class in determining the social position of African Americans in the United States today, Willie contends that race, not class, plays a central role in determining one's social position: "I would like to introduce a counterhypothesis," Willie writes,

> that the significance of race is increasing and that it is increasing especially for middle-class blacks who, because of school desegregation and affirmative action and other integration programs, are coming into direct contact with whites for the first time for extended interaction.[20]

Against Wilson's emphasis on the physical condition of the African American underclass affected by recent changes in the economic structure, which, together with favorable civil rights legislation, has led to improvements in the economic position of the emerging African American middle class, Willie focuses on the effects of race and race relations in general and argues that, despite recent economic gains, race continues to play a dominant role in the life experiences of African Americans, especially the middle class. Stressing the importance of psychological factors, those who suffer most from the effects of these changes, Willie argues, are members of the educated middle class, not the underclass: "The people who most severely experience the pain of dislocation due to the changing times are the racial minorities who are talented and educated and integrated, not those who are impoverished and isolated."[21]

Responding to Willie's emphasis on the significance of race in African American middle-class life, resulting from increased black–white contact within this class, Wilson writes,

> I do not disagree with the way in which Willie has proposed his counterhypothesis. Many educated blacks do experience psychological discomfort in new integrated situations. Willie and I could probably draw many personal examples

of this. We both are black and we both teach at elite universities. A few years ago almost no blacks were in such positions. But I am sure that neither of us would trade places with a poor black trapped in the ghetto and handcuffed to a menial, dead-end, and poorly paid job. That is the real problem in the black community and no cries about the psychological discomfort of the integrated black elite should distract our attention from the abominable and deleterious physical conditions of the isolated black poor.[22]

"Wilson does not disagree with the counterhypothesis that I offered about the increasing significance of race," Willie writes, "largely because my hypothesis is an attempt to explain the discomfort of some affluent blacks."[23] He adds, "In Wilson's judgment, however, this is not the real problem in the black community. The real problem, as he states it, is 'the abominable and deleterious physical condition of the isolated black poor'."[24]

## Poverty and the Plight of the Urban Underclass

In addressing the issues concerning the source(s) of poverty among the African American underclass, Willie and Wilson sharply differ on the role of race and class in affecting the "life chances" of segments of the African American population, leading to the formation of a large and impoverished underclass. "When I argue that 'the black experience has moved historically from economic racial oppression experienced by virtually all blacks to economic subordination for the black under-class'," Wilson writes, "Willie complains that I cancel 'out racial discrimination as a key cause of poverty among blacks' thereby making it difficult to explain the greater proportion of black families in poverty and the higher unemployment rate for younger blacks."[25] "Once again Willie overlooks or chooses to ignore one of my key arguments," he states, "namely that 'one of the legacies of the racial oppression in previous years is the continued disproportionate black representation in the under-class'."[26] Wilson explains,

In other words, patterns of racial subjugation in the past created a vast black under-class as the accumulation of disadvantages were passed on from generation to generation and the economic and technological revolution of modern industrial society threatens to insure it a permanent status. Accordingly, even if all racial discrimination were eliminated today, the situation of poor blacks will not be substantially improved unless something is done to remove the structural barriers to decent jobs created by changes in our system of production.[27]

Looking at poverty through the lens of class, Wilson examines the structural impediments that force the underclass into further economic deprivation and argues,

The current economic problems of the black urban underclass cannot be suffi-ciently addressed by programs based on the premise that race is the major cause of those problems. They are problems which are more appropriately associated with class subordination—problems which developed from previous experiences with racial oppression, problems which are now compounded by the economic changes of modern industrial society.[28]

Thus, Wilson continues,

the challenge of economic dislocation in modern industrial society calls for pub-lic policy programs to attack inequality on a broad class front, policy programs, in other words, that go beyond the limits of ethnic and racial discrimination by directly confronting the pervasive and destructive features of class subordination.[29]

To Willie, however, the predicament of the urban poor is directly related to race and racism that prolongs their misery. Consequently, Willie characterizes Wilson's con-ceptualization of the problem of poverty as "flawed." But Willie's argument is based more on his disagreement with Wilson concerning the solution(s) to poverty than the analysis itself.

Commenting on policy recommendations that Wilson made in both *The Declining Significance of Race* and his subsequent book, *The Truly Disadvantaged*, Willie crit-icizes Wilson for rejecting population-specific remedies in favor of "economic and social reforms [that] benefit all groups in the United States, not just poor minorities."[30] "Universal approaches may be helpful in preventing poverty but not in correcting the effects of poverty after it has been experienced," writes Willie. "The poor are placed at risk," he says, "when their self-interest and special needs are ignored or subordinated as could happen in a universal approach."[31] Thus, he concludes, Wilson's universal "action-strategy for dealing with poverty and the poor in the United States is wrong,"[32] a conclusion that is debatable due to its own built-in bias in favor of a population-spe-cific strategy based on race, which others have rejected as inadequate and ineffective given the current state of race relations in the United States.

### Wilson and Willie on Race, Class, and Poverty: Toward a Synthesis

Clearly, the Wilson–Willie debate on race and class has generated a number of important questions that have both historical and contemporary significance for understanding race relations in the United States today.

While the African American community has clearly undergone major transformations in its social structure and, thus, experienced class differentiation based on changes
in the labor force structure over the past hundred years, it is also clear that race continues to play an important role in determining the predicament of African Americans
in the United States today, albeit in different ways and forms within different classes
across the racial divide. Recent racist incidents resulting from police brutality in the
African American community and the responses that this has generated in Ferguson,
Baltimore, and elsewhere across the United States are clear indicators of the racial
divide that illustrate the continuation of racism and racial oppression in America today.

It is true, as Wilson contends, that in the economic sector "class has become more
important than race in determining black life chances,"[33] but, as Willie insists and
Wilson admits,

> This is not to deny the importance of racial antagonism in the social-political
> order, or even suggest that residential, social, and educational discrimination do
> not form a part of a vicious circle that feeds back to the economic sector. But
> this circular process is far more relevant for poor blacks than for more privileged
> blacks.[34]

"In terms of understanding life chances," Wilson continues,

> the economic mobility of privileged blacks has offset the negative consequences
> of racial discrimination in the social-political order. Indeed, one will only be able
> to understand the growing class divisions in the black community by recognizing
> that racial antagonisms in the sociopolitical order have far less effect on black
> individual or group access to those opportunities and resources that are centrally
> important for life chances than have racial antagonisms in the economic sector.[35]

Wilson argues that although racial antagonisms and tensions continue to characterize
the American social landscape, class divisions among African Americans yield differential results in advancing one's class interests. Thus, as the black class structure
increasingly resembles the white class structure, middle-class blacks will more and
more identify their interests with those of middle-class whites, as opposed to poor
blacks, notwithstanding the fact that they will continue to experience racial tensions
and conflict within the middle class itself for as long as racism in its various forms continues to exist in the United States. The point is that increasing class differentiation
within the African American community will make uniform, racially oriented policies

obsolete as the class nature of such policies becomes increasingly transparent. It is in this context that Wilson writes,

> Thus, as the class divisions of the black community grow, it will become increasingly difficult for Willie and other social scientists to mask these differences either by speaking of a uniform or single black experience or by presenting gross statistics that neither reflect significant variations in the resources of various subgroups within the black population nor the differences in the effects of race in the past and the effects of race in the present.[36]

Although Willie opts for a racial explanation when he argues that race is "a significant variable differentiating blacks from whites at all income levels," he nevertheless recognizes the validity of Wilson's class-based argument when he concedes that his "counterhypothesis" on the "increasing significance of race" actually pertains to "middle-class blacks" and is "an attempt to explain the discomfort of some affluent blacks,"[37] for it is the "talented and educated" blacks, "not those who are impoverished and isolated," Willie asserts, who "most severely experience the pain of dislocation due to changing times."[38]

Finally, in line with his emphasis on the declining significance of race in the economic sector, Wilson defends his position by saying,

> It would be shortsighted to view the traditional forms of racial segregation and discrimination as having essentially disappeared in contemporary America; the presence of blacks is still firmly resisted in various institutions and social arrangements. . . . However, in the economic sphere, class has become more important than race in determining black access to privilege and power.[39]

Wilson goes on to state, "[W]hen I speak of the declining significance of race, I am neither ignoring the legacy of previous discrimination nor am I arguing that racial discrimination no longer exists."[40] He writes, "My argument that race relations in America have moved from economic racial oppression to a form of class subordination for the less privileged blacks is not meant to suggest that racial conflicts have disappeared or have even been substantially reduced."[41]

Elsewhere, responding to his critics on this issue, Wilson insists,

> Nowhere in my book do I argue that race is "irrelevant or insignificant." It is not simply an either-or situation; rather it is a matter of degree. And I strongly emphasize that there is still a strong basis for racial antagonism on the social, community, and political level.[42]

## Conclusion

The analysis presented in these pages makes it sufficiently clear that despite differences in their respective positions regarding race and class, Wilson and Willie provide complementary perspectives that should be incorporated in some fashion into a synthetic whole so that we can better conceptualize and address issues of race and racism that affect different segments of society at various social-economic levels. Together, their seemingly opposed viewpoints, which appear contradictory at one level, are in fact reconcilable at another if one accepts their value in providing explanations for different aspects of race relations that are, in effect, complementary.

## Notes

1  William Julius Wilson, *The Declining Significance of Race*, 2nd ed. (Chicago, IL: University of Chicago Press, 1980), ix.
2  Wilson, *The Declining Significance of Race*, ix.
3  Wilson, *The Declining Significance of Race*, 1.
4  Wilson, *The Declining Significance of Race*, 2–3; italics in the original.
5  Wilson, *The Declining Significance of Race*, 1.
6  Wilson, *The Declining Significance of Race*, 1.
7  Wilson, *The Declining Significance of Race*, 1.
8  Wilson, *The Declining Significance of Race*, 1–2.
9  Wilson, *The Declining Significance of Race*, 23.
10  Wilson, *The Declining Significance of Race*, x.
11  Wilson, *The Declining Significance of Race*, x.
12  Wilson, *The Declining Significance of Race*, 152.
13  Wilson, *The Declining Significance of Race*, 151.
14  Wilson, *The Declining Significance of Race*, 151–2.
15  Wilson, *The Declining Significance of Race*, 152.
16  Charles V. Willie, ed., *The Caste and Class Controversy on Race and Poverty*, 2nd ed. (Dix Hills, NY: General Hall, 1989), 82.
17  Willie, *The Caste and Class Controversy on Race and Poverty*, 82.
18  Willie, *The Caste and Class Controversy on Race and Poverty*, 86.
19  Willie, *The Caste and Class Controversy on Race and Poverty*, 55.
20  Willie, *The Caste and Class Controversy on Race and Poverty*, 20.
21  Willie, *The Caste and Class Controversy on Race and Poverty*, 21.
22  William Julius Wilson, "The Declining Significance of Race: Revisited but Not Revised," in Willie, *The Caste and Class Controversy on Race and Poverty*, 36.
23  Willie, *The Caste and Class Controversy on Race and Poverty*, 39.
24  Willie, *The Caste and Class Controversy on Race and Poverty*, 39.
25  Wilson, "The Declining Significance of Race: Revisited But Not Revised," 31.
26  Wilson, "The Declining Significance of Race: Revisited But Not Revised," 31.
27  Wilson, "The Declining Significance of Race: Revisited But Not Revised," 31–2.
28  Wilson, *The Declining Significance of Race*, 165.

29  Wilson, *The Declining Significance of Race*, 154.
30  William Julius Wilson, *The Truly Disadvantaged: The Inner City, the Underclass, and Public Policy* (Chicago, IL: University of Chicago Press, 1987), 155.
31  Willie, *The Caste and Class Controversy on Race and Poverty*, 179.
32  Willie, *The Caste and Class Controversy on Race and Poverty*, 179.
33  Wilson, "The Declining Significance of Race: Revisited But Not Revised," 35.
34  Wilson, "The Declining Significance of Race: Revisited But Not Revised," 26.
35  Wilson, "The Declining Significance of Race: Revisited But Not Revised," 26–7.
36  Wilson, "The Declining Significance of Race: Revisited But Not Revised," 35.
37  Willie, *The Caste and Class Controversy on Race and Poverty*, 39.
38  Willie, *The Caste and Class Controversy on Race and Poverty*, 21.
39  Wilson, *The Declining Significance of Race*, 2.
40  Wilson, *The Declining Significance of Race*, 167.
41  Wilson, *The Declining Significance of Race*, 23.
42  Wilson, "The Declining Significance of Race: Revisited But Not Revised," 35–6.

# 24

# FEMINIST THEORY: YESTERDAY AND TODAY

*Martha E. Gimenez*

Contemporary feminism is a product of decades of struggle that women have waged to address and remedy inequalities in gender relations stemming from patriarchy and class divisions that continue to persist in capitalist society. This chapter provides an overview of feminist theory, focusing on various currents and perspectives that depict the range of analyses presented by feminists to deal with the oppression of women in capitalist society.

At the time the women's liberation movement was at its peak, from the mid-1960s to the early 1970s, it was possible to identify in the United States four main currents within feminist thought: (1) liberal (concerned with attaining economic and political equality within the boundaries of capitalist society); (2) radical (focused on men and patriarchy as the main causes of the oppression of women); (3) Socialist (critical of capitalism while skeptical of Marxism, resulting in dual systems theories postulating the interaction between capitalism and patriarchy; and (4) Marxist (a theoretical position that sought to develop the potential of Marxist theory to understand the capitalist foundations of the oppression of women).

These are, of course, oversimplified descriptions of a rich and complex literature that reflects important theoretical, political, and social cleavages among feminist academics and activists that continue to this date.[1] Divisions in feminist thought multiplied as the effects of poststructuralist and postmodern theorizing merged with grassroots challenges to a feminism perceived as the expression of the needs and concerns of middle- and upper-middle-class white women.[2] In the process, the subject of feminism became increasingly difficult to define, as the postmodern critique of "woman" as an essentialist category,[3] together with critiques grounded in racial, ethnic, sexual-preference, and national-origin differences, resulted in a seemingly never-ending proliferation of "subject positions," "identities," and "voices." Cultural and identity politics replaced the early Marxist and Socialist feminist focus on capitalism and (among Marxist feminists primarily) class divisions among women. Today, among most feminists, class has been reduced to another "ism" (i.e., to another form of oppression), which, together with gender and race, resulted in a sort of mantra, designating three variables that everyone ought to include in feminist theorizing and research.[4] Eventually, the trilogy was left behind, replaced by "intersectionality," which, today, is the dominant feminist approach to theorizing and research. This chapter describes the main concepts and issues that have characterized early feminist theories, followed by a lengthier discussion of more recent theoretical developments.

## Early Feminist Theory

The difference between earlier and current feminist thought is vast. To understand fully the changes feminist theory has undergone, it is important to understand the theoretical concerns feminist theory has raised over the past four decades.

Early theorizing about the origins of the inequality between men and women, the ongoing processes that reproduced inequality over time, and the objectives of women's political activities reflected the extent to which feminists were critical of the capitalist nature of American society, of the effects of capitalist processes upon the status and opportunities open to women, and of the relative usefulness of Marx's work to further feminist theoretical and political concerns.

### *Liberal Feminism*

Liberal feminists took capitalism for granted and believed that its institutions could be made to work to ensure that women would become full and equal participants in society. Acknowledging the coexistence of real inequalities (e.g., inequalities of talent, social class, race, gender, and ethnicity) with equality under the law and other important civil and political rights inherent in contemporary society, liberal feminists sought to remedy the inequalities affecting women through state action. Mid-twentieth-century liberal feminists struggled against the ideological and economic barriers to women's equality. Against the notion that gender differences were rooted in biology and created insurmountable differences between men and women, they insisted on the separation between biological sex and socially constructed gender and argued that, with the right socialization and opportunity structure, there was nothing men could do that women could not do just as competently. Dismantling the stereotypes about gender was an important step in the struggle against institutional barriers to women's educational and occupational opportunities. Liberal feminists focused their analysis on the barriers to women's right to equal access in every sphere of social activity to attain parity with men and to pursue educational and political objectives. In line with their uncritical acceptance of the existing capitalist system, liberal feminists saw nothing wrong with male patterns of occupational achievement and insisted that women had a right to have families and careers, even though the organization of work, education, and family conspire against women's ability to do so with ease. Despite the criticisms that other feminists addressed to liberal feminism, it is necessary to acknowledge that without their successes, such as Affirmative Action and Titles VII and IX, today there would not be as many women in higher education, in occupations commanding higher rank and pay, in fields previously closed to women (e.g., engineering, law, medicine), in business, or in politics.[5] The gender pay gap, however, has not closed; in 2014, women's annual median earnings were 79 percent of what men were paid, 20 cents on the dollar more than in 1974.[6]

### Radical Feminism

Radical feminists focused on women as women, exploring the implications of women's bodies and personality traits for the oppression of women. For radical feminists, the oppression of women is at the root of all forms of oppression; it is universal, ubiquitous, and deeply rooted in the biological and psychosexual differences between the sexes. Men's thirst for power and desire to dominate women (because of men's greater size and force), or men's need to control women's sexuality, reproductive capacity, and labor are the basis for the emergence of patriarchy, a system of male domination perpetuated through fear and physical and sexual violence. According to radical feminists, women, as women, regardless of class, race, ethnicity, and other differences, are vulnerable to rape, domestic violence, and homicide at the hands of their intimate partners. All women, as women, have largely common interests in healthcare, reproductive control, and control over their sexuality and can find common ground for organizing politically around those issues. Radical feminists have contributed to raising women's and society's consciousness about the commonality of women's needs and oppression, which, to some extent, they share despite their differences. The results of their efforts are visible in today's taken-for-granted research, legislation, and community organizing about sexual harassment, domestic violence, and reproductive rights. Finally, unlike liberal feminists, radical feminists celebrate what they perceive as the nurturant qualities inherent in most women. Because most women engage in a variety of caring activities, within and often outside their circle of family and friends, women are characterized by a "maternal thinking" that makes their views superior to those of aggressive and competitive males. Presumably, this maternal way of thinking and

relating to people and nature explains women's politics as more peaceful and environ-
mentally conscious than men's.[7]

### Socialist Feminism

Socialist feminism is a hybrid theoretical framework that combines Marxist and radical
feminist theories. Socialist feminists find Marxist theory inadequate to account fully
for the causes of the oppression of women because, in their view, Marxism reduces it
to an effect of class divisions and has to be supplemented by a theory that identifies the
basis for the oppression of women independently from the form of economic organization, namely, patriarchy. From this perspective, Marxism, as a theory of modes of
production, can only explain the economic exploitation of women; patriarchy, as a
theory of male domination, explains the oppression of women as women. Socialist
feminists argue that, in contemporary societies, capitalism and patriarchy interact in
a mutually supportive fashion to place women at a disadvantage in all spheres of life,
resulting in *capitalist patriarchy*, a concept that leads to the theorization of the complex
ways in which patriarchal practices, social relations, and ideologies inside and outside
the family intensify economic exploitation.[8]

    Socialist feminists have illuminated the ways women are oppressed at home, where
the products of their unpaid domestic labor are appropriated by their husbands or
partners, and in the workplace, where sex-segregated labor markets relegate most
women to the lowest-paid, lower-status, blue- and white-collar jobs. The outcome of
this unequal sexual division of labor outside and inside the home has resulted in working women's oppression through the "double shift":[9] while male workers tend to hold
only one job and each day look forward to returning home to a home-cooked meal and
rest, working women return home to continue working, for they continue to have primary responsibility for housework (cooking, cleaning, planning meals) and child care.
As a popular article from the late 1960s points out, "a woman's work is never done."[10]

### Marxist Feminism

The Socialist and Marxist theories of the oppression of women overlap substantially.
Marxist feminists have contributed to a lengthy debate on whether women's domestic
labor is paid (through the economic benefits conferred by marriage and their share of
their husbands' wages) or unpaid; whether it produces economic benefits appropriated by capitalists (who can pay lower wages to male workers because the workers'
quality of life and standard of living benefit from their wives' labor); or whether their
labor is appropriated only by their husbands or intimate partners. But there is a crucial

difference between Socialist and Marxist feminist theory. Marxist feminist theory rejects the notion that the oppression of women can be explained outside modes of production; consequently, it is a unitary, not a "dual systems," or hybrid, perspective that assumes the functional interaction between capitalism and patriarchy.[11]

The Marxist feminist alternative explanation of the oppression of women theorizes an aspect of the mode of production largely unexamined by Marx: the mode of reproduction. Marxist theory is usually misunderstood as a theory that reduces everything to the economy, meaning that everything, including the oppression of women, can be explained by identifying its function within the economic system. Marxist theory argues that there is a fundamental unity between the process of producing material life (e.g., transforming nature to produce food, clothing, shelter); the production of consciousness, self-understanding, language, and culture; and the reproduction of life biologically (i.e., procreation), physically (consumption of goods and services), and socially (the changing processes through which we learn the ideologies and practices corresponding to our place in the class structure and the division of labor).[12] This means that we cannot understand how things are produced in "the economy" without examining how different people located in different social classes and different socioeconomic strata within those classes are reproduced biologically, physically, and socially. Women are the crucial laborers in the processes of reproduction, and because of their demanding place in capitalist societies as paid and unpaid workers, they are disadvantaged in relationship to male workers.

Marxist theory's focus on working women highlights another difference between this theory and the others previously discussed. Marxist feminists point out that it is problematic to theorize the oppression of "women" in general as if all women share the same experiences and interests. They argue that while all women might, because of their sexual and reproductive characteristics, be exposed to similar forms of oppression (e.g., sexual harassment, rape, lack of control over their bodies), the female population is divided by class, race, ethnicity, and socioeconomic position. Upper-class, capitalist women have the social and economic power to protect themselves from many forms of oppression to which the average working woman is more vulnerable because her economic and social powerlessness makes her live under conditions that increase the likelihood of victimization. Women of color, who are disproportionately poor, are even more vulnerable to economic and sexual exploitation than other, better-off working women.[13] These four theoretical perspectives, which flourished from the late 1960s to the mid-1980s, eventually gave way to other theoretical trends that have been emerging since the late 1970s.

## New Trends in Feminist Theory

New trends that came to dominate feminist theory in the 1980s and 1990s reflect the influence of European postmodern thought, as well as criticisms from women of color who have felt the earlier theories do not address their actual conditions of existence and are based on the experiences and political concerns of white, middle- and upper-class women.

Perhaps the most important contribution of black feminist theorizing in this more recent period, which places the experience of African American women at the core of its analysis of oppression, is the idea of the simultaneity of oppression. African American women's experiences are shaped not only by male dominance but by class and racial structures of exploitation and domination. Rather than emphasizing the priority of one of these oppressions over the other two, black feminists argue that all of them are equally important and mutually interacting to give historically specific content to their experience of oppression. This form of theorizing eventually evolved into three main forms of theorizing inequality: the race, gender, and class perspective, multicultural or multiracial feminism,[14] and intersectionality, a term developed in the process of exploring how the elements of the trilogy operate together to shape individuals' experiences.

### *Race, Gender, and Class Approach*

The object of study of the race, gender, and class approach is the intersection of these three sources of inequality. Authors describe this intersection using different metaphors (e.g., triple oppression, interplay, interrelation, interlocking, cumulative effects, interconnections). Patricia Hill Collins, whose work has been foundational for this approach, identifies the following main elements: race, gender, and class are "distinctive yet interlocking structures of oppression";[15] "interlocking" refers to macro-level connections linking race, gender, and class;[16] "intersectionality" describes micro-level phenomena; groups and individuals can be located at the intersection of these structures;[17] everyone has a race, gender, and class identity; everyone is simultaneously oppressed and oppressor;[18] and oppressions are all equally important and should not be ranked.[19] From this perspective, one cannot understand either one of these oppressions without, at the same time, taking into account how the other two affect it. To some extent, this approach replaces feminist theory's focus on women or gender with a framework that places the study of gender or women in the context of class and racial/ethnic oppression.

## *Multiracial Feminism*

These principles are incorporated into multiracial feminism,[20] a feminist framework that does not rest upon a unified theory but seeks to map the range of experiences associated with the multiple intersections within which men and women of color live their lives. The issues, research objectives, and theoretical insights of multiracial feminism stem from the experience of U.S. women of color. Latina, Asian American, Native American, and African American women, despite historical and cultural differences, can write and speak with a common wisdom grounded in their unique insights as "outsiders within"; this means that they bring to bear, in their intellectual work and social and political activities, knowledge about the functioning of U.S. social institutions based on experiences qualitatively different from those of white intellectuals and activists.

Multiracial feminism is a pluralistic approach to feminist research and theory that has some fundamental principles. Gender is constructed in the "matrix of domination" constituted by the intersection of gender with class, race, and sexuality; these four sets of inequalities are interlocking aspects of the social structure and individuals' experience, thus calling attention to the need to avoid generalizations based on each taken in isolation from the others. All forms of inequality are not simply individual attributes but relations of domination and subordination, so that women's agency against oppression is always embedded in power struggles. Multiracial feminism is interdisciplinary and theoretically and methodologically diverse, despite sharing this common focus on the interlocking nature of oppression.[21]

It is important to note that as political and theoretical critiques of the earlier feminist theories deepened, an important qualitative conceptual change gradually took over the way these issues were framed in academic work. This was the change from theorizing the oppression of women as historical agents to theorizing the effects of gender (i.e., the social construction of biological/sex differences) upon inequality. U.S. women of color's political critique of "women" as a category of analysis, predicated on the experiences of white and relatively privileged women, found theoretical support in the postmodern critique of "woman" as an essentialist category of analysis that should be deconstructed to avoid generalizations rendered suspect by the heterogeneity of women's experiences.[22] Hence, this signifies the shift from theorizing the oppression of women to theorizing the social constructions of gender, which signals also the crucial political shift from concern with theorizing inequality to theorizing difference.

*Intersectionality*

Intersectionality, one among the several metaphors used to describe the relationship between race, gender, and class, eventually replaced the trilogy, becoming an over-arching approach to research and theorizing, as the number of politicized identities signifying oppression and inequality grew to include ethnicity, sexuality, or sexual preference, gender choice, national origin, citizenship status, immigrant status, age, disability, and socioeconomic status. Today, intersectionality is considered to be "the heart of feminist analysis,"[23] "the most important theoretical contribution to this date of feminism,"[24] "its leading paradigm . . . . Its indispensable tool."[25]

Another important metaphor is the notion of "co-construction": intersectionality is thus defined as the study of how the various dimensions of inequality, for example gender, race, class, ethnicity, and so forth, "co-construct" one another.[26] "Single axis" analyses, that is, those that privilege only one dimension of inequality, rest on the assumption that these dimensions can be studied independently from one another, and that one particular form of oppression, for example gender or class, is dominant and shapes the effects of the others. However, everyone is situated at the intersection of a "matrix" formed by the multiple oppressions and inequalities that simultane-ously affect everyone's experience, placing everyone in a position of oppressor and oppressed. For example, a Latino man is oppressed, in his relationship to white men, but is an oppressor in his relationship to women. It follows that no form of inequal-ity is more important than the others; as an "integrated approach," intersectionality "refutes the compartmentalization of hierarchization of the great axes of social dif-ferentiation through the categories of gender/sex, class, race, ethnicity, disability and sexual orientation."[27]

At the micro level of analysis, intersectionality is concerned with the analysis of how the effects of multiple, intersecting, or co-constituting oppressions affect indi-viduals' lives in unique ways. At a macro level of analysis, intersectionality examines the "matrix of domination"[28] formed by the interlocking structures of oppression and inequality in society.

Micro-level research that takes intersectionality into account, and awareness of the multiple channels through which individuals are oppressed and placed in unequal social positions, is most valuable for policy formation and activists' organization. On the other hand, even though scholars stress that inherent in intersectionality there is a critique of inequality and oppression, this perspective lends itself to being reduced to an acceptance of multiculturalism and diversity that blunts critique of the system.[29] In other words, through teaching and public policy intended to ensure diversity in the student population and the work force, identity politics are reinforced to the detriment of class awareness and class politics.

At the macro level of analysis, intersectionality is not linked to any specific social theory so intersectionality research is carried out by scholars from many different theoretical perspectives within the social sciences and feminism. Common to all, however, is the idea that all forms of oppression and inequality are equal in their importance and social effect and, consequently, that no form of inequality is more consequential than others. To make the point more clearly, neither class, gender, nor race, for example, is more important in its effects than other sources of inequality and oppression.

From a Marxist standpoint, however, class is central because in capitalist societies the great majority of the population (the working class) is exploited and oppressed by the owners of capital (the capitalist class) regardless of gender, race, ethnicity, and other forms of identity and oppression. Thus, the individual's place in the relations of production or class location determines, to a large extent, the effect of other forms of inequality. This critical stance does not negate the potential value of intersectionality studies if linked to a class analysis of capitalist relations of exploitation underlying the "matrix of domination" within which most people are situated.

## Materialist Feminism

The main themes of current feminist theorizing have emerged within the framework of a more recent theoretical trend referred to as "materialist feminism." Under the materialist feminist label, there are two very different kinds of feminist theorizing: postmodern, deconstructive feminism that affirms the materiality of discourse, gender, race, and so forth,[30] and a Marxist feminism that takes up the task of illuminating the determinants of the oppression of women in capitalist society.[31]

The main concept that postmodern materialist feminism uses to differentiate itself from Marxist feminism is "materiality." But it is not clear what the concept actually means. It could mean objective or real (e.g., gender is as real as class) or determinant, having causal effects (e.g., ideologies are just as central or have as much "material weight" as class). Postmodern materialist feminism seems to rest upon the claim that all elements of the social organization or structure of society are equally material, meaning they are equally real and important and have real consequences.[32] To the Marxist emphasis on the importance of capitalism in determining, through its economic, political, and cultural institutions, the limits within which social relations among individuals and groups take place, postmodern materialist feminism affirms the materiality or causal importance of discourse. Discourse is a postmodern way of referring to what mainstream sociologists call values, normative systems, and culture and what Marxist sociologists call ideologies. To say that discourse is "material" is to argue that it has objective and inescapable effects because everything, including gender and class, is "discursively constructed." While Marxist feminists theorize the relationship between the economy and the family and the capitalist organization of work and reproduction as the basis for the inequality between working men and women, such an analysis is perceived, from a postmodern standpoint, as a deterministic analysis that does not give due recognition to the importance of discourses in the construction of identities, including gender identity. Marxists refer to the mode of production and reproduction as the material conditions that generate inequality between men and women in class society. Postmodern materialist feminists argue that other aspects of the social system are equally important, such as ideologies of race and sexuality.[33]

Lise Vogel's analysis of reproduction as a basis for the oppression of women is firmly grounded within the Marxist tradition.[34] Her analysis is materialist, in the Marxist sense, because it highlights the key role of production (public and domestic) in determining the conditions leading to the oppression of women. Postmodern materialist feminists, on the other hand, stress the importance of material conditions based on social relations, which influence gender hierarchy and the materiality of the body and its sexual, reproductive, and other biological functions.

Rosemary Hennessy[35] traces the origins of materialist feminism in the work of British and French feminists who prefer the term materialist feminism to Marxist feminism because, in their view, Marxism must be transformed to explain the sexual division of labor.[36] In the 1970s, Hennessy states, Marxism was inadequate to the task because of its class bias and focus on production, while feminism was also problematic due to its essentialist and idealist concept of woman; this is why postmodern materialist feminism emerged as an alternative to Marxism and feminism.[37] The combined effects of the postmodern critique of the empirical self and the criticisms voiced by women who did not see themselves included in the generic woman subject of academic feminist theorizing resulted, in the 1990s, in postmodern materialist feminist analyses that, according to Hennessy, "problematize 'woman' as an obvious and homogeneous empirical entity in order to explore how 'woman' as a discursive category is historically constructed and traversed by more than one differential axis."[38] Furthermore, Hennessy argues, despite the postmodern rejection of metanarratives (i.e., theoretical analyses of social systems), materialist feminists need to hold on to the critique of the totalities that affect women's lives: patriarchy and capitalism. Women's lives are everywhere affected by world capitalism and patriarchy, and it would be politically self-defeating to replace that critique with localized, fragmented, political strategies and a perception of social reality as characterized by a logic of contingency.

## Social Construction Feminism

A second, and perhaps even more important, trend in contemporary feminist theory in terms of its impact on feminist theorizing is what Judith Lorber calls "social construction feminism."[39] Since Peter L. Berger and Thomas Luckman wrote their famous book, *The Social Construction of Reality*,[40] the idea that everything social (e.g., institutions, roles, patterns, identities, structures, systems, classes) is socially constructed has taken a powerful hold on U.S. mainstream sociological perspectives approaching the study of social reality, an approach earlier developed by Charles Horton Cooley. This constructionist perspective has become the dominant way of theorizing gender among American social scientists and feminists.

Social construction feminism "looks at the gendered social order as a whole and at the processes that construct and maintain it."[41] From this standpoint, social institutions, patterns of behavior, and individuals are gendered. Like all feminist theories, social constructionism also points out that gender is a key determinant of people's access to valued resources of all kinds (e.g., economic, social, political, cultural). But its distinctive contribution to feminist theory is the analysis of the processes through which individuals "do gender" and, so, contribute unavoidably and unintentionally to the persistence, pervasiveness, and continuity of gender differences and inequalities through time.

Social construction feminist theory is derived from ethnomethodology, a sociological perspective developed by Harold Garfinkel, according to which individuals, as they carry on their everyday activities, accomplish, or "construct," the variety of enduring patterns to which sociologists attribute objectivity, characterizing them as "social facts" and causal effects, for they determine what individuals in society do, think, and believe.[42] From the perspective of ethnomethodology, "social facts" are nothing but the artful accomplishment (i.e., "construction") of individuals; gender is "a routine, methodical, and recurring accomplishment."[43] In enacting their gender, people appear in ways congruent with the expected characteristics of their gender. It is the activity through which people claim membership in the male or female sex category. Furthermore, the sex category may or may not coincide with biological sex, but, as biological sex is never displayed, what matters in the process of everyday interaction is the competent display or performance of membership in a socially legitimate sex category. In this way, people also reproduce the gendered nature of the social order and its associated inequalities. For men, this means domination over women; for women, it entails submission, dependence, deference, and acceptance of secondary status.

Social constructionism argues that if gender, race, and class oppressions are simultaneously experienced, they can be considered "situated accomplishments" rather than the property of individuals, as "something that is accomplished or constructed in the process of interaction with others."[44] People simultaneously "do" difference (i.e., class, gender, and race) in the process of interacting with others and, through this process, contribute to the reproduction of those structures of inequality. This viewpoint, as Collins aptly criticizes, reduces oppressive structures to "difference" and thus leaves out "the power relations and material inequalities that constitute oppression."[45]

From the standpoint of Marxist feminist theory, social constructionism is open to the criticism that it overlooks the material bases of inequality and oppression, which stem not only from the different ways in which people may display the expected characteristics of gender (or class, or race) but from the unequal relations among people grounded in their unequal ownership and/or control of property, income, credentials, or other sources of economic, social, and political power. In other words, doing gender is not isolated from class location and from location in the occupational hierarchies; the appropriate accomplishment, or construction, of gender yields different results for women assembly line workers, upper-class women, or women at the top of the Hollywood film industry. However, despite these problematic aspects of social construction feminism, it remains an important perspective, first because it is compatible with its more sophisticated version in cultural or materialist feminism, which views gender as a discursively (i.e., ideologically) constructed identity, and second, because it legitimates the psychological and voluntaristic understanding of how society works, which is characteristic of the average person's worldview in advanced capitalist societies. If gender is a mere construction or performance,[46] something we do or are able to subvert, then the differences between men and women would seem to be a matter of choice or, at the very least, less rigid and open to individuals' willingness to deconstruct them.

There is, then, a deep chasm between earlier feminist theories, which called for women's collective mobilization and organizing to struggle for necessary changes in the social institutions affecting women's position and opportunities, and more recent theories, which, centered around gender as a discursively (materialist feminists) or socially constructed (constructionist feminism) category, can only offer deconstruction (i.e., ideological critique) or subversive performances as ways to challenge it or change it.

## Future Course of Feminist Thought

At the beginning of the twenty-first century, the world has been transformed in ways that would have been unthinkable twenty-five years ago. The disappearance of the Socialist bloc accelerated the untrammeled penetration of capitalist relations of production throughout the globe, and the notion that we live in the era of globalization dominates social science thinking and commonsense understandings of the world. While writers might disagree about the causes, significance, effects, and future trends of globalization, there is general agreement that this new world is fraught with conflicts and the exacerbation of existing problems and inequalities. Working-class and peasant women and their children have been the most negatively affected, though the situation of working-class men, especially in the countries of the Southern Hemisphere, is only marginally better. From the standpoint of the problems afflicting most working-class women today (e.g., unemployment, underemployment, economic inequality, cultural and political oppression, lack of education, lack of adequate healthcare for themselves and their children, lack of housing, lack of clean water), problems that are worsened by gender, age, racial, and ethnic discrimination, feminist theory seems to be a mere academic exercise, irrelevant to the lives of most working women.[47]

Whether globalization signals the eventual death of feminist theory or the emergence of a new kind of feminism is a matter that only future historical developments can decide. Replicating the same criticisms addressed to Western feminist theories by working-class women and women of color, women in the poorer countries are critical of feminist theories that represent the experience of white Western women, privileged by race, class, and culture. Liberal feminism, however, has continued to inform women's activities in the United States (e.g., through the National Organization for Women) and around the world (e.g., through the United Nations (UN)-sponsored World Conference on Women and other UN venues). The bedrock of the Beijing Declaration and Platform for Action, which expresses the goals of the world's women who met in the fourth UN-sponsored conference, is that "women's rights are human rights." It follows that the foundation of a just, developed, and sustainable society requires equality between the sexes "as a matter of human rights and a condition for social justice."[48]

The vocabulary of human rights and, it is important to add, workers' rights has a universalizing potential, for it can unite women who are otherwise divided by class, race, ethnicity, religion, culture, nationality, and so forth. As Valentine Moghadam points out, attendance at local, national, regional, and world conferences, involvement in non-governmental organization activities, and, above all, the vast possibilities for communications and organization opened up by the Internet have facilitated an amazing proliferation of transnational feminist networks and women's movements.[49] The emergence of these women's networks shows that the struggle for justice transcends national, cultural, linguistic, and other barriers to communication and understanding, for these networks struggle not only against patriarchy but against the hardships and intensification of the full gamut of inequalities affecting women wrought by the effects of economic globalization.[50]

## Conclusion

Women struggle for their rights as political agents embedded in economic, political, cultural, national, social, and racial relations, seeking solutions that entail the attainment of rights and the betterment of their working conditions, access to healthcare and reproductive rights, education and so forth. These ongoing developments are theoretically and politically important, and for this reason, various feminist theories have attempted to develop and provide answers to questions involving gender and women's oppression. From a broader global perspective, the new transnational women's networks challenge the parochial nature of Western feminist theories and suggest that gender equality might be attained to the extent that gender is no longer the only or the main category of analysis through which oppression is understood. Politically, they challenge the notion that under globalization, politics can only be local politics because of the complexities and divisions that shape the consciousness of the world's population. By changing women's consciousness and questioning their centuries-old oppression, contemporary feminist theory, despite its limitations, has prepared the way for social change.

## Notes

1  For mainstream accounts of these divisions, see Rosemary Tong, *Feminist Thought: A Comprehensive Introduction* (Boulder, CO: Westview Press, 1989). See also Judith Lorber, *Gender Inequality: Feminist Theory and Politics* (Los Angeles, CA: Roxbury Publishing Company, 2002).

2  See Caroline Ramazanoglu, *Feminism and the Contradictions of Oppression* (London: Routledge, 1989); and Ann Brooks, *Postfeminisms: Feminism, Cultural Theory, and Cultural Forms* (London: Routledge, 1997).

3  But see Lena Gunarsson, "A Defense of the Category 'Woman,'" *Feminist Theory* 12, no. 1 (2011): 23–37.

4  For a Marxist critique of this perspective see Martha E. Gimenez, "Marxism and Class, Gender and Race: Rethinking the Trilogy," *Race, Gender & Class* 8, no. 2 (2001): 23–33.

5  Lorber, *Gender Inequality*, 25–37; Tong, *Feminist Thought*, 11–38.

6  See, for example, AAUW, "The Simple Truth about the Gender Pay Gap," www.aauw.org/research/the-simple-truth-about-the-gender-pay-gap/ (accessed August 31, 2016).

7  Lorber, *Gender Inequality*, 77–97; Tong, *Feminist Thought*, 71–94; Shulamith Firestone, *The Dialectic of Sex: The Case for Feminist Revolution* (New York: Bantam Books, 1971); and Mary Daly, *Gyn/Ecology: The Metaethics of Radical Feminism* (Boston, MA: Beacon Press, 1978).

8  See Zillah R. Einsenstein, ed., *Capitalist Patriarchy and the Case for Socialist Feminism* (New York: Monthly Review Press, 1979); and Lydia Sargent, *Women and Revolution: A Discussion of the Unhappy Marriage of Marxism and Feminism* (Boston, MA: South End Press, 1981).

9  Arlie Hochschild, *The Second Shift* (New York: Avon Books, 1989).

10  Pat Mainardi, "The Politics of Housework," in *Sisterhood is Powerful*, ed. Robin Morgan (New York: Random House, 1970).

11  See, for example, Charnie Guettel, *Marxism and Feminism* (Toronto: The Hunter Rose Co, 1974); Martha E. Gimenez, "Marxism and Feminism," *Frontiers: A Journal of Women's Studies* 1, no. 1 (1975); Heleieth I. B. Saffioti, *Women in Class Society* (New York: Monthly Review Press, 1978); and Lise Vogel, *Marxism and the Oppression of Women: Toward a Unitary Theory* (New Brunswick, NJ: Rutgers University Press, 1983). For an excellent bibliography of the domestic labor debate, see Roberta A. Hamilton and Michele Barrett, eds., *The Politics of Diversity* (London: Verso, 1986), 465–7.

12  Vogel, *Marxism and the Oppression of Women*. See also Martha E. Gimenez, "The Mode of Reproduction in Transition: A Marxist Feminist Analysis of the Effects of Reproductive Technologies," *Gender and Society* 5, no. 3 (1991).

13  See Alliance Against Women's Oppression (AAWO), *Poverty: Not for Women Only: A Critique of the Feminization of Poverty* (AAWO discussion paper no. 3, September, 1983); Martha E. Gimenez, "The Feminization of Poverty: Myth or Reality?" *Social Justice* 17, no. 3 (1990); and Johanna Brenner, *Women and the Politics of Class* (New York: Monthly Review Press, 2000).

14  Lorber, *Gender Inequality*.

15  Patricia Hill Collins, "Toward a New Vision: Race, Class and Gender as Categories of Analysis and Connection," *Race, Sex & Class* 1, no. 1 (1993).

16  Patricia Hill Collins, "On West and Fenstermaker's 'Doing Difference,'" in *Women, Men and Gender: Ongoing Debates*, ed. Mary Roth Walsh (New Haven, CT: Yale University Press, 1997), 74.

17  Collins, "On West and Fenstermaker's 'Doing Difference,'" 74.

18  Collins, "Toward a New Vision," 28.

19  Collins, "On West and Fenstermaker's 'Doing Difference,'" 74.

20  See, for example, Gloria E. Anzaldua, *Borderlands/La Frontera: The New Mestiza* (San Francisco, CA: Aunt Lute Books, 1999); bell hooks, *Talking Back: Thinking Feminist, Thinking Black* (Boston, MA: South End Press, 1989).

21  Lorber, *Gender Inequality*.

22  See, for example, Denise Riley, *Am I that Name? Feminism and the Category of Women in History* (Minneapolis, MN: University of Minnesota Press, 1988).

23  Christie Launius and Holly Hassel, *Threshold Concepts in Women's and Gender Studies: Ways of Seeing, Thinking, and Knowing* (New York and London: Routledge, 2015), 114.

24  Sirma Bilge, "Recent Feminist Outlooks on Intersectionality," *Diogenes* 225, no. 1 (2010): 58.

25  Patrick R. Grzanka, ed., *Intersectionality: A Foundations and Frontiers Reader* (Boulder, CO: Westview Press, 2014), xiii.

26  Grzanka, *Intersectionality*, xiii.

27  Bilge, "Recent Feminist Outlooks on Intersectionality," 58.

28  Patricia Hill Collins, *Black Feminist Thought: Knowledge, Consciousness, and the Politics of Empowerment* (New York: Routledge, 1990), 18, cited in Bilge, "Recent Feminist Outlooks on Intersectionality," 60.

29  Grzanka, *Intersectionality*, xix.

30  See, for example, Toril Moi and Janice Radway, special issue eds., "Materialist Feminism," *The South Atlantic Quarterly* 93, no. 4 (1994).

31  An excellent collection of Marxist and socialist feminist articles published under the aegis of materialist feminism is Rosemary Hennessy and Chrys Ingraham, eds., *Materialist Feminism: A Reader in Class, Difference, and Women's Lives* (New York: Routledge, 1997).

32  Martha E. Gimenez, "What's Material about Materialist Feminism? A Marxist Feminist Critique," *Radical Philosophy* 101 (2000).

33  See Donald Landry and Gerald Maclean, *Materialist Feminisms* (London: Blackwell, 1993).

34  Vogel, *Marxism and the Oppression of Women.*

35  Rosemary Hennessy, *Materialist Feminism and the Politics of Discourse* (New York: Routledge, 1993).

36  Veronica Beechey, "Some Notes on Female Wage Labor in Capitalist Production," *Capital and Class*, 3 (1977), 45–66, cited in Annette Kuhn and Anne Marie Wolpe, eds., *Feminism and Materialism: Women and Modes of Production* (London: Routledge and Kegan Paul, 1977).

37  Hennessy, *Materialist Feminism and the Politics of Discourse*, xii.

38  Hennessy, *Materialist Feminism and the Politics of Discourse*, xii.

39  Lorber, *Gender Inequality*, 180.

40  Peter L. Berger and Thomas Luckman, *The Social Construction of Reality: A Treatise on the Sociology of Knowledge* (New York: Anchor Books, 1967).

41  Lorber, *Gender Inequality*, 180.

42  Harold Garfinkel, *Studies in Ethnomethodology* (Englewood Cliffs, NJ: Prentice Hall, 1967).

43  Candace West and Don H. Zimmerman, "Doing Gender," in *Gender: A Sociological Reader*, ed. Stevi Jackson and Sue Scott (London: Routledge, 2002), 42–7.

44  West and Zimmerman, "Doing Gender," 43.

45  Patricia Hill Collins, "On West and Fenstermaker's 'Doing Difference.'"

46  See, for example, Judith Butler, "Performative Subversions," in Stevi Jackson and Sue Scott, *Gender.*

47  See, for example, Jerry Mander, Debi Baker and David Korten, "Does Globalization Help the Poor?" *Third World Traveler* (International Forum on Globalization), *IFG Bulletin*, 1, no. 3 (2001), www.thirdworldtraveler.com/Globalization/DoesGlobaliz_HelpPoor.html (accessed September 2, 2016).

48  Beijing Declaration and Platform for Action, Fourth World Conference on Women (September 15, 2005), A/CONF.177/20, and A/CONF.17720Add.1, available at www1.umn.edu/humanrts/instree/beijingdec.htm (accessed January 15, 2005).

49  Valentine Moghadam, "Gender and Globalization: Female Labor and Women's Mobilization," *Journal of World-Systems Research* 5, no. 2 (1999).

50  Some of these networks are DAWN (Development Alternatives with Women for a New Era), WLUML (Women Living Under Muslim Laws), WIDE (Network on Women in Development Europe), and WEDO (Women's Environment and Development Organization). See Moghadam, "Gender and Globalization."

# 25

# WALLERSTEIN AND WORLD-SYSTEMS THEORY

Over the past four decades, since the publication in 1974 of his *The Modern World-System*, Immanuel Wallerstein has played a central role in the formulation of world-systems theory, a theory of the global political economy.[1] Providing a comparative-historical approach to the study of societies across national boundaries, Wallerstein has thus introduced a unique perspective to social analysis of states at the global level. This chapter focuses on the arguments presented by Wallerstein in favor of his world-systems perspective, which has become prominent among a group of social scientists who have developed an entire school of thought around this theory.

## World-Systems Theory

With the publication of *The Modern World-System*, Wallerstein launched a multivolume study of the origins and development of the modern world system in an effort to re-examine the transition from feudalism to capitalism in western Europe and capitalism's subsequent development and expansion to the rest of the world.[2] This was followed by Samir Amin's two-volume study of accumulation on a world scale and other studies of the world accumulation process from earlier times to the present.[3] Thus began the formation of the entire school of thought known as world-systems theory.[4]

Explaining his method in selecting the world system as the unit of analysis, Wallerstein argues that he

abandoned the idea altogether of taking either the sovereign state or that vaguer concept, the national society, as the unit of analysis. I decided that neither one was a social system and that one could only speak of social change in social systems. The only social system in this scheme was the world system.[5]

"Once we assume that the unit of analysis is such a world-system and not the state or the nation or the people," Wallerstein argues, "then much changes in the outcome of the analysis."

> Most specifically we shift from a concern with the attributive characteristics of states to concern with the relational characteristics of states. We shift from seeing classes (and status groups) as groups within a state to seeing them as groups within a world-economy.[6]

Conceptualizing global power struggles as those in accordance with the requirements of a world system that dominates the global political economy over an entire historical period, the world-systems approach attempts to provide analytic tools to examine contemporary global political developments in the context of the logic of the capitalist world economy that has come to dominate the structure of economic relations on a world scale since the sixteenth century.

The capitalist world economy, argues Wallerstein, brings capitalist and non-capitalist states alike under its sway and determines the nature and course of their development as dictated by the most powerful state in control of the world system in a given historical epoch. But competition and rivalry between the leading states engaged in the struggle for domination of the world system leaves open the possibility that another state will replace the dominant state in a particular historical period:

> While the advantages of the core-states have not ceased to expand throughout the history of the modern world-system, the ability of a particular state to remain in the core sector is not beyond challenge. The hounds are ever to the hares for the position of top dog. Indeed, it may well be that in this kind of system it is not structurally possible to avoid, over a long period of historical time, a circulation of elites in the sense that the particular country that is dominant at a given time tends to be replaced in this role sooner or later by another country.[7]

Moving beyond nation-states and formulating the problem in world-systemic terms, Wallerstein thus provides an alternative explanation of the rise and fall of world systems, which take place in much longer historical periods and constitute the very basis of world historical transformations. In "The Rise and Future Demise of the World Capitalist System," Wallerstein argues in favor of just such a conceptualization in explaining the origins, development, and future transformation of the capitalist world economy and system.[8] Likewise, situating the problematic in a broader historical context of systemic transformation, Wallerstein attempts, elsewhere, in *The Modern*

*World-System*, and later in *The Capitalist World-Economy*, to explain the transition from feudalism to capitalism in western Europe and the subsequent rise and development of the world capitalist system in such world-systemic terms.[9]

## The Three-Tiered Model

An essential element in the global analysis of the modern world system is the theory's three-tiered model of "core," "periphery," and "semiperiphery," which divides the world system into three areas, or zones, defined on the basis of a society's level of development and incorporation into the world system. Moreover, the political-economic content of such incorporation determines whether a given social formation is part of the core, the periphery, or the semiperiphery.[10]

> The organizing principle of this operation is the categorical differentiation of levels of the world-system: core, semiperiphery, and periphery. These zones, distinguished by their different economic functions within the world-economic division of labor . . . structure the assemblage of productive processes that constitute the capitalist world-economy.[11]

"On a world-scale," write Terence Hopkins and Wallerstein, "the processes of the division of labor that define and integrate the world-economy are . . . [those] which we designate as 'core' and 'periphery'."[12] Moreover, "although obviously derivative from the core-periphery conception," they add, "there exists a third category, structurally distinct from core and periphery": "Looking at the world-economy as a whole . . . [there exists] a basically triadic world-scale division of labor among, now, core states, semiperipheral states, and peripheral areas."[13] Thus,

> The world-economy became basically structured as an increasingly interrelated system of strong "core" and weak "peripheral" states, in which inter-state relations . . . are continually shaped and in turn continually shape the deepening and expanding world-scale division and integration of production.[14]

This brings up the question of "the network(s) of governance or rule in the area in question."[15] "In this respect," write Hopkins and Wallerstein, "incorporation entails the expansion of the world-economy's interstate system":

> Interstate relations and the interstate system overall, in part express and in part circumscribe or structure the world-scale accumulation/production process. In short, the relational networks forming the interstate system are integral to, not

outside of, the networks constitutive of the social economy defining the scope and reach of the modern world-system. . . .

Insofar as external areas are incorporated, then—and in the singular development of the modern world-system all have been—the transition period framing incorporation encloses definite directions of change in a once external area's arrangements and processes of rule or governance.[16]

The main feature of the modern world system is, in essence, the transfer of surplus from the periphery to the core of the system, conceptualized in a manner similar to Andre Gunder Frank's "metropolis-satellite" model of domination and "exploitation."[17] The mechanism whereby this transfer takes place is "unequal exchange,"[18] a mechanism made possible by the domination of peripheral states by those in the core:

> Once we get a difference in the strength of the state machineries, we get the operation of "unequal exchange" which is enforced by strong states on weak ones, by core states on peripheral areas. Thus capitalism involves not only appropriation of the surplus value by an owner from a laborer, but an appropriation of surplus of the whole-world-economy by core areas. And this was as true in the stage of agricultural capitalism as it is in the stage of industrial capitalism.[19]

More specifically, Wallerstein argues that without this process of unequal exchange, the capitalist world economy could not exist:

> Such a system [of unequal exchange] is *necessary* for the expansion of a world market if the primary consideration is *profit*. Without *unequal* exchange, it would not be *profitable* to expand the size of the division of labor. And without such expansion, it would not be profitable to maintain a capitalist world-economy, which would then either disintegrate or revert to the form of a redistributive world-empire.[20]

Despite the subordination of peripheral states to those in the core, and the exploitation of the former by the latter through surplus extraction, the modern world system allows, under certain conditions and in the context of certain political-economic processes, the transformation of some peripheral states into semiperipheral ones. But such transformation (or mobility) of states along the three-tiered continuum takes place within the context and logic of the system as a whole and as a consequence of the dictates of the dominant world system in a given historical period. Thus, the various parts of the system that make up its totality always function within the framework of the relationship of the parts to the whole.

## Conclusion

Although world-systems theory constitutes a major improvement over mainstream developmentalist theories of the world political economy, it nevertheless suffers from a number of fundamental flaws. The central flaw of this theory is its treatment of the world economy and the world system in strictly circulationist terms. Capitalism, defined as a system of accumulation for profit through the market, is conceptualized in the context of exchange relations. Thus, economic relations take place between states within the context of such market exchange. As a result, the question of the mode of production and its social component relations of production (i.e., class relations) is ignored or eliminated from analysis so that class struggles based on relations of production also disappear from analysis as irrelevant. We are thus left with the generalized, abstract notions of "world system" and "world economy" consisting of three zones (core, periphery, and semiperiphery) between which all major global social, political, and economic relations take place. Unfortunately, given its focus on the world system at the global level, the theory fails to provide an explanation of the underlying class logic of the world system, its class contradictions, and class conflicts. We will address these in the next chapter where we look at various theories of globalization to understand the class nature of the global capitalist system and the capitalist globalization process in the late twentieth and early twenty-first centuries.

## Notes

1  Immanuel Wallerstein, *The Modern World-System* (New York: Academic Press, 1974), 53.
2  Wallerstein, *The Modern World-System*, 53.
3  Samir Amin, *Accumulation on a World Scale*, 2 vols. (New York: Monthly Review Press, 1974); Richard Rubinson, ed., *Dynamics of World Development* (London: SAGE, 1981). See also the works of Terence Hopkins, Christopher Chase-Dunn, Albert Bergesen, Walter Goldfrank, and Terry Boswell.
4  For an in-depth analysis of the theoretical and methodological premises of world-systems theory, see Alvin Y. So, *Social Change and Development: Modernization, Dependency, and World-System Theories* (Newbury Park, CA: SAGE, 1990), pt. 3.
5  Wallerstein, *The Modern World-System*, 7.
6  Wallerstein, *The Modern World-System*, xi.
7  Immanuel Wallerstein, "The Rise and Future Demise of the World Capitalist System," *Comparative Studies in Society and History* 16, no. 4 (1974): 350.
8  Wallerstein, "The Rise and Future Demise of the World Capitalist System," 350.

9  See Wallerstein, *The Modern World-System*; and Immanuel Wallerstein, *The Capitalist World-Economy* (Cambridge: Cambridge University Press, 1979).

10  Wallerstein, *The Modern World-System*; and Wallerstein, "The Rise and Future Demise of the World Capitalist System."

11  Terence K. Hopkins and Immanuel Wallerstein, *World-Systems Analysis* (Beverly Hills, CA: SAGE, 1982), 77.

12  Hopkins and Wallerstein, *World-Systems Analysis*, 45.

13  Hopkins and Wallerstein, *World-Systems Analysis*, 47.

14  Hopkins and Wallerstein, *World-Systems Analysis*, 43.

15  Terence K. Hopkins and Immanuel Wallerstein, "Structural Transformations of the World-Economy," in Rubinson, *Dynamics of World Development*, 245.

16  Hopkins and Wallerstein, "Structural Transformations of the World-Economy," 245–6.

17  See Andre Gunder Frank, *Capitalism and Underdevelopment in Latin America* (New York: Monthly Review Press, 1967).

18  This process was first examined at length by Arghiri Emmanuel, *Unequal Exchange: A Study of the Imperialism of Trade* (New York: Monthly Review Press, 1972). Later, it was elaborated by Samir Amin, *Unequal Development: An Essay on the Social Formations of Peripheral Capitalism* (New York: Monthly Review Press, 1977).

19  Wallerstein, *The Capitalist World-Economy*, 18–19.

20  Wallerstein, *The Capitalist World-Economy*, 71.

# 26

# THEORIES OF GLOBALIZATION

Among recent prominent theories of society and social change in the late twentieth and early twenty-first centuries there has been a proliferation of theories that address issues concerning globalization. Coined in the early 1990s, the term "globalization" entered the academic vocabulary and became a central concept in international relations in a world that is more and more interconnected in many dimensions of social life. Although Immanuel Wallerstein and the world-system theorists had been theorizing about the world economy and the world system since the mid-1970s, theories of globalization and the global political economy began to dominate academic studies only after the process became obvious to many in the final decade of the twentieth century.

This chapter provides a critical analysis of theories of globalization and the evolving globalization process, highlighting its dynamics, contradictions, and impact on society in the late twentieth and early twenty-first centuries. It argues that the shift in production from the advanced capitalist centers to the peripheral areas of the world economy has occurred as part of the accelerated globalization of capital and capitalist expansion throughout the world. Such expansion, which is the basis of the accumulation of capital under global capitalism, has led to increased class conflict, class struggles, and, ultimately, to major social transformations on a global scale. Assessing the situation in broader political-economic terms, it is argued that the contradictions embedded in the structure of contemporary global capitalism will inevitably lead to the intensification of class struggles around the world that are bound to develop in response to the accelerated globalization of capital in this latest phase of global capitalist development.

## The Nature and Dynamics of Globalization

Among early theorists of contemporary globalization, Robert J. S. Ross and Kent C. Trachte in their pioneering book, *Global Capitalism: The New Leviathan* (1990), introduced to the academic world the enormity of the new and latest stage of capitalist development on a global scale, highlighting what they viewed as the epochal transition

of capitalism as a global economic system to a higher level of unprecedented proportions.[1] While this development, they argued, is fundamentally an extension of capitalism
from the national to the global level, hence it is at root a manifestation of the contradictions of capitalism now unfolding on a world scale, they did nevertheless argue that
this most recent stage of global capitalism is characterized by new features that make it
qualitatively different from its previous forms—a contention that has opened up a flood
of studies to explore the dynamics of this process from a variety of critical perspectives.

Scholars of globalization, such as Leslie Sklair, *Sociology of the Global System* (1991),
William I. Robinson, *A Theory of Global Capitalism* (2004), and David Harvey, *A
Brief History of Neoliberalism* (2007), are among those who have taken up a careful
study of the global system and have made major contributions to theories of globalization by focusing on different aspects of the globalization process.[2] Thus, while Sklair
has developed the analytical concept of "Transnational Practices" through which a
"Transnational Capitalist Class" operates to coordinate the global capitalist system,
Robinson has focused on transnational production by highlighting the active collabo-
ration of transnational capitalists and the transnational state to bring into play this
triangular global relationship that takes place beyond the traditional practices of established nation-states.[3]

In attempting to understand the many features of globalization, it becomes clear
that neoliberal capitalist globalization is the highest and most advanced stage of global
capitalist expansion facilitated by transnational capital throughout the world. James
Petras and Henry Veltmeyer in their book *Globalization Unmasked: Imperialism in the
21st Century* (2001) and Berch Berberoglu in his book *Globalization of Capital and the
Nation-State: Imperialism, Class Struggle, and the State in the Age of Global Capitalism*
(2003) make this point and argue that globalization today is an accelerated and much
more pervasive phase of advanced capitalism operating on a worldwide basis than
earlier stages of capitalist imperialism, and is, in this sense, a continuation of transnational capitalist expansion across the world, defined by its new and more characteristic
features (i.e., its speed and intensity) that are specific to this most current phase of
global capitalism.[4]

A central feature of this current phase of transnational capitalism, besides its speed
and intensity, is the increased privatization of various spheres of the economy and society with a proportionate decline in the power and ability of the state and other political
institutions to control their national economies relative to earlier periods. Under the
current wave of globalization, the state in the advanced capitalist societies (and increasingly in the less developed ones) has lost not only some of its traditional power in
controlling and regulating the various spheres of society, especially the economy, but

also other areas such as communications, information technology, education, and the cultural sphere, where privatization is becoming increasingly prevalent.[5] However, this does not mean that the state has lost its power completely, as it continues to be the chief administrator of power and holds on to its monopoly of force. Still, while the state persists in playing a prominent role in the public sphere, the current phase of global capitalist expansion has placed the transnational corporations in a more visible position where they have increasingly taken center stage in effecting changes in the global political economy, including some of the areas traditionally controlled by the state.[6]

The rate at which these changes have been taking place, and the vigor with which transnational capital has been exercising more power vis-à-vis the state, has led some to declare globalization a qualitatively new stage in the development of world capitalism.[7] However, these quantitative, surface manifestations of contemporary capitalism, no matter how pervasive they are, do *not* change the fundamental nature of capitalism and capitalist relations, nor the nature of the capitalist/imperialist state and the class contradictions generated by these relations, which are inherent characteristics of the system itself. They cannot change the nature of capitalism in any qualitative sense to warrant globalization a distinct status that these critics have come to assign as something fundamentally different than what Marxist political economists have always argued to be the "normal" operation and evolution of global capitalism in the age of imperialism.[8]

Globalization, then, much as during the earlier stages of capitalism, is driven by the logic of *profit* for the private accumulation of capital based on the exploitation of labor throughout the world. It is, in essence, the highest and most pervasive phase of transnational capitalism operating on a world scale. It is the most widespread and penetrating manifestation of modern capitalism in the age of the Internet—a development that signifies not only the most thorough economic domination of the world by the biggest capitalist corporations, but also increasingly direct military intervention by the chief capitalist states to secure the global economic position of their own corporations, especially in controlling sources of raw materials (such as oil), as in the 2003 invasion of and war against Iraq by the United States.

## Globalization: Its Particular Characteristics

Globalization today is a manifestation of worldwide capitalist expansion, but it involves a multitude of spheres within which it operates. These are economic, social, political, ideological, cultural, and environmental, to mention the most central. However, all of these spheres function within the class configurations of the prevailing social system and have immense political implications.

*Economic Basis*

It has already been pointed out that the economic essence of neoliberal capital-ist globalization is profit-making on a global scale. Hence, the central dynamic of globalization today is capital and its accumulation in private hands throughout the world. The export of capital by the transnational corporations of the advanced capital-ist countries to the Third World and elsewhere in the world for control of labor and resources of these regions has historically been part of the process of capitalist expan-sion worldwide that has led to the growth of giant capitalist conglomerates, cartels, and trusts that came to dominate the world economy over the course of the twentieth century.[9]

The accelerated rate of exploitation of labor through the expanded reproduction of surplus value (profits) on a world scale facilitates the rapid accumulation of capital by the transnationals at global proportions—a process that stimulates further capital accumulation worldwide, hence further economic domination by the transnationals.[10] It is this economic essence of neoliberal capitalist globalization, then, that sets into motion the social, political, and ideological contexts in which capitalism prospers.

*Social Impact*

In the social sphere, we find the global expansion of capital as transforming social rela-tions of production from precapitalist or semicapitalist ones to capitalist ones, where the main class contradictions become wage-labor and capital. The transformation of class relations through this process in a capitalist direction leads to the integra-tion of peripheral countries into the global capitalist economy and the restructuring of the international division of labor for purposes of extracting high rates of profit from superexploited wage-labor (Petras and Veltmeyer 2001). As female workers increasingly constitute the bulk of the low-wage laboring population worldwide, the exploitation of the working class takes on a gender dimension.[11]

The global domination of capital over wage-labor in this process of worldwide capitalist expansion fosters the subordination of the working class to the dictates of transnational capitalists, who not only extract surplus value (profits) from wage-labor, but are also the very source of the emerging inequalities in income, wealth, and power. These inequalities, in time, lead to contradictions and conflict in the social sphere, when class divisions become solidified to a point when class struggles between the opposing class forces begin to surface.[12]

## Political Dynamics

In the political sphere, power remains in the hands of the capitalist class and is exercised through its "executive committee"—the capitalist state. The transnational capitalist control of the state and major political institutions of society has led to the erosion of bourgeois democracy and to the rise of authoritarianism and political corruption.[13] However, rather than representing the unified interests of a newly emergent global capitalist class, the state under conditions of capitalist globalization continues to protect and advance the interests of "its own" monopoly capitalists, as against other capitalists, for supremacy over the global capitalist economy.[14]

Hence, despite a temporary commercial, monetary, and even military union, the leading capitalist state (currently the United States) continues to dominate the world political economy and dictates its terms over other capitalist states, including its chief rivals, thus giving rise to competition and rivalry between the major global capitalist powers.[15] While this competition takes place at the monopoly level, between rival transnational corporations as well as their states, it nevertheless affects the structure of social relations in general and has a direct impact on other sectors of society as well.

## Ideological Context

In the ideological sphere, global capitalism continues to propagate the superiority of capitalism and "free markets" in a private economy,[16] emphasizing the "victory" of capitalism over socialism and criticizing the public sphere as inefficient and undesirable—ideas that are a direct reflection of the class interests of the capitalist class. Such ideological propaganda disseminated by the capitalist media and the capitalist state was especially effective during the Cold War years and in the aftermath of the collapse of the Socialist block, as neoliberalism took hold of the global economy in the post-Cold War "new world order" that the capitalist media propagated in favor of global capitalism. Thus, the global capitalist media became an instrument to facilitate neoliberal capitalist globalization, hence acting as the mouthpiece of the global capitalist system.[17] However, as the power and legitimacy of capitalism and profit-making come under attack, as harmful to millions of working people around the world, the ideology behind capitalist globalization is bound to face opposition from the popular forces advocating an alternative to capitalism, imperialism, and globalization (the kind of opposition that took place, for example, in the protests and demonstrations against the World Trade Organization (WTO) in Seattle in November 1999, the International Monetary Fund (IMF), and the World Bank in Washington, DC, in April 2000, and similar such protests in Europe and the United States in 2001 and

2002).[18] Another round of protests and demonstrations that sprung up in the aftermath of the Great Recession of 2008–2009 culminated in the Occupy Wall Street movement that erupted into open rebellion by tens of thousands who rose up against the banks and the corporations that wreaked havoc on the economy and the people victimized by a system that they felt benefited only the few—the 1 percent.[19]

### Cultural Framework

In the cultural sphere, capitalist globalization fosters cultural imperialism.[20] This aspect of the global expansion of capital involves the imposition of capitalist cultural values on other precapitalist or noncapitalist societies to integrate them into the world capitalist system. The significance of the transformation of belief systems and cultural practices under the globalization project is such that the dominant values promoted by capitalist globalization (such as "privatization" and "free markets"—code words for capitalism) become the new values that are adopted by societies around the world.[21] Such values are easily translated into consumerism, private accumulation, and other individualistic practices, rather than collective/communal values that foster cooperation. Thus, the globalization of capital is able in this way to promote the globalization of capitalist values and capitalist culture to legitimize the capitalist system on a worldwide basis.[22]

### Environmental Impact

Finally, considering the impact of globalization on the environment, the destruction of the ecosystem and the living space (through pollution, contamination, and disposal) to reduce the cost of production has meant the gradual deterioration of the quality of air, water, and soil, with long-range negative consequences that are quite often irreversible.[23] While capitalism and the private accumulation of capital has in this way brought about the decline in the quality of the environment, the globalization of capital has accelerated this process and has led to an ecological crisis. In their reckless drive for private accumulation, the transnational corporations have turned much of the world into a dumping ground for the sole purpose of maximizing profits.[24] These profits have benefited only a small segment of the world's population while ruining the lives of billions of people throughout the globe. The destruction of the environment through this process has also meant the destruction of the lives and livelihoods of working people the world over and placed the future of our planet into great risk.[25]

## Globalization and its Transformation: The Prospects for Change

Looking at the class contradictions of the globalization process and the prospects for change in the world situation, one notes the resurgence of renewed anti-imperialist struggles through the formation of new revolutionary social movements in the Third World during this latest phase of capitalist globalization (e.g., the Zapatistas in Chiapas) and the radicalization of the labor movement in the advanced capitalist countries and the development of protest movements in mainland Europe, Britain, and, increasingly, North America.[26]

Unlike in earlier periods of anti-imperialist mobilization, however, when nationalism was the defining characteristic of the radical anti-imperialist movements, today popular movements in the Third World are led by the working class and its organizations. As a result, the struggle against neoliberal capitalist globalization in the Third World is moving beyond the anti-imperialist struggle and taking on more and more an anticapitalist character.[27] This is so because labor unions and other workers' organizations have increasingly taken the lead to initiate the kinds of mass movements that will evolve into a wider global effort to unite labor across national boundaries, so that a broader global unity of the working class can be built on a worldwide basis.[28]

Similar to developments in the Third World, in the advanced capitalist countries, too, there has been a resurgence of the labor movement, and workers' organizations (primarily labor unions in the United States and labor unions and workers' political parties in Europe and elsewhere) have taken the lead to mobilize workers to address the problems created by capitalist globalization in the heartlands of the global economy.[29] While these movements are stronger and play a more direct role in Europe and Britain, the move toward greater mobilization of labor to rally workers' support in the United States is becoming an important aspect of the struggle against neoliberal capitalist globalization and the global economic project of the transnationals—and, increasingly, on the very soil where their global reach took root. It is thus at the home base of the transnationals where we will more and more witness the kinds of opposition that is beginning to develop against them.[30]

These and other developments engendered by the globalization process lead one to the inescapable conclusion that the contradictions of the global political economy will result in increased class struggles in the years ahead, with the potential development of radical social transformations that are yet to come.

## Notes

1  Robert J. S. Ross and Kent C. Trachte, *Global Capitalism: The New Leviathan* (Albany, NY: State University of New York Press, 1990).
2  See Leslie Sklair, *Sociology of the Global System* (Baltimore, MD: Johns Hopkins University Press, 1991); William I. Robinson, *A Theory of Global Capitalism: Production, Class, and State in a Transnational World* (Baltimore, MD: Johns Hopkins University Press, 2004); and David Harvey, *A Brief History of Neoliberalism* (New York: Oxford University Press, 2007).

3   Leslie Sklair, *The Transnational Capitalist Class* (London: Blackwell, 2000); William I. Robinson, *A Theory of Global Capitalism*.

4   James Petras and Henry Veltmeyer, *Globalization Unmasked: Imperialism in the 21ˢᵗ Century* (London: Zed Books, 2001); Berch Berberoglu, *Globalization of Capital and the Nation-State: Imperialism, Class Struggle, and the State in the Age of Global Capitalism* (Boulder, CO: Rowman & Littlefield, 2003), 135.

5   C. P. Rao, ed., *Globalization, Privatization, and Free Market Economy* (Westport, CT: Quorum, 1998).

6   Malcolm Waters, *Globalization: The Reader* (New York: Routledge, 1995); Fred Halliday, *The World at 2000* (New York: St. Martin's Press, 2001); Robinson, *A Theory of Global Capitalism*.

7   Ross and Trachte, *Global Capitalism: The New Leviathan*.

8   Albert Szymanski, *The Logic of Imperialism* (New York: Praeger, 1981); Bill Warren, *Imperialism: Pioneer of Capitalism* (London: Verso, 1980); Nick Beams, *The Significance and Implications of Globalization: A Marxist Assessment* (Southfield, MI: Mehring Books, 1998).

9   Samir Amin, *Capitalism in the Age of Globalization* (London: Zed Books, 1997); Sam Gindin and Leo Panitch, *The Making of Global Capitalism: The Political Economy of American Empire* (London: Verso, 2013).

10  Ronaldo Munck, *Globalization and Labor* (London: Zed Books, 2002).

11  Deborah Barndt, ed., *Women Working the Nafta Food Chain: Women, Food and Globalization* (Toronto: Sumach Press, 1999); Shirin Rai, *Gender and the Political Economy of Development* (Cambridge: Polity Press, 2001).

12  Beams, *The Significance and Implications of Globalization: A Marxist Assessment*.

13  Greg Palast, *The Best Democracy Money Can Buy* (London: Pluto Press, 2002); Noreena Hertz, *Silent Takeover: Global Capitalism and the Death of Democracy* (New York: Free Press, 2002).

14  Theodore H. Cohn, Stephen McBride, and John Wiseman, eds., *Power in the Global Era: Grounding Globalization* (New York: Palgrave Macmillan, 2000).

15  Yang Xiaohua, *Globalization of the Automobile Industry: The United States, Japan, and the People's Republic of China* (Westport, CT: Praeger Publishers, 1995); Steven Weber, ed., *Globalization and the European Political Economy* (New York: Columbia University Press, 2001).

16  Rao, *Globalization, Privatization, and Free Market Economy*.

17  Edward S. Herman and Robert W. McChesney, *Global Media: The Missionaries of Corporate Capitalism* (New York: Bloomsbury, 2001); Tanner Mirrlees, *Global Entertainment Media: Between Cultural Imperialism and Cultural Globalization* (London: Routledge, 2013).

18  Amory Starr, *Naming the Enemy: Anti-Corporate Movements Confront Globalization* (London: Zed Books, 2001); George Katsiaficas and Eddie Yuen, eds., *The Battle of Seattle: Debating Capitalist Globalization and the WTO* (New York: Soft Skull Press, 2002).

19  Heather Gautney, "Occupy Wall Street: Repossession by Occupation," in *Protest and Organization in the Alternative Globalization Era*, by Heather Gautney (New York: Palgrave Macmillan, 2010).

20  James Petras, "Cultural Imperialism in the Late 20ᵗʰ Century," *Journal of Contemporary Asia* 23, no. 2 (1993); Herman and McChesney, *Global Media: The Missionaries of Global Capitalism*.

21  Richard Falk, *Predatory Globalization: A Critique* (Malden, MA: Blackwell Publishers, 1999); Richard Spinello, *Global Capitalism, Culture, and Ethics* (London: Routledge, 2014); Lane Crothers, *Globalization and American Popular Culture*, 3rd ed. (Lanham, MD: Rowman and Littlefield, 2012).

22  Falk, *Predatory Globalization*; Halliday, *The World at 2000*.

23 Peter Newell, *Globalization and the Environment: Capitalism, Ecology, and Power* (London: Polity, 2012); Naomi Klein, *This Changes Everything: Capitalism vs. the Climate* (New York: Simon and Schuster, 2015).

24 Joshua Karliner, *The Corporate Planet: Ecology and Politics in the Age of Globalization* (Los Angeles, CA: University of California Press, 1997); John Bellamy Foster, Brett Clark, and Richard York, *The Ecological Rift: Capitalism's War on the Earth* (New York: Monthly Review Press, 2011).

25 Julian E. Kunnie, *The Cost of Globalization: Dangers to the Earth and Its People* (New York: McFarland, 2015).

26 François Houtart and François Polet, eds., *The Other Davos: The Globalization of Resistance to the World Economic System* (London: Zed Books, 2001); Jackie G. Smith and Hank Johnston, eds., *Globalization and Resistance: Transnational Dimensions of Social Movements* (New York: Routledge, 2002).

27 James Petras, *The Left Strikes Back: Class Conflict in Latin America in the Age of Neoliberalism* (Boulder, CO: Westview Press, 1998); Starr, *Naming the Enemy: Anti-Corporate Movements Confront Globalization*.

28 Ronaldo Munck and Peter Waterman, eds., *Labor Worldwide in the Era of Globalization* (New York: Palgrave Macmillan, 1999); Munck, *Globalization and Labor*.

29 Smith and Johnston, eds., *Globalization and Resistance*.

30 Gus Bagakis, *Seeing through the System: The Invisible Class Struggle in America* (Bloomington, IN: iUniverse, 2013).

# 27

# THERBORN AND SZYMANSKI ON CONTEMPORARY MARXIST THEORY

In contrast to the neo-Weberian and world-systems theories discussed in previous chapters, in this chapter we present an overview of recent developments in contemporary Marxist theory by focusing on the works of Goran Therborn (1941– ) and Albert Szymanski (1941–1985), who provide an alternative, historical-materialist conceptualization of class, state, and society.[1] Incorporating some of the important Marxist theorizing of the late twentieth century into a class-analysis approach informed by the dialectics of the class struggle, Therborn and Szymanski make an important contribution to the resurgence of Marxist theory in recent decades.

### Historical Materialism and the Base–Superstructure Problematic

The origins of this recent wave of Marxist theorizing go back to the late 1970s, when Therborn, Szymanski, and a number of other Marxist intellectuals set forth their theoretical position and, thus, prepared the stage for the subsequent emergence of works raising questions of paramount importance originally formulated by Karl Marx, Frederick Engels, and V. I. Lenin.

"This renaissance of Marxist political analysis in the 1980's," writes Therborn, "will appear unexpected":

> The irony is that while many former protagonists and adherents of various "schools" of neo-Marxism are now proclaiming a post-Marxist, beyond-class stance, a new, vigorous self-confident class theory of politics and the state is being launched, impeccably dressed in the best clothes of modern empirical social science, while making no secret of its inspiring commitment to the working-class movement....
>
> There is, then, still a contingent of scholars arguing that states are a function of classes, rather than the other way round.[2]

To his credit, Therborn's contribution to this renaissance led to a flood of studies in Marxist political economy and class theory of the state and society in the 1980s and 1990s.

In his book *What Does the Ruling Class Do When It Rules?* Therborn argues in favor of the historical-materialist approach to the study of society, the state, and politics. The aim of such an approach, he writes, "is to show that different types of class relations and of class power generate corresponding forms of state organization, and to elucidate the way in which the class character of the state apparatus is determined and revealed."[3]

According to the axioms of historical materialism, class and state condition each other: where there are no classes, there is no state. In class societies, moreover, social relations are first and foremost class relations. Thus, by definition, every state has a class character, and every class society has a ruling class (or bloc of ruling classes).[4]

Contrary to Hegelian-Marxist and neo-Weberian notions of "state autonomy" and "state-centered" theories that assign primacy to the state and superstructural institutions in society, such as that advanced by Ellen Kay Trimberger, Fred Block, and Theda Skocpol (see Chapter 19), Therborn reintroduces into the debate the base–superstructure problematic interpreted in a new light, one that avoids economistic conceptualizations of politics on the one hand, while rejecting eclectic "codeterminist" notions of class and state on the other.

Basic to Therborn's analysis of the relationship of the economic base to the political superstructure is the role of the class struggle engendered by the dominant mode of production. "In very general terms," writes Therborn,

the character of state power is defined by the two fundamental processes of determination of the superstructure by the base—processes which in reality are two aspects of the same determination. One of these is the systemic logic of social modes of production, that is to say, the tendencies and contradictions of the specific dynamic of each mode. The other is the struggle of classes, defined by their position in the mode of production. These two forms of determination by the base are logically interrelated in the basic theory of historical materialism.[5]

In this formulation, the state is no longer viewed simply as a passive recipient of directives from the dominant class, but is actively involved in the reproduction of the dominant relations of production: "Invariably the state enters into the reproduction of the relations of production by providing the latter with a stabilizing legal framework backed by force."[6] Moreover, the relations of production, Therborn points out, are structured by legal boundaries that define relations between dominant and subordinate classes.[7]

To sum up Therborn's position, "the economic base determines the political superstructure by entering into the reproduction of state power and the state apparatus" and "shapes the character of state power by, among other things, providing the basic parameters of state action."[8] Further, because "exploitative relations of production need a repressive political apparatus as their ultimate guarantee,"[9] the state comes to assume this role to "promote and defend the ruling class and its mode of exploitation or supremacy."[10] Thus, "the ruling class exercises its ruling power over other classes and strata through the state—through holding state power."[11] In order to maintain its legitimacy and secure social order, however, "the state must *mediate* the exploitation or domination of the ruling class over other classes and strata."[12]

Viewing the base–superstructure problematic in these terms, Therborn bridges the gap between structuralist and instrumentalist formulations of the state and provides a dialectical analysis of the relationship between class and state, thus advancing the debate through a fresh look at historical materialism as the basis for a resurgent Marxist theory of society in the late twentieth and early twenty-first centuries.

## Theory of the State

In his book *The Capitalist State and the Politics of Class*, Szymanski makes a similar case in favor of the historical-materialist approach to the study of society and the state.[13] Citing the works of Marx, Engels, and Lenin on the state, Szymanski argues that the state plays a central role in society and that "a Marxist political sociology must thus give careful and detailed consideration to the nature of the state."[14]

Examining the nature and role of the state in class society in general and capitalist society in particular, Szymanski writes,

> The state is an instrument by which the exploitation of the economically subordinate class is secured by the economically dominant class that controls the state. . . . The social relationships and the social order that the state guarantees are thus the social relationships of inequality and the order of property and exploitation. . . .
>
> The state in capitalist society is a capitalist state by virtue of its domination by the capitalist class *and* in that it functions most immediately in the interests of capital.[15]

Moreover, the state must function within the confines of an economic, military, political, and ideological environment structured by capitalist relations of production.[16] This means that the logic of capitalist economic relations, reinforced by capital's ideological hegemony, dictates the policies the state must follow, which are formulated within a very limited range of options allowed by the capitalist mode of production. Thus, the capitalist class controls the state in capitalist society through both direct and indirect mechanisms that foster the interests of this class.

Far from providing a simple instrumentalist view of the state, Szymanski reveals the full range and complexity of the state's actions in response to the ensuing class struggles in society: "Political outcomes are the result of the relative size, social location, consciousness, degree of organization, and strategies followed by classes and segments of classes in their ongoing struggles."[17] He goes on to point out that "no one class or segment of a class is ever able totally to control all aspects of society."[18] Moreover, while the state

> is normally under the domination of the class that owns and controls the means of production, . . . the ruling class must take into account both the demands and likely responses of other classes when it makes state policy. If it does not it may suffer very serious consequences, including social revolution.[19]

"The degree of relative autonomy of the state bureaucracy from direct capitalist-class domination," writes Szymanski, "can either decrease *or* increase drastically during an economic and social crisis":

> A state that is too directly dominated by the majority bloc of the capitalist class may be unable to handle such a crisis, because the narrow-minded self-interest of this bloc prevents the state it dominates from adopting the policies necessary to save and advance the system. Domination of the state by these groups also tends to discredit the state, which because of such control is obviously not alleviating an economic crisis. The legitimating function of the state thus comes into increasing conflict with direct capitalist-class control.[20]

Providing an empirical path out of the structuralist–instrumentalist problematic, Szymanski argues that some states are dominated principally by direct mechanisms, while others are dominated by indirect mechanisms, and still others are dominated by both.

Commenting on the question of relative autonomy, David Gold, Clarence Y. H. Lo, and Erik Olin Wright make a similar argument when they point out that such autonomy "is not an invariant feature of the capitalist state":

> Particular capitalist states will be more or less autonomous depending upon the degree of internal divisiveness, the contradictions within the various classes and fractions which constitute the power bloc, and upon the intensity of class struggle between the working class and the capitalist class as a whole.[21]

Given the differential political development of some advanced capitalist societies (e.g., France, Italy, Spain, and Greece), where strong Socialist and Communist parties and radical social movements have developed and flourished, it has been difficult for capital to maintain direct, exclusive control of the state apparatus and to yield results always in line with its interests. In these societies, the state has been shaped not only by the various fractions of the capitalist class but also by the representatives of rival opposition forces, including the Socialists and the Communists, contending for state power. This situation has invariably been effected through the presence of opposition forces within the very organs and institutions of the state. As the power and influence of these parties have increased disproportionately vis-à-vis that of the capitalists, a resurgence of the class struggle and struggles for state power have occurred, sometimes leading to the possession of political power by Socialist and Communist forces in key state institutions, such as the parliament or the presidency and cabinet posts within the executive branch, as in Spain, France, Italy, and Greece, as well as elsewhere in Europe at various levels of government in local and national politics.

In contrast, in the United States except possibly during crisis periods (such as the Great Depression of the 1930s) when there has been a resurgence of class politics, the state has been completely dominated and controlled by the capitalist class, now especially by its monopoly fraction. This, coupled with the relative weakness of the U.S. labor movement, has led capital to control the U.S. state directly. This was clearly evident in the invasion of Afghanistan in 2001 and Iraq in 2003, when the major U.S. oil companies became the direct beneficiaries of the spoils of war in the Middle Eastern and Central Asian regions. Given the occurrence of similar events throughout much of the twentieth century, it is not surprising to find that an instrumentalist view of the state has become the predominant mode of state theorizing among Marxists in the United States.

The greater strength and militancy of the organized working-class movement and effective opposition of independent workers' parties and organizations in Europe, on the other hand, have effected the distribution of power among a multitude of political parties and coalition governments. Thus, it is likewise not surprising that a structural-ist theory of the state has emerged to provide an alternative explanation of the nature and dynamics of politics and the state in Europe during this same period.

Thus, the role of direct and indirect mechanisms of capitalist-class rule, as well as the degree of autonomy of the state, has varied considerably among formations dominated by the capitalist mode of production. These variations point to the need for a concrete analysis of states across national boundaries and over extended historical periods.

## Conclusion

The centerpiece of the resurgent Marxist theory of society and the state has been its focus on the nature of class relations, class struggles, and the class character of the state. Situated within the framework of the base–superstructure problematic of historical materialism, Marxist theory has taken center stage in social theorizing and is now experiencing a resurgence among a growing contingent of critical social theorists in addressing the pressing problems of contemporary capitalist society. Therborn and Szymanski were among the pioneers of this resurgence of critical thinking in sociology and the social sciences during the 1980s; others, promoting their views among a new generation of critical social theorists, are now playing a central role in the development of this important trend in social theory in the twenty-first century.

## Notes

1 For Therborn's most important works, see Goran Therborn, *Science, Class and Society* (London: New Left Books, 1976), esp. 317–429; Goran Therborn, *What Does the Ruling Class Do When It Rules?* (London: New Left Books, 1978); and Goran Therborn, *The Ideology of Power and the Power of Ideology* (London: New Left Books, 1980). For some of Szymanski's most important works, see Albert Szymanski, *The Capitalist State and the Politics of Class* (Cambridge, MA: Winthrop, 1978); Albert Szymanski, *The Logic of Imperialism* (New York: Praeger, 1981); and Albert Szymanski, *Class Structure: A Critical Perspective* (New York: Praeger, 1983).

2 Goran Therborn, "Neo-Marxist, Pluralist, Corporatist, Statist Theories and the Welfare State," in *The State in Global Perspective*, ed. A. Kazancigil (Aldershot, UK: Gower and UNESCO, 1986), 205–6.

3 Therborn, *What Does the Ruling Class Do When It Rules?* 35.

4 Therborn, *What Does the Ruling Class Do When It Rules?* 132.

5 Therborn, *What Does the Ruling Class Do When It Rules?* 162.

6 Therborn, *What Does the Ruling Class Do When It Rules?* 165.

7 Therborn, *What Does the Ruling Class Do When It Rules?* 165.

8 Therborn, *What Does the Ruling Class Do When It Rules?* 169.

9 Therborn, *Science, Class and Society*, 400–1.

10 Therborn, *What Does the Ruling Class Do When It Rules?* 181.

11  Therborn, *What Does the Ruling Class Do When It Rules?* 181.
12  Therborn, *What Does the Ruling Class Do When It Rules?* 181.
13  Szymanski, *The Capitalist State and the Politics of Class.*
14  Szymanski, *The Capitalist State and the Politics of Class,* 20–1.
15  Szymanski, *The Capitalist State and the Politics of Class,* 21, 25.
16  Szymanski, *The Capitalist State and the Politics of Class,* 24.
17  Szymanski, *The Capitalist State and the Politics of Class,* 27.
18  Szymanski, *The Capitalist State and the Politics of Class,* 27.
19  Szymanski, *The Capitalist State and the Politics of Class,* 27.
20  Szymanski, *The Capitalist State and the Politics of Class,* 273.
21  David Gold, Clarence Y. H. Lo, and Erik Olin Wright, "Some Recent Developments in Marxist Theories of the Capitalist State," *Monthly Review* 27, nos. 5–6 (1975): 38.

# 28

# FOUCAULT ON THE DIFFUSION OF POWER

*Pinar Kayaalp*

This chapter examines the contribution of Michel Foucault (1926–1984) to the study of social control in its trajectory from the mid-eighteenth century to postmodern society. Foucault's life-long project "to create a history of the different modes by which, in our culture, human beings are made subjects" has deeply influenced postmodern thought.[1] His work developed and substantiated this theme over three distinct periods, each displaying a different intellectual orientation. This chapter concentrates on Foucault's middle period characterized by his reliance on the genealogical method in explaining the historical transformations and manifestations of political power—more specifically, on his contribution to the study of the diffusion of power in its trajectory from the mid-eighteenth century to postmodern society.

## Theoretical and Historical Background

In his early writings, encompassing *The History of Madness* (1961), *The Birth of the Clinic* (1963), and *The Order of Things* (1966), Foucault espoused what he called the "archaeological method." The premise of this orientation was that any system of thought and knowledge (episteme) specific to a field of study was built upon a given power structure, which, operating underneath the consciousness of its subscribers, determined the tenor and breadth of their arguments. An episteme would change as the undergirding power/knowledge relation shifted from one historical era to another, like the epistemes on madness, sickness, or criminal justice did from ancient society to the postmodern world.

In the next decade, Foucault moved beyond the archaeological method. This occurred because, while finding this method useful in analyzing and comparing different epistemes, he found that approach lacking in identifying the causes of their

transformations. In the early 1970s, Foucault developed and adopted the genealogical approach, deriving the insight from Nietzsche's conceptualization of "effective
history," according to which the researcher transposes to the present a problem that
occurred in the past in order to transform the present.[2] This methodological property
allowed Foucault to study the provenience and formation of scientific discourses from
marginal, local, and dissenting historiographies. He gave "the term 'genealogy' to the
union of erudite knowledge and local memories which allows us to establish a historical knowledge of struggles and to make use of this knowledge tactically today."[3] This
methodology pointed to the enormous gap between genealogical knowledge and the
institutionalized one, and the necessity to fill that hiatus. Making extensive use of
genealogical knowledge, Foucault demonstrated in *Discipline and Punish* (1975) how
some fields of "the human sciences," especially economics, psychology, and criminology, "are tied to new forms of power, so that recognizing them as telling *the* truth about
human beings prevents us from seeing them as articulating and supporting forms of
domination."[4] Thus, Foucault made the power/knowledge relation the cornerstone
of his project, remarking: "[P]ower produces knowledge; . . . power and knowledge
directly imply one another; [and] there is no power relation without the correlative
constitution of a field of knowledge, nor any knowledge that does not presuppose and
constitute at the same time power relations."[5]

In his late period, Foucault turned his attention to the historical conditions that
have collectively presided over the formation of the modern individual as the self-
constituting subject, that is, as a creature contingently endowed with a historically
circumscribed complement of powers and potentialities.[6] He advocated a changed way
in which intellectuals should act and intervene in public policy, remarking:

> The work of an intellectual is not to form the political will of others; it is, through
> the analyses he does in his own domains, to bring assumptions and things taken
> for granted again into question, to shake habits, ways of acting and thinking, to
> dispel the familiarity of the accepted, to take the measure of rules and institutions
> and, starting from that re-problematization (where he plays his specific role as
> intellectual) to take part in the formation of a political will (where he has his role
> to play as citizen).[7]

This switch of methodology not only added to Foucault's work on the dimension of
ethics, but also to the reformulation of his line of investigation as one of "problematization," that is, as rendering an object of study.[8]

Foucault spelled out some ethical principles he believed intellectuals ought to adopt
against the dehumanizing dicta imposed by social institutions: (1) withdraw allegiance

from the negative sanctions inflicted on yourself and your cohorts and embrace the positive and multiple; (2) develop action by proliferation and disjunction rather than subdivision and hierarchization; (3) do not think that one has to be harmed personally in order to be militant; (4) do not demand of politics that it restore the "rights" of the individual as philosophy has defined them, for the individual is the product of power and what is needed is to "de-individualize" by means of multiplication and displacement; and (5) do not become enamored of power (and grab it yourself).[9] In Foucault's view, a fitting investigative approach to accommodate the ethical dimension into the examination of the power/knowledge relationship is to cast the relevant discourse as one of problematization; more specifically, to employ archaeology and genealogy as two complementary aspects of a critical-historical ontology of ourselves in such a way that archaeology attends to the *form* of a problematization while genealogy attends to the *formation* of a problematization and to the *transformations* it engenders.[10] Put differently, the new ontology is archaeological in its method and genealogical in its design so that archaeology promotes the study of conceptualizations of the real (as reflected in discursive practices), and genealogy the examination of action on the real (i.e., non-discursive practices) in the cultivation of an ethical attitude to propel human subjects to modify their actions and resist any exercise of power.[11]

Focusing on Foucault's middle period, relying on the genealogical method, we take up in this chapter Foucault's contribution to the study of the diffusion of power and its manifestations at the macro level and the imposition of this power on the individual as a mode of social control. Treating *Discipline and Punish* as the pivot of this orientation, the discussion moves both backward to delineate the macro transformations and manifestations of power/knowledge, and forward to show how this construct has effectively subjugated the individual at the micro level.

## The Nature of Disciplinary Power

Disciplinary power, previously exerted by the sovereign directly upon a particular subject, has permeated into a host of social organizations in the past three centuries. The result has been the insidious and continual alteration of the consciousness of members of society and the direction of their thoughts and actions toward prescribed modes of behavior. In *Discipline and Punish*, Foucault, deploying the genealogical method, shows how disciplinary power transformed in the second half of the eighteenth century into a new power/knowledge construct that thoroughly objectified the fields of criminology, social policy, and psychology, consequently objectifying the individual in society. In the first half of the book, Foucault describes in great detail the manner in which the sovereign exercised the power to punish until the mid-eighteenth century.

Reacting to a given contingency, the sovereign, acting in person or through his or her agents, would generate and enforce a fitting measure upon a subject or a group of subjects whose compliance was deemed necessary. One distinguishing characteristic of this mode of social control was that it occurred between two identifiable parties, one flexing its arm and the other receiving the thrust. The other characteristic was the intermittency of this exchange. Indeed, individuals would lead their lives beyond the control of the sovereign until such time when the ruler construed it necessary to inflict a corrective measure on some of them. In other words, the power to punish manifested itself in a partial and improvised mode, depending on the nature of the contingency under consideration and the breadth of the appropriate measure. As the locus of political power shifted from the sovereign to emerging social organizations—schools, hospitals, factories, armed forces—the power to punish became not only more diffuse, but also more effective, for disciplinary measures that were exerted upon larger and larger segments of subjects in a sustained manner resulted in the production of hosts of "docile bodies," all conforming to the required behavioral parameters.

Foucault explains in *Discipline and Punish* that when a convict was tortured and executed on the scaffold in the days of the direct application of sovereign power, it was because he affronted the ruler's authority. Hence, the public display was but an act of affirmation and restitution of that privilege. The downside of this spectacle from the point of view of the sovereign was that a hero sometimes emerged from the body of the condemned. Protests against public executions, and punishment by torture in general, gained momentum in the second half of the eighteenth century. It was not the *philosophes*, members of the clergy, or intellectuals who rose to arms against these acts; calls for reform came from insiders, particularly magistrates who were seeking more efficient forms of punishment.[12] A sea change soon took place in the criminal justice system during which the scaffold disappeared and prisons proliferated. The result was a subtler and more generalized, hence a more effective, form of punishment. For one thing, the sovereign no longer needed to devise alternative forms of punishment since the same sanction, deprivation of liberty, was uniformly applicable to all human bodies. For another, the length of incarceration could be meted out according to the perceived seriousness of the offense. Finally, this form of punishment would simultaneously allow for the rehabilitation of the criminal along socially desirable parameters. In the end, a political economy of punishment was born.

The rules drawn up in the first half of the nineteenth century for the management of emerging social organizations—prisons, schools, orphanages, poor houses, hospitals—readily displayed a reliance on these characteristics. The code of behavior written for the House of Young Prisoners in Paris, for instance, reveals a seemingly benign timetable regulating inmates' daily activities: prisoners would rise at six (five in summer), work for nine hours, receive instruction for two hours, attend two half-hour prayer sessions, eat two square meals, and have multiple short breaks between these activities.[13] But it would be a gross mistake to construe these rules, and the penal code reform in general, as if the sovereign power was subscribing to more equitable principles of criminal justice. In fact, according to Foucault, the new correctional system was establishing nothing but

> a new "economy" of power to punish, with a more efficient distribution system, so that it should be neither too concentrated at certain privileged points, nor too divided between opposing authorities; so that it should be distributed in homogeneous circuits capable of operating everywhere, in a continuous way, down to the finest grain of the social body. The reform of criminal law must be read as a strategy for the rearrangement of the power to punish, according to modalities that render it more regular, more effective, more constant, and more detailed in its effects; in short, which increase its effects while diminishing its economic cost (that is to say, dissociating it from the system of property, of buying and selling, of corruption in obtaining not only offices, but the decisions themselves) and its political cost (by dissociating it from the arbitrariness of monarchical power). The new juridical theory of penality corresponds in fact to a new "political economy" of the power to punish.[14]

This conclusion thus reveals a new overlying schema, the objectification of the subject, which constitutes the main theme of Foucault's subsequent researches. By classifying certain members of society as inmates and sequestering them not only in prisons, but also in hospitals, poor houses, and barracks, the sovereign is in effect reducing these individuals to mere objects monitored through his or her invisible gaze. As such, the sovereign is shielding him- or herself from the reciprocal gaze that would emanate from the observed, and the concomitant risk of resistance and rebellion. Bolstered by a panoptic arrangement, disciplinary power thus acquires a discipline-forming function in addition to its traditional crime-prevention function.

> There are two images, then, of discipline. At one extreme [is] the discipline-blockade—the enclosed institution, established on the edges of society, turned inwards toward negative functions: arresting evil, breaking communications, suspending time. At the other extreme, with panopticism, is the discipline-mechanism: a functional mechanism that . . . improve[s] the exercise of power by making it lighter, more rapid, more effective, a design of subtle coercion for

a society to come. The movement from . . . a schema of exceptional discipline to one of generalized surveillance, rests on a historical transformation: the gradual extension of the mechanisms of discipline throughout the seventeenth and eighteenth centuries, their spread throughout the whole social body, the formation of what might be called in general the disciplinary society.[15]

## Disciplinary Society

In the days of sovereign power, individuals clearly discerned the locus of disciplinary power and unmistakably directed their resentment toward its occupier. With the emergence of impersonal and invisible forms of punishment, open resentment and the correlative urge to revolt dampened in people's hearts and minds. In fact, as disciplinary power has become pervasive and continual, not only in prisons but all forms of social environments, the individual has been effectively transformed into an object, that is, an artifact fully conforming to the prototype created and perpetuated by the dominant discourse. At the end of this transformational process, individuals have come to believe that the modes of behavior they have espoused are nothing but the manifestations of normal conduct, a demeanor they discern in all their cohorts, one that they consider not only normal, but also natural.

Put differently, the sustained and generalized monitoring of a group of individuals—students, workers, patients, soldiers, convicts—by someone who exercises a supervisory power over these individuals—teacher, foreman, physician, military officer, prison guard—gives rise to knowledge that, characterized by unrelenting monitoring and corrective action, and grounded in the norms deduced from this very activity of surveillance and control, binds the individual to a process of production unilaterally established by the producer.[16] In this turn of events, the individual living in disciplinary society falls prey not only to the "dividing practices" in accordance with which he or she is separated from society with the purpose of normalization, but also to "scientific classification" arising from the human sciences which objectify the person as a speaking subject (philology or linguistic), productive subject (economics or management), or living subject (natural history or psychology).[17] With the establishment and advancement of these disciplines, coupled with the formation of self-knowledge substantiated and promoted by the same modes of inquiry, the human being has altered itself by taking on the character of a rational creature, changing its living conditions and, in fact, its entire life in the process.[18]

In *The Order of Things*, which constitutes an interface between two investigative approaches, archaeological and genealogical, Foucault had already shown how the discourses of language, labor, and life came to be structured within the framework of philology, economics, and biopsychology, respectively; how in this manner these discourses achieved a high degree of internal autonomy and coherence; and how they came to be viewed as dealing with universals of human social life, and, therefore, as progressing logically and refining themselves in the course of history, notwithstanding the fact that they actually changed abruptly at several junctures, displaying a conceptual discontinuity from preceding discourses.[19] In fact, Foucault had explicated even earlier in *The Birth of the Clinic* how the body of the infirm came to be treated as an object in the previous century and a half, substantiating the effect of the process of objectification with the clinic's spatial, temporal, and social compartmentalizations.[20] With the proliferation of diagnostic tests and efficient medical technologies, the gaze of the doctor attained further keenness with the inevitable result that what was previously not obvious suddenly opened itself to the brightness of the new gaze, as though this was a natural consequence of a more highly developed experience on the part of the gazer.[21] As such, the human sciences have served to define and enforce normality by creating subjects who conform to certain standards such as sanity, docility, and accommodation that are not part of their nature.[22]

This theme was established earlier still, in Foucault's first major work, *Madness and Civilization*. In it, Foucault exhibited the changing cultural constructs of madness. In the ancient world, the mad were not banished from the community. Considered mere eccentrics, they shared the public sphere with other unconventional personalities, such as drunkards, gamblers, and libertines. In the Renaissance the concept of madness took on an esoteric veneer and the mad were characterized as people who were affected by some mysterious cosmic force. In the seventeenth century madness came to be perceived as a social problem. This time around, the mad were confined to jails, retreats, and poor houses along with the sick, idle, and promiscuous. Evidently, madness was now deemed a pernicious social problem instead of a harmless oddity. From the nineteenth century onward, madness acquired the status of mental illness while asylums assumed the characteristics of a space of diagnosis and therapeutics as well as a juridical space in which the mentally ill were condemned and locked up.

In summary, Foucault considered institutionalized settings—hospitals, asylums, prisons, schools, churches, barracks—as spaces in which individuals are branded and punished. The branding relegates the individual to the lowly status of invalid, mad, criminal, truant, sinner, or conscript. Accepting this as turn of fate, the branded individual submits to this derogatory identity, losing his or her own in the process. To make objectification complete, individuals in disciplinary society take charge to *willingly* turn themselves into objects. This development seems counterintuitive considering that in the previous two modes of objectification, produced by "dividing practices" and "scientific classification," the individual lacked the power to resist the objectification process initiated by those who were at the locus of social control. How could an individual, evidently bestowed with free will, consciously turn her- or himself into an object? Yet this process obviously takes place in disciplinary society, such as when men learn to recognize themselves as subjects of sexuality.[23]

## Disciplinary Society and the Private Domain

The process of self-formation has a complicated genealogy. It takes place in an individual's own body, soul, thought, and conduct, entailing an internal mechanism of self-assessment and understanding, though always under the tutelage of an external authority figure, be that a confessor, psychoanalyst, or paterfamilias.[24] The social sphere in which this process unfolds most manifestly is gender and sexuality. Foucault takes up these questions in his *The History of Sexuality* and *The Use of Pleasure.*

Sexuality has been repressed in Western society since the beginning of the seventeenth century. Characterized as an unmentionable human trait, hence presumed to be condemned to silence, sexuality actually gave rise to a discursive explosion during that century and the next. In fact, there occurred a steady growth in discourses concerning sex on the part of individuals, coupled with a determination on the part of the agencies of power to hear it spoken about.[25] In Foucault's words, in those days,

> a certain frankness was still common, it would seem. Sexual practices had little need of secrecy; words were said without undue reticence, and things were done without too much concealment; one had a tolerant familiarity with the illicit. Codes regulating the coarse, the obscene, and the indecent were quite lax compared to those of the nineteenth century. It was a time of direct gestures, shameless discourse, and open transgressions, when anatomies were shown and intermingled at will, and knowing children hung about amid the laughter of adults.[26]

This lively discourse all but stopped with the dawn of the Victorian age when sexuality was confined to the household, as the conjugal family took custody of it after having absorbed it into the solemn function of reproduction.[27] As the state law encroached into the realm of human sexuality, silence became the rule. Speaking of sex was confined either to the confessional, where the sinner met with the redeemer, or to the podium, when a figure of authority spoke publicly and in a manner that was not determined by the division between licit and illicit, even if the speaker maintained the distinction for himself (which is what these solemn and preliminary declarations were intended to show) [and spoke] of it as of a thing to be not simply condemned or tolerated but managed, inserted into systems of utility, regulated for the greater good of all, [and] made to function according to an optimum.[28]

Foucault points out that the spectacle in the arena of sexuality is not essentially different today, though the bond that holds together the moral theology of concupiscence and obligation of confession is loosened and diversified with the concurrent emergence of "a whole series of tensions, conflicts, efforts at adjustment, and attempts at retranscription."[29] But the vestiges of the old "regime of power-knowledge-pleasure [still] sustains the discourse on human sexuality in our part of the world," which directs Foucault

to locate the forms of power, the channels it takes, and the discourses it permeates in order to reach the most tenuous and individual modes of behavior, the paths that give it access to the rare or scarcely perceivable forms of desire, how it penetrates and controls everyday pleasure—all this entailing effects that may be those of refusal, blockage, and invalidation, but also incitement and intensification, in short, the "polymorphous techniques of power."[30]

## Conclusion

In the light of discourses fashioned and perpetuated by the seat of authority, normality boils down to the instillation in individual members of society the consciousness that a certain type of behavior is not just something that is expected of them, but something that is natural. In other words, the desired, defined, and ultimately enforced rules of normality are construed by affected individuals not as some extraneous dicta, but as natural manifestations of the actual world around them. Thus, disciplinary power has transcended the status of a mere art of distributing bodies and extracting from them due compliance—it has become a science with the disconcerting objective of creating an efficient machine.[31]

Foucault's arguments with respect to the diffusion of power prompted criticism from many directions. Much of it focused on Foucault's eclectic social perspective, neglect of the examination of the formal power of the state, lack of class analysis in his exploration of the modus operandi of the social organization, and anarchistic political orientation. One postmodern theorist proposed that we forget Foucault altogether because although Foucault understood that power is complex and pluralized, he failed to see that it has become completely abstract, no longer located in any institutions whatsoever, be they macro or micro.[32] Other detractors were more focused in their criticism, such as one who has found Foucault's wide angle of vision concerning society and the human sciences as too dispersed to be used as a passkey for unlocking the discursive practices pertaining to any given community or scientific discipline.[33] Another remarked:

> For Foucault there seems to be no focal point, but rather an endless network of relations . . . so we all live to a time schedule, get up to an alarm, work to a rigid routine, live in the eye of authority, are periodically subject to examination and inspection, [and] no one is entirely free from these new forms of social control; . . . however, subjection to these new forms is not the same thing as being in prison.[34]

This critic finds Foucault's anarchistic political orientation counterproductive because it misses the point that the abolition of power systems would entail the abolition of both moral and scientific categories:

> Foucault does not believe, as earlier anarchists did, that the free human subject is a subject of a certain sort, naturally good, warmly sociable, kind and loving. Rather, there is for [Foucault] no such thing as a free human subject, no natural man or woman. Men and women are always social creations, the products of codes and disciplines. And so Foucault's radical abolitionism, if it is serious, is not anarchist so much as nihilistic. For on his own arguments, either there will be nothing left at all, nothing visibly human; or new codes and disciplines will be produced, and Foucault gives us no reason to expect that these will be any better than the ones we now live with. Nor, for that matter does he gives us any way of knowing what "better" might mean.[35]

Embedded in this line of criticism is the fear that freeing people to do whatever they want will lead to a natural condition in which weaker individuals will be dominated by the stronger, a problem that Foucault neglects to address.[36] Foucault's answer to this criticism was that his call for individuals to exercise their will not to be governed was nothing but a call for expressing the will not to be governed *thus*.[37] He asserted that, in the way that he expressed it, the will not to be governed is a sort of general cultural form, at once a moral and political attitude, a way of thinking, which I would simply call the art of not being governed or again the art of not being governed like that, or at that price.[38]

Notwithstanding such criticisms, Foucault has not faded into obscurity, as he often stated he wished. His vision serves well those who use historiographies of dissent as well as assent to explain power relationships affecting not only the human community in general, but also the body and mind of single individuals. Indeed, more than thirty years after his death, Foucault continues to inspire researchers in all social sciences and humanities, as well as transdisciplinary fields of scholarship.

## Notes

1 Michel Foucault, "The Subject and Power," in *Power*, ed. J. D. Faubion (New York: The New Press, 1994), 326.
2 D. Owen, "Power, Knowledge and Ethics: Foucault," in *The Edinburgh Encyclopedia of Continental Philosophy*, ed. S. Glendinning (Edinburgh: Edinburgh University Press, 1999), 596.
3 Michel Foucault, "Genealogy and Social Criticism," in *The Postmodern Turn: New Perspectives on Social Theory*, ed. S. Seidman (Cambridge: Cambridge University Press, 1994), 42. First published in Michel Foucault, *Power/Knowledge – Selected Interviews and Other Writings 1972–1977* (New York: Pantheon Books, 1980).
4 Owen, "Power, Knowledge and Ethics," 596. Emphasis in the original.
5 Michel Foucault, *Discipline and Punish: The Birth of the Prison* (New York: Vintage Books, 1995a), 27.
6 D. Conway, "Foucault, Michel," in *The Encyclopedia of Philosophy, Supplement*, ed. D. M. Borchert (New York: Simon & Schuster Macmillan, 1996), 201.
7 C. Gordon, "Introduction," in *Power*, xxxiv, referring to Foucault's "Le souci de la verité," in volume IV of D. Defers and F. Ewalt, eds., *Dits et écrits: 1954–1988/Michel Foucault* (Paris: Editions Gallimard, 1994), 676–7.
8 Owen, "Power, Knowledge and Ethics," 599.
9 Michel Foucault, "Preface to Anti-Oedipus," in *Power*, 108–9.
10 Owen, "Power, Knowledge and Ethics," 599. Emphases in the original.
11 Owen, "Power, Knowledge and Ethics," 599, drawing on Michel Foucault, "What is Enlightment?" in *The Foucault Reader*, ed. P. Rabinow (New York: Pantheon Books, 1984), 46.
12 Foucault, *Discipline and Punish*, 81.
13 Foucault, *Discipline and Punish*, 6–7.
14 Foucault, *Discipline and Punish*, 80–1.
15 Foucault, *Discipline and Punish*, 209.
16 Michel Foucault, "Truth and Juridical Forms," in *Power*, 59, 71.
17 P. Rabinow, "Introduction," in *The Foucault Reader*, ed. Rabinow, 8–9.
18 Michel Foucault, "Interview with Michel Foucault," in *Power*, 256.
19 Rabinow, "Introduction," 9.
20 Rabinow, "Introduction," 10.

21  Michel Foucault, *The Birth of the Clinic: An Archaeology of Medical Perception* (New York: Vintage Books, 1995), 195.

22  D. Jones, "The Genealogy of the Urban Schoolteacher," in *Foucault and Education: Discipline and Knowledge*, ed. S. J. Ball (New York: Routledge, 1990), 57.

23  Foucault, "The Subject and Power," 327.

24  Rabinow, "Introduction," 11.

25  Michel Foucault, "The Repressive Hypothesis," in *The Foucault Reader*, ed. Rabinow, 302. Reprinted from Michel Foucault, *The History of Sexuality*, vol. I (London: Allen Lane, 1976).

26  Michel Foucault, "We 'Other Victorians,'" in M. Foucault, *The History of Sexuality*, vol. I (London: Allen Lane, 1976), 292.

27  Foucault, "We 'Other Victorians,'" 292.

28  Foucault, "The Repressive Hypothesis," 307.

29  Foucault, "We 'Other Victorians,'" 299.

30  Foucault, "We 'Other Victorians,'" 299.

31  Foucault, *Discipline and Punish*, 164.

32  Jean Baudrillard, *Forget Foucault* (New York: Semiotext(e), 1987), 59, as cited in Steven Best and Douglas Kellner, *Postmodern Theory, Critical Interrogations* (New York: The Guilford Press, 1991), 123.

33  E. Said, "Michel Foucault as an Intellectual Imagination," in *Michel Foucault (1): Critical Assessments*, ed. B. Smart (New York: Routledge, 1998), 37.

34  M. Walzer, "The Politics of Michel Foucault," in *Foucault: A Critical Reader*, ed. David C. Hoy (Oxford: Basil Blackwell, 1986), 55, 59.

35  Walzer, "Politics of Michel Foucault," 61.

36  David C. Hoy, "Introduction," in *Foucault: A Critical Reader*, 9.

37  Gordon, "Introduction," xxxix, referring to Michel Foucault, "Qu'est-ce que la critique? Critique et Aufklärung," *Bulletin de la Société Française de Philosophie* 84, no. 2 (1990): 35.

38  Gordon, "Introduction," xxxix.

# 29

# HARVEY AND CALLINICOS ON POSTMODERNISM AND ITS CRITIQUE

During the past three decades, contemporary social theory has undergone some important changes resulting from the emergence of various forms of critical discourse. Among these, one finds postmodernist theory. Those opting for this alternative to both mainstream and Marxist approaches to the study of modern capitalist society have introduced into their analysis the theory and practice of *postmodernity*, an era that allegedly characterizes contemporary, postindustrial society.

This chapter presents a critical analysis of postmodernism and postmodernist theory through David Harvey's and Alex Callinicos's piercing critique of this latest fad in contemporary social theory. Harvey and Callinicos confront what they characterize as the myths surrounding this most recent theoretical expression of a group of disaffected intellectuals searching for answers in a period of societal crisis and decline in the late twentieth and early twenty-first centuries. In doing so, they reaffirm the validity of historical materialism as a viable theoretical alternative that has stood the test of time.

## Postmodernism

What is postmodernism, and what does it represent? What are its origins and the fault lines that define the limits of its usefulness in advancing contemporary social theory? And, why has it become so popular among a group of intellectuals at a particular historical conjuncture characterized by epochal decline, reflected in the pessimism of our time? Harvey and Callinicos take up these and other questions surrounding the controversy over postmodernist theory in their books, *The Condition of Postmodernity* and *Against Postmodernism: A Marxist Critique*, respectively, and provide a critical analysis of postmodernism's underlying assumptions and arguments through a theoretical discourse that is at once complex and comprehensible.[1]

"Does postmodernism . . . represent a radical break with modernism, or is it simply a revolt within modernism against a certain form of 'high modernism'?" asks Harvey.

Is postmodernism a style . . . or should we view it strictly as a periodizing concept . . .? Does it have a revolutionary potential by virtue of its opposition to all forms of meta-narratives (including Marxism, Freudianism, and all forms of Enlightenment reason) and its close attention to "other worlds" and to "other voices" that have for too long been silenced (women, gays, blacks, colonized peoples with their own histories)? Or is it simply commercialization and domestication of modernism, and a reduction of the latter's already tarnished aspirations to a *laissez-faire*, "anything goes" market eclecticism? Does it, therefore, undermine or integrate with neo-conservative politics? And do we attach its rise to some radical restructuring of capitalism, the emergence of some "postindustrial" society, view it, even, as the "art of an inflationary era" or as the "cultural logic of late capitalism" (as Newman and Jameson have proposed)?[2]

"Postmodernism," Callinicos points out, "represents the convergence of three distinct cultural trends. . . . Postmodern art, poststructuralist philosophy, and the theory of postindustrial society":

The first involved certain changes in the arts over the previous couple of decades—in particular, the reaction against the International Style in architecture associated with such names as Robert Venturi and James Sterling which first brought the term "Postmodern" into popular usage. . . . Secondly, however, a certain current in philosophy was thought to be giving conceptual expression to the themes explored by contemporary artists. This was a group of French theorists who came in the 1970s to be known in the English-speaking world by the shared label of "poststructuralism"—in particular, Gilles Deleuze, Jacques Derrida and Michel Foucault. . . . But, thirdly, art and philosophy seemed to reflect (somewhat at odds with poststructuralism's anti-realism) changes in the social world. A version of the transformations supposedly undergone by Western societies in the past quarter century was provided by the theory of postindustrial society developed by sociologists such as Daniel Bell and Alain Touraine.[3]

While representing a qualitatively new development in society that appears to be distinct from that characteristic of modernity, postmodernism's adherents nevertheless view it as an outgrowth of modernist thought and practice transformed into new forms of expression and going beyond the original parameters of modernity itself. In fact, as Table 29.1 listing the dichotomies of modernism and postmodernism illustrates, the postmodernist project turns out to be quite the opposite of the modernist mode—a classic dialectical resolution of its original contradictions. Postmodernity, then, arises

*Table 29.1* **Selected Dichotomies of Modernism and Postmodernism**

| *Modernism* | *Postmodernism* |
| --- | --- |
| Romanticism/symbolism | Paraphysics/Dadaism |
| Form (conjunctive, closed) | Antiform (disjunctive, open) |
| Design | Chance |
| Hierarchy | Anarchy |
| Art object/finished work | Process/performance/happening |
| Totalization/synthesis | Deconstruction/antithesis |
| Semantics | Rhetoric |
| Paradigm | Syntagm |
| Root/depth | Rhizome/surface |
| Narrative/grande histoire | Antinarrative/petit histoire |
| Metaphysics | Irony |
| Determinacy | Indeterminacy |

Source: Hassan 1985: 123–4.

out of its modern origins, and in doing so it becomes something quite different. But such a view is not entirely consistent with the thinking of all its proponents, some of whom differ on the nature, magnitude, and historic context of postmodernism's decisive break with modernity.

"For postmodernists," writes Callinicos, "the decisive break is usually with the Enlightenment, with which . . . Modernism tends to be identified."[4] In the economic sphere, however, this break is marked by the shift from industrial production to services and information technology, hence, from the industrial to the postindustrial stage. An argument based largely on Daniel Bell's conception of postindustrial society, this aspect of postmodernist thought identifies a manifestation of late capitalist development as a qualitatively distinct stage of human development that warrants the "postindustrial" or "postmodernist" label. "What runs through all the various—mutually and often internally inconsistent—accounts of Postmodernism," writes Callinicos, "is the idea that recent aesthetic changes (however characterized) are symptomatic of a broader, radical novelty, a sea-change in Western civilization."[5]

"This sea-change," Harvey points out, "is bound up with the emergence of new dominant ways in which we experience space and time."[6] He writes,

While simultaneity in the shifting dimensions of time and space is no proof of necessary or casual connection, strong a priori grounds can be adduced for the proposition that there is some kind of necessary relation between the rise of postmodernist cultural forms, the emergence of more flexible modes of capital accumulation, and a new round of "time-space compression" in the organization of capitalism.[7]

"A little before the postmodern boom got into full swing," Callinicos reminds us, "Daniel Bell noted the widespread 'sense of an ending' among the Western intelligentsia 'symbolized . . . in the widespread use of the word *post* . . . to define, as a combined form, the age into which we are moving'."[8] "Bell illustrated this proliferation of 'posts-'," Callinicos notes,

> by listing the following examples: post-capitalist, post-bourgeois, post-modern, post-civilized, post-collectivist, post-Puritan, post-Protestant, post-Christian, post-literature, post-traditional, post-historical, post-market society, post-organization society, post-economic, post-scarcity, post-welfare, post-liberal, post-industrial.[9]

Although, as Harvey points out, "traditional neo-conservatives, such as Daniel Bell, fear rather than welcome" any affinity to postmodernist thought, as "Bell plainly regrets the collapse of solid bourgeois values, the erosion of the work ethic in the working class, and sees contemporary trends less as a turn towards a vibrant postmodernist future and more as an exhaustion of modernism,"[10] the postmodernists have nevertheless been influenced just as much by Bell's postindustrialism as Jean-François Lyotard's leftwing anti-institutionalism.

Counterposed to Bell's bourgeois critique of postindustrial developments that have engendered "the cultural contradictions of capitalism" that Bell despises, Lyotard provides an alternative view of such developments that welcomes an era when new forms of cultural practice are "supplanting permanent institutions in the professional, emotional, sexual, cultural, family, and international domains, as well as in political affairs."[11]

Despite the divergent political views embodied in the two politically contradictory positions, the convergence of these two positions on the nature of the postindustrial, postmodern condition defines for the postmodernists the cultural parameters of postmodernism in the late twentieth and early twenty-first centuries.

## Critique of Postmodernism

In providing a critique of postmodernism and postmodernist thought, Callinicos and Harvey raise a number of important issues that are central to an understanding of what postmodernism is and what the postmodernist intellectuals propose in their antimodernist project.

In seeing themselves as part of "a willful and rather chaotic movement to overcome all the supposed ills of modernism," Harvey argues, "postmodernists exaggerate when they depict the modern as grossly as they do."[12] He writes that

> postmodernism, with its emphasis upon the ephemerality of *jouissance*, its insistence upon the impenetrability of the other, its concentration on the text rather than the work, its penchant for deconstruction bordering on nihilism, its preference for aesthetics over ethics, takes matters too far. It takes them beyond the point where any coherent politics are left, while that wing of it that seeks a shameless accommodation with the market puts it firmly in the tracks of an entrepreneurial culture that is the hallmark of reactionary neoconservativism.[13]

"Postmodernist philosophers tell us," Harvey continues, "not only to accept but even to revel in the fragmentations and the cacophony of voices through which the dilemmas of the modern world are understood."[14] He says,

> Obsessed with deconstructing and delegitimating every form of argument they encounter, they can end only in condemning their own validity claims to the point where nothing remains of any basis for reasoned action. Postmodernism has us accepting the reifications and partitionings, actually celebrating the activity of masking and cover-up, all the fetishisms of locality, place, or social grouping, while denying that kind of meta-theory which can grasp the political-economic processes (money flows, international divisions of labor, financial markets, and the like) that are becoming ever more universalizing in their depth, intensity, reach and power over daily life.[15]

"Worst of all," Harvey concludes,

> while it opens up a radical prospect by acknowledging the authenticity of other voices, postmodernist thinking immediately shuts off those other voices from access to more universal sources of power by ghettoizing them within an opaque otherness, the specificity of this or that language game. It thereby disempowers those voices (of women, ethnic and racial minorities, colonized peoples, the unemployed, youth, etc.) in a world of lop-sided power relations.[16]

Lending support to Harvey's contentions, Callinicos argues that while postmodernists' rejection of anything associated with the modernist past and their self-defined affinity with the powerless appears to be revolutionary, postmodernism in reality turns its back on social revolution, providing support instead to those longing for individual expression that is anti-institutional and self-centered—a postmodern version of the anarchy of thought that supports an intellectual discourse in a society that lacks an aesthetic identity and logic. The chaos that emerges from all this is what identifies the nature and purpose of eclecticism of the mind, prompting Frank Kermode to call postmodernism "another of those period descriptions that help you to take a view of the past suitable to whatever it is you want to do."[17]

"Postmodernity," Callinicos points out, "is merely a theoretical construct, of interest primarily as a symptom of the current mood of the Western intelligentsia."[18] Its roots lie in the pessimism prevalent in a period of decline and decay in centers of world capitalism in the closing decades of the twentieth century, a condition reinforced by the perceived failure of Socialist revolution in the advanced capitalist countries.

> The discourse of postmodernism is best seen as the product of a socially mobile intelligentsia in a climate dominated by the retreat of the Western labor movement and the "overconsumptionist" dynamic of capitalism in the Reagan-Thatcher era. From this perspective the term "postmodern" would seem to be a floating signifier by means of which this intelligentsia has sought to articulate its political disillusionment and its aspiration to a consumption-oriented lifestyle. The difficulties involved in identifying a referent for this term are therefore beside the point, since talk about postmodernism turns out to be less about the world than the expression of a particular generation's sense of an ending.[19]

"The political odyssey of the 1968 generation," Callinicos writes, "is, in my view, crucial to the widespread acceptance of the idea of a postmodern epoch in the 1980s."

> This was the decade when those radicalized in the 1960s and early 1970s began to enter middle age. Usually they did so with all hope of socialist revolution gone—indeed, often having ceased to believe in the desirability of any such revolution. Most of them had by then come to occupy some sort of professional, managerial or administrative position, to have become members of the new middle class, at a time when the overconsumptionist dynamic of Western capitalism offered this class rising living standards (a benefit often denied the rest of the workforce: hourly real wages in the US fell by 8.7 percent between 1973 and 1986). This conjuncture—the prosperity of the Western new middle class combined with the political disillusionment of many of its most articulate members—provides the context to the proliferating talk of postmodernism.[20]

Postmodernity, then, is a reaction to the reality of late twentieth-century capitalism as it is translated into a mythical future to cope with the material contradictions of modernity that the Western intelligentsia now confronts. And in this way, the post-modernist discourse claims to transcend the boundaries of what has until now been real and to venture into what is claimed to be in the making in the postmodernist journey that we are purported to have begun and are destined to travel.

Critics of postmodernism, however, disagree with such claims of the occurrence of a great sociocultural transformation. For Frederic Jameson, for example, postmodern-ism and all that it embodies is a product of the cultural logic of late capitalism, and the accompanying changes that it has effected in society do not constitute a social or cultural transformation of epochal proportions.[21] "If there has been some kind of transformation in the political economy of late-twentieth-century capitalism," writes David Harvey, "then it behooves us to establish how deep and fundamental the change might be."[22]

> Signs and tokens of radical changes in labor processes, in consumer habits, in geographical and geopolitical configurations, in state powers and practices, and the like, abound. Yet we still live, in the West, in a society where production for profit remains the basic organizing principle of economic life. We need some way, therefore, to represent all the shifting and churning that has gone on since the first major post-war recession of 1973, which does not lose sight of the fact that the basic rules of a capitalist mode of production continue to operate as invariant shaping forces in historical-geographical development.[23]

Thus, "there is much more continuity than difference between the broad history of modernism and the movement called postmodernism." Harvey concludes,

> It seems more sensible to me to see the latter as a particular kind of crisis within the former, one that emphasizes the fragmentary, the ephemeral, and the chaotic side of Baudelaire's formulation (that side which Marx so admirably dissects as integral to the capitalist mode of production) while expressing a deep skepticism as to any particular prescriptions as to how the eternal and immutable should be conceived of, represented, or expressed.[24]

Hence,

> Whether or not the new systems of production and marketing, characterized by more flexible labor processes and markets, of geographical mobility and rapid

shifts in consumption practices, warrant the title of a new regime of accumulation, and whether the revival of entrepreneurialism and of neo-conservatism, coupled with the cultural turn to postmodernism, warrant the title of a new mode of regulation, is by no means clear. There is always a danger of confusing the transitory and the ephemeral with more fundamental transformations in political-economic life.[25]

Callinicos likewise criticizes postmodernist claims of a qualitative social transformation by arguing that the sociocultural changes the postmodernists allude to do not represent the arrival of a "new age"; rather, the changes that we are now witnessing are part of the process of modern capitalist development over the past two centuries. He writes,

> I do not believe that we live in "New Times," in a "postindustrial and postmodern age" fundamentally different from the capitalist mode of production globally dominant for the past two centuries. I deny the main theses of poststructuralism, which seem to me in substance false. I doubt very much that Postmodern art represents a qualitative break from the Modernism of the early twentieth century. Moreover, much of what is written in support of the idea that we live in a postmodern epoch seems to me of small caliber intellectually, usually superficial, often ignorant, sometimes incoherent.[26]

"Whatever else we do with the concept," concludes Harvey, "we should not read postmodernism as some autonomous artistic current. Its rootedness in daily life is one of its most patently transparent features."[27]

This, in essence, is the critique of postmodernism and postmodernist thought that, as both Callinicos and Harvey have shown, is part of a larger critique of the most recent contradictions of capitalism in the late twentieth and early twenty-first centuries.

### Return to Historical Materialism?

Callinicos and Harvey counter the postmodernist myth of a postindustrial society by stressing the necessity of returning to an analysis of society and social relations provided by historical materialism.

Highlighting the superiority of historical materialism over postmodernist modes of thought, "Marx's greater optimism about the scope for human emancipation," writes Callinicos, "rested on his deeper historical understanding of the transitory nature of the social structures that have shaped our existence for the past few millennia."[28] In this context, Callinicos states, "perhaps we should think of modernity as the kind of civilization formed by the development and global dominance of the capitalist mode of production."[29] And, as an extension, one could view postmodernity as a continuation of the capitalist mode of production and its contradictions in the late twentieth and early twenty-first centuries.

Historical materialism, Harvey reminds us,

> is an open-ended and dialectical mode of enquiry rather than a closed and fixed body of understandings. Meta-theory is not a statement of total truth but an attempt to come to terms with the historical and geographical truths that characterize capitalism both in general as well as in its present phase.[30]

Clearly, such a reasoning would force us to confront the dialectical logic of capitalism's inherent class contradictions, which, according to this logic, could be resolved only by a working-class revolution.

Callinicos's and Harvey's perceptive analysis of postmodernism and postmodernist thought shows the invaluable contribution of historical materialism as the only viable approach that helps us understand the nature and dynamics of the modern world and its postmodern variants through an analysis of society that probes deeply into the human condition, without resorting to the intellectual detours and confusion invoked by contemporary postmodernist discourse that has become fashionable among the intellectual elite.

## Notes

1 See David Harvey, *The Condition of Postmodernity* (Cambridge, MA: Basil Blackwell, 1990); and Alex Callinicos, *Against Postmodernism: A Marxist Critique* (New York: St. Martin's Press, 1989).
2 Harvey, *The Condition of Postmodernity*, 42.
3 Callinicos, *Against Postmodernism*, 2–3.
4 Callinicos, *Against Postmodernism*, 25.
5 Callinicos, *Against Postmodernism*, 25.
6 Harvey, *The Condition of Postmodernity*, vii.
7 Harvey, *The Condition of Postmodernity*, vii.
8 Callinicos, *Against Postmodernism*, 25.
9 Callinicos, *Against Postmodernism*, 25.
10 Harvey, *The Condition of Postmodernity*, 113.
11 Jean-Francois Lyotard, *The Postmodern Condition* (Minneapolis, MN: University of Minnesota Press, 1984), 66.
12 Harvey, *The Condition of Postmodernity*, 115.
13 Harvey, *The Condition of Postmodernity*, 116.
14 Harvey, *The Condition of Postmodernity*, 116.

15  Harvey, *The Condition of Postmodernity*, 116–17.

16  Harvey, *The Condition of Postmodernity*, 117.

17  Frank Kermode, *History and Value* (Oxford: Clarendon Press, 1988), 132.

18  Callinicos, *Against Postmodernism*, 9.

19  Alex Callinicos, "Reactionary Postmodernism?" in *Postmodernism and Social Theory*, ed. R. Boyne and A. Rattansi (New York: St. Martin's Press, 1990), 168.

20  Callinicos, *Against Postmodernism*, 168.

21  Frederic Jameson, "Postmodernism, or the Cultural Logic of Late Capitalism,' *New Left Review* 146 (1984): 53–92.

22  Harvey, *The Condition of Postmodernity*, 121.

23  Harvey, *The Condition of Postmodernity*, 121.

24  Harvey, *The Condition of Postmodernity*, 116.

25  Harvey, *The Condition of Postmodernity*, 124.

26  Callinicos, *Against Postmodernism*, 4–5.

27  Harvey, *The Condition of Postmodernity*, 63.

28  Callinicos, *Against Postmodernism*, 172–3.

29  Callinicos, *Against Postmodernism*, 36.

30  Harvey, *The Condition of Postmodernity*, 355.

# 30

# SOCIAL MOVEMENTS AND TRANSFORMATION

Social movements have been struggling against repressive states that advance the interests of dominant classes throughout history. Over time, the great majority of the people have organized and become empowered to bring about social transformations across the globe. This chapter provides an analysis of the conditions that lead to the emergence and development of social movements struggling to bring about transformation of society. It examines the origins, nature, dynamics, and challenges of social movements as they struggle to transform the prevailing dominant social, economic, and political institutions. After a brief historical background and an analysis of Howard J. Sherman and James Wood's and Albert J. Szymanski's theoretical insights on conditions leading to the development of social movements, the chapter explores the dynamics of movement organization and mobilization with examples of concrete cases of social movements that have succeeded in transforming societies in the twentieth and early twenty-first centuries.

Recent mobilization, protests, and political responses by various social movements are leading to protracted struggles that threaten entrenched dominant class interests that have held on to power for decades. The significance of the success of the Arab Spring of 2011 is more for its inspirational value to social movements across the globe than the simple replacement of authoritarian regimes to secure civilian, multi-party rule. It is for this reason that the rebellions across North Africa and the Middle East have had a ripple effect in triggering similar uprisings in other countries when millions across the world have shed their fears and found their way to express their will through collective political action.

## Historical Background

Many diverse social movements have emerged and developed in different societies throughout history. Some of these movements have developed spontaneously and without any prior preparation in terms of organization, strategy, and tactics, such as slave rebellions in Ancient Rome and peasant revolts in medieval Germany. Uprisings have occurred in old despotic empires, just as they have under slavery, feudalism, and other oppressive systems, where states ruled by despots, slave masters, and landlords have often repressed attempts to alter the existing order to prevent the people from coming to power. But they have not always succeeded in keeping the people down. There have been instances when the oppressed have risen and put up a determined fight, and occasionally won, through a series of rebellions and revolutions that have brought about social transformations across the globe.[1]

In the transition from feudalism to capitalism in Europe and elsewhere, a variety of social movements have come to challenge existing states and have transformed them to serve the interests of the victorious classes that have succeeded in taking state power. Among these we find the great bourgeois revolutions of the eighteenth and nineteenth centuries, such as the French Revolution, when the nascent national bourgeoisies of Europe rose up in arms to smash the old (feudal) system and to rule over society by unfurling the banner of "freedom" across the continent for free trade, investment, and economic activity that later facilitated the accumulation of private capital through the exploitation of wage-labor.[2] This victory assured the domination of moneyed wealth that came to assume state power to advance its own interests against that of the landlords. Thus, the rule of capital over the state was established in Europe, followed by a similar development in North America, where slavery and the rule of the slave-owners were replaced by that of capital after the victory of the latter in the Civil War that allowed them the full control of the state in the United States in the late nineteenth century.[3]

The domination of society by the new ruling classes in Europe and North America, which facilitated the development of capitalism in these regions of the world, thus led to the development of a labor movement through the formation of trade unions that came to organize workers to wage a determined struggle against the new oppressive system.[4]

Many of the benefits that organized labor has secured for itself over the past century have been the result of such struggles. While the balance of class forces under capitalism in Europe and the United States came close to (but did not quite result in) workers taking state power to transform society during the Great Depression in the early twentieth century, social movements in other parts of the world did succeed in effecting change that led to the construction of new societies across the globe.[5]

Some of these movements succeeded in taking state power despite the unrelenting onslaught by the dominant forces to crush them, while others failed, facing the counter-revolutionary machinations of foreign and domestic subversion. Ironically, a few decades later, a number of these failed movements were able to regroup and retake state power and survive attempts to derail their efforts to rebuild their societies (as in Chile, Argentina, Nicaragua, and El Salvador). Others, such as Venezuela, Bolivia, Ecuador, Uruguay, and several other Latin American countries, as well as Brazil, led by grassroots people's movements, have taken a critical path and turned to the left, adopting policies that are against neoliberalism and in favor of the interests of the great majority of the people in these countries. We will have more to say about some of these movements later in this chapter, but first we must examine the factors contributing to the formation and success of social movements in transforming contemporary capitalist society.

## Factors Leading to the Emergence of Social Movements

Much has been written by social theorists on the factors contributing to the emergence and development of social movements. The conditions leading to the rise of social movements that challenge the established order are both objective and subjective. The objective conditions include the prevailing class structure of society (the prevalence of dominant and oppressed classes), the political structure and the nature of the state, and existing social and economic conditions. The subjective conditions include the level of class consciousness among the oppressed classes; the emergence of leading figures, organizations, and political parties of the oppressed; the response of the government and the dominant classes; and the balance of class forces and mass mobilization. In considering the opposing classes engaged in struggle, it is important to know the nature and composition of the dominant class, including its various fractions, who (i.e., which fraction of the dominant class) the state represents, who the oppressed classes are that want to replace the established order, and what the class alliances are in the social movement in question.

Howard J. Sherman and James Wood provide a list that specifies the conditions that are required before a social movement can emerge:[6]

1   *Social structural conditions* must lead to certain stresses and strains between classes or other groups in society. This can occur as a result of economic and political crises in society, or as an outcome of general decline and decay of society and societal institutions that affect various classes, leading to conflict between them.
2   Objective economic, political, or social *deprivation*, resulting from the above structural conditions, must occur. This means that the unfolding crises in society are affecting an important segment of society in a negative way, leading to a decline in their standard of living.

3   These objective deprivations must lead to *conscious feelings of deprivation*, which will crystallize into an ideology. Here, the increasing awareness of one's condition conveyed by the gravity of the situation transformed into consciousness leads to the formation of an ideology that shows the way out of the crisis.

4   This ideology must lead to the *organization* and *mobilization* of the discontented group to become a powerful political force that can bring about change. As such, the mobilization necessary to take political action becomes a critical component of the struggle being waged to transform society.

5   The structural conditions must also include *weakened social control* by the dominant class. Here, the depth of the societal crisis weakens the ability and the will of those in power to effectively control society.

6   Given these five conditions, many kinds of *precipitating events* can lead to the emergence of a social movement. Such events can trigger mass protests and demonstrations that quickly translate into action and serve as a catalyst to bring about change.[7]

Sherman and Wood go on to argue that the above conditions for social movements to develop flow from the prevailing social structure: society is built on a certain economic base on which arises social and political institutions—such as the state—as well as ideologies, and that these institutions and ideologies play a vital role in supporting and justifying the present societal arrangements.[8]

Albert J. Szymanski in his book *The Capitalist State and the Politics of Class*[9] provides additional insight into this process and argues that the material conditions necessary for the emergence of social movements in contemporary society must include the following:

1   *Felt oppression*: The economic oppression and political repression of large segments of society is increasingly felt to be unnecessary and intolerable (as the possibilities of living differently become more apparent).

2   *Decline of the dominant class's ideological hegemony*: The ideological hegemony of the dominant class spontaneously breaks down, as the masses become increasingly bitter and disillusioned with their present existence. The dominant class itself becomes cynical about its ability and right to rule. It increasingly resorts to manipulation and repression to preserve its rule. Internally, it becomes increasingly divided and demoralized, and hence incapable of adequately dealing with the social movements.

3   *The failure of non-revolutionary solutions to a social crisis:* The various alternative solutions being offered as solutions to the oppression of the masses (such as nationalism, fascism, liberal reformism, social democracy, etc.) lose credibility among the oppressed as these solutions reveal themselves to be incapable of actually relieving the oppression of the people.

4   *Decline of the dominant class's ability to solve social, economic, and political crises and counter the growth of social movements:* The ability of the dominant class to handle both a social crisis and a rising social movement is a product of its internal cohesion, the intensity of its belief in the legitimacy of its rule, and its willingness to use force when necessary. When a ruling class cannot unify around and implement a rational program to handle the crisis or the social movement, it is likely to be driven from power.[10]

5   *Efficient organization and adoption of scientific strategy and theory by social movements:* In order to succeed, social movements create organizations that can mobilize the masses into a common united front, provide them with a realistic analysis of the causes of their oppression, a proposal about the historical alternatives, and a program to realize an alternative—that is, an organizational form, a strategy, and a set of tactics to bring about social change and transformation.[11]

These five important conditions set the stage for the emergence and development of social movements in contemporary capitalist society and facilitate the process that leads to social transformation, according to Szymanski.[12]

## Social Movements in the Twentieth and Early Twenty-First Centuries

The twentieth century saw the emergence and development of numerous social movements, and many of these movements turned into full-blown social revolutions. The Mexican Revolution of 1910, as the first great peasant revolution of the twentieth century, had a major impact on all other subsequent rebellions and revolutions, as the peasants with the support of labor rose up to rid themselves of the feudal oligarchy that enslaved and oppressed them. The Russian Revolution of 1917—the first workers' revolution of the twentieth century—was not far behind, while Europe itself was embroiled in revolutionary fervor following the First World War. Whereas movements on the left came close to toppling some of the major capitalist states (e.g., Germany), the ruling classes were quick to respond with their own fascist regimes in Italy, Germany, and Spain, where civil wars across the continent divided states into rival forces that fought to impose their rule while crushing their enemies. This momentum of uprisings in various countries continued during the Great Depression and its aftermath, when dominant classes everywhere were challenged through the Second World War and in the postwar period to the century's end—which included the Chinese, Vietnamese, Cuban, Nicaraguan, and Iranian revolutions, to name the most prominent.[13]

The emergence of the people's movements during the 1960s—when the civil rights, women's, antiwar, peace, student, environmental, and other related progressive movements coalesced—led to the many gains that these movements were able to secure through collective political action. The lull of the 1970s and 1980s reversed these trends, and a period of resignation set in under the right-wing, conservative forces in power led by Reaganism in the United States and Thatcherism in the United Kingdom, as well as right-wing military and civilian dictatorships that came to power elsewhere during this period (e.g., in Chile and Argentina in the mid-1970s; in Egypt, Iran, Turkey, the Philippines, and others in the late 1970s or early 1980s; and across Eastern Europe at the end of the 1980s, when anti-communist counterrevolutions in Hungary, Poland, the Czech Republic, East Germany, Romania, Bulgaria, and later in the Soviet Union in the early 1990s shifted power away from communism and toward the capitalist West), which seemed to bring an end to the radical social movements of the previous periods. But, merely three years after the collapse of the Soviet Union in 1991, the first "postmodern rebellion"[14] erupted in Chiapas, in the hinterland of Mexico, led by the Zapatista National Liberation Army and its leader Subcommandante Marcos, in response to the signing of the North American Free Trade Agreement (NAFTA), which they argued would devastate the small impoverished peasantry.[15] This unexpected people's rebellion signaled the rise of the first organized mass struggle against neoliberal globalization in Latin America, across the border from the United States. This was followed by a series of protests and demonstrations against neoliberal globalization that had by then come to dominate the policies and practices of many states in Latin America and around the world.[16] Inspired by these movements struggling against neoliberal capitalist globalization, social movements across the global south took the lead to confront global capital in every corner of the world.[17]

The World Social Forum (WSF) and other similar organizations led efforts to build global solidarity focused on issues related to the effects of neoliberal globalization on a world scale. The first meeting of the WSF took place in 2001 in Porto Alegre, Brazil, with some 15,000 participants from 117 countries; by the 2005 meetings of the WSF, there were 155,000 participants from 135 countries. Since then, the WSF has met at various venues each year and engaged in movement activities that involve tens of thousands of activists at hundreds of grassroots organizations that are part of a global political network operating across the world.[18]

People's movements around the world—from Seattle to Prague, Quebec City, Genoa, Barcelona, Washington, DC, and other cities around the globe—have gone into action to protest against neoliberal globalization to counter the economic domination of the world by a handful of transnational corporations and their supportive institutions—above all, the political and military machinery of their respective states.[19] These protests, which were quite successful in disrupting the World Trade Organization (WTO) meetings in Seattle in 1999, and derailing corporate efforts to impose their policies on the people, reached new heights when over 15 million people across the globe protested against U.S. intervention in Iraq in 2003.

The global economic crisis of 2008–2009, which entered its seventh year in 2014, has devastated the economies and societies of many countries across the world, especially those most severely affected by the sovereign debt crisis in Europe (Greece, Spain, Portugal, Ireland, and Italy). And this has led to a crisis of the Euro-zone, affecting the very stability of the European Union (EU) itself. The deepening recession in the EU and the depression in Greece, Spain, and other countries in Europe's periphery have led to the mobilization of millions of working people who are fighting back against the austerity measures that are being imposed on them. And the expanding mass protests and struggles of working people in these countries are galvanizing the popular social movements to wage battle against the state—a development that has immense political implications for the situation in Europe.[20]

Elsewhere across the globe, most notably in North Africa and the Middle East, the people have been fighting back and are determined to take back their countries from the dominant classes that have used despots to maintain their power and to keep the people in check. The Arab Spring of 2011 has ushered in a period of mass rebellion and revolution across this region: in Tunisia, Egypt, Yemen, Bahrain, Libya, and Syria, the people have risen up and toppled, or are in the process of toppling, regimes and rulers that were considered untouchable only a few years before.[21] This is an unprecedented development in the history of the Middle East and will have a great impact on many other regions of the world in coming years.

In North America, the anti-WTO and anti-corporate globalization demonstrations in Seattle in 1999 and Toronto in 2010 became the training grounds for the Occupy Wall Street movement of 2011, which mobilized hundreds of thousands of people across twenty states and many cities throughout the United States and in eighty countries around the world.[22] The biggest and most vocal protest movement of recent times, the Occupy Wall Street movement was no doubt inspired by the Arab Spring and the people's struggles across the globe and became a symbol of the struggle against the big banks, corporations, and the dominant class (the top 1 percent of the population) who made billions of dollars in profits, while a large segment of the 99 percent has struggled to survive in the midst of an economic crisis that has devastated the lives of millions of people across the globe. Clearly, the millionaires and billionaires have seen their wealth and income grow and expand during these depression-ridden times, while millions of working people have lost their jobs, been foreclosed and thrown out of their homes, are without healthcare, and are in desperate condition.[23] It is this dire situation in the United States and elsewhere that has finally forced people to the streets to fight back and reclaim their communities, their government, and their nation.

As social movements emerge, develop, and expand, the necessity for organized collective political action to succeed becomes more and more evident. And as the material conditions of life under the present economic, political, and social system deteriorate and the situation becomes unbearable, more and more people are bound to come together to express their frustration and anger to force the state to meet their demands—demands that the state cannot meet as long as it remains dominated and controlled by powerful class forces that benefit from their exploitation and oppression. Therein one faces both the problem *and* the solution to the crisis of contemporary capitalist society and the state: the economic crisis that has affected millions of working people in the United States and the rest of the world cannot be resolved without a thorough transformation of our societies. And this transformation requires the full participation of people who must gain control of their government so that it can become a truly democratic people's government—a "government of the people, by the people, for the people".[24]

## Notes

1  Kenneth Neill Cameron, *Humanity and Society: A World History* (New York: Monthly Review Press, 1977).
2  Rodney Hilton, *The Transition from Feudalism to Capitalism* (London: New Left Books, 1976).
3  Herbert Aptheker, *The Unfolding Drama: Studies in U.S. History* (New York: International Publishers, 1978). See also Charles Beard and Mary Beard, *The Rise of American Civilization* (New York: Macmillan, 1930).
4  Richard Boyer and Herbert Morais, *Labor's Untold Story*, 3rd ed. (New York: United Electrical, Radio, and Machine Workers of America, 1980).
5  These include the numerous revolutions in the periphery of the global capitalist system throughout the course of the twentieth century (such as Russia, China, Cuba, and Nicaragua, to name a few). See Jack Goldstone, *Revolutions: Theoretical, Comparative, and Historical Studies*, 3rd ed. (New York: Cengage, 2002); Stephen K. Sanderson, *Revolutions: A Worldwide Introduction to Social and Political Contention*, 2nd ed. (Boulder, CO: Paradigm Publishers, 2010); and James Defronzo, *Revolutions and Revolutionary Movements*, 4th ed. (Boulder, CO: Westview Press, 2011).
6  Howard Sherman and James Wood, *Sociology* (New York: Harper Collins, 1989), chap. 18.
7  Sherman and Wood, *Sociology*, chap. 18.

8  Sherman and Wood, *Sociology*, chap. 18.

9  Albert Szymanski, *The Capitalist State and the Politics of Class* (Cambridge, MA: Winthrop, 1978), 293–318.

10 This could occur because of a loss at war, the disaffection of many upper-class youth and their rejection of upper-class traditions, widespread corruption, encroaching decadence and loss of will, or demoralizing internal antagonisms that cannot be contained by a strong sense of class solidarity.

11 Szymanski, *The Capitalist State and the Politics of Class*, 293–318.

12 Szymanski, *The Capitalist State and the Politics of Class*, 294.

13 Goldstone, *Revolutions: Theoretical, Comparative, and Historical Studies*; Sanderson, *Revolutions: A Worldwide Introduction to Social and Political Contention*; and Defronzo, *Revolutions and Revolutionary Movements*.

14 R. Burbach, "Roots of the Postmodern Rebellion in Chiapas," *New Left Review* 1, no. 205 (1994).

15 Neil Harvey, *The Chiapas Rebellion: The Struggle for Land and Democracy* (Durham, NC: Duke University Press, 1998).

16 James Petras and Henry Veltmeyer, *Social Movements in Latin America* (New York: Palgrave-Macmillan, 2011).

17 Francois Polet, ed., *The State of Resistance: Popular Struggles in the Global South* (London: Zed Books, 2007); Valentine Moghadam, *Globalization and Social Movements* (Lanham, MD: Rowman and Littlefield, 2009).

18 See Jackie Smith et al., *Global Democracy and the World Social Forums* (Boulder, CO: Paradigm, 2008), xi–xii, 3–4; and Moghadam, *Globalization and Social Movements*, 106.

19 Martin Orr, "The Struggle Against Capitalist Globalization: The Worldwide Protests Against the WTO," in *Globalization and Change: The Transformation of Global Capitalism*, ed. Berch Berberoglu (Lanham, MD: Lexington Books, 2005). See also Jackie Smith, "Globalizing Resistance: The Battle of Seattle and the Future of Social Movements," in *Globalizing Resistance: Transnational Dimensions of Social Movements*, ed. Jackie Smith and H. Johnston (Lanham, MD: Rowman & Littlefield, 2002).

20 Mike-Frank Epitropoulos, "The Global Capitalist Crisis and the European Union, with Focus on Greece," in *Beyond the Global Capitalist Crisis: The World Economy in Transition*, ed. Berch Berberoglu (Farnham, UK: Ashgate Publishing, 2012), 83–101.

21 Mark L. Haas and David W. Lesch, eds., *The Arab Spring: Change and Resistance in the Middle East* (Boulder, CO: Westview Press, 2012). See also James Petras and Henry Veltmeyer, *Beyond Neoliberalism: A World to Win* (Farnham, UK: Ashgate, 2011), 175–97.

22 Todd Gitlin, *Occupy Nation: The Roots, the Spirit, and the Promise of Occupy Wall Street* (New York: It Books, HarperCollins, 2012).

23 Howard Sherman, *The Roller Coaster Economy: Financial Crisis, Great Recession, and the Public Option* (Armonk, NY: M. E. Sharpe, 2010).

24 From President Abraham Lincoln's "Gettysburg Address" during the U.S. Civil War, November 24, 1863.

# CONCLUSION

Social theory is the foundation for the critical study of society. Classical and contemporary social theories have played a central role in advancing our understanding of society and social structure. The varieties of social theory discussed in this book represent a sampling of the rich heritage of diverse perspectives in sociology and related disciplines. They provide us with a multitude of explanations on different aspects of social life, encompassing the economy, society, and polity. While the traditions of classical social theory inform contemporary theorizing in sociology, thus cultivating the contributions of the great social thinkers of the past century and a half, modern social theorists of the late twentieth and early twenty-first centuries have made their own unique contribution to the study of society, providing answers to the burning questions of our time from a variety of diverse theoretical perspectives.

This book has provided a glimpse of classical and contemporary social theory by highlighting the views of a variety of social theorists who have attempted to tackle the central questions of our time, questions that define the human condition in all its complexities. Theorists with differing views on human nature, the nature of society and social structure, the role of the individual and social institutions, as well as other dimensions of social, economic, and political life that define the totality of social relations and the social order, have made eloquent arguments in favor of their positions on these questions, which were critically examined throughout this book.

Much of the theoretical discourse among the classical social theorists of the late nineteenth and early twentieth centuries were in reaction to the arguments advanced by Karl Marx on a variety of questions concerning society. Emile Durkheim, Max Weber, Vilfredo Pareto, Gaetano Mosca, George Herbert Mead, Sigmund Freud, Thorstein Veblen, Antonio Gramsci, and a host of other social theorists of this period developed their theories as an extension of, or in direct opposition to, the ideas expounded by Marx, who is viewed by many as the greatest social theorist of the nineteenth century. Through a brilliant transformation of the Hegelian dialectic and a dynamic reconceptualization of classical materialism, Marx went on to develop a materialist conception of history and explained it dialectically. Going a step further, he insisted that "the philosophers have only *interpreted* the world, in various ways; the point, however, is to *change* it." Thus, dialectical and historical materialism, committed to a scientific analysis of society and its transformation, became the hallmark of the Marxist approach, which has established the broader framework of discussion and debate in social theory for more than a century.

The ongoing controversies in sociology and the other social sciences on the nature of contemporary society, economy, and polity are an extension of these earlier debates and have yielded a variety of diverse theoretical approaches, including Parsonian, Millsian, Althusserian, neo-Weberian, neo-Marxist, feminist, and postmodernist formulations. Herein lies the importance of classical and contemporary social theory, which has contributed in different ways to the totality of the knowledge we have come to obtain about society, a knowledge that is a direct product of the constant subjection of theory to the test of social reality.

The constant interaction of this continuously expanding theoretical knowledge with the changing conditions of social reality (i.e., between theory and practice) in the end informs our conception of different aspects of life in contemporary capitalist society, a process that highlights the importance of social theory as a tool for critical analysis to sort out the complex phenomena that define the nature and scope of human relations in modern society.

# BIBLIOGRAPHY

Abrahamsson, Bengt. "Homans on Exchange." *American Journal of Sociology* 76, no. 2 (1970).

Addams, Jane. *Twenty Years at Hull-House*. New York: Macmillan, 1910.

—— "Tolstoy and Gandhi." *Christian Century* 48, no. 47 (1931).

Addams, Jane, Emily G. Balch, and Alice Hamilton. *Women at The Hague: The International Peace Congress of 1915*. Amherst, NY: Humanity Books, 2003.

Adorno, Theodor. *The Stars Down to Earth*. New York: Routledge, 1994.

Adorno, Theodor, Else Frenkel-Brunswik, Dan Levinson, and Nevitt Sanford. *The Authoritarian Personality*. New York: Harper and Row, 1950.

Alexander, Jeffrey C. *Fin de Siècle Social Theory*. London: Verso, 1995.

Alford, C. Fred. *Melanie Klein and Critical Social Theory*. New Haven, CT: Yale University Press, 1989.

Alliance Against Women's Oppression (AAWO). *Poverty: Not for Women Only: A Critique of the Feminization of Poverty*. AAWO Discussion Paper No. 3, September, 1983.

Althusser, Louis. *For Marx*. London: Penguin, 1969.

—— "Ideology and Ideological State Apparatuses." In *Lenin and Philosophy and Other Essays*, edited by Louis Althusser, 127–86. London: New Left Books, 1971.

—— *Lenin and Philosophy and Other Essays*. New York: Monthly Review Press, 1971.

—— *Essays in Self-Criticism*. London: New Left Books, 1976.

Althusser, Louis, and Etienne Balibar. *Reading Capital*. London: New Left Books, 1970.

Amin, Samir. *Accumulation on a World Scale*. 2 vols. New York: Monthly Review Press, 1974.

—— *Unequal Development: An Essay on the Social Formations of Peripheral Capitalism*. New York: Monthly Review Press, 1977.

—— *Capitalism in the Age of Globalization*. London: Zed Books, 1997.

Antonio, Robert. *Marx & Modernity*. Hoboken, NJ: Wiley-Blackwell, 2002.

Anzaldua, Gloria E. *Borderlands/La Frontera: The New Mestiza*. San Francisco, CA: Aunt Lute Books, 1999.

Appelrouth, Scott A., and Laura Desfor Edles. *Classical and Contemporary Sociological Theory: Text and Readings*. 3rd ed. Thousand Oaks, CA: SAGE, 2015.

Aptheker, Herbert. *The World of C. Wright Mills*. New York: Marzani and Munsell, 1960.

—— *Annotated Bibliography of the Published Writings of W. E. B. Du Bois*. Millwood, NY: Kraus-Thomson, 1973.

—— *The Unfolding Drama: Studies in U.S. History*. New York: International Publishers, 1978.

—— "W. E. B. Du Bois: Struggle Not Despair." *Clinical Sociology Review* 8, no. 1 (1990).

Ashley, David, and David Michael Orenstein. *Sociological Theory: Classical Statements*. 5th ed. Boston, MA: Allyn and Bacon, 2001.

Avineri, Shlomo. *Hegel's Theory of the Modern State*. Cambridge: Cambridge University Press, 1972.

Bagakis, Gus. *Seeing through the System: The Invisible Class Struggle in America*. Bloomington, IN: iUniverse, 2013.

Balibar, Etienne. *On the Dictatorship of the Proletariat*. London: NLB, 1977.

Barndt, Deborah, ed. *Women Working the Nafta Food Chain: Women, Food and Globalization*. Toronto: Sumach Press, 1999.

Baudrillard, Jean. *Forget Foucault*. New York: Semiotext(e), 1987.

Beams, Nick. *The Significance and Implications of Globalization: A Marxist Assessment*. Southfield, MI: Mehring Books, 1998.

Beard, Charles, and Mary Beard. *The Rise of American Civilization*. New York: Macmillan, 1930.

Beechey, Veronica. "Female Wage Labor in Capitalist Production." *Capital and Class* 1, no. 3 (1977).

Beijing Declaration and Platform for Action. Fourth World Conference on Women, A/CONF.177/20, and A/CONF.17720Add.1, www.umn.edu/humanrts/instree/beijingdec.htm

Bellah, Robert N. "Durkheim and History." *American Sociological Review* 24, no. 4 (1959).

Benjamin, Walter. *Illuminations*. New York: Houghton Mifflin, 1969.

Berberoglu, Berch. *The Legacy of Empire: Economic Decline and Class Polarization in the United States*. New York: Praeger, 1992.

—— *The Political Economy of Development*. Albany, NY: SUNY Press, 1992.

—— *Critical Perspectives in Sociology*. 2nd ed. Dubuque, IA: Kendall/Hunt, 1993.

—— *The Labor Process and Control of Labor: The Changing Nature of Work Relations in the Late 20th Century*. New York: Praeger, 1993.

—— *Class Structure and Social Transformation*. New York: Praeger, 1994.

—— *The National Question: Nationalism, Ethnic Conflict, and Self-Determination in the 20th Century*. Philadelphia, PA: Temple University Press, 1995.

—— *Political Sociology: A Comparative/Historical Approach*. 2nd ed. Boulder, CO: Rowman & Littlefield, 2001.

—— *Labor and Capital in the Age of Globalization*. Boulder, CO: Rowman & Littlefield, 2002.

—— *Globalization of Capital and the Nation-State*. Boulder, CO: Rowman & Littlefield, 2003.

—— *Nationalism and Ethnic Conflict: Class, State, and Nation in the Age of Globalization*. Boulder, CO: Rowman & Littlefield, 2004.

Berger, Peter L., and Thomas Luckman. *The Social Construction of Reality: A Treatise on the Sociology of Knowledge*. New York: Anchor Books, 1967.

Best, Steven, and Douglas Kellner. *Postmodern Theory, Critical Interrogations*. New York: The Guilford Press, 1991.

Bilge, Sirma. "Recent Feminist Outlooks on Intersectionality," *Diogenes* 225, no. 1 (2010).

Birnbaum, Norman. *Toward a Critical Sociology*. New York: Oxford University Press, 1971.

Blackwell, James E., and Morris Janowitz, eds. *Black Sociologists: Historical and Contemporary Perspectives*. Chicago, IL: University of Chicago Press, 1974.

Bloch, Ernst. *The Principle of Hope*. Vols. 1–3. Cambridge, MA: MIT Press, 1986.

Block, Fred. "The Ruling Class Does Not Rule: Notes on the Marxist Theory of the State." *Socialist Review*, no. 33 (1977).

—— "Marxist Theories of the State in World System Analysis." Paper, First Annual Political Economy of the World System Conference, American University, Washington, DC, 1977.

—— "Class Consciousness and Capitalist Rationalization: A Reply to Critics." *Socialist Review*, nos. 40–1 (1978).

—— *Revising State Theory*. Philadelphia, PA: Temple University Press, 1987.

Bottomore, Tom. *Elites and Society*. Baltimore, MD: Penguin, 1966.

Bottomore, Tom, and Robert J. Brym, eds. *The Capitalist Class: An International Study*. New York: New York University Press, 1989.

Boyer, Richard, and Herbert Morais. *Labor's Untold Story*. 3rd ed. New York: United Electrical, Radio, and Machine Workers of America, 1980.

Brenner, Johanna. *Women and the Politics of Class*. New York: Monthly Review Press, 2000.

Bronner, Steve. *Critical Theory: A Short Introduction*. New York: Oxford University Press, 2011.

Brooks, Ann. *Postfeminisms: Feminism, Cultural Theory, and Cultural Forms*. London: Routledge, 1997.

Bryson, Valerie. *Feminist Political Theory*. 2nd ed. New York: Palgrave Macmillan, 2003.

Burbach, R. "Roots of the Postmodern Rebellion in Chiapas." *New Left Review* 1, no. 205 (1994).

Burke, Edmund. *Reflections on the Revolution in France*. New Rochelle, NY: Arlington House, 1966.

Butler, Judith. "Performative Subversions." In *Gender: A Sociological Reader*, edited by Stevi Jackson and Sue Scott. London: Routledge, 2002.

Callinicos, Alex. *Against Postmodernism: A Marxist Critique*. New York: St. Martin's Press, 1989.

—— "Reactionary Postmodernism?" In *Postmodernism and Social Theory*, edited by R. Boyne and A. Rattansi. New York: St. Martin's Press, 1990.

Calvert, Peter. *The Concept of Class*. New York: St. Martin's Press, 1982.

Cameron, Kenneth Neill. *Humanity and Society: A World History*. New York: Monthly Review Press, 1977.

Carnoy, Martin. *The State and Political Theory*. Princeton, NJ: Princeton University Press, 1984.

Carritt, E. F. "Hegel and Prussianism." In *Hegel's Political Philosophy*, edited by Walter Kaufmann. New York: Atherton, 1970.

Clarke, S. "Marxism, Sociology and Poulantzas's Theory of the State." *Capital and Class* 2, nos. 21–31 (1977).

Cohn, Theodore H., Stephen McBride, and John Wiseman, eds. *Power in the Global Era: Grounding Globalization*. New York: Palgrave Macmillan, 2000.

Collins, Patricia Hill. *Black Feminist Thought: Knowledge, Consciousness, and Empowerment*. Boston, MA: Unwin Hyman, 1990.

—— "Toward a New Vision: Race, Class and Gender as Categories of Analysis and Connection." *Race, Sex & Class* 1, no. 1 (1993).

—— "On West and Fenstermaker's 'Doing Difference.'" In *Women, Men and Gender: Ongoing Debates*, edited by Mary Roth Walsh. New Haven, CT: Yale University Press, 1997.

—— *Fighting Words: Black Women and the Search for Justice*. Minneapolis, MN: University of Minnesota Press, 1998.

Collins, Randall. *Four Sociological Traditions*. New York: Oxford University Press, 1994.

Collins, Randall, and Michael Makowsky. *The Discovery of Society*. New York: Random House, 1972.

Comte, Auguste. *The Positive Philosophy*. London: Kegan Paul, 1893.

Conway, D. "Foucault, Michel." In *The Encyclopedia of Philosophy, Supplement*, edited by D. M. Borchert. New York: Simon & Schuster Macmillan, 1996.

Cooley, Charles Horton. *Human Nature and Social Order*. New York: Scribner's, 1902.

—— *Social Organization*. New York: Scribner's, 1909.

—— *Social Process*. New York: Scribner's, 1918.

Cooper, John Milton, Jr. "Foreword." In *W. E. B. Du Bois: Black Radical Democrat*, by Manning Marable, vi–vii. Boston, MA: Twayne, 1986.

Copleston, Frederick. *A History of Philosophy*. Vol. 7. New York: Doubleday, 1994.

Coser, Lewis A. *Masters of Sociological Thought: Ideas in Historical and Social Context*. New York: Harcourt Brace Jovanovich, 1971.

Coser, Lewis A., and Bernard Rosenberg, eds. *Sociological Theory: A Book of Readings*. 2nd ed. New York: Macmillan, 1962.

Cowling, Mark, and James Martin, eds. *Marx's "Eighteenth Brumaire."* London: Pluto Press, 2002.

Crompton, Rosemary, and Jon Gubbay. *Economy and Class Structure*. New York: St. Martin's Press, 1978.

Crothers, Lane. *Globalization and American Popular Culture*. 3rd ed. Lanham, MD: Rowman and Littlefield, 2012.

Dahms, Harry. "Affinities between the Project of Dynamic Theory and the Tradition of Critical Theory: A Sketch." In *Theorizing the Dynamics of Social Processes*, edited by Harry Dahms, 81–9. Bingley: Emerald, 2010.

Dahrendorf, Ralph. *Class and Class Conflict in Industrial Society*. Palo Alto, C.A.: Stanford University Press, 1959.

Daly, Mary. *Gyn/Ecology: The Metaethics of Radical Feminism*. Boston, MA: Beacon Press, 1978.

Davis, Allen F. *American Heroine*. New York: Oxford University Press, 1973.

Davis, Kingsley, and Wilbert E. Moore. "Some Principles of Stratification." *American Sociological Review* 10, no. 2 (1945).

Dazhina, I. M. *Alexandra Kollontai: Selected Articles and Speeches*. New York: International Publishers, 1984.

Deegan, Mary Jo. "Women in Sociology, 1890–1930." *Journal of the History of Sociology* 1 (1978).

——— *Jane Addams and the Men of the Chicago School, 1892–1918*. New Brunswick, NJ: Transaction Press, 1988.

——— ed. *Women in Sociology*. Westport, CT: Greenwood Press, 1991.

——— "Play from the Perspective of George Herbert Mead." In *Play, School, and Society*, edited and introduction by Mary Jo Deegan. New York: Peter Lange, 1999.

——— *Race, Hull-House, and the University of Chicago: A New Conscience against an Ancient Evil*. Westport, CT: Greenwood Press, 2002.

——— "Katharine Bement Davis: Her Theory and Praxis of Feminist Pragmatism." *Women & Criminal Justice* 14, nos. 2–3 (2003).

——— "Jane Addams." In *Fifty Key Sociologists: The Formative Theorists*, edited by John Scott. London: Routledge, 2007.

——— *Self, War, and Society: The Macrosociology of George Herbert Mead*. New Brunswick, NJ: Transaction Publishers, 2008.

——— "Jane Addams on Citizenship in a Democracy." *Journal of Classical Sociology* 10, no. 3 (2010).

——— *Gender at Hull-House and the University of Chicago: Exploring the Origins and Influence of Feminist Pragmatism, 1889–2011*. Amherst, NY: Cambria Press, 2014.

——— *Annie Marion MacLean and the Chicago Schools of Sociology, 1894–1934*. New Brunswick, NJ: Transaction Press, 2014.

Deegan, Mary Jo, and Christopher Podeschi. "The Ecofeminist Pragmatism of Charlotte Perkins Gilman: The Herland Sagas." *Environmental Ethics* 23, no. 1 (2001).

Deegan, Mary Jo, and Ana-Maria Wahl. "Introduction: Ellen Gates Starr and Her Journey Toward Social Justice and Beauty." In *On Art, Labor, and Religion*, edited and introduction by Mary Jo Deegan and Ana-Maria Wahl. New Brunswick, NJ: Transaction Publishers, 2003.

Defers, D., and F. Ewalt, eds. *Dits et écrits: 1954–1988/Michel Foucault*. Paris: Editions Gallimard, 1994.

Defronzo, James. *Revolutions and Revolutionary Movements*. 4th ed. Boulder, CO: Westview Press, 2011.

Delaney, Tim. *Classical Social Theory*. New York: Pearson, 2003.

—— *Contemporary Social Theory*. New York: Pearson, 2004.

Deutsch, Morton. "Homans in the Skinner Box." *Sociological Inquiry* 34, no. 2 (1964).

Dillon, Michele. *Introduction to Sociological Theory*. 2nd ed. Malden, MA: Wiley-Blackwell, 2014.

Dobb, Maurice. *Studies in the Development of Capitalism*. New York: International Publishers, 1963.

Domhoff, G. William. *Who Rules America?* Englewood Cliffs, NJ: Prentice Hall, 1967.

—— *The Higher Circles: The Governing Class in America*. New York: Vintage, 1971.

—— *The Powers That Be: Processes of Ruling Class Domination in America*. New York: Vintage, 1978.

—— *Who Rules America Now? A View for the 80's*. New York: Simon & Schuster, 1983.

—— *The Power Elite and the State*. New York: Aldine de Gruyter, 1990.

Domhoff, G. William, and Hoyt B. Ballard, eds. *C. Wright Mills and the Power Elite*. Boston, MA: Beacon Press, 1968.

Draper, Hal. *Karl Marx's Theory of Revolution: State and Bureaucracy*. Pts. 1 and 2. New York: Monthly Review Press, 1977.

Du Bois, W. E. B. "The Freedman's Bureau." *The Atlantic Monthly* 87 (1901).

—— "Negroes and the Crisis of Capitalism in the United States." *Monthly Review* 4, no. 12 (1953).

—— "The Class Struggle." In *W. E. B. Du Bois: A Reader*, edited by Meyer Weinberg. New York: Harper & Row, 1970.

—— "The Social Effects of Emancipation." In *W. E. B. Du Bois: A Reader*, edited by Meyer Weinberg. New York: Harper & Row, 1970.

—— "The White Masters of the World." In *The Writings of W. E. B. Du Bois*, edited by Virginia Hamilton, 199–210. New York: Crowell, 1975.

Durkheim, Emile. *Suicide: A Study in Sociology*. New York: Free Press, 1951.

—— *Education and Sociology*. Glencoe, IL: Free Press, 1956.

—— *The Elementary Forms of Religious Life*. London: Allen & Unwin, 1957.

—— *Professional Ethics and Civic Morals*. Glencoe, IL: Free Press, 1958.

—— *Moral Education*. New York: Free Press, 1961.

—— *The Division of Labor in Society*. New York: Free Press, 1964.

—— *The Rules of the Sociological Method*. New York: Free Press, 1964.

Einsenstein, Zillah R., ed. *Capitalist Patriarchy and the Case for Socialist Feminism*. New York: Monthly Review Press, 1979.

Eisenstadt, N., ed. *Modernization: Protest and Change*. Englewood Cliffs, NJ: Prentice Hall, 1966.

Ekeh, Peter. *Social Exchange Theory: The Two Traditions*. Cambridge, MA: Harvard University Press, 1974.

Emmanuel, Arghiri. *Unequal Exchange: A Study of the Imperialism of Trade*. New York: Monthly Review Press, 1972.

Engels, Frederick. "The Origin of the Family, Private Property and the State." In *Selected Works*, by Karl Marx and Frederick Engels. New York: International Publishers, 1972.

—— "Ludwig Feuerbach and the End of Classical German Philosophy." In *Selected Works*, by Karl Marx and Frederick Engels. New York: International Publishers, 1972.

—— *The Peasant War in Germany*. New York: International Publishers, 1973.

—— *Anti-Duhring*. New York: International Publishers, 1976.

Epitropoulos, Mike-Frank. "The Global Capitalist Crisis and the European Union, with Focus on Greece." In *Beyond the Global Capitalist Crisis: The World Economy in Transition*, edited by Berch Berberoglu. Farnham, UK: Ashgate Publishing, 2012.

Esping-Andersen, Gosta, Roger Friedland, and Erik Olin Wright. "Modes of Class Struggle and the Capitalist State." *Kapitalistate* nos. 4–5 (1976).

Falk, Richard. *Predatory Globalization: A Critique*. Malden, MA: Blackwell Publishers, 1999.

Farganis, James. *Readings in Social Theory*. 7th ed. New York: McGraw-Hill, 2013.

Farr, Arnold. *Critical Theory and Democratic Vision: Herbert Marcuse and Recent Liberation Philosophies*. Lanham, MD: Lexington Books, 2009.

Feagin, Joe R., Hernan Vera, and Kimberly Ducey. *Liberation Sociology*. 3rd ed. Boulder, CO: Paradigm, 2014.

Feenberg, Andrew. *Transforming Technology: A Critical Theory Revisited*. Oxford: Oxford University Press, 2002.

—— *The Philosophy of Praxis: Marx, Lukács and the Frankfurt School*. London: Verso Press, 2014.

Filmer, Paul, Michael Phillipson, David Silverman, and David Walsh. *New Directions in Sociological Theory*. Cambridge, MA: MIT Press, 1973.

Fiori, Giuseppe. *Antonio Gramsci, Life of a Revolutionary*. London: New Left Books, 1970.

Firestone, Shulamith. *The Dialectic of Sex: The Case for Feminist Revolution*. New York: Bantam Books, 1971.

Foster, John Bellamy, Brett Clark, and Richard York. *The Ecological Rift: Capitalism's War on the Earth*. New York: Monthly Review Press, 2011.

Foucault, Michel, *The History of Sexuality*, vol. I. London: Allen Lane, 1976.

—— *Power/Knowledge – Selected Interviews and Other Writings 1972–1977*. New York: Pantheon Books, 1980.

—— "What is Enlightment?" In *The Foucault Reader*, edited by P. Rabinow. New York: Pantheon Books, 1984.

—— "The Repressive Hypothesis." In *The Foucault Reader*, edited by P. Rabinow. New York: Pantheon Books, 1984.

—— "Qu'est-ce que la critique? Critique et Aufklärung." *Bulletin de la Société Française de Philosophie* 84, no. 2 (1990).

—— "Genealogy and Social Criticism." In *The Postmodern Turn: New Perspectives on Social Theory*, edited by S. Seidman. Cambridge: Cambridge University Press, 1994.

—— "Interview with Michel Foucault." In *Power*, edited by J. D. Faubion. New York: The New Press, 1994.

—— "Preface to Anti-Oedipus." In *Power*, edited by J. D. Faubion. New York: The New Press, 1994.

—— "The Subject and Power." In *Power*, edited by J. D. Faubion. New York: The New Press, 1994.

—— "Truth and Juridical Forms." In *Power*, edited by J. D. Faubion. New York: The New Press, 1994.

—— *Discipline and Punish: The Birth of the Prison*. New York: Vintage Books, 1995.

—— *The Birth of the Clinic: An Archaeology of Medical Perception*. New York: Vintage Books, 1995.

Frank, Andre Gunder. *Capitalism and Underdevelopment in Latin America*. New York: Monthly Review Press, 1967.

Fraser, Nancy, "Rethinking the Public Sphere: A Contribution to the Critique of Actually Existing Democracy," *Social Text* 25/26 (1990), 56–80.

Frazier, E. Franklin. *The Negro Family in the United States*. Chicago, IL: University of Chicago Press, 1939.

—— *The Negro in the United States*. New York: Macmillan, 1949.

—— *Race and Culture Contacts in the Modern World*. New York: Knopf, 1957.

—— *Black Bourgeoisie*. Glencoe, IL: The Free Press, 1957.

Freud, Sigmund. *An Outline of Psychoanalysis*. New York: Norton, 1949.

—— *New Introductory Lectures on Psychoanalysis*, edited and translated by James Strachey. New York: Norton, 1990.

—— *The Question of Lay Analysis*. Garden City, NY: Doubleday Anchor, 1950.

—— *The Future of an Illusion*. Garden City, NY: Doubleday Anchor, 1961.

—— *Civilization and Its Discontents*. New York: Norton, 1962.

Friedrich, C. J., ed. *The Philosophy of Hegel*. New York: Modern Library, 1953.

Fromm, Erich. *Escape from Freedom*. New York: Holt, Rinehart, 1941.

—— *Beyond the Chains of Illusion*. New York: Simon and Schuster, 1962.

—— *The Crisis of Psychoanalysis*. New York: Holt, Rinehart, Winston, 1970.

Garfinkel, Harold. "Perception and the Other." Unpublished PhD dissertation, Harvard University, 1952.

—— *Studies in Ethnomethodology*. Englewood Cliffs, NJ: Prentice Hall, 1967.

Garner, Roberta, and Black Hawk Hancock, eds. *Social Theory: Continuity and Confrontation: A Reader*. 3rd ed. Toronto: University of Toronto Press, 2014.

Gautney, Heather. "Occupy Wall Street: Repossession by Occupation." In *Protest and Organization in the Alternative Globalization Era*, by Heather Gautney. New York: Palgrave Macmillan, 2010.

Giddens, Anthony. *Capitalism and Modern Social Theory*. New York: Cambridge University Press, 1971.

Gilsenan, Tom. "Peacemakers and Friends: Jane Addams and Gandhi," www.mkgandhi-sarvodaya. org/articles/addamsgandhi.htm (accessed 8 February 2007).

Gimenez, Martha E. "Marxism and Feminism." *Frontiers: A Journal of Women's Studies* 1, no. 1 (1975).

—— "The Feminization of Poverty: Myth or Reality?" *Social Justice* 17, no. 3 (1990).

—— "The Mode of Reproduction in Transition: A Marxist Feminist Analysis of the Effects of Reproductive Technologies." *Gender and Society* 5, no. 3 (1991).

—— "What's Material about Materialist Feminism? A Marxist Feminist Critique." *Radical Philosophy* no. 101 (2000).

—— "Marxism and Class, Gender and Race: Rethinking the Trilogy," *Race, Gender & Class*, 8, no. 2 (2001).

Gindin, Sam, and Leo Panitch. *The Making of Global Capitalism: The Political Economy of American Empire*. London: Verso, 2013.

Gitlin, Todd. *Occupy Nation: The Roots, the Spirit, and the Promise of Occupy Wall Street*. New York: It Books, Harper Collins, 2012.

Goffman, Erving. *The Presentation of Self in Everyday Life*. Garden City, NY: Doubleday, 1959.

—— *Asylums: Essays on the Social Situation of Mental Patients and other Inmates*. Garden City, NY: Doubleday, 1961.

—— *Encounters*. Indianapolis, IN: Bobbs-Merrill, 1961.

—— *Behavior in Public Places*. New York: Free Press, 1963.

—— *Stigma: Notes on the Management of Spoiled Identity*. Englewood Cliffs, NJ: Prentice Hall, 1963.

—— *Interaction Ritual: Essays in Face-to-Face Behavior*. Garden City, NY: Doubleday, 1967.

—— *Strategic Interaction*. New York: Ballantine, 1969.

—— *Frame Analysis: An Essay on the Organization of Experience*. Cambridge, MA: Harvard University Press, 1974.

Gold, David, Clarence Y. H. Lo, and Erik Olin Wright. "Some Recent Developments in Marxist Theories of the Capitalist State." Pts. 1 and 2. *Monthly Review* 27, nos. 5–6 (1975).

Goldstone, Jack. *Revolutions: Theoretical, Comparative, and Historical Studies.* 3rd ed. New York: Cengage, 2002.

Gonos, George. "'Situation' Versus 'Frame': The 'Interactionist' and the 'Structuralist' Analyses of Everyday Life." *American Sociological Review* 42, no. 6 (1977).

Gordon, C. "Introduction." In *Power*, edited by J. D. Faubion. New York: The New Press, 1994.

Gouldner, Alvin W. *The Coming Crisis of Western Sociology.* New York: Avon Books, 1970.

Gramsci, Antonio. *Prison Notebooks.* New York: International Publishers, 1971.

—— *Selections from Political Writings: 1921–1926.* London: Lawrence & Wishart, 1978.

Grzanka, Patrick R., ed. *Intersectionality. A Foundations and Frontiers Reader.* Boulder, CO: Westview Press, 2014.

Guettel, Charnie. *Marxism and Feminism.* Toronto: The Hunter Rose Co., 1974.

Gunarsson, Lena. "A Defense of the Category 'Woman.'" *Feminist Theory* 12, no. 1 (2011).

Haas, Mark L., and David W. Lesch, eds. *The Arab Spring: Change and Resistance in the Middle East.* Boulder, CO: Westview Press, 2012.

Habermas, Jürgen. *Legitimation Crisis.* Boston, MA: Beacon Press, 1975.

—— *The Theory of Communicative Action.* Boston, MA: Beacon Press, 1984.

—— *Knowledge and Human Interests.* London: Polity Press, 1986.

—— *The Structural Transformation of the Public Sphere.* Cambridge, MA: MIT Press, 1989.

Halliday, Fred. *The World at 2000.* New York: St. Martin's Press, 2001.

Hamilton, Roberta A., and Michele Barrett, eds. *The Politics of Diversity.* London: Verso, 1986.

Hart-Landsberg, Martin. *Capitalist Globalization: Consequences, Resistance, and Alternatives.* New York: Monthly Review Press, 2013.

Harvey, David. *The Limits to Capital.* Cambridge, MA: Basil Blackwell, 1982.

—— *The Condition of Postmodernity.* Cambridge, MA: Basil Blackwell, 1990.

—— *A Brief History of Neoliberalism.* New York: Oxford University Press, 2007.

Harvey, Neil. *The Chiapas Rebellion: The Struggle for Land and Democracy.* Durham, NC: Duke University Press, 1998.

Hassan, I. "The Culture of Postmodernism." *Theory, Culture, and Society* 2, no. 3 (1985).

Hegel, G. W. F. *Selections*, edited by J. Loewenberg. New York: n.p., 1929.

—— *Philosophy of Right.* Oxford: Knox, 1942.

—— *The Philosophy of History.* New York: Dover, 1956.

—— *Science of Logic.* London: Allen and Unwin, 1969.

—— *Hegel: Political Writings*, edited by Lawrence Dickey and H. B. Nisbet. Cambridge: Cambridge University Press, 1999.

Hennessy, Rosemary. *Materialist Feminism and the Politics of Discourse.* New York: Routledge, 1993.

Hennessy, Rosemary, and Chrys Ingraham, eds. *Materialist Feminism: A Reader in Class, Difference, and Women's Lives.* New York: Routledge, 1997.

Herman, Edward S., and Robert W. McChesney. *Global Media: The Missionaries of Corporate Capitalism.* New York: Bloomsbury, 2001.

Hertz, Noreena. *Silent Takeover: Global Capitalism and the Death of Democracy.* New York: Free Press, 2002.

Hilton, Rodney. *The Transition from Feudalism to Capitalism.* London: New Left Books, 1976.

Hochschild, Arlie. *The Second Shift.* New York: Avon Books, 1989.

Holloway, John, and Sol Picciotto. "Capital, Crisis and the State." *Capital and Class* 1, no. 2 (1977).

—— "Introduction: Towards a Marxist Theory of the State." In *State and Capital*, edited by John Holloway and Sol Picciotto, 1–31. London: Edward Arnold, 1979.

Holt, Alix, ed. *Selected Writings of Alexandra Kollontai*. Westport, CT: Lawrence Hill, 1978.

Homans, George C. "Social Behavior as Exchange." *American Journal of Sociology* 63, no. 6 (1958).

—— "Contemporary Sociological Theory." In *Handbook of Modern Sociology*, edited by Robert E. L. Faris. Chicago, IL: Rand McNallly, 1964.

—— *Social Behavior: Its Elementary Forms*. Revised ed. New York: Harcourt, Brace and Jovanovich, 1974.

Homans, George C., and David Schneider. *Marriage, Authority, and Final Causes*. Glencoe, IL: Free Press, 1955.

hooks, bell. *Talking Back: Thinking Feminist, Thinking Black*. Boston, MA: South End Press, 1989.

Hopkins, Terence K., and Immanuel Wallerstein. "Structural Transformations of the World-Economy." In *Dynamics of World Development*, edited by Richard Rubinson. London: SAGE, 1981.

—— *World-Systems Analysis*. Beverly Hills, CA: SAGE, 1982.

Horkheimer, Max. "Traditional and Critical Theory." In *Critical Theory: Selected Essays*, edited by Max Horkheimer, 188–243. New York: Continuum, [1937] 1972.

—— "Authority and the Family." In *Critical Theory: Selected Essays*, edited by Max Horkheimer, 47–128. New York: Continuum, 1972.

Horkheimer Max, and Theodor W. Adorno. *The Dialectic of Enlightenment*. Palo Alto, CA: Stanford University Press, [1944] 2002.

Horne, Gerald. *Black & Red: W. E. B. Du Bois and the Afro-American Response to the Cold War, 1944–1963*. Albany, NY: SUNY Press, 1986.

Horowitz, Irving Louis, ed. *Power, Politics and People*. New York: Oxford University Press, 1963.

Houtart, François, and François Polet, eds. *The Other Davos: The Globalization of Resistance to the World Economic System*. London: Zed Books, 2001.

How, Alan. *Critical Theory*. New York: Palgrave Macmillan, 2003.

Hoy, David C. "Introduction." In *Foucault: A Critical Reader*, edited by David C. Hoy. Oxford: Basil Blackwell, 1986.

—— ed. *Foucault: A Critical Reader*. Oxford: Wiley-Blackwell, 1991.

Hume, David. *A Treatise of Human Nature*. Oxford: Clarendon Press, 1949.

Jackson, Stevi, and Sue Scott, eds. *Gender: A Sociological Reader*. London: Routledge, 2002.

Jameson, Frederic. "Postmodernism, or the Cultural Logic of Late Capitalism." *New Left Review* 146 (1984).

Jay, Martin. *The Dialectical Imagination*. Boston, MA: Little, Brown, 1973.

Jenkins, Richard. *Foundations of Sociology*. New York: Palgrave Macmillan, 2002.

Jessop, Bob. *The Capitalist State*. New York: New York University Press, 1982.

Johnson, Harry M. *Sociology: A Systematic Introduction*. New York: Harcourt, Brace, 1960.

Jones, D. "The Genealogy of the Urban Schoolteacher." In *Foucault and Education: Discipline and Knowledge*, edited by S. J. Ball. New York: Routledge, 1990.

Jones, Pip, Liz Bradbury, and Shaun Le Boutillier, eds. *Introducing Social Theory*. 2nd ed. Cambridge: Polity, 2011.

Kagarlitsky, Boris. *New Realism, New Barbarism: Socialist Theory in the Era of Globalization*. London: Pluto Press, 1999.

—— *The Twilight of Globalization: Property, State and Capitalism*. London: Pluto Press, 2000.

Kant, Immanuel. *Critique of Pure Reason*. New York: St. Martin's Press, 1929.

Karliner, Joshua. *The Corporate Planet: Ecology and Politics in the Age of Globalization*. Los Angeles, CA: University of California Press, 1997.

Katsiaficas, George, and Eddie Yuen, eds. *The Battle of Seattle: Debating Capitalist Globalization and the WTO*. New York: Soft Skull Press, 2002.

Kellner, Douglass. *Critical Theory, Marxism, and Modernity*. Baltimore, MD: Johns Hopkins University Press, 1989.

—— ed. *Collected Papers of Herbert Marcuse*. Vols. 1–6. New York: Routledge, 2005–2014.

Kermode, Frank. *History and Value*. Oxford: Clarendon Press, 1988.

King, Roger. *The State in Modern Society*. Chatham, NJ: Chatham House, 1986.

Kivisto, Peter. *Social Theory: Roots and Branches*. 5th ed. New York: Oxford University Press, 2012.

—— *Illuminating Social Life: Classical and Contemporary Theory Revisited*. 6th ed. Thousand Oaks, CA: SAGE, 2013.

Klein, Naomi. *This Changes Everything: Capitalism vs. the Climate*. New York: Simon and Schuster, 2015.

Kloby, Jerry. "Increasing Class Polarization in the United States: The Growth of Wealth and Income Inequality." In *Critical Perspectives in Sociology*, edited by Berch Berberoglu. Dubuque, IA: Kendall/Hunt, 1991.

Kollontai, Alexandra. "The Social Basis of the Women's Question." In *Selected Writings of Alexandra Kollontai*, edited by Alix Holt, 58–73. Westport, CT: Lawrence Hill, 1978.

—— "Sexual Relations and the Class Struggle." In *Selected Writings of Alexandra Kollontai*, edited by Alix Holt, 237–49. Westport, CT: Lawrence Hill, 1978.

Kuhn, Annette, and Anne Marie Wolpe, eds. *Feminism and Materialism: Women and Modes of Production*. London: Routledge and Kegan Paul, 1977.

Kuhn, Thomas S. *The Structure of Scientific Revolutions*. 2nd ed. Chicago, IL: University of Chicago Press, 1970.

Kunnie, Julian E. *The Cost of Globalization: Dangers to the Earth and Its People*. New York: McFarland, 2015.

Landry, Donald, and Gerald Maclean. *Materialist Feminisms*. London: Blackwell, 1993.

Langman, Lauren, and George Lundskow. *God, Gold, Guns and Glory*. Leiden, Netherlands: Brill Press, 2016.

Launius, Christie, and Holly Hassel. *Threshold Concepts in Women's and Gender Studies. Ways of Seeing, Thinking, and Knowing*. New York and London: Routledge, 2015.

Leacock, Eleanor B. "Introduction." In *The Origin of the Family, Private Property and the State*, by F. Engels. New York: International Publishers, 1972.

Lemert, Charles, ed. *Social Theory: The Multicultural, Global, and Classic Readings*. 5th ed. Boulder, CO: Westview Press, 2013.

Lengermann, Patricia Madoo, and Jill Niebrugge, eds. *The Women Founders: Sociology and Social Theory, 1830–1930*. New York: McGraw-Hill, 1998.

Lenin, V. I. *Works*. Vol. 31. Moscow: Foreign Languages Publishing House, 1947.

—— *Selected Works*. New York: International Publishers, 1971.

—— "What Is to Be Done?" In *Selected Works*, by V. I. Lenin. New York: International Publishers, 1971.

—— "Imperialism, The Highest Stage of Capitalism." In *Selected Works*, by V. I. Lenin. New York: International Publishers, 1971.

—— "The Three Sources and Three Component Parts of Marxism." In *Selected Works in One Volume*, by V. I. Lenin. New York: International Publishers, 1971.

—— "The State." In *On Historical Materialism*, by Karl Marx, Frederick Engels, and V. I. Lenin. New York: International Publishers, 1974.

—— "The State and Revolution." In *Selected Works in Three Volumes*. Vol. 2. Moscow: Progress Publishers, 1975.

Lenski, Gerhard. *Power and Privilege*. New York: McGraw-Hill, 1966.

Levine, Donald N., Ellwood B. Carter, and Eleanor Miller Gorman. "Simmel's Influence on American Sociology, I." *American Journal of Sociology* 81, no. 4 (1976).

Lipset, Seymour Martin. "Introduction." In *Political Parties*, by Robert Michels. New York: Free Press, 1968.

Longhofer, Wesley, and Daniel Winchester, eds. *Social Theory Re-Wired: New Connections to Classical and Contemporary Perspectives*. New York: Routledge, 2012.

Longhurst, Brian. *Karl Mannheim and the Contemporary Sociology of Knowledge*. New York: St. Martin's Press, 1989.

Lorber, Judith. *Gender Inequality: Feminist Theory and Politics*. Los Angeles, CA: Roxbury Publishing Company, 2002.

Loyal, Steven. *The Sociology of Anthony Giddens*. London: Pluto Press, 2003.

Luke, Timothy. *Ecocritique: Contesting the Politics of Nature, Economy, and Culture*. Minneapolis, MN: University of Minnesota Press, 1997.

Lyotard, Jean-François. *The Postmodern Condition*. Minneapolis, MN: University of Minnesota Press, 1984.

McNall, Scott G., ed. *Theoretical Perspectives in Sociology*. New York: St. Martin's Press, 1979.

Mainardi, Pat. "The Politics of Housework." In *Sisterhood is Powerful*, edited by Robin Morgan. New York: Random House, 1970.

Mander, Jerry, Debi Baker and David Korten, "Does Globalization Help the Poor?" *Third World Traveler (International Forum on Globalization), IFG Bulletin*, 1, no. 3 (2001), www.thirdworldtraveler.com/Globalization/DoesGlobaliz_HelpPoor.html (accessed 2 September 2016).

Mannheim, Karl. *Ideology and Utopia: An Introduction to the Sociology of Knowledge*, Preface by Louis Wirth, translated by Louis Wirth and Edward A. Shils. New York: Harcourt, Brace and Company, 1949.

—— *Essays in the Sociology of Culture*, edited and translated by Ernest Mannheim and Paul Kecskemeti. London: Routledge & Kegan Paul, 1956.

—— *Structures of Thinking*, edited by David Kettler, Volker Meja, and Nico Stehr, translated by Jeremy J. Shapiro and Shierry Weber Nicolsen. Boston, MA: Routledge & Kegan Paul, 1982.

Manuel, Frank E. *The New World of Henri Saint-Simon*. Cambridge, MA: Harvard University Press, 1956.

Marable, Manning. *W. E. B. Du Bois: Black Radical Democrat*. Boston, MA: Twayne, 1986.

Marcuse, Herbert. *Reason and Revolution: Hegel and the Rise of Social Theory*. New York: Oxford University Press, 1941.

—— *One-Dimensional Man*. Boston, MA: Beacon Press, 1964.

—— *Eros and Civilization*. New York: Vintage Books, 1968.

—— *Essay on Liberation*. Boston, MA: Beacon Press, 1969.

Marger, Martin N. *Elites and Masses: An Introduction to Political Sociology*. 2nd ed. Belmont, CA: Wadsworth, 1987.

Markham, F. M. H. *Henri Comte de Saint-Simon*. Oxford: Basil Blackwell, 1952.

Marx, Karl. *The Poverty of Philosophy*. New York: International Publishers, 1963.

—— *Pre-Capitalist Economic Formations*. New York: International Publishers, 1965.

—— *Capital*. 3 vols. New York: International Publishers, 1967.

—— "Critique of the Gotha Programme." In *Selected Works*, by Karl Marx and Frederick Engels. New York: International Publishers, 1972.

—— "Preface to *A Contribution to the Critique of Political Economy*." In *Selected Works*, by Karl Marx and Frederick Engels. New York: International Publishers, 1972.

Marx, Karl, and Frederick Engels. *The German Ideology*. New York: International Publishers, 1947.

—— "Manifesto of the Communist Party." In *Selected Works*, by Karl Marx and Frederick Engels. New York: International Publishers, 1972.

Mead, George Herbert. "Suggestions Toward a Theory of Philosophical Disciplines." *Philosophical Review* 9 (1900): 2.

—— *Mind, Self, and Society: From the Standpoint of a Social Behaviorist*. Chicago, IL: University of Chicago Press, 1934.

—— *Play, School and Society*. Edited and introduction by Mary Jo Deegan. New York: Peter Lang, 1999.

—— *Essays in Social Psychology*. Edited and introduction by Mary Jo Deegan. New Brunswick, NJ: Transaction Publishers, 2001.

Meltzer, Bernard N. *The Social Psychology of George Herbert Mead*. Kalamazoo, MI: Western Michigan University Center for Sociological Research, 1964.

Meltzer, Bernard N., John W. Petras, and Larry T. Reynolds. *Symbolic Interactionism: Genesis, Varieties and Criticism*. London: Routledge & Kegan Paul, 1975.

Merton, Robert K. *Social Theory and Social Structure*. New York: Free Press, 1968.

Michels, Robert. *Political Parties*. New York: Free Press, 1968.

Miliband, Ralph. *The State in Capitalist Society*. New York: Basic Books, 1969.

—— "The Capitalist State—Reply to Nicos Poulantzas." *New Left Review*, no. 59 (1970).

—— "Poulantzas and the Capitalist State." *New Left Review*, no. 82 (1973).

—— "Political Forms and Historical Materialism." In *Socialist Register, 1975*, edited by R. Miliband and J. Saville, 308–18. London: Merlin Press, 1975.

—— *Marxism and Politics*. London: Oxford University Press, 1977.

—— *Capitalist Democracy in Britain*. London: Oxford University Press, 1982.

Mills, C. Wright. *White Collar: The American Middle Classes*. New York: Oxford University Press, 1951.

—— *The Power Elite*. New York: Oxford University Press, 1956.

—— *The Sociological Imagination*. New York: Oxford University Press, 1959.

—— "The Structure of Power in American Society." In *Power, Politics, and People: The Collected Essays of C. Wright Mills*, edited by Irving Louis Horowitz. New York: Oxford University Press, 1963.

Mirrlees, Tanner. *Global Entertainment Media: Between Cultural Imperialism and Cultural Globalization*. London: Routledge, 2013.

Mitchell, Jack N. *Social Exchange, Dramaturgy, and Ethnomethodology: Toward a Paradigmatic Synthesis*. New York: Elsevier, 1978.

Moghadam, Valentine. "Gender and Globalization: Female Labor and Women's Mobilization." *Journal of World-Systems Research* 5, no. 2 (1999).

—— *Globalization and Social Movements*. Lanham, MD: Rowman and Littlefield, 2009.

Moi, Toril, and Janice Radway, special issue eds. "Materialist Feminism." *The South Atlantic Quarterly* 93, no. 4 (1994).

Mollenkopf, John. "Theories of the State and Power Structure Research." *Insurgent Sociologist* 5, no. 3 (1975).

Morse, Chandler. "The Functional Imperatives." In *The Social Theories of Talcott Parsons*, edited by Max Black. Englewood Cliffs, NJ: Prentice Hall, 1961.

Mosca, Gaetano. *The Ruling Class*. New York: McGraw-Hill, 1939.

Mullins, Nicolaus. "Text of a Speech Delivered at the ASA Convention." In *The Sociology of Sociology*, edited by Larry T. Reynolds and Janice Reynolds. New York: McKay, 1973.

Munck, Ronaldo. *Globalization and Labor*. London: Zed Books, 2002.

Munck, Ronaldo, and Peter Waterman, eds. *Labor Worldwide in the Era of Globalization*. New York: Palgrave Macmillan, 1999.

Needham, Rodney. *Structure and Sentiment: A Test Case in Social Anthropology*. Chicago, IL: University of Chicago Press, 1962.

Neeley, Elizabeth, and Mary Jo Deegan. "George Herbert Mead on Punitive Justice: A Critical Analysis of Contemporary Practices." *Humanity & Society* 29, no. 1 (2005).

Newell, Peter. *Globalization and the Environment: Capitalism, Ecology, and Power*. London: Polity, 2012.

Oberndorf, C. P. *A History of Psychoanalysis in America*. New York: Grune, 1953.

Orr, Martin. "The Struggle against Capitalist Globalization: The Worldwide Protests Against the WTO." In *Globalization and Change: The Transformation of Global Capitalism*, edited by Berch Berberoglu. Lanham, MD: Lexington Books, 2005.

Owen, D. "Power, Knowledge and Ethics: Foucault." In *The Edinburgh Encyclopedia of Continental Philosophy*, edited by S. Glendinning. Edinburgh: Edinburgh University Press, 1999.

Palast, Greg. *The Best Democracy Money Can Buy*. London: Pluto Press, 2002.

Palmer, Bryan D. *Descent into Discourse*. Philadelphia, PA: Temple University Press, 1990.

Parenti, Michael. "Power and Pluralism: The View from the Bottom." *Journal of Politics* 32, no. 3 (1970).

—— *Democracy for the Few*. 5th ed. New York: St. Martin's Press, 1988.

Pareto, Vilfredo. *The Mind and Society*. 4 vols. New York: Harcourt, Brace, 1935.

Parker, John, Leonard Mars, Paul Ransome, and Hilary Stanworth, *Social Theory*. New York: Palgrave Macmillan, 2003.

Parsons, Talcott. *The Social System*. New York: Free Press, 1951.

—— *Essays in Sociological Theory*. Revised ed. Glencoe, IL: Free Press, 1954.

—— *Structure and Process in Modern Societies*. New York: Free Press, 1960.

—— *Societies: An Evolutionary Approach*. Englewood Cliffs, NJ: Prentice Hall, 1966.

—— "On the Concept of Political Power." In *Sociological Theory and Modern Society*, by Talcott Parsons. New York: Free Press, 1967.

Petras, James. "Cultural Imperialism in the Late 20th Century." *Journal of Contemporary Asia* 23, no. 2 (1993).

—— *The Left Strikes Back: Class Conflict in Latin America in the Age of Neoliberalism*. Boulder, CO: Westview Press, 1998.

Petras, James, and Henry Veltmeyer. *Globalization Unmasked: Imperialism in the 21st Century*. London: Zed Books, 2001.

—— *Beyond Neoliberalism: A World to Win*. Farnham, UK: Ashgate, 2011

—— *Social Movements in Latin America*. New York: Palgrave-Macmillan, 2011

Picciotto, Sol. "The Theory of the State, Class Struggle, and the Rule of Law." In *Capitalism and the Rule of Law*, edited by Bob Fine, Richard Kinsey, John Lea, Sol Picciotto and Jack Young. London: Hutchinson, 1979.

Platt, Anthony M. *E. Franklin Frazier Reconsidered*. New Brunswick, NJ: Rutgers University Press, 1991.

Polanyi, Karl. *The Great Transformation*. Boston, MA: Beacon, 1957.

Polet, Francois, ed. *The State of Resistance: Popular Struggles in the Global South*. London: Zed Books, 2007.

Popper, Karl R. *The Open Society and Its Enemies*. Princeton, NJ: Princeton University Press, 1950.

Postone, Moishe. *Time, Labor and Social Domination*. Cambridge: Cambridge University Press, 1996.

Poulantzas, Nicos. "The Problem of the Capitalist State." *New Left Review*, no. 58 (1969).

—— *Political Power and Social Classes*. London: Verso, 1973.

—— *Fascism and Dictatorship*. London: New Left Books, 1974.

—— *Classes in Contemporary Capitalism*. London: New Left Books, 1975.

—— "The Capitalist State: A Reply to Miliband and Laclau." *New Left Review*, no. 95 (1976).

—— *The Crisis of the Dictatorships*. London: New Left Books, 1976.

—— *State, Power, Socialism*. London: Verso, 1978.

—— "The Political Crisis and the Crisis of the State." In *Critical Sociology: European Perspectives*, edited by J. W. Freiberg, 357–93. New York: Irvington, 1979.

Rabinow, P. "Introduction." In *The Foucault Reader*, edited by P. Rabinow. New York: Pantheon Books, 1984.

Rai, Shirin. *Gender and the Political Economy of Development*. Cambridge: Polity Press, 2001.

Ramazanoglu, Caroline. *Feminism and the Contradictions of Oppression*. London: Routledge, 1989.

Rao, C. P., ed. *Globalization, Privatization, and Free Market Economy*. Westport, CT: Quorum, 1998.

Reich, Wilhelm. *Character Analysis*. New York: Orgone Institute Press, 1949.

—— *The Mass Psychology of Fascism*. New York: Farrar, Strauss, and Giroux, 1970.

—— *Sex Pol: Essays, 1929–1934*. New York: Random House, 1972.

Remmling, Gunter W. "Marxism and Marxist Sociology of Knowledge." In *Towards the Sociology of Knowledge: Origin and Development of a Sociological Thought Style*, edited by Gunter W. Remmling. New York: Humanities Press, 1973.

Residents of Hull-House. *Hull-House Maps and Papers*. New York: Crowell, 1895.

Reynolds, Larry T. *Interactionism: Exposition and Critique*. 3rd ed. Dix Hills, NY: General Hall, 1993.

Reynolds, Larry T., and Janice M. Reynolds, eds. *The Sociology of Sociology*. New York: McKay, 1970.

Riley, Denise. *Am I that Name? Feminism and the Category of Women in History*. Minneapolis, MN: University of Minnesota Press, 1988.

Ritzer, George. *Modern Sociological Theory*. 5th ed. New York: McGraw-Hill, 2000.

—— *Classical Sociological Theory*. 3rd ed. New York: McGraw-Hill, 2000.

Ritzer, George, and Barry Smart, eds. *Handbook of Social Theory*. London: SAGE, 2001.

Ritzer, George, and Jeff Stepnisky. *Contemporary Sociological Theory and Its Classical Roots: The Basics*. 4th ed. New York: McGraw-Hill, 2012.

—— *Sociological Theory*. 9th ed. New York: McGraw-Hill, 2013.

Robinson, William I. *A Theory of Global Capitalism: Production, Class, and State in a Transnational World*. Baltimore, MD: Johns Hopkins University Press, 2004.

Rogers, Mary, ed. *Contemporary Feminist Theory: A Text/Reader*. New York: McGraw-Hill, 1998.

Ross, Robert J. S., and Kent C. Trachte. *Global Capitalism: The New Leviathan*. Albany, NY: SUNY Press, 1990.

Rousseau, Jean Jacques. *The Social Contract*. New York: Dutton, 1950.

Rowbotham, Sheila. *Women, Resistance, and Revolution*. New York: Penguin, 1972.

Rubinson, Richard, ed. *Dynamics of World Development*. London: SAGE, 1981.

Rucker, Darnell. *The Chicago Pragmatists*. Minneapolis, MN: University of Minnesota Press, 1969.

Russell, James W. *Introduction to Macrosociology*. Englewood Cliffs, NJ: Prentice Hall, 1992.

Saffioti, Heleieth I. B. *Women in Class Society*. New York: Monthly Review Press, 1978.

Said, E. "Michel Foucault as an Intellectual Imagination." In *Michel Foucault (1): Critical Assessments*, edited by B. Smart. New York: Routledge, 1998.

Saint-Simon, Henri de. *Social Organization, the Science of Man and Other Writings*, edited and translated with an introduction by Felix Markham. New York: Harper & Row, 1964.

Sanderson, Stephen K. *Revolutions: A Worldwide Introduction to Social and Political Contention*. 2nd ed. Boulder, CO: Paradigm Publishers, 2010.

Sargent, Lydia. *Women and Revolution: A Discussion of the Unhappy Marriage of Marxism and Feminism*. Boston, MA: South End Press, 1981.

Screpanti, Ernesto. *Global Imperialism and the Great Crisis: The Uncertain Future of Capitalism*. New York: Monthly Review Press, 2014.

Sherman, Howard. *The Roller Coaster Economy: Financial Crisis, Great Recession, and the Public Option*. Armonk, NY: M. E. Sharpe, 2010.

Sherman, Howard, and James Wood. *Sociology*. New York: Harper Collins, 1989.

Simmel, Georg. "Superiority and Subordination as Subject Matter of Sociology." *American Journal of Sociology* 2, no. 2 (1896).

—— "Domination, a Form of Interaction." In *The Sociology of Georg Simmel*, edited by Kurt H. Wolff. Glencoe, IL: The Free Press, 1950.

—— "The Dyad and the Triad." In *The Sociology of Georg Simmel*, edited and translated by Kurt H. Wolff. Glencoe, IL: The Free Press, 1950.

—— "The Web of Group Affiliations." In *Conflict and the Web of Group Affiliations*, translated by Kurt H. Wolff and Reinhard Bendix. New York: The Free Press, 1955.

Simonds, A. P. *Karl Mannheim's Sociology of Knowledge*. Oxford: Clarendon Press, 1978.

Skidmore, William. *Theoretical Thinking in Sociology*. Cambridge: Cambridge University Press, 1975.

Sklair, Leslie. *Sociology of the Global System*. Baltimore, MD: Johns Hopkins University Press, 1991.

—— *The Transnational Capitalist Class*. London: Blackwell, 2000.

Skocpol, Theda. *States and Social Revolutions: A Comparative Analysis of France, Russia and China*. Cambridge: Cambridge University Press, 1979.

—— "Political Response to Capitalist Crisis: Neo-Marxist Theories of the State and the Case of the New Deal." *Politics and Society* 10, no. 2 (1981).

Smith, David Norman. "Charisma and Critique." In *Current Perspectives in Social Theory*, edited by Harry Dahms. Bingley: Emerald, 2011.

Smith, Jackie. "Globalizing Resistance: The Battle of Seattle and the Future of Social Movements." In *Globalizing Resistance: Transnational Dimensions of Social Movements*, edited by Jackie Smith and H. Johnston. Lanham, MD: Rowman & Littlefield, 2002.

Smith, Jackie G., and Hank Johnston, eds. *Globalization and Resistance: Transnational Dimensions of Social Movements*. New York: Routledge, 2002.

Smith, Jackie, Marina Karides, Marc Becker, Dorval Brunelle, Christopher Chase-Dunn, and Donatella Della Porta. *Global Democracy and the World Social Forums*. Boulder, CO: Paradigm, 2008.

Smith, Tony. *The Logic of Marx's Capital*. Albany, NY: SUNY Press, 1990.

So, Alvin Y. *Social Change and Development: Modernization, Dependency, and World-System Theories*. Newbury Park, CA: SAGE, 1990.

Spinello, Richard. *Global Capitalism, Culture, and Ethics*. London: Routledge, 2014.

Staples, William G., and Clifford L. Staples. *Power, Profits, and Patriarchy*. Boulder, CO: Rowman & Littlefield, 2001.

Starr, Amory. *Naming the Enemy: Anti-Corporate Movements Confront Globalization*. London: Zed Books, 2001.

Stinchcombe, Arthur L. "Some Empirical Consequences of the Davis-Moore Theory of Stratification." *American Sociological Review* 28 (1963).

Stryker, Sheldon. *Symbolic Interactionism*. Menlo Park, CA: Benjamin Cummings, 1980.

Suchting, W. "Knowledge and Practice: Towards a Marxist Critique of Traditional Epistemology." *Science and Society* 47, no. 1 (1983).

Szymanski, Albert. "The Revolutionary Uses of Freudian Theory." *Social Praxis* 5, nos. 1–2 (1976).

—— *The Capitalist State and the Politics of Class*. Cambridge, MA: Winthrop, 1978.

—— *The Logic of Imperialism*. New York: Praeger, 1981.

—— *Class Structure: A Critical Perspective*. New York: Praeger, 1983.

Tew, Jerry. *Social Theory, Power and Practice*. New York: Palgrave Macmillan, 2002.

Therborn, Goran. *Science, Class and Society*. London: New Left Books, 1976.

—— "The Rule of Capital and the Rise of Democracy." *New Left Review*, no. 103 (1977).

—— *What Does the Ruling Class Do When It Rules?* London: New Left Books, 1978.

—— *The Ideology of Power and the Power of Ideology*. London: New Left Books, 1980.

—— "Neo-Marxist, Pluralist, Corporatist, Statist Theories and the Welfare State." In *The State in Global Perspective*, edited by A. Kazancigil. Aldershot, UK: Gower and UNESCO, 1986.

Thompson, Michael. *The Domestication of Critical Theory*. Lanham, MD: Rowman and Littlefield, 2016.

Tong, Rosemary. *Feminist Thought: A Comprehensive Introduction*. Boulder, CO: Westview Press, 1989.

Trimberger, Ellen K. *Revolution from Above: Military Bureaucrats and Development in Japan, Turkey, and Peru*. New Brunswick, NJ: Transaction Books, 1978.

Tumin, Melvin. "Some Principles of Stratification: A Critical Analysis." *American Sociological Review* 18, no. 4 (1953).

—— "Reply to Kingsley Davis." *American Sociological Review* 18, no. 6 (1953b)

Turner, Jonathan H. *The Structure of Sociological Theory*. Homewood, IL: Dorsey Press, 1974.

United States Bureau of the Census. *Statistical Abstract of the United States, 1990*. Washington, DC: Government Printing Office, 1990.

Vaughan, Ted R., Gideon Sjoberg, and Larry T. Reynolds, eds. *A Critique of Contemporary American Sociology*. Dix Hills, NY: General Hall, 1993.

Veblen, Thorstein. "On the Nature of Capital: Investment, Intangible Assets, and the Pecuniary Magnet." *Quarterly Journal of Economics* 23, no. 1 (1908).

—— *The Instinct of Workmanship*. New York: Macmillan, 1914.

—— *The Theory of the Leisure Class: An Economic Study of Institutions*. New York: The Macmillan Company, [1899] 1915.

Vogel, Lise. *Marxism and the Oppression of Women: Toward a Unitary Theory*. New Brunswick, NJ: Rutgers University Press, 1983.

Wallace, Ruth A., and Alison Wolf, eds. *Contemporary Sociological Theory: Expanding the Classical Tradition*. 5th ed. Upper Saddle River, NJ: Prentice Hall, 1999.

Wallerstein, Immanuel. *The Modern World-System*. New York: Academic Press, 1974.

—— "The Rise and Future Demise of the World Capitalist System." *Comparative Studies in Society and History* 16, no. 4 (1974).

—— *The Capitalist World-Economy*. Cambridge: Cambridge University Press, 1979.

Walsh, Mary Roth, ed. *Women, Men and Gender: Ongoing Debates*. New Haven, CT: Yale University Press, 1997.

Walton, John. *Sociology and Critical Inquiry*. 2nd ed. Belmont, CA: Wadsworth, 1990.

Walzer, M. "The Politics of Michel Foucault." In *Foucault: A Critical Reader*, edited by David C. Hoy. Oxford: Basil Blackwell, 1986.

Warren, Bill. *Imperialism: Pioneer of Capitalism*. London: Verso, 1980.

Waters, Malcolm. *Globalization: The Reader*. New York: Routledge, 1995.

Weber, Max. *The Protestant Ethic and the Spirit of Capitalism*. New York: Scribner's, 1948.

—— *The Theory of Social and Economic Organization*, edited and with an introduction by Talcott Parsons. New York: Free Press, 1964.

—— *From Max Weber. Essays in Sociology*. Edited and translated with an introduction by H. H. Gerth and C. Wright Mills. New York: Oxford University Press, 1967.

—— *Economy and Society*. 3 vols. New York: Bedminster Press, 1968.

Weber, Steven, ed. *Globalization and the European Political Economy*. New York: Columbia University Press, 2001.

Weinberg, Meyer, ed. *W. E. B. Du Bois: A Reader*. New York: Harper & Row, 1970.

Wells, Harry K. *The Failure of Psychoanalysis*. New York: International Publishers, 1963.

West, Candace, and Don H. Zimmerman. "Doing Gender." In *Gender: A Sociological Reader*, edited by Stevi Jackson and Sue Scott. London: Routledge, 2002.

West, Cornel. *The American Evasion of Philosophy*. Madison, WI: University of Wisconsin Press, 1989.

Westby, David L. *The Growth of Sociological Theory*. Englewood Cliffs, NJ: Prentice Hall, 1991.

Wiggershaus, Rolf. *The Frankfurt School: Its History, Theories, and Political Significance*. Cambridge, MA: MIT Press, 1994.

Williams, Fannie Barrier. *A New Woman of Color: The Collected Writings of Fannie Barrier Williams*. Edited and introduction by Mary Jo Deegan. DeKalb, IL: Northeastern Illinois University, 2002.

Willie, Charles V., ed. *The Caste and Class Controversy on Race and Poverty*. 2nd ed. Dix Hills, NY: General Hall, 1989.

Wilson, William Julius. *The Declining Significance of Race*. 2nd ed. Chicago, IL: University of Chicago Press, 1980.

—— *The Truly Disadvantaged: The Inner City, the Underclass, and Public Policy*. Chicago, IL: University of Chicago Press, 1987.

—— "The Declining Significance of Race: Revisited but Not Revised." In *The Caste and Class Controversy on Race and Poverty*, edited by Charles V. Willie. Dix Hills, NY: General Hall, 1989.

Woldring, Henk E. S. *Karl Mannheim: The Development of his Thought: Philosophy, Sociology and Social Ethics, with a Detailed Bibliography*. New York: St. Martin's Press, 1986.

Wolff, Kurt H., ed. *Emile Durkheim, 1858–1917*. Columbus, OH: Ohio State University Press, 1960.

Wright, Erik Olin. "To Control or to Smash Bureaucracy: Weber and Lenin on Politics, the State, and Bureaucracy." *Berkeley Journal of Sociology* 19 (1974–1975).

—— *Class, Crisis and the State*. London: New Left Books, 1978.

—— *Classes*. London: Verso, 1985.

Yang, Xiaohua. *Globalization of the Automobile Industry: The United States, Japan, and the People's Republic of China*. Westport, CT: Praeger Publishers, 1995.

Zeitlin, Irving M. *Ideology and the Development of Sociological Theory*. Englewood Cliffs, NJ: Prentice Hall, 1968.

—— *Rethinking Sociology: A Critique of Contemporary Sociology*. Englewood Cliffs, NJ: Prentice Hall, 1973.

—— *The Social Condition of Humanity*. New York: Oxford University Press, 1981.

# INDEX

# ABOUT THE AUTHOR

Dr Berch Berberoglu is Professor of Sociology and Director of Graduate Studies in the Department of Sociology at the University of Nevada, Reno. He received his PhD from the University of Oregon in 1977. He has been teaching and conducting research at the University of Nevada, Reno, for the past thirty-nine years. Dr Berberoglu has written and edited thirty-two books and many articles. His most recent books include *Class and Class Conflict in the Age of Globalization* (2009); *Globalization in the 21st Century* (2010); *Beyond the Global Capitalist Crisis: The World Economy in Transition* (2012); *Political Sociology in a Global Era* (2013); and *The Global Capitalist Crisis and Its Aftermath* (2014). His areas of specialization include political economy, class analysis, development, comparative-historical sociology, and social movements and transformation. Dr Berberoglu is currently writing a new book, *America After Empire: The Promise and the Vision for a New America in the 21st Century*, which will be published by Routledge in 2018.

Made in the USA
Monee, IL
01 September 2023

41975242R00168